SUNY series in

James N. Rosenau, editor

POLITICAL SPACE

POLITICAL SPACE

Frontiers of Change and Governance in a Globalizing World

EDITED BY

Yale H. Ferguson
and
R. J. Barry Jones

State University of New York Press

Published by
State University of New York Press, Albany

For information, address State University of New York Press,
90 State Street, Suite 700, Albany, NY 12207

Production by Diane Ganeles
Marketing by Patrick Durocher

Library of Congress Cataloging-in-Publication Data

Political space : frontiers of change and governance in a globalizing world / edited by Yale H. Ferguson and R. J. Barry Jones.
    p. cm. — (SUNY series in global politics)
  Includes bibliographical references and index.
    ISBN 0-7914-5459-2 (alk. paper) — ISBN 0-7914-5460-6 (pbk. : alk. paper)
    1. Globalization. 2. International relations. 3. Political geography. I. Ferguson, Yale H.
II. Jones, R. J. Barry. III. Series.

JZ1320 .P65 2002
327.1'01—dc21

                                                                    2001055122

10 9 8 7 6 5 4 3 2 1

Contents

Political Space and Global Politics

Yale H. Ferguson
and
R. J. Barry Jones

The concept of *political space*, already familiar to political geographers, has lately received increasing attention from political scientists and other social scientists who are concerned with what has traditionally been called "international relations" (IR) theory.[1] That attention, in part, reflects a sense that we need new ways of thinking about and describing change and the actors, structures, and processes that shape politics and patterns of governance in the contemporary world.

There is a new agenda of concerns that arises from a host of such interrelated developments as the end of the Cold War; the much lower cost and vast expansion of transnational transportation and communication; a related information revolution; the increased internationalization, regionalization, and substantial globalization of the world economy; the recognition of growing threats to the global environment; a resurgence of ethnic identity, religious fundamentalism, and localisms of many kinds; migration and refugee flows; and the proliferation of terrorist and other criminal networks.[2] Distinctions between and among the various academic disciplines are eroding even as are those between the external and internal dimensions of states and societies. The response in the IR field has been heightened interest in international political economy (IPE), the proliferation of critical perspectives upon the nature and role of the state— and now, we submit, concern with changing patterns of political space.

The concept of political space, let alone changing political space, may appear to be unnecessarily abstract or even abstruse. To the contrary, the editors regard it as an especially useful concept for the task of ground-clearing. Thinking about political space forces us to reconsider the degree to which politics and territory continue to be related, possible shifts in that relationship and the sources of change, as well as the extent to which important aspects of global politics and governance transcend territory or are effectively deterritorialized. In this way we can help free ourselves from what John Agnew and Stuart Corbridge felicitously labeled "the territorial trap."[3]

1

Different Maps of Global Politics

Contemporary analysts urgently need to "remap" the world politically. We must consider other borders than those reflected in the map all of us grew up with, with neat sovereign state boxes. Certainly, that map still has considerable utility, but it is seriously misleading in many respects and definitely is not the only map we need to comprehend the political complexities of the present-day world. A useful starting exercise might be to ask ourselves whether if were we to wake one morning and not be able to find the familiar map, how might *we* redraw the political map of the world? The short and obvious answer is that it all depends on what *we* want or need to show. We are reminded of the map in souvenir shops in New York City purporting to be "A New Yorker's View of the World," which today is not nearly so focused on just a few traditional tourist destinations for New Yorkers as it used to be. Indeed, most of the nationalities that comprise New York City's multiethnic population now follow daily events in their former homelands via their own newspapers, television channels, and web sites.

The editors cannot stress too strongly that one map will not serve for all persons and purposes, any more than it has for the contributors to this volume. As Harold and Margaret Sprout pointed out decades ago[4] and constructivists of all persuasions[5] continue to remind us, although the "real world" is definitely "out there" somewhere and misreading its "true" nature sometimes can lead to severe consequences, it is also a fact that all of us are constrained in what we see.[6] We are limited by the "glasses behind our eyes," not least the various "schools" of theory that presume to tell us what we should find worthy of particular attention and what we can safely ignore. Theory leads us to certain kinds of puzzles, issues, actors, and background forces shaping behavior—and, equally significantly, not to others.

Traditionally, realism and neorealism focused us on a world of sovereign states with differing power capabilities and interests, an international system structure that arises from the distribution of such capabilities, and a systemwide condition of anarchy that makes states competitive and fearful for their security. Let us be clear that we do *not* intend this book to be read as some sort of antirealist manifesto. First, the many problems of realism and neorealism are well-known, including a tendency to generate self-confirming behavior of decision makers who accept their tenets.[7] To review all the old debates would be pointless and boring. Second, there is no denying that there are times in global politics—especially but not exclusively during periods of heightened concern for security—when the realist model seems to be a reasonable description of observable behavior. Decision-makers may be convinced they perceive "objective" national interests, seek to extend the power/influence of their states at the expense of their neighbors, build up their armed forces, and regularly rattle the saber. China's frequently belligerent posture regarding Taiwan and strident reaction early in 2000 to the collision of its military jet with a U.S. reconnaissance plane might be considered examples. Yet such cases nearly always highlight some of the severe limitations of any realist perspective. How do we explain why Peking's approach to Taiwan has sometimes been much more accommodative? Was what some observers considered to be an overreaction to the collision less a reassertion of enduring national security interests than a product of short-term competition among elites at a time of domestic political transition? Similarly, it is tempting to regard the sudden rapprochement among such strange bedfellows as the United States, Russia, Pakistan, India, and China after the terrorist attack on the World Trade Center as a classic exercise in realist political opportunism. Although the others no doubt sincerely deplored the brutal attack on the United States, each obviously hoped to exact a "price" from the superpower for supporting the war on terrorism. The war itself was in defense of the security of a state but otherwise was almost wholly outside the scope of traditional realist doctrine—fought with broad international support against the transnational al-Queda network and their Taliban protectors, and in a so-called country, Afghanistan, that is a volatile conglomeration of rival ethnicities, warlord bands, and religious factions.

To be sure, there are still interstate conflicts in the world, like the India/Pakistan perennial dispute over Kashmir, but in recent years such conflicts have appeared to be dramatically on the decline. Moreover, until the war on terrorism, a host of economic, environmental, and humanitarian issues seemed to be pushing matters military out of the headlines—and they are likely to do so again. Even as the war continued, the World Trade Organization (WTO) held a major successful conference in Qatar, and 160 countries concluded a new pact on global warming (albeit without the U.S.). We clearly need other approaches than realism to explain the remarkable amount of order, cooperation, rulemaking, institution-building, and other forms of political, economic, and social integration in the contemporary world. These sorts of subjects, of course, realists once assigned to those whom they contemptuously labeled "idealists," but such matters are plainly central to any *genuinely* realistic worldview today. Unfortunately, there is still no consensus among IR theorists as to the extent to which order and cooperation are virtually inevitable outcomes of interdependence and produced by a variety of actors or are almost entirely dependent upon the perceptions and "interest" calculations of state decision-makers.[8]

What follows next in this introduction is not so much the editors' prescription as a modest checklist of categories of things we might we need or want to show on a political map that would serve as a guide for the early twenty-first century. It is meant to be nothing more than food for thought, and the editors themselves and contributors actually offer a wide range of more specific and complex conceptions of political space in their respective essays. *In fact, the novelty and diversity of such conceptions—and the appropriateness of novelty and diversity at this stage in the development of theories of global politics—are the main themes of this collection.*

Now to the features on our hypothetical map: *Legal boundaries* clearly persist, but not only those of states (countries). What traditional theorists have often overlooked, or at least underplayed, is that legal boundaries also lie within states, and increasingly overarch and transcend them as well. Within many national governments, a single executive, various executive bureaucracies, legislative bodies, and courts have their separate and to some extent overlapping, legally defined realms of authority. Nonetheless, their actual influence and control varies with particular issues and the political currents of the day. As is the case in the United Kingdom, some political systems enshrine parliamentary sovereignty and may even have no written constitution. Yet the UK does now provide for limited "devolution" for historical regions like Scotland and Wales. Most countries also have political subdivisions with varying degrees of autonomy, like the states in federal regimes, provinces or departments, counties, cities and towns, and so on.

Moreover, in most relatively open and economically developed societies, private property rights, a host of firms and financial institutions, and myriad interest groups that constitute "civil society" all enjoy a degree of autonomy and protection enshrined in law. Companies, banks, and NGOs are increasingly establishing organizational structures, alliances, and networks that cross national boundaries, as are an ever-growing number of international organizations (IOs) and less-formal regimes created by treaties and other agreements. Many IOs, too, have internal administrative and legislative subdivisions as well as a variety of linkages to member-states, other IOs and regimes, and global civil society. Continuing subjects for debate are the degree to which IOs and regimes are separate actors or merely the sum of their member parts, and whether at the end of the day (when and if such ever comes) "final" power and authority resides with states. In practice, however, analysts today might do best perhaps just to raise the questions of how and where effective decisions are customarily made and implemented, only in the relatively infrequent extreme, by means of coercion.

There are also many characteristics of the contemporary world which, while not themselves directly "political" in any conventional sense of the term, nevertheless bear strongly on the pressures on traditional governments, their capacities to act effectively, and on general patterns of advantage and disadvantage. It is thus possible to emphasize various *topographical or ecological characteristics* that seem to have important relevance for global politics, however difficult the task sometimes is to establish the precise nature of that connection—for example, the loci of petroleum deposits and other natural resources, principal mountain ranges, climate zones, fishing grounds, threatened flora and fauna, major rivers, deserts, and straits.

Another approach is to highlight *economic, social, and technological features*—GNP performance; national public and private debt; the centers of petroleum production and consumption; arms possession and production; the loci of certain "ethnicities"; language groupings; regions or countries of unusual affluence and extreme poverty; class divisions demarcated by income; the concentrations of personal computers, televisions, telephones, internet accounts—and many more.

An additional useful set of features on our map might be actual *transaction flows*. Who is interacting with whom (i.e., "diplomacy" broadly conceived)?—such as summit meetings between heads of state, bureaucratic politics, intergovernmental relations; relations between and among firms, between firms and governments, or between NGOs and IOs. What do we observe about trade, in general and with respect to specific commodities, goods, and services? To what extent is it bilateral or increasingly globalized, concentrated regionally, intercity, or intrafirm? We could ask similar questions about direct investment, loans from development banks, personal mail, telephone calls, hits on World Wide Web sites, and other sorts of interactions. For instance, Susan Strange's early differentiation of worldwide knowledge structures, production structures, and financial structures—from the more conventional notion of a power structure—illuminated the variable structures and spaces in the area of economics and transactions.[9]

Then there is what we might term the *subjective* dimension of global politics. For example, maps supposedly identifying concentrations of certain ethnic groups can be extremely misleading. Although "ethnicity" may sometimes rest on such factors as a common history or language, there is no escaping the fact that it is largely a social construct like most other identities. The degree to which an individual or a group regards itself as "Scottish," "Kurdish," "Hispanic," "Mayan," "Slavic," "Ukrainian," or another ethnicity, almost always depends on a much broader context and often varies over time. The same might be said for the concept of "nation," despite the fact that most states define their own nationals and citizens by law. A key question is: With whom or what do individuals and groups actually identify? Religions have their faithful, internal schisms, and heretics. Firms have their local and often far-flung facilities and markets. Scholars have their professions and arcane specializations. Women and gays, their respective and (in the case of lesbians) overlapping constituencies, and so on. Identities are normally not mutually exclusive. However, as a category like "women" strongly suggests, what perhaps matters most is not identity as such, but intensity of identification and loyalty. To what extent are identities shaped by local and global culture? How do identities affect political behavior, and the other way around? Where do true loyalties lie, particularly when identities do seem to conflict and cannot all be equally served?—and why?

Viewed in the ways we have proposed, the global political map becomes at once considerably more complex, but, we continue to insist, far more "realistic" than the map reflected in traditional IR theory. Nonetheless, responsible analysts cannot stop with the statement that the world is, indeed, a complex place politically. The task of theory building is finding better means to "read" the map, make greater sense of its complexities, identify significant patterns, and establish relationships either between the whole and its parts or at least among aspects of the whole. For instance, a concern with specific *issues* brings into focus certain actors, legal boundaries, system characteristics, transaction flows, identities, and loyalties—and, again by implication, not others. If one's preoccupation is with the issue of protecting whales, for example, the relevant world of political actors and environment influencing their behavior is far different from what it might be, say, if the issue is nuclear nonproliferation. Likewise, deep-sea mining, rather than stabilization of global financial markets, control of AIDS, stopping genocide, ending traffic in women, halting the flow of heroin, combatting bioterrorism, or improving airline safety.

Patterns of Governance

Another way of discerning a measure of order in otherwise apparent chaos is to map political space in terms of patterns of *governance*. A familiar approach to that task is to keep sovereign-state boxes but distinguish domestic regime types. We may map the world's democracies, governments undergoing apparent transitions from authoritarianism, personal dictatorships, military regimes, and others. An unfortunate number of dysfunctional political systems or "failed states" might also have to be identified and charted. Such a map would be helpful to those studying, for example, the often-proposed connection between democracy and peace, or progress of human rights in the sense of political freedoms.

The territorial state has been the primary focus for students of international relations and politics in the past, and certainly many states remain important actors in global politics. It is difficult to generalize because the classification "state" embraces everything from superpower to failed states and ministates. However, if there is any emerging consensus in the current literature, it is that states are not becoming obsolete but that they—like all polities (and there are many types)[10]—are continually evolving and adapting. Contemporary developments may be tending to undermine some traditional state functions (e.g., control of some aspects of the national economy) and to enhance others (e.g., the provision of infrastructure and services that improve competitiveness). In any event, states have never been the only significant political actors in global politics, and it is now increasingly apparent that states must share the stage with a variety of other polities and even with forms of governance like markets and networks that are somewhat amorphous with regard to their identity and institutions.

Especially today we need to reconsider the relationship between territory and governance. All individuals and collectivities are situated in physical space, and for most nationalist movements the notion of a specific homeland remains strong. Yet much of what is important in global politics and surely the world economy is increasingly incongruent with state boundaries, or put another way, lies within or transcends those boundaries. Not only (as Saskia Sassen reminds us) is the global embedded in the national (and vice versa),[11] but there is also a significant and perhaps growing degree of "deterritorialization." Cyberspace, for example, gives a new meaning to the more familiar legal concept of "offshore." Markets are continually shifting and often volatile, and although particular transactions happen in specific places on any given day, it is the flow of transactions that matters most. Likewise, the subjective dimension we mentioned earlier—for example, identities and cultural norms—is hard to pin down geographically but can be remarkably effective in governing human behavior.

If we conceive of "governance" as those polities and processes that effectively allocate values, that is, collective goods, we open up a wide range of possibilities. To be sure, patterns of governance widely seen as "legitimate"—that is, as proceeding from some legal or moral "authority"—are for that reason all that more secure. However, Ferguson and Mansbach[12] and others insist that governance need not be legitimate to be effective. A contributor to this volume and the editor of the series in which it appears, James N. Rosenau, has put it that "systems of rule can be maintained and their controls successfully and consistently exerted even in the absence of established legal or political authority." One might well ask how long such informal authorities can persist and under what conditions? In any event, Rosenau's own premise is that "the world is not so much a system dominated by states and national governments as a cogeries of spheres of authority (SOAs) that are subject to considerable flux and not necessarily coterminous with the division of territorial space." The foundation of such authority is not legitimacy per se, rather a capacity to "evoke compliance" within their respective domains.[13] Similarly, Benjamin J. Cohen writes: "In fact, authority may be manifested through any number of de facto channels of control. . . . By no means is it true, therefore, that we are left with a 'yawning hole of non-authority' just because power has shifted away from national governments." "Governance," in his view, "may not even call for the presence of explicit actors, whether state-sponsored or private, to take responsibility for rulemaking and enforcement." "Market forces may be impersonal, but that does not make them any less capable of governance."[14]

Barry Jones argues to the contrary that, even if recent developments have weakened the capacities of established governments, "private" agents of governance will not prove capable of effective governance in many of the areas traditionally undertaken by states or statelike public authorities. A "democratic deficit" is only one of the palpable deficiencies of private authorities.[15] Still others might rejoinder, whether private authority is anywhere near an acceptable substitute, state control is weakening and we have to get used to thinking about global governance in additional nonstate terms. Others might stress that many states, as well, have had and continue to have a grave democratic deficit of their own.

As the foregoing suggests, the familiar distinction between "*public*" and "*private*" governance has begun to blur.[16] It has become, for some, less a firm dividing line than a vague and shifting political boundary between those who make the rules and effectively allocate goods in particular domains. Each attempts to justify their capacity to evoke compliance by reference to the collectivities that are putatively being served. State bureaucrats will claim to enhance "the public interest" when they are providing needed services and also when they are merely spending taxpayers' money for hopelessly inefficient and self-serving programs that should have been terminated long ago. Likewise, Wall Street will sing the praises of the public good supposedly being served by "private" markets that profit numerous small investors, make the superrich even richer, and benefit the poorest of the poor hardly at all.

"*Global governance*" in this perspective becomes not so much a reference to the control exercised by effective authorities on a truly global scale, than a concept that invites investigators of political space in today's world to map the patterns and consider the source(s) of whatever order and compliance they may observe.[17] Craig N. Murphy, for example, comments: "Certainly it matters that global norms have an impact on and help to construct national interests, just as it matters that some intergovernmental agencies and private institutions are increasingly powerful, but we are not going to be able to explain the nature of global governance without understanding the ways in which powerful states construct and pursue their grand strategies." "[I]t is in the most powerful state agencies (the Treasuries) and the most powerful clubs of states (the WTO, IMF, and World Bank) that neoliberalism is triumphant."[18] Of course, this perceptive statement nonetheless brings us back to questions like whether the state as an actor is really identical with one of its ministries, or whether "state" behavior is fundamentally altered by participation in "clubs" or international organizations, or whether both treasury ministries and "clubs" may simply be acting at the behest of private institutions who (rather than states) are the actual source of "neoliberalism." In any event, it is possible that any search for a *dominant* actor or form of governance in the contemporary world—and perhaps often throughout all of political history,[19] including the Westphalian era[20]—will be nothing more than an exercise in frustration that obscures far more than it clarifies. In each and every period, and certainly the present one, governance has proceeded not only at various levels of the global system—local, regional, national, and so on—but also as a consequence of ever-widening and complex networks of actors and interconnected systems.[21] As Martin Hewson observes, a "node-and-network space [among distinct yet interconnected power centers] ... encompasses the world" today and, indeed, did much to displace localism and regionalism from the fifteenth through eighteenth centuries onward.[22] Christer Jönsson, Sven Tägil, and Gunnar Törnqvist similarly explain that a relationship between regions, networks, and cities has long been a feature of Europe and continues in the present-day European Union.[23]

There is increasing recognition in at least some social science literature that a global system of states is but one type of many important social systems, whose fluid nature and frequent linkages shape the political complexity we observe.[24] Governance emanates sometimes from discrete and identifiable actors, but as often than not, from their complicated relationships on various levels. Liora Salter, for example, describes the "standards regime" for communication and information technologies as "a hybrid regime": "It is still very local or national, even while it is global in orientation. Even as it becomes more commonplace to speak of global developments, it is also easier to identify the national or local allegiances of those involved. Even though some national organizations have been eclipsed, others have been strengthened, and new ones have emerged that are demonstrably powerful within the standards regime. At any moment in time, and with respect to any particular decision about a standard, it is exceptionally difficult to locate the epicenter of action, the degree to which any standard is national, local, or global in origin."[25]

Thus far we have been discussing what might be termed the "supply-side" of governance, that is, those existing patterns that we need to muster our analytical skills, information, and consensus-building in order to map. A more prescriptive, or "demand-side," approach might attempt to highlight those needs and requirements that have yet to be met. What aspects of global politics evince inadequate patterns of governance, in either one of two possible senses: (1) there is as yet too little in the way of order and compliance, or (2) the order and compliance that currently prevails is in some respect or another manifestly unjust? The latter concern is central to what is sometimes referred to as the current "backlash" against globalization. Normative concerns of that sort are considered only in an oblique fashion in this volume, but they are plainly important for both the present and future. It is impossible to deny that our contemporary political space is becoming increasingly globalized (as well as localized) and complex, but who benefits and who does not benefit, in what respects, from prevailing trends, and how can more truly collective goods be provided to an ever-wider constituency?[26] These are fundamental demand-side questions, and addressing them will continue to provide a crucial challenge for analysts and policy makers in a variety of settings.

Charting Political Space in this Volume

Most of the essays in this volume are substantially revised versions of papers that were first presented at the Third Pan-European International Relations Conference (of the Standing Group on International Relations, European Consortium of Political Research) that met jointly with the International Studies Association in Vienna, Austria, in mid-September 1998. Vienna provided an intriguing venue in terms of its own political space. Austria had been part of one of the world's most polyglot empires, suffered a brief civil war in 1934, was forcefully annexed by Hitler in his campaign for an expanded Third Reich, after World War II was divided into sectors administered by the victorious Allies, became a sovereign state again only in 1955, struggled to reconcile strong regional identities with an Austrian identity (separate as well from German), perceived its security to be threatened by the breakup of Yugoslavia and refugees from the resulting conflicts, joined the European Union after a long national debate, and recently found itself the object of considerable EU and world condemnation because of the rise of Haider's neofascist Freedom Party.

The panel series on "Political Space" at the Vienna meeting brought together an unusually distinguished and diverse group of theorists of global politics, political geography, and international political economy. Those of us who participated had a genuine sense of an "occasion" and even a milestone in the progress of social science theory. The nature of the "milestone" was *not* that anyone thought we were building or reconstructing some bold new paradigm or even theoretical approach on which we all could *or should* agree—quite the contrary! The reader who expects the essays that follow to sing from the same songbook in that sense will thus not only be disappointed but also will have sadly missed one the key points of the exercise. *What we conferees did all agree on was that "political space" is a worthy subject for investigation, that we need to move beyond the constraints of traditional IR theories in attempting to chart that space (or spaces), and that at this stage of new departures a diversity of approaches is to be both expected and encouraged.*

Conversations on the panels over several days were substantive, spirited, and almost always constructive in tone. Everyone made a sincere effort to communicate across disciplines and different theoretical positions. Although the participants might be loosely classified as realists, neorealists, constructivists, and postinternationalists,[27] in fact it is evident that such established theoretical "schools" are themselves rapidly evolving and, happily, few of the essays produced fit neatly into the usual pigeonholes. These essays, we believe, literally do explore the frontier of the field of global politics and all of them deal imaginatively with some aspect of political space. The only other common denominators are an implied continued faith in empirical research and a shared sense of excitement in pioneering and discovery.

The four essays in Part I of this collection offer us historical perspectives on political space and invite us to weigh carefully claims of the uniqueness, fundamental nature, and rapidity of change in contemporary global politics. Kal Holsti quips that change, "like beauty and good skiing condition, is in the eye of the beholder." Microlevel change is, by definition, not macrochange, but it is often the accumulation of change by such microincrements that make for important major shifts over what Fernand Braudel termed the *longue durée*. Particularly under the confusing conditions of the present, Holsti suggests, we have an urgent need for markers of change, but there is a lack of consensus as to what those markers should be. We may search for certain trends, yet the scales we use to measure those trends are both "quantitatively arbitrary" and "qualitatively constructed." Similarly, we may highlight certain "great events," "great achievements," and "significant social/technical innovations," without being able to agree whether or not they have inaugurated truly "new eras or epochs." In Holsti's view, at the very least, we need to be clear when we refer to change, whether we are asserting that there has been "replacement," "addition," "dialectical change," or a full-fledged "transformation."

According to Richard Little, the best approach in assessing the degree to which political space today is "undergoing fundamental change" is to develop much greater historical perspective, in his words, for IR theory "to develop closer links with the evolving study of world history."[28] He insists that two of the leading schools of theory, neorealism and neoliberal institutionalism, have suffered because "they have adopted an ahistorical approach to the conceptualization of political space." Little considers several other theorists who, by contrast, have made extensive use of world history, and he explains and critiques their findings. Ferguson and Mansbach's "polities" model he regards as a bit too drastic in treating political space as "seamless web." His prefers to retain a "dichotomized" distinction between hierarchical and anarchical structures in the global system, but to generate "more empirical detail" by establishing "deeper and more elaborate theoretical foundations." The work that he and Barry Buzan have now completed[29] proceeds from a neorealist foundation, yet acknowledges the existence of a variety of actors (including "acephalous units") and relationships throughout history. Little also admires the contribution that constructivists have made that stresses "the importance of ideas in structuring political space." For example, the anarchical political space of the Greek city-states and that of modern states are profoundly different, not least because the former was conditioned by a Greek normative cultural context.

Ken Dark's essay similarly maintains that it is important to view patterns of global political and geopolitical change both over the longest possible time span and with sensitivity to the unique characteristics of each era. He makes the case for greater attention to insights and data from such disciplines as archaeology and anthropology as well as world history, noting that contemporary IR theorists focus almost exclusively on the post-Westphalian era of the sovereign-state system and ignore the fact that most of the 6,000-year geopolitical record is one of nonstate polities. Different types of polities and relationships among them have prevailed in different periods. Dark's principal explanation for these shifts over time, from his perspective of "macrodynamic theory"—an interdisciplinary "synthesis" from the social, biological, and physical sciences—is the effect of changes in communication and information-processing. He writes that "changes in the mode of information-processing and communication [have] not merely enabled . . . polities to operate efficiently, but actually permitted the existence of particular sorts of political form." The current "revolution" in information and communication raises the question of whether we may be witnessing the birth of yet another era in global politics. As he sees it, the modern state is less likely to become "redundant" than to have to "co-exist" with "new political forms." However, "the 'death of distance' inherent in transformed time [means that] geographies of the global system well may constitute a 'death of warning' also." If transnational governance mechanisms do not keep up with the accelerating pace of change, global collapse could become a real possibility.

Yale Ferguson and Richard Mansbach suggest in the last essay of Part I that "remapping political space" in an adequate fashion should be seen as a two-step process. First, they argue for abandoning most of the current "great debates" in IR theory, nearly all of which they regard as fundamentally misguided, irrelevant, inconsequential, or ready for closure. Those controversies targeted for abandonment include empiricism versus relativism, agent-structure, objective versus constructed worlds, democracy and peace, the novelty and existence of a globalized world, the autonomy of international regimes from their state members, and the demise versus continued viability of the state. The second step advocated by Ferguson/Mansbach is for theorists to focus on the three matters that they define as "the real issues" in the study of global politics. One such issue is the assessment of change in the contemporary world, seen (in Holsti's terms) as an interrelated process of both "addition" and "transformation." In every instance, they insist, it is crucial to specify exactly how the present is "both similar to the past and also different." Another key issue is governance. Ferguson/Mansbach propose that analysts of global politics admit as actors a wide range of "polities" or "authorities" and ask two central questions: "What polities control or significantly influence what issues in the world arena—and why?" The final "real issue" is identities and loyalties. What Strange called "the retreat of the state"[30] is bound to have a powerful long-range influence on identities and loyalties, as she herself recognized. Ferguson/Mansbach remark: "Our conceptions of ourselves and others will be continually changing, or sometimes will be ages old, and the task for us political scientists is to explain what the limited range of choices are, which are likely to prevail—and, again as always, why?"

The three essays in Part II, although otherwise quite different in focus, all strongly emphasize the contingent, ever-fluid nature and significance of political space. Political geographer John Agnew disputes the common notion that "power . . . is fixed in given territorial units." Rather, he argues that power "changes both its character and spatial significance as different geographical scales (local, regional, national-state, world-regional, international and global) change their relationships to one another as the political practices of the global geopolitical order change." He describes four different models of "the spatiality of power . . . each of which has dominated in different epochs of geopolitical order." As he puts it, power thus "has a history" that "can *only* be understood through its changing geography." Agnew closes by pointing up the normative implications of such an understanding, the historical contingency of the "moral geography of state-based political power." In other epochs, he observes, "there was widespread acceptance of the idea of a hierarchy of communities with specified purposes and overlapping spatial jurisdictions." Is the present just such an epoch?

Robert Latham begins his essay with a simple yet important observation that most thought about political life has focused on the state. We therefore tend to "end up with a global realm that is thin, fluid, and lacking an accountable center, and yet in its diffusion is rich with varied forms, political projects, and discourses." He shares the view of some theorists that it is possible to discern various structures at the global level, but he regards his own work as a somewhat less "top down" and different approach to that task. He identifies three "basic dimensions within which interactions occur across human spaces: namely, international arenas, translocal networks, and transterritorial deployments." The first is the familiar locus where "states meet to hammer out treaties, conventions, war settlements, alliances, regimes, and where NGOs attempt to influence those activities and define new ones." Translocal networks involve "the transmission of one form of capital or another (political, symbolic, informational, financial, etc.)" from one local node and place to another. Such networks thus are "specialized pathways of flows of messages, knowledge, and goods . . . along a trajectory that is not open to the view of a public." Transterritorial deployments (TDs), by contrast, are the actual embedding or "installation in a local context of agents from outside that context," for example, the headquarters of a UN agency or an office or production facilities of a transnational corporation. Latham devotes the balance of his essay to TDs, especially their "interface with the local," including translocal networks, and consequent impact on local order, political centers, and the state.

At first glance, Stuart Corbridge's essay on Hindu nationalism in India might appear to be a rather traditional look at a leading country in the developing world and its great-power aspirations; however, in actuality, his analysis is an extremely radical departure from traditional theory. Here we have the same territorial space, India, utterly transformed by ideology—what we have termed shifts in the subjective dimension of political space—which, in turn, has broad implications for much of the Southeast Asian region. The BJB Party has "imagined India anew," reinventing it as Hindustan, "an ancient country whose boundaries are set by fixed geographical features and whose rivers and landscapes are indicative of the mythological unity of India." Part of the ideological shift involves "gendered rituals of pilgrimage and spatial representation" that "position Mother India (Bharat Mata) as a geographical entity under threat from Islam" and in need of protection by the military might of Lord Rama, "the [now] very masculine incarnation of Vishnu." The BJP also manipulates "representations of India's domestic spaces . . . to fashion a new conception of India as a Great Power." Yet that selfsame Hindu India faces serious challenges from within, from "an ideology of secularism" as well as "a rainbow coalition of popular movements which disavow the dirigiste projects of Nehruvian modernity and militant Hinduism." The reader cannot help but come away from Corbridge's provocative treatment with a very fluid view of "India" as a modern "state" or perhaps as a complex polity that almost defies classification.

Three essays in Part III each offer their own assessments of the effects of recent globalizing trends in the world economy on the relative significance of the state and a variety of other actors. Saskia Sassen identifies what she variously describes as "a new cross-border field for public and private actors," "a new geography of power," or a "new institutional spatio-temporal order." States are not so much phasing out as being transformed and repositioned with reconfigured tasks "in a broader field of power." She sees "the emergence of a mostly, but not exclusively private institutional order whose strategic agents are not the national governments of leading countries but a variety of non-state actors." Former state capacities and policy agendas are being substantially "denationalized," and a "new normativity" of free markets has eroded the old Keynesian rules of the game. Not only is economic globalization relocating national public governance functions to transnational private arenas, but also there are profound developments "inside national states—through legislative acts, court rulings, executive orders—of the mechanisms necessary to accommodate the rights of global capital." Sassen rightly cautions that "moving from territorial organizations such as the modern state to spatial orders is no easy analytic task." The main reason, as she points out, is that space "is not a mere container or tabula rasa" but "is itself productive of the new dynamics of power and control as well as produced by these."

In what was, sadly, to be Susan Strange's last essay, she reflects on the status of the field of international political economy that she helped to found and also draws some additional theoretical conclusions from her famous book on *Casino Capitalism* as well as her final volume on *Mad Money*. In characteristically caustic style, she decries the "myopia" of international relations theorists preoccupied with issues of military security and the "equal myopia" of Western political theorists concerned only with values of political liberalism. What they are missing, "astonishingly," is "the role of finance, and financial policy, in deciding the 'who benefits?' question at the heart of international political economy." The primary changes in the modern era, she maintains, are two, the role of technology in "shifting power over trade and production from governments to firms" and "the involvement of organized crime in the international financial system." One result is that the traditional specific goals of regulation have blurred to such an extent that the supposedly regulated are essentially writing their own rules. Strange repeats her long-held view that states themselves are largely to blame for their own decline, in that their decision and nondecisions have led to the contemporary ascent of private power. "Bad theories" of declining U.S. hegemony and the benefits of capital mobility—against which she believes students must be warned!—have also mislead policy makers. Her essay (and career) closed with a clarion call to economists and other social scientists to exercise their "social responsibility" in setting the record straight, building better theory, and both fashioning and advocating more effective policies.

Ronen Palan also highlights the degree to which states have themselves been responsible for creating the legal space—in his example, the concept of "offshore"—for globalization to blossom and expand. Although he acknowledges that cyberspace linkages have been a prominent feature of globalization, he takes strong issue with any notion that global finance, for instance, has been a "space-less" phenomenon. Indeed, he points to Sassen's work on global cities[31] as illustrating the territorial embeddedness of the global financial system. Asserting that "space is not simply there" but is "in fact a social construction," Palan urges us to think about the "proper spaces of globalization" and how they came about. In his view, "the growing integration of the market within the context of a state system . . . created a series of problems [and] attempted solutions." States came up with legal constructs like tax havens and "offshore" as a means of withholding some or all of their regulations in certain enclaves while preserving the general principle of state sovereignty. Much of global economic activity now takes place (literally) in or through such enclaves. "Offshore is the quintessential global market," writes Palan, "and yet contrary to globalists, it is a juridical space that operates within the context of a particularistic political system."

The primary concern of the final four essays that constitute Part IV are shifting patterns of governance. R. J. Barry Jones's lead essay offers an important caution that we need "a disciplined approach to the notion of political space" as well as to whatever changes in such space and difficulties we might foresee as a consequence. "Governance," he stresses, is *the* issue," and we must be careful not to confuse the "supply side" thereof with the "demand side." As he expresses it, "ubiquitous information technologies or mass long-distance transportation do not necessarily lead to the emergence of new patterns of political association or public governance," nor "does the emergence of new needs and problems within the human condition guarantee the emergence of appropriate structures of public governance." He "highlights the importance of the distinction between public governance and private governance and, in consequence, between formal and informal governance."To be sure, "history reveals a complex and changeable pattern of political structures" and contemporary states are a highly varied lot, but, when all is said and done, the state remains "one of the most potent forces, for good and ill, within the modern world system."Yet today's states face formidable challenges from forces of internationalization and globalization, nested polities, and private governance. Under such circumstances, how will the various collective goods and minority needs states have traditionally supplied and met continue to be served? "Global governance," as Jones sees it, is not an effective substitute; rather, it is "poised delicately between a potentially expanding realm of private governance and a dense, but often fragile, structure of inter-governmental public governance." "Popular democratic representation is largely (possibly necessarily) absent from the former; tenuous, and rarely more than indirect, in the case of the latter." In sum, complexity itself is less to be feared than the prospect that "states will further weaken, or even dissolve as effective central agencies, without the prior, or simultaneous, emergence of alternative agencies of public governance to deal with a wide range of human requirements, at societal as well as global levels."

Mark Boyer's essay considers together the separate notions of clubs, socially constructed identities, and international institutions, with the goal of establishing "how the divergent theoretical approaches complement one another in their challenges to realist approaches to understanding the prospects for international cooperation." He observes that "the greater the overlap among the clubs in the policy space, the greater the likelihood that there will be cooperation among the clubs in search of common goals and policy outcomes"; and, by extension, "for issues that lie outside the shaded overlapping policy space, it is likely that as cooperation emerges on issues within the area of overlap, club members will tend to make decisions on other policy issues that are also in concert with overlap issues." A variety of factors could intervene to make the relationship between overlapping clubs and cooperation somewhat more tenuous, but the connection is still likely to remain significant. In the contemporary system, Boyer identifies a core set of perceived interests among various clubs in military stability, liberal trading policies, and international financial stability. Whether that degree of consensus will persist long into the twenty-first century is, of course, uncertain.

James Rosenau in his essay probes the role of transnational nongovernmental organizations (NGOs) in "the emergent global system," which subject he regards as "both central and controversial," as a bridge to wider issues of understanding "the underlying nature of world affairs." He begins, in fact, by reflecting on the meaning and significance of key concepts, including one that we met earlier in Holsti's essay, "change"—the others are "complexity," "structural erosion," "state capabilities," and the "NGO" concept itself. Rosenau sees the world as "a globalized space—a space that is not disaggregated in terms of specific geographic territories so much as it consists of a wide range of fast-moving, boundary-spanning actors whose activities cascade erratically across amorphous ethnoscapes, mediascapes, ideoscapes, technoscapes, and financescapes." The second half of the essays addresses the nature of "authority" in such a world. For Rosenau, the essence of authority is its capacity to elicit "varying kinds and degrees of compliance." That formulation accommodates both states and many other authority structures, and it allows for "change in response to the feedback loops and complex adaptation of collectivities in diverse situations." The essay closes with an examination of five types or sources of authority on which NGOs can draw to gain compliance and thereby enhance their role in global politics.

In the last essay of the volume, Rey Koslowski and Antje Wiener observe that the "modern democratic context" has changed dramatically in the second half of the twentieth century, owing to "border crossing by a variety of non-state actors" and "international interdependence expressed by institutional arrangements." The "democratic deficit" potentially inherent in a world in which states are less predominant has, of course, been the subject of considerable discussion in IR literature. Koslowski and Weiner explore some of the conditions traditionally presumed to be associated with democratic practices and suggest, optimistically, that there may at least be hope for a substantial measure of democracy to evolve beyond the state or transnationally. The second section of their essay traces the way the European Union has tried to deal with the issue of democracy as part of its decades-old process of integration. Subsequent sections examine "new forms of democratic practices" in several additional important "sites" in global politics, including international nongovernmental organizations, transgovernmental relations between regions and localities within two or more states, and transnational corporations. Our volume thus closes with a glimpse of the possibility that at least some future nonstate patterns of governance within global political space may become participatory, regularized, and even routinized. With all of the uncertainty, turbulence, and complexity of the contemporary world, that comes as a rather comforting thought.

Notes

1. See, for example, Christer Jönsson, Sven Tägil, and Gunnar Törnqvist, *Organizing European Space* (London: Sage, 2000); and Stephen Rosow, et al., eds., *The Global Economy as Political Space* (Boulder: Lynne Rienner, 1994).

2. On recent trends, see especially: Yale H. Ferguson and Richard W. Mansbach, "Global Politics at the Turn of the Millennium: Changing Bases of 'Us' and 'Them,'" *International Studies Review*, vol. 1, no. 2 (Summer 1999), 76–107; Yale H. Ferguson and Richard W. Mansbach, "History's Revenge and Future Shock: The Remapping of Global Politics," in Martin Hewson and Timothy J. Sinclair, eds., *Approaches to Global Governance Theory* (Albany: State University of New York Press, 1999), 197–238; Thomas L. Friedman, *The Lexus and the Olive Tree: Understanding Globalization*, rev. ed. (New York: Anchor Books, 2000); Robert Gilpin, *The Challenge of Global Capitalism: The World Economy in the Twenty-first Century* (Princeton: Princeton University Press, 2000); David Held, Anthony McGrew, David Goldblatt, and Jonathan Perraton, *Global Transformations: Politics, Economics and Culture* (Oxford: Polity, 2000); R. J. Barry Jones, *The World Turned Upside Down? Globalization and the Future of the State* (Manchester, UK: Manchester University Press, 2000); Robert O. Keohane and Joseph S. Nye, *Power and Interdependence*, 3rd ed. (New York: Longman, 2001); Richard Langhorne, *The Coming of Globalization: Its Evolution and Contemporary Consequences* (New York: Palgrave, 2001); Richard Rosecrance, *The Rise of the Virtual State: Wealth and Power in the Coming Century* (New York: Basic Books, 1999); Jan Aarte Scholte, *Globalization: A Critical Introduction* (New York: Palgrave, 2000); and Herman M. Schwartz, *States Versus Markets: The Emergence of a Global Economy*, 2nd ed. (New York: St. Martin's Press, 2000).

3. John Agnew and Stuart Corbridge, *Mastering Space: Hegemony, Territory and International Political Economy* (New York: Routledge, 1995), chap. 4.

4. Harold and Margaret Sprout, *The Ecological Perspective on Human Affairs with Special Reference to International Politics* (Princeton: Princeton University Press, 1965).

5. See, for example, Friedrich V. Kratochwil, *Norms and Decisions: On the Conditions of Practical and Legal Reasoning in International Relations and Domestic Affairs* (Cambridge, UK: Cambridge University Press, 1989); Vendulka Kubálková, Nicholas Onuf, and Paul Kowert, eds., *International Relations in a Constructed World* Armonk, NY: M. E. Sharpe, 1998); and Alexander Wendt, *Social Theory of International Relations* (Cambridge, UK: Cambridge University Press, 1999).

6. Extreme relativist among postmodernists would insist that the "real world" is entirely an illusion, precisely because it can never be truly known, but we part company with them on that score and side with the constructivists.

7. See, for example, John A. Vasquez, *The Power of Power Politics From Classical Realism to Neotraditionalism* (Cambridge: Cambridge University Press, 1998).

8. Compare, for example, the famous liberal institutionalist manifesto of Robert O. Keohane, *After Hegemony: Cooperation and Discord in the World Economy* (Princeton: Princeton University Press, 1984) with the constructivists cited in footnote #3. See also constructivists John Gerard Ruggie, *Constructing the World Polity: Essays on International Institutionalism* (London: Routledge, 1998); and Martha Finnemore, *National Interests in International Society* (Ithaca: Cornell University Press, 1996). Wendt's state-centric position is closer to Keohane's than the other constructivists, although Finnemore and Ruggie also stress the role of powerful states in shaping norms and institutions to their lik-

ing. An earlier influence on all who write about these subjects was Hedley Bull's *The Anarchical Society: A Study of Order in World Politics* (New York: Columbia University Press, 1977). Nevertheless, Bull was somewhat more venturesome in speculating about the possible emergence of a "new medievalism."

9. Susan Strange, *States and Markets* (London: Pinter, 1988).

10. On this subject see Yale H. Ferguson and Richard W. Mansbach, *Polities: Identities, Loyalty, and Change* (Columbia: University of South Carolina Press, 1996).

11. Saskia Sassen, "Embedding the Global in the National: Implications for the Role of the State," in David A. Smith, et al., eds., *States and Sovereignty in the Global Economy* (London: Routledge, 1999), 158–171.

12. Ferguson and Mansbach, *Polities*, 35.

13. James N. Rosenau, *Along the Domestic-Foreign Frontier: Exploring Governance in a Turbulent World* (Cambridge, UK: Cambridge University Press, 1998), 39, 147.

14. Benjamin J. Cohen, *The Geography of Money* (Ithaca, NY: Cornell University Press, 1998, 145.

15. See R. J. Barry Jones, *The World Turned Upside Down: Globalization and the Future of the State* (Manchester, UK: Manchester University Press, 2000), especially chaps. 8, 9, and 11.

16. See especially A. Claire Cutler, Virginia Haufler, and Tony Porter, eds., *Private Authority and International Affairs* (Albany: State University of New York Press, 1999).

17. See, for example: Hewson and Sinclair, *Approaches to Global Governance Theory*; Robert W. Cox and Timothy J. Sinclair, *Approaches to World Order* (Cambridge, UK: Cambridge University Press, 1996); Joseph S. Nye and John D. Donahue, eds., *Governance in a Globalizing World* (Washington: Brookings Institution Press, 2000); and Oran F. Young, *Governance in World Affairs* (Ithaca: Cornell University Press, 1999).

18. Craig N. Murphy, "Global Governance: Poorly Done and Poorly Understood," *International Affairs*, Vol. 76, No. 4 (October 2000), 797.

19. See Ferguson and Mansbach, *Polities*.

20. See Stephen D. Krasner, *Sovereignty: Organized Hypocrisy* (Princeton, NJ: Princeton University Press, 1999).

21. On the more recent era, see, for example, Mark W. Zacher and Brent A. Sutton, *Governing Global Networks: International Regimes for Transportation and Communications* (Cambridge, UK: Cambridge University Press, 1996); and Mark W. Zacher, *The United Nations and Global Governance* (New York: United Nations Department of Public Information, 1999).

22. Martin Hewson, "Did Global Governance Create Informational Globalism?" in Hewson and Sinclair, *Approaches to Global Governance Theory*, 109.

23. Jönsson, et al., Organizing European Space.

24. cf. Niklas Luhmann, *Social Systems*, trans. by John Bednarz, Jr. with Dirk Baecker (Stanford, CA: Stanford University Press, 1995); and Robert Jervis, *System Effects: Complexity in Political and Social Life* (Princeton, NJ: Princeton University Press, 1997).

25. Liora Salter, "The Standards Regime for Communication and Information technologies," in Cutler, Haufler, Porter, eds. *Private Authority and International Affairs*, 117.

26. See, for example, Murphy, "Global Governance," Robert O'Brien, et al, *Contesting Global Governance: Multilaterial Economic Institutions and Global Social Movements* (Cambridge UK: Cambridge University Press, 2000); Margaret E. Kock and Kathyrn Sikkink, *Activists Beyond Borders* (Ithaca: Cornell University Press, 1998); Jackie Smith, et al., eds. *Transnational Social Movements and Global Politics: Solidarity Beyond the State* (Albany: State University of New York Press, 1999); James H. Mittelman, *The Globalization Syndrome; Transformation and Resistance* (Princeton: Princeton University Press, 2000); David Harvey, *Spaces of Hope* (Berkeley: University of California Press, 2000); and Andrew Heron, et al., eds., *An Unruly World?: Globalization, Governance, and Geography* (London: Routledge, 1998).

27. We lacked liberal institutionalists and "critical" theorists, and there was only one postmodernist (Cynthia Weber), whose paper, unfortunately, was unavailable for this volume.

28. On the need to study history to understand change, see also especially Robert A. Denemark et al., *World System History: The Social Science of Long-Term Change* (London: Routledge, 2000).

29. Barry Buzan and Richard Little, *International Systems in World History: Remaking the Study of International Relations* (Oxford, UK: Oxford University Press, 2000).

30. Susan Strange, *The Retreat of the State: The Diffusion of Power in the World Economy* (Cambridge, UK: Cambridge University Press, 1996).

31. Saskia Sassen, *The Global City: New York, London, Tokyo* (Princeton: Princeton University Press, 1991).

PART I

The Problem of Change
in Historical Perspective

CHAPTER 1

The Problem of Change
in International Relations Theory

K. J. Holsti

Because we have an inadequate basis for comparison, we are tempted to exaggerate either continuity with the past that we know badly, or the radical originality of the present, depending on whether we are more struck by the features we deem permanent, or with those we do not believe existed before. And yet a more rigorous examination of the past might reveal that what we sense as new really is not, and that some of the "traditional" features are far more complex than we think.[1] (Since) no shared vocabulary exists in the literature to depict change and continuity, ... we are not very good as a discipline at studying the possibility of fundamental discontinuity in the international system.[2]

These observations about the nature of inquiry in international relations point directly to a fundamental, if often hidden, dimension of all international theory. It is the problem of change. Ruggie is right: we do not have even the beginning of a consensus on what constitutes change or transformation in international relations.

The great debates among theorists of international relations have been implicit arguments about the nature of change, its possibilities, and its consequences.[3] Along with other dimensions that distinguish the various schools and strains of international theory, mutability has been a major area of disagreement.[4] Realists commonly believe that anarchy creates a realm that predisposes states to behave in certain ways irrespective of national attributes and policymakers' wishes. Thucydides, Meinecke, von Gentz, Gilpin, and Waltz share a view of recurrence in international politics, and are skeptical about the possibilities of transcending the consequences of anarchy through international institutions, learning, or sociological and technological changes at the unit or transnational levels. Whatever their differences, change in international relations is limited to narrow parameters such as alterations in the balance of power, the poles of power, or the cast of great power characters.

Many castigate Realists for not acknowledging that some things in international life have fundamentally changed and that, therefore, the conceptual apparatus that may have been useful for understanding and even explaining diplomatic/military life in eighteenth- and nineteenth-century Europe will not help us a great deal today.[5] Proponents of the view that the quality of international life today is fundamentally different are equally criticized for failing to acknowledge continuities.[6] Absent some agreement on what we mean by change, how we identify it, and for what purposes, these debates are likely to continue and to come to no resolution.

Liberals and constructivists emphasize the variability of state interests, the capacity of policy makers to learn, and the prospects for progress away from standard scenarios of realists such as security dilemmas and stag hunts.[7] Even some postmodernists join a variety of positivist-oriented critics in claiming that the main conceptual categories of the realist tradition—for example sovereignty and anarchy—are no longer consistent with the observed facts of international life. R. B. J. Walker, for example, charges that mainstream versions of IR theory "remain caught within the discursive horizons that express spatiotemporal configurations of another era."[8] Susan Strange argues that "social scientists, in politics and economics especially, cling to obsolete concepts and inappropriate theories. These theories belong to a more stable and orderly world than the one we live in."[9] The result is "one-eyed social science."[10] It is thus incumbent on us to accomplish an intellectual "jailbreak,"[11] to move beyond ritual invocations of concepts that once had theoretical and descriptive uses, but that are no longer able to capture those things that are truly new and novel in the world.

But there is more than just change in the theoretical air. Increasingly, scholars of International Relations are claiming fundamental *transformations*. We live in an era not of marginal alterations and adaptations, of growth and decline, but in an era of discontinuity with the past. Rosenau speaks of post-international politics[12] and of a contemporary "epochal transformation."[13] Yoshikazu Sakamoto characterizes the contemporary scene as a *new era* involving fundamental transformations.[14] Rey Koslowski and Friederich Kratochwil suggest that the end of the Cold War constituted a "transformation" of the international system—not a change within the system but a change *of* system.[15]

Postmodernists and many critical theorists read our intellectual predicament somewhat differently. Rosenau and Strange, they might suggest, do not go far enough because they remain wedded to positivism and to the idea that the trained observer can through a variety of rigorous procedures encapsulate the amazing complexity of the world into totalizing theoretical projects such as Rosenau's "two worlds of world politics."[16] The world, they claim, cannot be rendered intelligible through "grand" theoretical projects that attempt to distill complexity, paradox, and change into neat theoretical packages and categories.

Rather, we now have to acknowledge that everything is in flux, paradox prevails, and we can only know what we ourselves experience.[17] Generalization is a Western logocentric practice that invariably contains a political program. To know, literally, is to act, and since the record of action on the diplomatic front in the twentieth century is not one to be proud of, it is probably better not to know in the sense of generalization. Postmodernists basically claim that change has rendered the pursuit of knowledge as we have known it since Aristotelian times not only a fool's game, but also ethically dangerous. The human mind is incapable of understanding the complexity of the world, and since change is ubiquitous, any attempt to characterize it in general terms is bound to fail.

Analysis of change, then, has become almost a constant in the academic field of international theory. A whole new vocabulary of clichés or analogies has invaded debate. "Globalization," the "global village," "new mediaevalism," "post-Westphalia," "the borderless world," and the like, suggest that we have entered, or are entering, a new era or epoch in which contemporary ideas, practices, institutions, and problems of international politics are fundamentally different from their predecessors. But popular monikers, while evocative of things that are different, do not substitute for rigorous analysis. Lacking in all of this claim of novelty is a consensus not only on *what* has changed but also on *how we can distinguish* minor change from fundamental change, trends from transformations, and growth or decline from new forms. The intellectual problems are both conceptual and empirical. This essay addresses two questions: (1) What do we mean by change? and (2) What, exactly, has changed in the fundamental institutions of international politics? This implies a subquestion, namely, what has *not* fundamentally changed?

Markers of Change

Change, like beauty and good skiing conditions, is in the eye of the beholder. From a microperspective, the international events recorded in today's headlines constitute change because they are not identical to yesterday's news. The media, to perhaps a greater extent than ever before, run on a twenty-four-hour cycle that militates against notions of continuity, that emphasizes novelty, and that encourages pessimistic framing of issues for analysis.[18] To a historian of civilizations, on the other hand, today's events do not even appear on the intellectual radar screen. Nothing in daily events suggests any sort of fundamental alteration of the persisting dynamics and patterns of power, achievement, authority, status, and the nature of social institutions. Somewhere between these micro- (media) and macro- (philosophical) extremes, observers may note certain types of markers where, typically, things appear to be done differently than they were previously.

Trends

Trends record one kind of change. Population grows, the membership in the United Nations increases, communications networks and the messages they carry proliferate and speed up (space and time are compressed), the volume of international trade grows at a much faster rate than total economic production, and the numbers of people traveling abroad increases annually. Moving in the other direction, the incidence of terrorist acts and airline hijacking declined before September 11, 2001, as continue to do the number of nuclear warheads and the incidence of interstate wars. What are we to make of such trends? That they are noticeable or that they occur over a relatively short period of time does not necessarily make them theoretically significant. Change must have significant consequences. Otherwise the claim of change is no more than one observer's arbitrary judgment that things in a quantitative sense are not the same as they used to be. We have many notable trends over the past half-century, but their implications are by no means obvious. Population, international trade, number of sovereign states, number of intergovernmental organizations (IGOS) and nongovernmental organizations (NGOS), investment flows, citizen competence, and the like may increase. But individually or collectively, what is their import? This is the Hegelian and Marxist problem: At what point does quantitative change lead to qualitative consequences?[19]

Traditional markers are also subjective and selective. How do we interpret the dramatic growth of World Wide Web use against the less well-known fact that one-half of the world's three billion souls have never made a telephone call? If you choose the first trend you will infer very different characteristics of the world than if you choose the second. Thus, inferring systemwide transformations from increases or decreases of selective quantitative trends is a tricky business indeed. Few of the advocates of the "new" international politics (or new paradigm, or whatever) have made a convincing case that all the quantitative changes since 1945 or 1989—to pick arbitrary dates—somehow constitute a revolution, a new era, or a transformation in the world.

Great Events

Others favor "great events" as the main markers of change. Change is not an accumulation of many little acts, seen as trends. What matters are not quantities of standard practices, but great variations from the typical. Significant change, many argue, tends to be dramatic and compressed. The practices, ideas, and institutions of international politics assume reasonably fixed patterns over the long haul, until a major historical event—usually cataclysmic—changes them. Lord Bolinbroke defined epochs in terms of chains of events (indicating regular patterns) being so broken "as to have little or no real or visible connection with that which we see continue."[20] Historians often use the device of a major *discontinuity* to organize their narratives. Since 1800 to 1900 would be a purely arbitrary designation of the "nineteenth century," most historians prefer the period 1815 to 1914. The markers of change here are the end of one great period of European war and the beginning of another. An era or period is configured around major events that ostensibly caused major disruptions or changes of previous patterns. They are also the sources of entirely new patterns. James Der Derian has termed these "monster years," for they mark a fundamental transition, not just some arbitrary point on a quantitative scale.[21] Notice, however, that the marker is still a chronological artifact and there is no guarantee that major events in fact alter typical patterns.

The problems of major events as markers of change are nicely (if unwittingly) summarized in Ian Clark's *Globalization and Fragmentation: International Relations in the Twentieth Century*. He summarizes a number of historians' use of periodization to characterize the twentieth century. Most use the great events of 1914, 1919, 1939, 1945, and/or 1989–1991 as demarcating significant changes, even transformations, rather than continuities.[22] But there is no agreement on these dates. That they all contained significant events is beyond dispute, but there is no consensus—indeed there is wide disagreement—as to whether or not these events were the sources of change or transformation. As with trends, choices tend to be arbitrary.

Did 1815 or 1919 really constitute some sort of discontinuity? Woodrow Wilson's wartime and postwar perorations would certainly lead one to believe that after 1919 the world would enter some sort of new age. Yet, the record of war, imperialism, and national chauvinism in the 1920s and 1930s would justifiably give rise to skepticism. Was 1945 a major marker separating significantly different epochs of twentieth century history? Many analysts have made a compelling case that it was; others have simply assumed it. Yet others, such as Clark himself, vigorously dispute the dichotomization of the twentieth century into two clear-cut parts. Thus one person's discontinuity or great event is not necessarily a sign of transformation for others. Arbitrary decisions remain, and because this is so, theorists of international relations are not likely to agree on their import.

Great Achievements

Another common marker is the "great achievement(s)" which stands in contrast to the ordinary and mundane. Unlike "great events," they suggest an ongoing pattern of difference from previous eras. New patterns of social practice deriving from these great achievements do not necessarily outlive their originators, however, and so change in this sense may be ephemeral. In eras marked by greater opportunities for heroism or the unique contributions of leaders, the markers can correspond to a dynastic reign, such as the Han dynasty[23] or the age of Louis XIV. Or it can refer to an era of great popular social, artistic, and cultural achievement as in the case of the "golden age" of Greece in the fifth century B.C.

Significant Social/Technological Innovations

In the twentieth century, analysts have used many other types of events as historical markers suggesting fundamental change. After 1945 there was a good deal of talk about the "nuclear revolution," a technological innovation that nullified the Clausewitzian conception of war . . . or so it was believed. The record of war since 1945 is inconsistent with the conclusion, however. The "nuclear revolution" altered the nature of relations between great powers, to be sure, but it did not terminate violence between states.

Today, the computer has reputedly replaced the atomic bomb as the causal agent of change or transformation. The bomb could only alter traditional security thinking—away from how to win wars to how to prevent them— whereas the microelectronic revolution has changed the daily life of several billion people. Its influences are more ubiquitous, and therefore more transformative than nuclear weaponry. Most of the discussion of "globalization," "the global village" or "borderless world" derives specifically from a technological innovation. As with "great events," however, there is little consensus on the consequences of the innovation. For some, "globalization" results in the erosion of sovereignty; for others it has strengthened the state. And there are innumerable positions between these two extremes.

Concepts of Change

Markers only identify when or what causes significant change. They do not specify what kinds of change are involved. Theorists in our field, perhaps astonishingly, rarely take the trouble to define what they mean by change. But there are several major conceptions of change. These include change as replacement, change as addition, dialectical change, and transformation.[24] Most authors fail to specify which kind they have in mind, yet the differences between them are theoretically important, perhaps even crucial in estimating the validity of claims.

Change as Addition

Change can be *additive*—a new phenomenon not necessarily a *replacement, but only adds complexity*. It means, for example, that while behaviors consistent with elements of realism persist in many areas of the world, new forms of collaboration, cooperation, and governance are also developing. Stag hunts, security dilemmas, and prisoners' dilemmas (India-Pakistan, the South China Sea) coexist with international regimes, global governance, integration, and the development of pluralistic security communities (Sweden-Norway, Canada and the United States, the European Union, and the like). Global "civil society" does not replace national-level political activity; it only complements it. A significant proportion of the debates about theories of international relations over the past several decades do not claim that realism is wrong, but that it is incomplete. It is not the only game in town and for the sake of comprehensiveness we need to add other perspectives and other forms of activity. Similarly, diplomacy is today much more complex and involves substantially more people than before, but this complexity has not led to a transformation, that is, the obliteration of older practices, norms, and etiquette.

Dialectical Change

Dialectical concepts do not solve all the problems of identifying change, establishing markers, distinguishing quantitative from qualitative changes, the problems of micro- versus macroperspectives, and the like. But they do handle in a unique way the old and the new. Change does not displace. But it is more than additive, meaning greater complexity. It can represent *new forms* built on the old. Thus, there is both novelty *and* continuity. It can combine the new and the old without total replacement. But we must be wary of any teleological elements to dialectical notions of change. In the Marxist idiom, the synthesis arising from the contradictions between old forms always led to a "higher" form. This progressivist notion of change may sound nice, but a synthesis can also signify reversal, corruption, or decline.

Change as Transformation

Transformation can result from quantitative changes which, when accumulated over a period of time, bring new forms to life. But, logically, the new forms must derive from old patterns. They can partly *replace* old forms, but by definition they must include residues or legacies of the old. One cannot transform from nothing. In the case of social and political institutions, a transformation is distinguished from obsolescence in the sense that old ideas, practices, and norms may remain reasonably similar over long periods of time, but the *functions* of the institution change. A good example is monarchy. In the Scandinavian countries, Japan, and perhaps less so in England, many of the practices of monarchy, as well as protocol, norms, and ideas remain similar over the centuries, but the functions of the monarchy have changed from ruling, to symbolism and national identity. There has been a transformation of an institution, but not its replacement. The old and the new coexist.

Change as Replacement

The end of the Cold War stimulated a large industry of projections for the future. Most of these heralded significant changes in the texture, structures, and practices of international relations as we reach a new millennium. For Goldgeier and McFaul, Singer and Wildavsky, and Koslowski and Kratochwil, the end of the Cold War constituted, minimally, a fundamental change in the way the superpowers relate to each other and, maximally, a true transformation of the international system.[25] For Francis Fukuyama, also, we are in the midst of a major historical transformation where for a variety of ideational and technological reasons, something resembling perpetual peace—the dream of thinkers since at least the duc de Sully in the seventeenth century—will come to pass.[26] For Samuel Huntington, in contrast, war and violence do not end with the Cold War.[27] Only the fault lines of international conflict have changed from conflicts between states and their encapsulated ideologies, to conflicts between civilizations. Notice that one common practice of international politics, namely war, does not disappear; only the types of actors that engage in it do. For Alain Minc, there is yet another area of change.[28] The breakdown of political authority in many Third World states and in the OECD countries is giving rise to "le nouveau moyen age," an era where we can expect less safety of life and property than we have seen in almost a millennium. If Minc's prognostication comes to pass, clearly there will have been more than just a quantitative change. The patterns and structures of the past will be *replaced* by vast sets of novel conditions.

For Fukuyama, peace replaces war. For Huntington, civilizational wars replace interstate wars. For Goldgeier and McFaul, Singer and Wildavsky, Minc, and Kaplan, the relative stability of the Cold War is replaced by the "coming chaos" characteristic of armed conflict in the Third World.[29] Whether or not these changes are true transformations can be debated endlessly, but all the authors take a common stand in their implicit notion of change. *A significant change is something new, and that new thing is usually the antithesis of something old.*

This is a *discontinuous* idea of change: new patterns replace old forms, so the problem of transformation does not arise. Certainly nothing new develops without a past, but the characteristics of the new may be so fundamentally different from anything proceeding that transformation is not an appropriate word. Replacement means novelty. Anthony Giddens, though focusing on macrosocial phenomena rather than contemporary international politics, adopts the discontinuist view of history on the grand scale when he argues:

> [O]riginating in the West but becoming more and more global in their impact, there has occurred a series of changes of extraordinary magnitude when compared with any other phases in human history. What separates those living in the modern world from all previous types of society, and all previous

epochs in history, is more profound than the continuities which connect them to the longer spans of the past. . . . [T]he contrasts which can be made will often prove more illuminating than the continuities that may be discerned. It is *the* task of sociology . . . to seek to analyze the nature of that novel world which, in the late twentieth century, we now find ourselves. . . . In a period of three hundred years, an insignificant sliver of human history as a whole, *the face of the earth has been wiped clean* (my italics).[30]

This is not an organic view of historical change. It is not similar to Braudel's concept of the "*longue durée.*" It is not analysis of trends, of systemic change at the margins, or of the transformation of old institutions. In elaborating his social theory, Giddens makes it clear that contemporary social formations, and in particular the modern state, *have virtually nothing in common with what has preceded.* For Giddens, meaningful modern history is the story of discontinuity and replacement, not of transformation.

Much of the International Relations rhetoric of the past decade implicitly makes the case for concepts of change as replacement or transformation. This seems natural following great events such as the end of the Cold War. Human propensities to optimism are particularly pronounced when long eras of tension, war, and violence seemingly come to an end. But previous claims to a "new world order," whether in 1815, 1919, 1945, or 1989–1991 have usually turned out to be somewhat premature. Most often, the claims of replacement and transformation would better be classified as additions or dialectical syntheses, where elements of the old and the new coexist. For example, if we do indeed live in a "Post-Westphalian" order, then there must be few traces of Westphalia remaining in it. We cannot use "Post-Westphalia" legitimately if there are only new elements added to the old. Similarly, if, as Rosenau suggests, we now live in a new epoch of postinternational politics,[31] then the main characteristics of international politics as we knew them for about three centuries must be demonstrated to have disappeared and to have been replaced by other (or new) practices, ideas, and norms. That we have more states, that we communicate more rapidly, or that we trade more within the context of a vastly expanded global population does not automatically entitle us to claim either discontinuity or transformation. Yet, this is exactly the tone of much IR scholarship today.

Systemic and Lower Levels of Change

Much of the popular discourse on contemporary change refers to systemic phenomena. The indicators of change, be they trends, transformations, or replacements, are universal. A new era in international relations, for example, does not refer to a single country's foreign policy alteration, but to properties of the entire system. Population growth, compression of time and space, decline in the incidence of interstate wars, or the waning authority of states are in most of the literature statements about universal trends. The spatial hallmark of almost all International Relations theory, indeed, is its unabashed—and therefore inappropriate—universalism.[32]

There is, however, an approach to change that begins at the state or individual levels. It is a theory of learning. We now have a large, mostly American-based, literature of this genre.[33] It examines the ways that foreign policy-makers redefine state interests as a result of learning through participation in international organizations and their encompassed epistemic communities. Change here is at the unit level, whether a policy-maker or a state's definition of interests. But it does not automatically warrant claims of systemic change. This would be the ecological fallacy in reverse. Although Lebow claims that "[é]lite learning at the unit level has systemic consequences," it would require a very muscular state indeed to change the entire texture of international relations in a given time period.[34] Even the most revolutionary leaders like Hitler and Stalin were unable to alter the fundamental institutions of international relations although they tried. World War II, among other purposes, was a war to sustain the Westphalian system, which means a group of institutions that sustain the sovereignty and independence of distinct political communities called states. Change at the unit level is not likely to alter such a system, although when many states begin to emulate the changes of some "leaders," there may well be some form of system change or even transformation.

A Source of Confusion: Defining International Relations

Assertions of change and novelty abound in contemporary international relations theory and in more descriptive and policy-relevant analyses. Regrettably, the assertions are often more notable for their stridency than for their sensitivity to important distinctions between concepts of change or to systematic empirical evidence. We all seem to acknowledge obvious trends and tendencies, but we are much less certain as to their consequences for international relations. Time and space have been compressed; economics are being globalized; frontiers erode; autonomy is constrained; sovereignty is dead; an international civic society is developing to challenge the authority of the state; there are elements of a "new medievalism," and global problems have rendered solutions in terms of national priorities obsolete.

Not everyone, of course, accepts these assertions. Adherence to "eternal verities," whether conceptual or empirical, remains striking in both academic discourse and in the ways that states conduct their foreign relations. Claims of a new world order or escaping "conceptual jails" notwithstanding, the behavior of Pakistanis and Indians, Israelis and Arabs, or Greeks and Turks toward each other is strikingly reminiscent of Soviet and American relations during the Cold War, or of the Anglo-German rivalry before 1914. Chinese military activities in the South China Sea could be reasonably compared to French/Spanish/British struggles to control the Balearic Islands in the late eighteenth and early nineteenth centuries. Current textbooks in international relations have not jettisoned concepts such as power, the state, national interest, conflict, security, or international organizations despite many claims that such ideas are dated, outworn, or part of an obsolete and closed "modernist discourse."

How are we to judge this proliferation of assertions and warnings? How are we to distinguish the significant from the passing and ephemeral? How can we assess the rival claims that changes constitute additions versus replacements and/or transformations? How can we judge whether conceptual "jailbreaks" are worth the effort?

One of the reasons the great disputes in international theory cannot be easily resolved is because analysts have fundamentally different conceptions of the world that we are trying to characterize, interpret, and explain. Realists are interested in the classical problems of peace and war and consequently concentrate on the official relations between states and between states and their international organizations. Others, in contrast, are not comfortable with the world of international politics. They want to examine "world politics," "global politics," or "globology," that is, any activities that cross state boundaries. The intellectual mandate of world or global politics runs from the activities of the secretary-general of the United Nations to African market women and the wives of Zapatista rebels in Chiapas. The purview of "globology"[35] is no less than the grand project of global social change. Since these perspectives are so different from the focus of the "classical tradition"—that is, the relations between states as they revolve around issues of war, peace, and security—they are incommensurable. They are not right or wrong, but different. There cannot be, therefore, some consensus on what has changed and what continues. For the global sociologist, all sorts of trends suggest change, though not many would qualify as evidence of a new epoch or transformation in the relations between states.[36] On the other hand, because many governments behave in ways approximating the tenets of realism or liberalism, those characterizations have a ring of truth that hints more at continuities than at transformation.

Change and International Institutions

Though we cannot judge between conceptions of the world, we must, as Rosenau insists, develop benchmarks from which significant deviations can be noted. International institutions are one important candidate. This choice may not be accepted by all because it is political rather than economic or sociological, and because it is state-centric. However, an essential foundation of a society of states is the international institution. If, on the one hand, the fundamental institutions of international relations, collectively, change to the point of transformation, as many contemporary analyses argue or imply, then with some authority we can make the case that we are seeing the emergence of a new kind of international system. We must specify, however, whether the change is a replacement, addition, transformation, or synthesis. If, on the other hand, most international institutions maintain their essential characteristics, though with some degrees of change such as added complexity, then we have no solid basis for making the claim that in terms of international politics, we live in a new world.

The institutions of international politics are fundamental. They are not to be confused with organizations, such as the United Nations. I follow Hedley Bull's use of the term institution which, while not exact, implies the critical importance of the combination of *ideas, practices,* and *norms*:

> A *society of states* (or international society) exists when a group of states, conscious of certain common interests and common values, form a society in the sense that they conceive themselves to be bound by a common set of rules in their relations with one another, and share in the working of common institutions. . . . In international society . . . the sense of common interests . . . does not in itself provide precise guidance as to what behaviour is consistent with these goals; to do this is the function of rules. These rules may have the status of international law, of moral rules, of custom or established practice, or they may be merely operational rules or 'rules of the game,' worked out without formal agreement or even without verbal communication. It is not uncommon for a rule to emerge first as an operational rule, then to become established practice, then to attain the status of a moral principle and finally to become incorporated in a legal convention. . . . States communicate the rules through their official words. . . . But they also communicate the rules through their actions, when they behave in such a way as to indicate that they accept or do not accept that a particular rule is valid.[37]

I do not adopt the teleological aspects of this definition, because institutional growth, development, and decline are not always accounted for by common purposes.[38]

We can distinguish *foundational institutions* of the states system that emerged in the seventeenth century from procedural institutions. Foundational institutions have allowed analysts of virtually all persuasions—from realists to liberal institutionalists and constructivists—to claim or assume that there is an international states system (or society of states, to use Bull's term) that is markedly distinguishable from empires, migrant clans and lineages, the complex medieval system of overlapping jurisdictions, leagues of cities, suzerainty systems, and other formats for organizing distinct political communities.[39] Without these foundational institutions, we could not make the claim. Political space would be organized on different principles and, presumably, on different institutional formats. Foundational institutions define (1) legitimate actors; (2) the fundamental principles on which they are based; and (3) the major norms, assumptions, and/or rules on which their mutual relations are based. The foundational institutions of the Westphalian international system includes states, sovereignty, territoriality, and the fundamental norm of all international law, *pacta sunt servanda*.

Procedural institutions are those repetitive practices, ideas, and norms that underlie and regulate interactions and transactions between the separate actors. These institutions refer not to questions of "who are we" and "how do we claim status and legitimacy," but to more instrumental issues of how we behave toward one another. They are important in helping us describe the essential characteristics of an international system, but they are of secondary significance compared to the foundational institutions. A procedural institution such as war could disappear without fundamentally altering the foundational institutions. A warless (in the sense of interstate war) world would be a wonder, but would it also be something other than a world of states? The states system has survived the demise of the international slave trade and colonialism, and with the new technologies available today, we can at least conceive of the death of traditional diplomatic institutions, but the foundational institutions might endure without substantial transformation.

Institutions are comprised, adding to Bull's definition, of a combination of (1) common *practices*; (2) a *consensus of ideas underlying those practices*; and (3) commonly observed and accepted *norms, rules, and etiquette*. All three interconnected components must be present to constitute an international institution. Diplomacy is a procedural institution of international politics because it is a common and patterned *practice* in the sense that thousands of government officials are in daily contact for the purposes of representation, exchanging information, persuasion, and formal negotiation. We can also predict with almost complete certainty that they will do exactly the same tomorrow, this date next year, and probably this date in 2015. It is precisely because diplomacy is practiced so widely, so frequently, and according to such common procedures that we take it for granted. Taking practices for granted provides one clue that they have become institutionalized. If political units went to war to see which ones could send diplomats abroad, if they regularly imprisoned, assassinated, or poisoned emissaries, and if major crises erupted over issues of diplomatic precedence, then we could not claim that the practice was either regular or institutionalized. Second, the practices of diplomacy are founded on or surrounded by (1) concepts that command common understanding (e.g., diplomat, ambassador, conference, and the like) and (2) sets of ideas and expectations about how governments should deal with each other. There is no ideology of diplomacy, but there is something we can call a "diplomatic vocabulary" or "diplomatic culture" that is based on ideas that command common recognition and understanding. Finally, diplomacy is surrounded by an extensive and commonly observed network of norms, protocols, regulations, and etiquette. Many of these have reached the status of law, as contained in the Vienna Convention on Diplomatic Privileges, Intercourse and Immunities (1961) which gave concrete form to and amended the conventional laws and practices of diplomacy developed in 1815 and subsequently. Although the *practices* of diplomacy may have changed in many ways—for example in the incorporation of representatives of nongovernmental organizations or individual citizens in official diplomatic delegations—the institution of diplomacy has not been replaced or transformed. The ideas, norms, regulations, and conventions of diplomacy remain largely intact.

Possibilities of Institutional Change

There are four possibilities for institutional change. Institutions can (1) arise; (2) change (add complexity); (3) transform, perhaps through dialectical processes; and (4) disappear.

Institutions seldom just appear suddenly. They are themselves the consequences of previous practices. When we say that they have arisen, we mean only that those practices (1) have become generalized, predictable, and patterned; (2) have been suffused with ideological justification or adorned with a commonly understood set of concepts and ideas; and (3) have become surrounded with norms, regulations, and etiquette.

Once institutionalized, a practice or activity may change quantitatively. Today diplomacy encompasses the activities of hundreds of thousands of officials (compared to hundreds in the eighteenth century), taking place annually in thousands of multilateral meetings, and mostly practiced by issue-based experts in constant touch with their superiors. This pattern contrasts with the few "gentlemen" who received general instructions from their sovereign and then disappeared to a foreign capital for a decade or more to bring those instructions to life. The ideas, conventions, and purposes or functions of diplomacy have not transformed, but the practices have become much more complex.

Transformation is the third possibility. This is the case when change in the three defining variables has been so profound—once again, an arbitrary judgment—that even though the activity retains its original name, what really goes on is no longer the same. A further indicator of transformation is change in function[40] or purposes. Forms, rules, and ideas may remain, but the practices and purposes of the practices become transformed. War may be a current example of institutional transformation. In the eighteenth century, it was characterized by a set pattern of activities (training, mobilization, battle, command, and control), a commonly accepted set of justifications (e.g., *raison d'etat*), definitions (e.g., Clausewitz), and other ideas. War was highly regulated by conventions, protocols, and etiquette (e.g., surrender ceremonies, treatment of prisoners and wounded, respect for civilian life, uniforms, ranks, declarations of war, and the like). The purpose of war was, according to its main philosopher of the period, Clausewitz, to promote and protect the interests of the state. Recent wars in Liberia, Sierra Leone, Tajikistan, and other places have only killing in common with nineteenth-century wars. In every other way they are a different phenomenon. Their purpose, or function, is not the pursuit of state interests "by other means," but to enrich small groups of kleptocrats whose private interests are paramount. Mercenaries have reappeared. The distinction between war and criminality has become increasingly blurred, as has the distinction between combatants and civilians. One of the major post-1945 trends that does suggest fundamental change is the pronounced waning of interstate, Clausewitzian-type wars, and the luxurious growth of domestic violence where the practices, ideas, and norms of classical warfare are notable by their absence.[41] There is plenty of evidence to sustain an argument of the institutional transformation of contemporary war.

Finally, institutions can disappear. Colonialism was a late-nineteenth-century practice that became surrounded with norms and regulations, and was propped up with an elaborate set of social and political justifications (e.g., *la mission civilisatrice*), an elaborate anthropological taxonomy that clearly demarcated superiors and inferiors, and ideological principles. By the early twentieth century, notions of self-determination gained currency as moral justification for the creation of new European states from old empires. The rules of the colonial game also changed. The main idea of the League of Nations Mandates system was to prepare colonial peoples for self-government, if not independence. This was an idea that only one-half century earlier would have been unheard of. By the end of World War II, statehood became the great goal of liberation policies and the ideological props of colonialism had been discredited by the barbarism of intra-Europan wars, by the spread of liberalism, and by forms of protonationalism in places like India. With no further ideological legitimacy, colonial practices gave way to the birth of over 130 countries in a matter of two decades. By 1960 colonialism was rendered illegitimate by the fiat of United Nations resolutions.

The four possibilities—new institutions, institutional change (complexity), institutional transformation, and institutional demise—do not necessarily take place simultaneously in the international system. Some institutions die off as new ones arise. All institutions change over time, but some may do so more quickly than others. And some changes may lead to transformations, while others do not alter the three generic characteristics we use.

Table 1.1
Continuity and Change in International Institutions

Foundational Institutions	Major Changes	Current Status
Sovereignty	Increased complexity; some delegation of (EU); UN practices on humanitarian intervention; quasistates; international criminal activity	In process of transformation?
State	Reduced autonomy; growth of multiple loyalties; retrenchment of state functions; fragmentation of weak states	Slow transformation?
Territoriality	Increasing permeability but firmer legal status; reduced incidence of territorial change; outlaw change by force	Persisting/strengthening
International law	Growing complexity; foundational principles (*pacta sunt servanda*, reciprocity, equality) remain	Complexity (change)

Process Institutions		
Diplomacy	Growing complexity; "democratization"; foundational principles increasingly elaborated and legalized	Complexity (change)
Commerce	Growing complexity; quantitative increase; increasingly rule-bound; political influence of TNCs; rise of drug trade and international crime	Complexity (change); increased institutionalization, thus strengthening
Colonialism	Collapse of an institution	Obsolescence
Slave trade	Only few vestiges remain (traffic in women)	Obsolescence
War	Primarily within states; mostly civilian casualties; laws of war not observed; violence combined with criminality	Transforming or replacement
Conflict management	Role of IGOs in controlling conflicts; elaboration of PKO functions; delegitimization of use of force in IR	Arising (compared to pre-1945)
Governance	Vast elaboration of international regimes and management organizations; G-7, IMF, environmental regulations, etc.	Arising (compared to pre-1919)

From the perspective of system change, presumably transformations in foundational institutions are more important than those of procedural institutions. We can chronicle institutional transformation in the practice of war, but this may not have system-changing consequences. If, in contrast, the institution of sovereignty is transforming, as an increasing number of analysts claim,[42] then there is a case for the view that we are in the midst of epochal change in the fundamental characteristics of international relations. We are in the process of systems rather than systemic change. Such a determination would provide a major filip for those who maintain that older generalizations about the fundamental characteristics of international politics are woefully out of date.

I conclude with a brief list of the major institutions of contemporary international relations (Table 1.1). I have no rigid selection criteria (nor does Bull), but while all may not agree that the list is exhaustive, there would probably be a reasonable consensus that the main foundational and procedural institutions are included. In the right column, I offer impressionistic observations about the kind of change that we have seen in each institution during approximately the period since 1945.

This discussion will not end the debate about change in both the practice and theory of international politics but it may help to discipline the proliferation of claims about novelty, "new eras," "new world orders," transformations, and post-this or post-that. On the one hand, one detects in these claims a large component of wishful thought that seems to be replacing serious, empirically based, and authoritative analysis. On the other hand, those who see nothing new and who continue to think that Thucydides, Machiavelli, or Morgenthau described the eternal verities of international politics will note, when examining international institutions, significant changes and even the demise of some institutions that were considered normal and quite permanent during their heydays. Not all may support the notion of international institutions as the only or most appropriate benchmark for noting change and continuity. But benchmarks of some kind are essential. In their absence, we have little but trends of debatable consequences, arbitrary dates, unsubstantiated epochs, eras, or systems, and no discrimination about types of change. In the midst of the current cacophony of countering claims, now is a good time to begin thinking systematically and in a disciplined fashion about the problem of change in international politics.

Notes

1. Stanley Hoffman, "An American Social Science: International Relations," *Daedelus* (1977): 57.

2. John Ruggie, "Territoriality and Beyond Problematizing Modernity in International Relations," *International Organization* 47, no. 4 (1993): 140–174.

3. Barry Buzan and R. J. Barry Jones, eds., *Change and the Study of International Relations: The Evaded Dimension* (London: Frances Pinter, 1981), 2.

4. Yale H. Ferguson and Richard W. Mansbach, *The Elusive Quest: Theory and International Politics* (Columbia, SC: University of South Carolina, 1988).

5. See, for example, K. J. Holsti, "The Post-Cold War 'Settlement' in Comparative Perspective," in *Discord and Collaboration in a New Europe: Essays in Honor of Arnold Wolfers*, ed. Douglas T. Stuart and Stephen F. Szabo (Washington, DC: The Paul H. Nitze School of Advanced International Studies, 1994), 37–70. See also Susan Strange, *The Retreat of the State: The Diffusion of Power in the World Economy* (Cambridge: Cambridge University Press, 1996).

6. See, for example, Hedley Bull, *The Anarchical Society: A Study of Order in World Politics* (London: Macmillan, 1977), chap. 10. See also John J. Mearsheimer, "Back to the Future: Instability in Europe after the Cold War," *International Security* 15, no. 1 (1990): 5–56.

7. See, for example, Emmanuel Adler and Beverly Crawford, eds., *Progress in Postwar International Relations* (New York: Columbia University Press, 1991).

8. R. B. J. Walker, *Inside/Outside: International Relations as Political Theory* (Cambridge: Cambridge University Press, 1993), x.

9. Strange, *Retreat of the State*, 3.

10. Ibid., 175.

11. James N. Rosenau, *Turbulence in World Politics* (Princeton: Princeton University Press, 1990), chap. 2.

12. Rosenau, *Turbulence in World Politics*, chap. 1.

13. James N. Rosenau, *Along the Domestic-Foreign Frontier: Exploring Governance in a Turbulent World* (Cambridge: Cambridge University Press, 1997), 7.

14. Yoshikazu Sakamoto, "A Perspective on the Changing World Order: A Conceptual Prelude," in *Global Transformation: Challenges to the State System*, ed. Yoshikazu Sakamoto (Tokyo: United Nations University Press, 1994), 15, 16.

15. Rey Koslowski and Friedrich Kratochwil, "Understanding Change in International Politics: The Soviet Empire's Demise and the International System," *International Organization* 48, no. 2 (1994): 215–248.

16. Rosenau, *Turbulence in World Politics*.

17. Sandra Harding sums up this view: "Coherent theories in an incoherent world are either silly and uninteresting or oppressive and problematic, depending on the degree of hegemony they manage to achieve. Coherent theories in an *apparently* coherent world are even more dangerous, for the world is always more complex than such unfortunately hegemonic theories can grasp" (Sandra Harding, *The Science Question in Feminism* [London: Milton Keynes, 1986], 164). For similar sentiments, see Richard Ash-

ley and R. B. J. Walker, "Reading Dissidence/Writing the Discipline: Crisis and the Question of Sovereignty in International Studies," *International Studies Quarterly* 34 (September 1990): 367–416. See also Jim George, *Discourses of Global Politics: A Critical (Re)Introduction to International Relations* (Boulder, CO: Lynne Rienner, 1995).

18. See, for example, Thomas E. Patterson, "Time and News: The Media's Limitations as an Instrument of Democracy," *International Political Science Review* 19, no. 1 (1998): 55–68.

19. See, for example, R. J. Barry Jones, "Concepts and Models of Change in International Relations," in *Change and the Study of International Relations*, ed. R. J. Barry Jones and Barry Buzan (London: Frances Pinter, 1981), 11–29.

20. As quoted in Ruggie, *Territoriality and Beyond*, 148.

21. James Der Derian, James, "Post-Theory: The External Return of Ethics in International Relations," in *New Thinking in International Relations Theory*, eds. Michael Doyle and John Ikenberry (Boulder, CO: Westview Press, 1997), 54–76.

22. Ian Clark, *Globalization and Fragmentation: International Relations in the Twentieth Century* (Oxford: Oxford University Press, 1997).

23. Even in contemporary Japan, official dates are recorded not according to the Western calendar, but to the year of the emperor's reign.

24. This list is not necessarily exhaustive. It does not include the jargon of contemporary debates, such as "shift," "move," or "moment." These terms are so nebulous that they cannot add to conceptual clarity.

25. James Goldgeier and Michael McFaul, "A Tale of Two Worlds: Core and Periphery in the Post-Cold War Era," *International Organization* 46, vol. 1 (1992): 467–492; Max Singer and Aaron Wildavsky, *The Real World Order: Zones of Peace Zones of Turmoil* (Chatham, NJ: Chatham House Publishers, 1993); Koslowski and Kratochwil, "Understanding Change in International Politics."

26. Francis Fukuyama, "The End of History?" *National Interest* (Summer 1989): 3–18.

27. Samuel Huntington, "The Coming Clash of Civilizations?" *Foreign Affairs* 72: 22–49.

28. Alain Minc, *Le Nouveau Moyen Age* (Paris: Gallimard, 1993).

29. Goldgeier and McFaul, "Tale of Two Worlds"; Singer and Wildavsky, *Real World Order*; Minc, *Nouveau Moyen Age*; Robert D. Kaplan, "The Coming Anarchy," *The Atlantic Monthly* (February 1994): 44–76.

30. Anthony Giddens, *The Nation-State and Violence* (Berkeley and Los Angeles: University of California Press, 1987), 33–34.

31. Rosenau, *Turbulence in World Politics*.

32. K. J. Holsti, "International Relations Theory and Domestic War in the Third World: The Limits of Relevance," in *International Relations and the Third World*, ed. Stephanie G. Neuman (New York, St. Martin's, 1998), 104–109.

33. Robert O. Keohane, *After Hegemony: Cooperation and Discord in the World Political Economy* (Princeton, NJ: Princeton University Press, 1984); Peter Haas, *Saving the Mediterranean: The Politics of Environmental Cooperation* (New York: Columbia University Press, 1990); Martha Finnemore, *National Interests in International Society* (Ithaca, NY: Cornell University Press, 1997).

34. Ned Lebow, "The Long Peace, the End of the Cold War, and the Failure of Realism," *International Organization* 15, no. 2 (1994): 276.

35. Sociology on a world scale, see Saurin (Julian Saurin, "The End of International Relations? The State and International Theory in the Age of Globalization," in *Boundaries in Question: New Directions in International Relations*, eds. Andrew Linklater and John MacMillan [London: Pinter Publishers, 1995], 257).

36. Saurin, among others, seeks to eliminate the privileged status of states in these analyses and to view social change from a global perspective. Hence his call for the "end of International Relations" (Saurin, "The End of International Relations?"). The lack of agreement on the scope of the field is reflected in Jim George's critical survey of the field. He implies that the attempt to describe and explain the behavior of states is not a high-priority intellectual activity because it is "framed" in a "closed modernist discourse" based on positivism and state-centrism. Resistance to "brutality" at the "everyday, community, neighborhood and interpersonal levels" is the proper focus of the field in his view. We should study family violence rather than interstate or intrastate wars (George, *Discourses of Global Politics*, 116, 1991, 214–215).

37. Bull, *The Anarchical Society*, 13, 67, 71.

38. There is no consensus on the meaning of the term *institution*. I prefer Bull's version because it refers to ideas and practices as well as to rules. An important analysis of the concept of international institutions is in Wendt and Duvall. They contrast the "English School" notion of institutions—similar to the idea of *Gemeinschaft*—with the neorealist notion that is akin to *Gesellschaft*. Wendt and Duvall emphasize that institutions both regulate practice and are constituted through practices. "Fundamental" institutions "represent the shared intersubjective understandings about the . . . preconditions for meaningful state action" and are thus more than simply the results of calculations of state interests or the desire to reduce transactions costs (Alexander Wendt and Raymond Duvall, "Institutions and International Order," in *Global Changes and Theoretical Challenges*, eds. James N. Rosenau and Ernst-Otto Czempiel [Lexington, MA: Lexington Books, 1989], 53). Kratochwil also emphasizes the combination of practices and norms (Friedrich Kratochwil, *Rules, Norms and Decisions: On the Conditions of Practical and Legal Reasoning in International and Domestic Affairs* [Cambridge: Cambridge University Press, 1989], 64).

39. Adam Watson, *The Evolution of International Society: A Comparative Historical Analysis* (London: Routledge, 1992).

40. Ronald J. Deibert, "*Exorcismus Theoriae*: Pragmatism, Metaphors and the Return of the Medieval in IR Theory," *European Journal of International Relations* 3, no. 2 (June 1997): 184.

41. K. J. Holsti, *The State, War, and the State of War* (Cambridge: Cambridge University Press, 1996), chaps. 2–3.

42. See, for example, Rosenau, *Turbulence in World Politics*; Ruggie, *Territoriality and Beyond*; Strange, *Retreat of the State*; Christopher Clapham, "Degrees of Statehood," *Review of International Studies* 24, no. 2 (April 1998): 143–158.

CHAPTER 2

Reconfiguring International Political Space: The Significance of World History

Richard Little

This book is premised on the assumption that IR theorists need to be more sensitive to the conception of political space because we are ostensibly living through an era when political space is undergoing fundamental change. In the European Union, for example, it is argued that individuals are having to accommodate to the idea of multilevel governance and it is often unclear where political power now lies. At the other extreme, there are countries like Sierra Leone where centralized power has collapsed. Although there is very little consensus about the extent to which the Westphalian conception of political space in under challenge or what political space is going to look like in fifty years time, many analysts are convinced that the idea of international political space being conceptualized in terms of an arena where a stable set of discrete and autonomous nation states interact is already a thing of the past. Indeed, for some analysts, this conception of political space has always been a fiction.[1] IR theorists, perhaps surprisingly, have failed to shed very much light on this debate. But this is primarily because neorealism and neoliberal institutionalism, which still represent two of the most dominant theoretical perspectives in the discipline, have managed to stand aloof from debates about the changing nature of political space in the contemporary international system. This is not because they have avoided analyzing the concept, but because, while eschewing the terminology, they have adopted an ahistorical approach to the conceptualization of political space.

The aim of this chapter, however, is not to draw on the idea of political space to provide yet another critique of neorealism and neoliberal institutionalism. On the contrary, it is suggested that their ahistorical approach to political space provides a useful entry point for opening up the concept. But the chapter will go on to suggest that it is a mistake not to move beyond an ahistorical assessment of political space. Progress will only be made in our understanding of political space if the concept is historicized. In other words, we have to appreciate that the meaning ascribed to political space has varied at different points in time and in different locations. Fortunately, IR theorists from various schools of thought, but in particular, constructivists and Marxists, are

45

becoming increasingly sensitive to the importance of historicizing our view of the world. Recent research is specifically helping to formulate an historicized conception of political space. Necessarily, however, the researchers have to move outside of the familiar Eurocentric spatial and temporal framework habitually drawn on by IR theorists and there is a growing interest in world history amongst IR theorists. These theorists, however, are not preoccupied with world history simply for the sake of finding distinctive and unfamiliar examples of political space in eras before the Eurocentic, Westphalian conception of political space was consolidated. On the contrary, interest is often focused on relatively familiar cases like the Greek and Italian city-states. The attraction of these cases is that they have so frequently been co-opted by neorealists to demonstrate the relevance and utility of their ahistorical conception of political space. Once the conception of political space has been historicised, however, it becomes very clear where the problems with the ahistorical approach to political space lie.

The chapter is divided into three sections. The first explores the ahistorical conception of political space as formulated by the neorealists and then developed by the neoliberal institutionalists. The second section examines some of the recent attempts by theorists to historicise the conception of political space, and it also demonstrates the importance of the underlying comparative methodology for this approach. The third section then assesses the extent to which these historicized conceptions stand up when examined from a world historical perspective.[2]

Interest in world history by IR theorists is beginning to develop as it becomes clear that IR theory can benefit by adopting a long view of history. Whether IR theory can return the favor and give a helping hand to world historians remains to be seen.

Neorealism and the Ahistorical Conception of Political Space

Neorealists, and Waltz in particular, have not resorted to the terminology of political space.[3] Nevertheless, if it is accepted that the idea of a political system coincides with the conception of political space, then there is no doubt that neorealists have already made a considerable contribution to our understanding of political space. Indeed, it can be argued that it is the pervasive and, as critics see it, constricting influence of neorealist terminology that has encouraged the search for new labels, like political space, in the attempt to reorient the way that IR theorists conceptualize and describe the world.

From a neorealist perspective political space represents the area where power is located and the analysis of political space identifies how power is distributed and organized. Neorealists insist that if we want to develop a theoretical understanding of politics, then not only must we focus on the conception of political space, but we also need to acknowledge that, deductively, there are only two logical ways that political space can be organized: either as a hierarchy or as an anarchy. There are no other ways, it is argued, to conceptualize the distribution and organization of power. Of course, it is accepted that these are theoretical extremes and it is readily acknowledged that, empirically, systems often contain elements of both hierarchy and anarchy. But it is insisted that if we want to understand how political systems operate, then it is essential to focus on the two extremes where the power that defines political space can be seen to flow along either on a vertical or a horizontal plane with the distribution of power generating either a hierarchy or an anarchy.

Neorealists make two important theoretical assumptions about the relationship between these conceptions of political space. First, anarchic political space provides an arena where units characterized by hierarchical political space can interact.[4] Second, any attempt to understand the interaction among these hierarchical units must start from the assumption that they are constrained by the structure of the anarchic political space within which they operate. It follows, according to Waltz, that political space needs to be theorized on a very different basis to physical space. To understand how atoms interact, we must move to a lower level of analysis and look inside the atoms, whereas to understand how political hierarchies interact with each other, we need to move to a higher level of analysis, and explore the dynamics of anarchical political space.

Hierarchical political space, argue the neorealists, is defined by three characteristics: first, functional differentiation, with different functions being performed by separate and independent actors or "unlike units" as Waltz puts it; second, the various actors operating within this political space are related on the basis of subordinate and superordinate relations; and third, relations between different functional actors are determined by the distribution of power. Within the modern state, for example, we find generals and judges performing radically different functions but both are lodged in a complex hierarchy. Where judges and generals stand in the hierarchy depends on the overall distribution of power. But there is also a strong presumption that in hierarchical political space actors very often interact on the basis of authority rather than power. In other words, political actors follow orders because they accept that their superiors have the right to issue the orders, rather than because the units in a superordinate position possess the resources to compel subordinates to follow orders. In anarchical political space, by contrast, actors are functionally undifferentiated or "like units" that refuse to acknowledge that they are components operating in hierarchical political space. The units are differentiated, therefore, not by the functions they perform, or their position in a hierarchy, but in terms of the power they possess. The primary goal of such units is to retain their independence of action and to achieve this goal, they need constantly to monitor the way that power is distributed across the political space within which they operate. If the distribution of power is moving against them, then they must either endeavor to increase their own internal power capabilities or seek new allies.

What the neorealists have succeeded in doing, therefore, is, first, to map out two archetypical conceptions of political space and, second, to expose the nature of the relationship that exists between them. Although the neorealist formulation of political space has been endlessly criticized, no one has succeeded is formulating an alternative approach that has resonated so widely or has generated anything like the same degree of theoretical interest in IR. Ferguson and Mansbach, for example, who have made one of the most ambitious attempts to rearticulate the conception of political space, ultimately fail in their attempt to dislodge the dichotomized approach to political space that has been institutionalized by the neorealists.[5] They insist that global politics has always been characterized by interaction among an extraordinarily rich set of polities, from families and pressure groups to tribes and empires. Global political space is depicted as a consequence in terms of a "seamless web, encompassing numerous layered, overlapping, and interacting political authorities."[6] By drawing attention to the way that polities overlap with each other, Ferguson and Mansbach make it impossible to sustain the dichotomized approach to political space adopted by the neorealists. But not only do they dispense with the neorealist's sharply differentiated approach to political space but they also do away at the same time with the idea of competing levels of analysis. Although they still acknowledge the utility of horizontal analysis that looks at ties between polities and vertical analysis that focuses on hierarchical links within polities, their analysis presupposes a single conception of political space. From the neorealist perspective, what Ferguson and Mansbach have done—and neorealists would extend the same assessment to many of the other attempts to counter their position—is to trade empirical accuracy for the theoretical purchase that can be derived from unequivocally dichotomizing political space. Waltz would certainly not regard the exchange as providing a very good bargain.

Historicizing the Conception of Political Space

Not everyone has been convinced, however, that the divide between empirical accuracy and theoretical purchase can or, perhaps it would be better to say, ought to be sustained. Significant attempts are now being made to refine the conception of political space. Instead of following the route mapped out by Ferguson and Mansbach, however, the separation between hierarchical and anarchical modes of political space is accepted as providing a useful starting point for thinking about political space. But close attention is now being paid to the neorealist maneuver of transforming what should be a tactical division between anarchical and hierarchical political space into a strategic buffer which is then used to resist all attempts to establish conceptions of political space that are more theoretically as well as empirically refined. Critics coming from a variety of directions all make the same point that the main weakness of the neorealist position is its lack of historical sensitivity. Neorealists, however, insist on portraying the putative weakness as a strength. They argue that one of the cardinal virtues of their approach is that they can apply their dichotomized conception of political space to systems as different as the Greek city states, the Diadochi Empires that formed in the wake of Alexander the Great's death, and the system of states that emerged in 1648 after the Treaties of Westphalia were signed. In each case, neorealists assert, the units can be characterized in terms of hierarchical political space, while the relations that formed between the units can be characterized in terms of anarchical political space.

An emerging body of critics while ready, in contrast to Ferguson and Mansbach, to accept the dichotomized conception of political space insist on rejecting the way that neorealism effectively closes off all routes, apart from polarity, to differentiating anarchical political space. These critics argue that differentiating anarchical political space in terms of bipolarity and multipolarity is insufficiently refined because such distinctions still makes it impossible, for example, to distinguish between the political space occupied by Athens and Sparta in the system of Greek city states and the political space opened up by United States and the Soviet Union during the Cold War era. Neorealists, however, can counter this criticism, by arguing that their approach still makes it possible to account for both the commonalities and the differences between these two systems. From the neorealist perspective, the commonalities become apparent when attention is focused on anarchic political space where the very substantial differences between the Greek city states and the Cold War superpowers are submerged; but when the level of analysis is changed, and attention is turned to hierarchical political space, then the very significant variations that separate the two sets of units can come into focus. Concentrating on anarchical political space, therefore, highlights the features that political systems have shared across time. By contrast, looking at hierarchical political space allows us to see how political systems have varied from one historical period to another. Neorealists, however, have failed to draw on or develop this argument because they are primarily interested in a systemic level of analysis and wish to account for the common processes that have ensured the continuous reproduction of anarchical political space. It is important to note, nevertheless, that their epistemology and ontology do establish a legitimate division of labor between theorists who are concerned with hierarachical political space and those, like the neorealists, who wish to concentrate on anarchical political space.[7]

The advocates of an historicized approach to theorising in IR do not appear to be interested in challenging the dichotomised approach to political space, instead, what they want to do is to extend the conception of anarchical political space in such a way that will admit more empirical detail without simultaneously weakening the theoretical framework. To do this, they have to establish deeper and more elaborate theoretical foundations. Ruggie showed the way when he argued that Waltz had made an error in excluding the concept of functional differentiation from his theoretical conception of anarchy.[8] But a more radical trail has been blazed by the members of the emerging school of constructivism. The initial constructivist foundations laid down by Wendt may appear at first sight, however, to challenge the neorealist formula that hierarchical and anarchical political space must be conceptualized on different levels of analysis.[9] The constructivists propose that the identity of the units that interact in anarchical political space is inextricably linked to the way that anarchical political space is structured.

On the face of it, the constructivists would seem to be locking hierarchical and anarchical political space together, following along similar steps to those taken by Ferguson and Mansbach and thereby eliminating the ontological distinction made by the neorealists in the process. But the apparent challenge to neorealism's dichotomized conception of political space fades when it is recognized that the constructivists are thinking of identity in purely ideational terms. It is being suggested, in other words, that there can be a common set of ideas that help to structure both hierarchical and anarchical political space. The idea of sovereignty provides the most familiar example of such an idea because it is widely recognized as structuring both hierarchical and anarchical political space. Even the neorealists acknowledge that sovereignty has an internal and an external face and that the idea can be applied to both hierarchical and anarchical political space.

The key theoretical contribution introduced by the constructivists, therefore, is the importance of ideas in structuring political space. The introduction of ideas enables the constructivists to increase the theoretical depth of their analysis of anarchical political space. Their theoretical orientation pulls them apart from the neorealist approach to the analysis of anarchy because the neorealists only take account of material forces. The constructivists, by contrast, are interested in the reciprocal impact of material and ideational forces. The role attributed to ideas means that constructivists can accept the neorealist claim that material power has always helped to structure anarchical political space without reaching the neorealist conclusion that anarchy is an unchanging feature of international relations. Taking account of ideas and recognizing that very different ideas have helped to structure anarchical political space has made it possible for constructivists to compare and contrast anarchy in different historical eras.

An example of this approach is provided by Reus-Smit who compares and contrasts the identity of Greek city states with modern states and in the process he also differentiates the anarchical political space within which these two divergent types of unit interact.[10] According to Reus-Smit the identity of any set of units is generated by the constitutional structure that prevails in the anarchical political space where the units interact. By constitutional structure, he means the established metavalues that define what constitutes legitimate statehood and rightful state action within an anarchical political space. Reus-Smit presupposes, therefore, that anarchical political space is defined by a normative structure that is maintained on the basis of an intersubjective agreement established amongst the component units. In the absence of a constitutional structure, a state of nature would prevail, whereas the existence of such a structure ensures that the units can cooperate and generate a degree of order within the anarchical political space where they interact.

What Reus-Smit demonstrates is that although neorealists have frequently argued that the anarchical political space occupied by Greek city-states, on the one hand, and modern states on the other, takes exactly the same form, the assessment is based on an impoverished understanding of political space. It fails to take account of the very different normative foundations that underpin the way that the Greek city-states interacted when compared to the way that modern states interact. He reveals that whereas the Greek city-states relied on arbitration to maintain international order, modern states have relied on multilateralism. He shows that these are very different institutional mechanisms and they derive from radically different normative frameworks. In both cases, moreover, the ideas that generated these institutional mechanisms are seen initially to have informed and constrained interaction within hierarchical political space. But over time, as the institutions came to symbolize the legitimacy of the state and define what is meant by right conduct, so the ideas started to constrain the way in which both types of state began to interact with each other.

At the heart of this constructivist project, therefore, is the recognition that Greek city-states and modern states possess radically different identities with the consequence that political space is articulated in very different ways. The normative role of the Greek city-states was to preserve a particular form of communal life where differences between individuals were resolved by public debate and deliberation rather than by the application of codified law. Reus-Smit argues that the same discursive norm was extended to relations between the city-states so that when disputes arose, they were habitually adjudicated by an arbiter who worked on the basis of debate and deliberation rather than having recourse to codified rules. By contrast, the normative role of the modern state is to promote an environment where individuals can pursue their own ends. This conception of the state, however, only began to emerge in the eighteenth century. Before then, the role of the European state was to preserve a rigid and dynastic social order. With the enlightenment, however, states across Europe began to adopt a very different normative stance, whereby it was acknowledged, first, that laws were only considered legitimate if they were established by those who would also be subject to them and, second, that the laws would be binding on everyone. Again, Reus-Smit argues that during the course of the nineteenth century, this normative stance began to filter into the international domain and thereby structure anarchical political space. This development resulted in the very rapid growth in multilateral treaties and organizations.

Constructivism, however, is not the only school of thought to have attacked attempts to study political space in ahistorical terms. Coming from a Marxist perspective, Rosenberg, for example, has endeavored to demonstrate that the use of the neorealist theoretical framework to identify transhistorical continuities across the Greek and Italian city-states as well as the modern nation states rests on a "gigantic optical illusion."[11] The illusion arises, Rosenberg argues, because in each case it is possible to demonstrate that the units are defined by the existence of autonomous political space. Realists, he insists, do not find this condition surprising. On the contrary, they take the existence of autonomous political space for granted. It is treated as an ahistorical given that does not require explanation. Marxists, by contrast, do not take the autonomy of political space for granted and they recognize that autonomous political space has only emerged under very special historical circumstances. They acknowledge, for example, that throughout the feudal era, it is not possible to draw a clear distinction between economic activity and the exercise of political authority. Rosenberg argues, therefore, that the conception of autonomous political space needs to be historicized and that it is necessary to look closely at the specific historical circumstances that have generated autonomous political space. He focuses on Greek, Italian, and modern states and demonstrates that the nature of the autonomous political space that emerged in each case was quite distinct. Rosenberg's approach also problematizes the way that neorealists have dichotomized political space. Rosenberg accepts that political space has been dichotomized but he sees it as an essentially modern phenomenon. Before exploring this aspect of his thinking, however, we shall focus on his assessment of autonomous political space in the Greek and Italian city states.

On initial inspection, Rosenberg argues that there seems to be a good reason for suggesting that the Greek city-states must have lacked any autonomous political space because the units did not possess any of the independent bureaucratic machinery that is usually employed to identify the existence of the state. In the absence of such conventional structures, it is not obvious how to locate the "autonomous" political space where the independent interests of the state are formulated and where decisions are made about how to promote and defend these interests. To find this autonomous political space, Rosenberg concludes that it is necessary to investigate the nature of social relations rather than searching for nonexistent state structures. He draws attention to the fact that the Greeks identified city-states as bodies of people rather than named political units: Athenians and Spartans rather than Athens and Sparta. It follows that there was no distinction drawn between state and society. The state consisted of a collection of landowners who derived their wealth from slavery. Having no need to work, the landowners were able to devote their time to the creation of political democracy, and political space is associated with their exercise of power in the Assembly. As Marx paradoxically puts it "civil society was the *slave* of political society."[12] What this case illustrates, according to Rosenberg, is the existence of autonomous political space formed in the absence of a state.

A very different kind of political space is shown to have evolved in the case of Renaissance Italy. The key factor behind this difference is shown to be the vital role played by trade in the Italian city-states. During the feudal era, merchants came to play a crucial role in the running of the Communes or Italian cities that had succeeded in escaping the power of the church. A consequence of this development, however, was that rivalry between merchants became a source of instability in the way that the city states were governed. To overcome this problem, institutions were designed to insulate government from the private power of individuals. But with the creation of these institutions to ensure a division between private and public realms in Renaissance Italy, the autonomy of the state underwent a significant expansion. So in Renaissance Italy, it was the state that eventually provided the source of autonomous political space. As a consequence, Rosenberg insists that although we can identify the existence of autonomous political space in classical Greece and Renaissance Italy, it took on radically different forms.

According to conventional wisdom, relations among the Italian city-states provided the model that was eventually to be extended to the rest of Europe. Rosenberg endeavors to counter this claim. From his perspective, the autonomous political space that formed in modern Europe had its own distinctive character and it emerged from an independent historical route. Rosenberg's starting point is the mercantilist empires that formed on the Iberian peninsula in the fifteenth and sixteenth centuries. In these empires, politics and economics are seen to be fused, with commercial activity being dictated by the crown which had no interest in or intention of encouraging the emergence of an autonomous political space. The separation of economics and politics that eventually took place across Europe is seen to be the product of a unique set of historical circumstances that resulted in the formation of capitalism. Following Marx, therefore, Rosenberg acknowledges that capitalism represents a unique mode of production that presupposes the existence of separate economic and political domains. In contrast to empires of the past, where economic surplus is appropriated by political means, capitalism is associated with the emergence of the state as a purely political and public institution that co-exists alongside and forms the necessary counterpart to a set of privatized "nonpolitical" economic mechanisms of surplus appropriation. Rosenberg insists, however, that despite the autonomy of these economic and political spaces, they cannot be studied separately because they form opposite sides of the same coin.

He explores the symbiosis linking economic and political space by highlighting two overlapping phases associated with the emergence of the modern state in Europe. During the first phase, the absolutist monarchs in Europe built up their states by suppressing rival centers of power and creating strong central bureaucracies. In the second phase a liberal transformation took place that involved a transfer of power from the state to civil society. In particular, the transformation resulted in the state divesting some of its public power into a newly constituted capitalist market, thereby leaving an autonomous political space where residual state power can be exercised in purely public and communal terms. On the other side of the coin, therefore, civil society was expanded through the unique development of a private capitalist market. Marx viewed this capitalist market as an entirely new social development. What distinguishes it from precapitalist markets is the creation of autonomous economic space where a compulsory association of legal equals can buy and sell their labor. This expanded function of the market meant that the state's traditional task of surplus appropriation could now be reconstituted as a private activity of civil society that takes place through the "nonpolitical" market mechanism. But state and market, although autonomous, need to be examined in conjunction because the public power of the state, for example, is still needed to support the private power that is exercised in the market.

Having established that the autonomy of the modern state derives from unique historical circumstances, Rosenberg extends his analysis to examine international political space. Ironically, when examining the contemporary international system, he has no difficulty accepting the way that neorealists dichotomize political space into hierarchy and anarchy with anarchy being regulated by an impersonal balance of power. But the neorealist account is considered to be fatally flawed because the neorealists lack the theoretical insight to see, first, that the autonomy they ascribe to hierarchical and anarchical political space is not an ahistorical given, but the product of a unique set of historical circumstances that only evolved in the eighteenth century; and, second, that the balance of power is also a product of the eighteenth century and that it only represents half of the power equation. Before the eighteenth century, Rosenberg argues, Europe was dominated by expansionist mercantilist empires that occupied both economic and political space. Only with the liberal transformation did the Waltzean states-system defined by anarchic and autonomous public political space come into existence. And only at this point did the necessary preconditions for a Waltzean balance of power emerge. But Rosenberg goes further and argues that to make sense of this development it must be examined in conjunction with the formation of a transnational capitalist market that was governed by the impersonal private power located in civil society. And just as public international power is regulated by the balance of power, so transnational private power is constrained by what Adam Smith referred to as the hidden hand. From Rosenberg's Marxist perspective, moreover, the international balance of public power that maintains order in the states-system is depicted as a necessary counterpart to the hidden hand that regulates the private transnational power that underpins the global market.[13]

Although operating on the basis of radically different research agenda, Reus-Smit and Rosenberg both succeed in presenting accounts of political space that provide a fundamental challenge to the ahistorical conception offered by the neorealists. The major strength of their approaches over the one adopted by the neorealists is that they provide the foundations for a progressive research agenda.

The ahistoricism of neorealism encourages the belief that its approach to international political space can be applied anywhere and anytime. If the associated balance of power theory fails to apply, then all that can be suggested is that a reassessment will be required at a different level of analysis. But there is no way that the theory can be elaborated. By contrast, adopting an historicized approach presupposes that the nature of political space varies and will take on different characteristics in different times and places. Following the comparative method, therefore, our understanding of political space can be progressively expanded and deepened. It would seem to follow then, that even if the accounts provided by Reus-Smit and Rosenberg fail to stand up under closer scrutiny, the progressive orientation of their analysis generates an overwhelming case in favor of historicizing our basic concepts. Before giving unequivocal support to this assessment, however, we need to explore the implications of historicizing the conception of political space from a world historical perspective.

Political Space and World History

Coinciding with the emergent interest in the need to historicize the concepts used to study international relations, there is a growing interest in studying international relations from a world historical perspective. At first sight, it seems obvious that these two developments must be mutually supporting but on closer inspection it becomes apparent that a world historical perspective poses problems, albeit of a different kind, for both the ahistorical and the historicized approaches to international relations. The nature of these problems can be illustrated by examining the light that world historical frameworks throw on the conception of political space.

Neorealists start from the premise that the study of world history reinforces their ahistorical position because it is said to demonstrate the "striking
sameness in the quality of international life through the millennia."[14] What
Waltz is referring to here is the centrality of polarity in the world history of
international systems. In other words, neorealists presuppose that international
political space has been organized on a habitual basis in terms of either bipolarity or multipolarity. It is acknowledged, therefore, that there will be a persistent tendency for system change to occur. As dominant states rise and fall, the
system will then stabilize through the operation of the balance of power on the
basis of either bipolarity and multipolarity. Because of the effectiveness of the
balance of power as a self-regulating mechanism, it is unlikely, although not
impossible, for the system to transform from an anarchy into a hierarchy.
Recent systematic analyses of world history, however, fail to substantiate the
neorealist position. Although there are examples of polarised systems in world
history, they are found to be very unstable. The evidence from world history
suggests that the balance of power is a remarkably ineffective mechanism for
maintaining polarized international systems and such systems are seen to give
way habitually to hegemonic empires.[15] McNeill argues, moreover, that once
imperial state structures emerged in world history, they proved to be incredibly
resilient.[16] Although they could be disrupted by revolts or invasion, given time,
they almost invariably reconstituted themselves. Whether the focus is on Eurasia, Pre-Columbia America, or Africa, McNeill concludes that from a world historical perspective the norm for civilized governance was "laminated polyeth-
nic empire." Such empires look much more like international systems than
states and there is a growing recognition that such empires should be defined
as international systems and brought within the purview of IR.[17] There is no
reason in principle why the neorealists should not endorse this move, since
their conceptual apparatus makes provision for the analysis of both hierarchical
and anarchical political space. But Waltz is adamant that his approach can shed
no light on the process of system transformation from anarchy to hierarchy.
More damaging, however, is the inability of Waltzean neorealism either to highlight or explain the emergence of a more stable balance of power system in
Europe from 1500 onward.

World history, however, also poses problems for the emerging literature
that aims to historicize the study of international relations. Although the comparative method drawn on by this literature is very effective at making use of
the length of the temporal reach provided by world history, it has not so far
been as effective at taking advantage of the breadth of the spatial reach offered
by world history. So, for example, Reus-Smit adopts a very Eurocentric perspective on the Greek city states, treating them effectively as a closed system.
But such an assessment ignores the very significant ties that existed between
Greece and Persia on the one hand and between the Greeks and the Scythi-

ans on the other. In particular, it ignores the argument that the emergence of the international society identified by Reus-Smit was a product of the fifth century wars with Persia.[18] In other words, a world historical perspective encourages us to see that the Greek international society was itself a unit in a larger system.

It can be suggested that world history poses Rosenberg's analysis with even greater problems. In the first place, it helps to highlight a powerful Eurocentric bias that runs through the analysis of all three case studies. Like Reus-Smit, Rosenberg also effectively treats the Greek city states as a closed system and ignores the fact that they had to interact with the Scythian nomadic tribes, on the one hand, and the vast bureaucratic empire of Persia, on the other. This does not, of course, invalidate his claim that the Greek cities were not states, but at the very least world history makes it necessary to recognize that they were part of a system that did unequivocally contain a state. More problematic is Rosenberg's argument that for most of world history politics and economics have been effectively fused. The argument is identical to the one made by Wallerstein who argues that a world economy was only consolidated in 1500 A.D.[19] Before then he suggests that world history was dominated by world empires where economic transactions coincided with political expropriation. But this position makes it impossible to explore the development of trade beyond the boundaries of these empires. So, for example, the passage of goods by merchants along the silk routes from China to Europe gets ignored. But what world history demonstrates is that economic systems have until very recently always extended far beyond the reach of political systems.[20]

It is apparent, nevertheless, that the conventional IR approach to political space also has very little purchase on the past. It is worth noting, therefore, that despite the tendency of IR theorists to berate geopolitics as a "pseudo-science" because of its geographic determinism, the early geopoliticians did at least make the attempt to provide a conception of political space on a world historical scale.[21] From Halford Mackinder's perspective, for example, the land mass of Eurasia provided the starting point for world history and, prior to 1500 A.D., constituted "a closed political system" according to Mackinder that was divided in terms of a heartland that was sparsely populated by highly mobile nomadic tribes who posed a constant threat to the oceanic crescent that was highly populated by sedentary people who inhabited states of various kinds.[22] With the emergence of ocean going boats, Eurasia is then depicted as an open political system and it remained so until the time Mackinder was writing when, with the European control over the "outer crescent" completed, political space became closed once more. Of course, there is more than a whiff of Eurocentrism about this account of political space, but it nevertheless provides a world historical assessment of political space that conventional IR cannot begin to match.

Conclusion

It is becoming increasingly evident that IR as a discipline has suffered by failing to take sufficient notice of world history. The importance attached to polarity, for example, is no doubt justified if attention is focused on the European state system. But as soon as a world historical perspective is taken on board then the significance of the concept is immediately put into question. It is equally clear that although the attempts to historicize the conception of political space have opened the way to increasing the theoretical depth of the concept, this approach has not and does not seem likely to help to provide an account of political space that can generate a world historical narrative. Indeed, from a world historical perspective there are problems with both the ahistorical and the historicizing approaches to the conceptualization of political space. But it would be a mistake to conclude that theorists as perceptive as Waltz, Ferguson and Mansbach, Reus-Smit, and Rosenberg do not have important contributions to make to the understanding of political space. There is a need for greater receptivity to methodological pluralism and for finding ways that will not only allow islands of research to coexist but also allow bridges to be built to establish connections between the islands. Buzan and Little argue that a more comprehensive conception of the international system can provide an ideal framework for carrying out such an exercise.[23] Certainly the international system makes provision for the conception of political space. By adopting a more enriched conception of the international system, acknowledging, for example, that international political space can take the form of either an anarchy or a hierarchy, then it becomes possible to see how IR theory can start to develop closer links with the evolving study of world history that could prove to be mutually beneficial.

Notes

1. For a useful overview, see "The Road to 2050: A Survey of New Geopolitics" a supplement in *The Economist* 31.7 (1999): 1–16.

2. I am grateful to Martin Hall for pointing out the importance of distinguishing between world historical approaches that rely on comparative methodology and those that aim to provide a narrative of world history.

3. See K. N. Waltz, *Theory of International Politics* (New York: Random House, 1979).

4. The neorealists make no allowance for the possibility of a political space occupied by acephalous units. See the discussion of this possibility in Barry Buzan, Charles Jones, and Richard Little, *The Logic of Anarchy: Neorealism to Structural Realism* (New York:

Columbia University Press, 1993), pp. 138–140; and Barry Buzan and Richard Little, *International Systems in World History: Remaking the Study of International Relations* (Oxford: Oxford University Press, 2000), part 2. Nor do they make any allowance for the possibility that hierarchy can give way to anarchy. See the discussion of "quasi-states" by Robert Jackson, *Quasi-States: Sovereignty, International Relations and the Third World* (Cambridge: Cambridge University Press, 1990).

5. See Yale H. Ferguson and Richard W. Mansbach, *Polities: Authorities, Identities and Change* (Columbia: University of South Carolina Press, 1996).

6. Ibid., pp. 33–34.

7. Of course, Waltz does not always wear his neorealist hat and devotes an entire book to exploring how the hierarchical political space in the United States and Britain diverge. See Kenneth N. Waltz, *Foreign Policy and Democratic Politics: The American and British Experience* (Boston: Little, Brown, 1967).

8. See J. G. Ruggie, "Theory of World Politics: Structural Realism and Beyond," *World Politics*, 35(2) (1983): 261–285

9. See Alexander Wendt, "Anarchy Is What States Make of It: The Social Construction of Power: Politics," *International Organization*, 46:2 (1992): 391–425.

10. See Christian Reus-Smit, "The Constitutional Structure of International Society and the Nature of Fundamental Institutions," *International Organization* 51(4) (1997), 555–589; and Christian Reus-Smit *The Moral Purpose of the State: Social Identity and Institutional Action* (Princeton: Princeton University Press, 1999).

11. See Justin Rosenberg, *The Empire of Civil Society: A Critique of the Realist Theory of International Relations* (London: Verso, 1994), p. 90.

12. Cited in ibid., p. 79.

13. Although following a very different route, this conclusion is almost identical to the one reached by Karl Polani, *The Great Transformation* (Boston: Beacon Press, 1957). Rosenberg ibid., pp. 192–193 acknowledges the similarities but argues that Polanyi lacks a social theory to account for the transformation.

14. See Waltz, *Theory of International Politics*, p. 66.

15. See, for example, Adam Watson, *The Evolution of International Society* (London: Routledge, 1992); Buzan, Jones and Little, *The Logic of Anarchy*; Barry Buzan and Richard Little, "The Idea of International System: Theory Meets History," *International Political Science Review*, 15:3 (1994): 231–256; Stuart Kaufman, "The Fragmentation and Consolidation of International Systems" *International Organization* 51(2) (1997): pp. 173–208; William H. McNeill, "Introductory Historical Commentary," in Geir Lundestad, ed., *The Fall of Great Powers: Peace, Stability and Legitimacy* (Oslo: Scandinavian University Press, 1994); Buzan and Little, *International Systems in World History*.

16. McNeill, "Introductory Historical Commentary," in Lundestad, *The Fall of Great Powers*, p. 4.

17. See, for example, Robert Gilpin, *War and Change in World Politics* (Cambridge: Cambridge University Press, 1981). Barry Buzan and Richard Little, "The Idea of International System: Theory Meets History," *International Political Science Review*, 15:3 (1994): 231–256; Barry Buzan and Richard Little, "Reconceptualizing Anarchy: Structural Realism Meets World History," *European Journal of International Relations* 2:4 (1996): 403–438; Buzan and Little *International Systems in World History*; Kaufman, "The Fragmentation and Consolidation of International Systems," pp. 173–208.

18. See Edith Hall, *Inventing the Barbarian: Greek Self-definition Through Tragedy* (Oxford: Clarendon Press, 1989); and S. Hornblower, "Greeks and Persians: West against East," in Beatrice Heuser, ed., *Thinking War, Peace and World Orders: From Antiquity to the Twenty-first Century* (London: Routledge, 2001).

19. Immanuel Wallerstein, *The Modern World-System* (New York: Academic Press, 1974).

20. See Andre Gunder Frank, *Reorient: Global Economy in the Asian Age* (Berkeley: University of California Press, 1998), and Buzan and Little, *International Systems in World History*.

21. Hans J. Morgenthau, *Politics Among Nations*, 5th ed. (New York: Knopf, 1973).

22. Halford J. Mackinder "The Geographical Pivot of History" *Geographical Journal* 1904, 13 (1904): 428.

23. Buzan and Little, *International Systems in World History*.

CHAPTER 3

The Informational Reconfiguring
of Global Geopolitics

Ken Dark

Global geopolitics might be understood as the worldwide spatial expression of political organization.[1] The division of space in ways relating to political organization has characterized human communities since at least the Mesolithic period, if not before, and no single brief account could do justice to the vast scope of this subject.[2] So, this contribution will seek only to investigate two major and related themes in global geopolitics. These are: the extent to which large-scale geopolitical transformations in the past and present are amenable to a unitary explanation, and—if so—what this might tell us about the future of global geopolitics.

Statehood and its Alternatives

Most accounts of global geopolitics focus on the state, and here too statehood is a convenient starting point.[3] That many types of state have existed in the past, not simply the so-called nation-states of the modern "Westphalian system," implies that political space was repeatedly reconfigured, as different types of state involved different types of spatial organization. Moreover, throughout the whole period in which states have existed—from the Fourth millennium B.C. to the end of the twentieth century A.D.—they have coexisted with other forms of political organization.[4] Two of these may hold special interest for us here: kin-based "hunter-gatherer" polities, and the "chiefdom"—the earliest form of hierarchical centralized political organization.[5] The former was the predominant form of political organization for 90 percent of human history, while the latter was the most widespread political form globally, prior to the global growth of statehood in the nineteenth century.[6]

A general pattern of global political development seems to have occurred in which kin-based polities were replaced by chiefdoms, and chiefdoms by states.[7] But this process took many millennia, and is not entirely complete even now. In the meantime, a wide variety of specific types of hunter-gatherer bands and chiefdoms are known to have existed, and such polities frequently replaced

61

each other. While individual polities were often short-lived, each of these preceding forms of political organization lasted much longer than statehood has to date.[8] Each was—for long time spans—the most common form of global geopolitical organization, before the emergence of the new form of political organization that ultimately superseded it.[9] Even after new political forms emerged, older forms did not simply wither away, but remained coexisting (and competing) polities in "international political systems" still comprising more than one political form.[10] These were not only multi-actor systems but multi-formal systems: systems encompassing more than one political form.

The Geopolitics of Nonstate Polities

Thus, most of the history of global geopolitics has not been about the geography of states. While states have come to predominate in global geopolitics today, this has taken about 6,000 years of political history.[11] In that time, the scale and organization of states have changed very dramatically, and often not in a directly linear fashion.[12] As Kosse and Carneiro have shown, there may be a broad trend toward fewer and larger polities over this time.[13] But many contemporary states (e.g., Fiji) would be extremely small-scale entities compared to some chiefdoms (such as the Anglo-Saxon kingdom of Northumbria in the seventh century A.D.) which existed in earlier millennia.

Each of these preceding political forms is associated with a distinct geopolitics. Anthropological and archaeological evidence combine to demonstrate that kin-based polities characteristically have "hunter-gatherer" economies that usually—although not universally—necessitate, that such polities are "mobile."[14] That is, they usually move from one area to another exploiting resources, and these areas are divided between different "bands" (kin-based hunter-gatherer groups) by means both of competition (including warfare) and intergroup cooperation. Kin-based societies of this sort are continually expansive, always seeking out new territories and resources.[15] In fact, it was exactly this sort of polity that was spread globally in the first phase of human colonization—the earliest "globalization" of politics perhaps![16]

The geopolitical structure of kin-based polities is not reliant on exclusive access to land or resources.[17] However, hunter-gatherers will wage war to retain access to territory or resources, and may have very strong cultural commitments to retaining exclusive access to specific zones or landmarks within their territories (e.g., ritual—or burial—places). These rights and claims are usually expressed through the customary regulation of movement or access for other bands or particular groups within their own polity, and may be designated by marking these places in some way. Thus, hunter-gatherer polities can be said to aspire to the control of definable territories, albeit frequently with ill-defined boundaries, and to the exercise over this territory of their own customs and cultural values.

In so-called complex hunter-gatherer societies these attitudes toward property and access are somewhat strengthened by the emergence of sedentism (continual settlement in a specific location), contextual leadership, or tribalism.[18] These may consolidate notions of exclusive access and definable resources or territory, for instance, as we find—at least until very recently—in the classic "big-man" political organization in the Highlands of Papua New Guinea.[19] These "complex" kin-based polities show evidence of regularized political leadership, and are generally seen as precursors of the chiefdom.[20]

In chiefdoms—such as Contact–Period Hawaii or early Christian Ireland—the relationship between polity, land, and resources is usually seen in a more exclusive fashion.[21] This is not least because most chiefdoms have an agricultural or pastoral basis, although other factors—such as enhanced concepts of the hereditary rights of individuals—also play an important role.[22] Boundaries among chiefdoms tend to be more clear-cut than among hunter-gatherers but, nevertheless, chiefdom boundaries are frequently in the forms of "boundary zones" rather than "lines in the sand." Continually competing to gain new territory and resources, chiefdoms are no less expansionist than kin-based polities, but are more bound to specific territories and to specific resources, and usually more constrained by the territorial claims of neighboring chiefdoms or states.[23] As a result, competition for land and resources now becomes strongly associated with warfare between chiefdoms over the control of resources.

One exception is those mobile chiefdoms (such as the Hunnic or Mongol invaders of Roman and medieval Europe) who are able to exploit resources more widely, by moving the whole political unit across the countryside.[24] These groups chose to disregard the competing claims of states or other chiefdoms to resources, acquiring what they needed or desired through warfare. Interestingly, this shows that, just as not all kin-based groups are mobile, so too not all not all chiefdoms are sedentary. It is one of several points which undermine the credibility of a narrow association between each of these forms and specific economic modes of production and exchange.[25]

However, geopolitical reconfiguration does not simply concern the consolidation of territoriality and the growth of violent competition for land and other resources. The internal restructuring of political units is also an important aspect of geopolitical change. Hunter-gatherer kin-based units have their ritual and ceremonial centers, and "special places" for burial or which carry particular associations. Within chiefdoms of all sorts, particular locations are assigned special meaning too, and chiefs and their associated aristocracies frequently monumentalize these with public works.[26] Chiefs and aristocracies also, of course, require their own residences, which frequently become foci for the expression of prestige and legitimacy. So, "courtly" sites are visible within many chiefdoms, and other localities might be developed for the inauguration of chiefs or the dispensation of law by them, as at Tara, Clogher, and Emain Macha in early Christian and late Iron Age Ireland.[27] Similarly, special trading places for regular markets or fairs may be established, which facilitate the chiefly control of long-distance exchange of all sorts. These more fixed centers understandably enhance the association between the chiefdom and territory, and further the desire of chiefly dynasties to retain control of specific localities in order to retain legitimacy, prestige or access to particular types of goods or services.[28]

These patterns suggest a growing association between polity and territory, and the willingness of political leaderships to compete (often violently) for land and other resources, prior to the origins of the state.[29] However, with the origins of the state these trends were intensified still further. Urban-based government, the need for local secondary centers associated with bureaucratic administration, and the more precise definition of political boundaries through mapping and written treaties, all intensified the association between place and political organization.[30]

The consolidation of these trends into a geopolitical structure based on states allowed little scope for territorial expansion without either violence or the mutual agreement between states to merge. The exception, of course, was when states were able to expand at the expense of political forms with a less strongly developed sense of territoriality.[31] Aggression by states against both kin-based polities and chiefdoms is, in this context, hardly surprising. States would, then, be expected on these grounds alone, to have acquired additional territory mostly through the conquest of nonstate polities. The growth of states into empires, as a consequence of warfare almost entirely against nonstate polities, therefore, represented the culmination of millennial processes toward the identification between political and territorial identity and of political limitations on geopolitical expansionism.

Consequently, it is clear that kin-based polities, chiefdoms, and states emerged successively in prehistory, and have coexisted until the present.[32] The existence of first kin-based, then chiefdom, and then state, forms of political organization can be used to divide global politics into three ages: an age of kin-based polities, an age of the chiefdom, and an age of the state.[33] All of these ages were extremely long-lived, yet each ended with the rapid emergence of a successive form of political organization, giving the overall pattern a sequential character.[34] In each of these "ages" of global politics not only were the political units involved different in nature, but each saw interpolity interactions conducted in a fundamentally different way.[35] This has created a series of chronologically overlapping geopolitical logics, both within and between polities. Each "age" can be associated, more specifically, with different concepts of territoriality and different internal geopolitical structures within the polities concerned. The survival of other political forms meant that several different "geopolitics" long coexisted, while new political forms gradually came to dominate global politics as a whole.

This broad categorization of global geopolitical history focuses attention on the transitions between these "ages" of world politics. It highlights the possibility for fundamental political and geopolitical transformations to occur, and suggests that discernable patterns and processes may exist in long-term global political change.[36] Such patterns and processes, in turn, might inform us of the possible consequences of geopolitical transitions underway at present.[37] The prospect of studying such large-scale and long-term processes is made all the more likely because of a new explanatory and analytical framework presently emerging within International Relations theory. This would enable us to discern the dynamics of large-scale processes in world politics, and is beginning to have a broader interdisciplinary impact.

The Growth of an Interdisciplinary Agenda

One of the most surprising developments in recent scholarship is that a convergence of theory has been taking place between the social, physical, and biological sciences.[38] This has been based on a new synthesis of research and analysis involving a range of disciplines: physics, mathematics, and biology, on the one hand, with economics, organizational analysis, anthropology, and archaeology, on the other.[39] All of these, apparently contrasting, disciplines share an interest in explaining and understanding the emergence of form ("morphogenesis"), order and dynamics in "complex systems" comprised of several interacting parts.[40] Such entities include biological and physical systems, economies, human societies, and political organizations.[41]

This conceptual convergence has led to a new synthesis ("macrodynamics") of the differing theoretical approaches developed within the social, biological, and physical sciences.[42] As macrodynamic theory is still somewhat new, the next section aims to give a very brief summary of some of the main points of this new synthesis.[43] Then, this analytical framework will be used to examine the problems posed at the start of this paper, with reference to the large-scale geopolitical changes already discussed. Naturally, any discussion of either this new synthesis or its application to these questions in a paper of this length can only be a provisional and outline account, in the latter case more exploratory in nature than attempting to offer any final conclusions. Moreover, it should be stressed that this new approach has far wider applicability to the study of global politics than simply to geopolitical change alone, and it might be employed to investigate change in almost any aspect of international relations.

Information and Organization

In recent years, the relationship between communication, information-processing and organizational form has been a particular topic of renewed study among economists, organizational analysts, anthropologists, and archaeologists.[44] At the core of this work has been a growing understanding of the central importance of information and communication to the strategic development, competition, coordination, and management of any organization—including polities of all sorts.[45]

All organizations have information requirements in order to operate.[46] All also require communications sufficient to transfer that information, and those people and materials, necessary for their operation.[47] It would be impossible to operate any sort of organization without fulfilling these needs. One way to conceptualize organizations of all sorts is, therefore, in terms of the flow of information and communication through them. This is not to say that organizations are only capable of conceptualization in this way, but simply that this is one way of thinking about them.

This simple point has been the basis of a very large number of empirical and theoretical studies on the (mostly unintended) consequences of such flows. These studies range from historical and anthropological investigations, through work undertaken for military or business purposes, to formal experimentation, mathematical analysis, and computer simulation.[48] The results of this wide range of analytical activity have been surprisingly consistent, so that several general conclusions emerge from this large body of work, which have already been debated extensively in theory outside of international relations theory and are supported by a wide range of empirical studies.[49]

To begin with, it is clear that organizational form and scale are highly dependent on communication and information-processing.[50] It is equally clear that problems in these two areas routinely result in organizational crises.[51] Conversely, more efficient communication and information-processing act greatly to the favor of those organizations that can achieve them, both in terms of efficiency and competitive success. Successful communication and information-processing strategies usually impart strong competitive advantages, whether—for example—in obtaining market shares or war-fighting.[52] However, when information-processing cannot keep pace with the requirements of growth or expansion, difficulties ("scalar stress") begin to show in the fabric of organizations.[53] While contexts alter their specific consequences, in general such stresses can be shown to lead to internal dissent, conflict and division.[54] If unchecked, such fission often places severe strains on any organization and can lead to rapid and dramatic organizational collapse.[55] So, in order to run smoothly—or even to survive—all organizations must operate within the specific limits of their information-processing and communication capabilities.[56] Ways of coping with information and communication are, therefore, closely connected to the competitive success and survival of any organization.

In order to achieve an adequate level of information-handling, several strategies may be employed. First, hierarchical ordering of information-processing can "soften" its organizational impact or facilitate efficiency.[57] This can often be associated with other forms of hierarchy within organizations, such as the managerial structure of a firm. Second, new technologies or means of communication and information-processing can have a similar effect. This can enable those organizations with access to those technologies or new modes of operation to obtain a competitive "edge" on their rivals and cope internally with greater information-flows. Third, internal differentiation can spread information-processing throughout an organization more effectively.[58] This is clearly illustrated by differentiated departments within a firm or state bureaucracy. Fourth, cooperation with other organizations might have a similar result to differentiation, in spreading information-processing between several organizations.[59] All of these strategies are, of course, commonly found both in firms and polities as ways of handling information.[60] Pursuing these strategies is in the interest of organizations because they enable not only survival but permit organizations to compete more effectively.[61]

However, this multidisciplinary work has also shown that the coexistence of organizations also has other consequences than simple competition. When two or more organizations continuously interact so as to exchange information, whether competitively or cooperatively, they begin to display convergence.[62] This convergence may be part of conscious strategies of competition, or a result of cooperative communication, or it may be entirely unintended on the part of those involved, for example as a result of transnational cultural contacts. Whatever the specific cause(s), sustained interaction will tend to produce a greater degree of similarity between the actors involved through time. In this way, even competing organizations will (in general terms) tend to share more common characteristics the longer they coexist, often including norms of behavior or values.[63]

More important still, the rate of information-flow may relate both to the rate of innovation within organizations, and to the rate of organizational change. It appears that the greater the rate of information-flow and information-processing, the faster change occurs.[64] That is, the rate of change itself may well bear a close relationship to the rate of information-flow and of information-processing.[65] As well as restructuring within organizations, completely new organizations can emerge from the need to cope with massive increases in information-flow, by the formation of new and separate information-processing hierarchies above the level of already existing organizations.[66] It seems clear that polities can be understood as organizations in this sense, so the relevance of this work to the study of global politics seems obvious.[67] Moreover, the importance of these developments is enhanced by another multidisciplinary body of recent work, that on complexity theory.[68]

Unfolding Complexity

The rise of complexity theory has been no less than a theoretical revolution in several fields, especially mathematics, physics, and biology.[69] Complexity theory attempts to understand the dynamics of "complex systems." A "complex system" may be variously defined, but a relatively uncontentious definition would be that such a system is comprised of many interacting and differentiated parts, all of which are related to one or more of the others constituting the system.[70] A complex system is, therefore, unlike the classic "system" of "general systems theory" in several respects, not least because each part of a complex system does not need to have a functional relevance to every other.[71] In a complex system, each part has the potential to affect the system as a whole, but need not.

Complex systems also exhibit an internal hierarchical ordering, so that above the lowest divisible unit of analysis, each system is comprised of what can be termed a "system of systems," a ranked series of systems, with each system "nested" in each other.[72] In this "nested hierarchy" of systems, each part of each system may (but need not) directly constitute more than one layer of the whole system of systems. As a result, complex systems are infinitely divisible down to their lowest unit of analysis and simultaneously are never simply the sum of their parts.[73]

One "counterintuitive" aspect of such systems is that concepts of atomism and holism are irrelevant in their discussion, because they are both "atomistic" and "holistic" simultaneously. However, this is not the only "counterintuitive" aspect of complexity. Complex systems exhibit some interesting, and at first sight possibly perplexing, dynamics deriving from their complexity alone.[74] While much work remains to be done, aspects of these dynamics are now extremely well-attested. Important here, there is no reason to doubt that these dynamics are universal to all complex systems, no matter what their constituent parts may be.[75] Recent applications of complexity theory in economics and other disciplines, make it clear that such systems include human societies, despite the additional dimensions added by conscious agency.[76] Unless one wishes to claim that polities and international systems are not complex systems (in this sense) at all, there are, therefore, no rational grounds whatsoever for arguing that complexity theory is irrelevant to international relations theory.

Although aspects of this theoretical revolution have already been applied to the analysis of global politics (notably in Rosenau's work[77]) many misconceptions still appear to surround complexity theory. One common mistake is to conflate nonlinear dynamics (including complexity theory) as a whole, and "chaos theory," perhaps because of the popularity of Gleick's book on the latter subject.[78] It is worth noting, then, that "chaos" is merely one of several distinct states that can be produced by the nonlinearities inherent in complex systems.[79] Strictly speaking, chaos is characterized by extreme unpredictability produced by systems that are so sensitive to minute changes that their outcomes are entirely uncertain.[80] However, complex systems can exhibit a range of other dynamical properties, also deriving from their nonlinearity. Some of these are, perhaps, even more interesting for international relations theory than mathematical chaos.[81] Rather than showing turbulent disorder and extreme volatility, instead they are characterized by the spontaneous emergence of order from complexity, what is termed *self-organization*.[82]

Self-organization is perhaps the most remarkable single feature of complex systems.[83] This is the property of complex systems to develop form and order that is not the deliberate outcome of agency. Instead, it is the unintended consequence of the many interactions that constitute the system, simply the outcome of the interrelationship of its parts. These interactions may take place for intentional reasons—as the product of deliberate agency—or as a result of unintentional contact, but they can be shown to have unintended consequences that give rise to systemwide processes.[84] In this way, form and order can derive from complexity alone, and this can—in turn—be subject to further transformations, as it too gives rise to further processes of self-organization.[85] Such "emergent forms" need not be volatile as in a chaotic system, but nor does this order need to be static: it too can self-organize.

Characteristically, complex systems are also expansive, in that they have an internal dynamic (deriving from similar processes of internal interaction) to colonize available spaces.[86] That is, they will "abhor vacuums" between different systems, and move into unoccupied space unless circumstance (such as ecological factors) or competition with other systems prevents them. So, complex systems tend to increase in size and become more extensive through time, and generally too, self-organization will lead to more hierarchically structured entities. In this sense complexity is usually progressive as well as expansive.[87]

To put it another way, complex systems can "just grow." Without other factors being involved they can expand and can develop apparently sophisticated structure and geometry.[88] Moreover, the geometries involved may be repeated over time, so that such form need not itself seem at any given time volatile at all. So, if polities or international systems are complex systems, they can—almost certainly—be expected to exhibit such dynamics.[89]

But the significance of self-organization to international relations theory does not end there. A particularly important aspect of complexity for world politics may be the propensity for complex systems to exhibit what is termed *self-organized criticality.*[90] When a critical threshold is reached, beyond which the existing state of the system cannot be sustained, the system will suddenly and dramatically shift its form into another state of existence (a "phase transition").[91] Similar rapid transformations are also found in work on the mathematics of "catastrophe theory," and in the property of "hypercoherence" (the overdependence of interrelated parts).[92] These different strands of analysis combine to suggest that transformations of this sort result from "triggering events" after long periods of cumulative (although often unperceived) "option-narrowing" on the systems involved. They are characteristically rapid and dramatic and are due to the overdependence of each part of the system on all others. When any one part changes, therefore, the consequences can be systemwide. So, wholesale systemic change can suddenly emerge from the unintended consequences of the interactions of a system after long periods of apparent "equilibrium."

Complex systems not only respond to internal dynamics but also evolve.[93] This is not to say that pure Darwinian logic can be applied to them, but they can exhibit dynamics consistent with "neo-evolutionary" concepts, such as those of Gould and Eldredge.[94] These dynamics include punctuated equilibrium, contingent selection, and adaptation.[95] That is, complex systems can grow, develop form and structure, shift between different states of existence, collapse, and disappear, entirely as a consequence of dynamics that are endogenous to the systems involved and they can also respond to the circumstances created for them by other coexisting systems. If states and international systems may be classified as complex systems, then it seems inescapable that such dynamics play some part in global political change, including global geopolitical transformations.

Toward a New Synthesis

These two strands of theoretical development have emerged independently from each other. However, they share so many features in common that it is easy to bring them together into a single macrodynamic synthesis. This, as will already be clear, has the potential to afford significant new contributions to the study of global political, and geopolitical, change.[96] The key link between these theoretical developments is provided by the role of information.

In complexity theory the flow of information between each constituent part of each system constitutes that system as a whole.[97] That is, complex systems are also always networks of information flow. Likewise, it is easy to conceptualize as networks of information flow and, of course, as complex systems, in the sense used here. Organizations of all sorts are, therefore, themselves (by definition) complex systems, and complex systems and organizations are both networks of information flow.

The key elements of each of these theoretical strands are so alike that they can be tied tightly together very effectively and simply by drawing attention to this point. As such a new synthesis of these approaches can be constructed, where communication and information are the critical links between work on organizational dynamics and the processes identifiable through complexity theory. Informational perspectives on organization may help us understand exactly how the dynamics of complex systems reconfigure world politics, and how processes of self-organization and self-criticality are expressed in political contexts.

This "macrodynamic synthesis" offers us an approach to IR theory that is not derived from any of the "three traditions" often used to characterize alternative paradigms within the discipline.[98] This is not to suggest that it need replace, but simply complement, other perspectives on the subject (it might, for example, be used along with liberal, realist, structuralist, constructivist, or feminist approaches to IR theory), although it can be employed alone as a framework of analysis, as here.

At this point we may return to the question of global geopolitical change. Using this new synthesis it is possible to reinterpret both past transformations and future prospects. This will enable us too see how the informational limits of political organization have shaped—and are shaping—global geopolitics.

The Informational Reconfiguration of Geopolitics

Earlier, we saw that the shifts from kin-based hunter-gather polities to chiefdoms and from chiefdoms to states, produced fundamental transformations in the spatial organization of world politics. If information-handling and communication affect political organization so profoundly, then this should be visible in these past transitions.

It has long been recognized by anthropologists that perhaps the best guide to any possible connection between communication and information-handling and political change in hunter-gatherer societies and chiefdoms comes from demographic data.[99] This is because all such societies are based on face-to-face modes of communication and these are necessarily constrained by population size. It is only possible to talk to so many people at once!

In fact, kin-based forms of political organization do seem to be associated with a clear-cut demographic range, in that all such groups include under 500 individuals.[100] This upper limit of 500 people correlates closely with the limits for face-to face communication established in anthropological work. Furthermore, the first evidence of emergent political stratification occurs at another clear demographic range, in this case of 300–500 people.[101]

Population growth and territorial expansion—especially in the search for additional food-sources—may well be triggers to the growth of "complexity" and political hierarchy at as hunter-gatherer groups approach the scalar limit of 500 individuals.[102] Increasing intergroup conflict might also have a role in promoting individualistic leadership, as competing polities fight each other for land or other resources.[103] But expansion in this way cannot be sustained indefinitely. As kin-based polities approach the scalar limit of 500 people, imposed by the limitations of face-to-face communication, political changes begin to occur.

This scalar limit for face-to-face communication necessitates that any polity with a larger population must cope with information flows in new ways. We have seen that there is only a limited number of different strategies that might potentially be employed to achieve this: new communication technologies, greater hierarchization, or increased differentiation.

Chiefdoms are not associated with new communication technologies.[104] But these polities are characterized by the growth of political hierarchy and of social and economic differentiation. These might well be seen as alternative strategies for coping with the problems of communication and information-processing in larger-scale polities. In all chiefdoms, many more layers of information-processing hierarchy exist than in kin-based polities, and decision-making is separated into different specialized areas of activity (craftsworkers, food-producers, ritual specialists, etc.) which had previously been less markedly differentiated within kin-based units.

The origin of chiefdoms is, therefore, associated specifically with the changed handling of information within these polities.[105] To put it another way, chiefdoms might be said to emerge as a response to the requirements of information-processing and communication among polities that were now too large to handle their informational requirements in existing ways, and that did not employ technological strategies of information management.[106]

When we come to the origins of the state, a different—but still consistent—pattern is found.[107] Here, informational requirements were not only met be organizational restructuring, but simultaneously by the use of a new technology of communication: writing.[108] All known states are associated with some form of literacy.[109] Recent work has also reasserted the association between the earliest known writing and the requirements of the earliest state-bureaucracy.[110] This has demonstrated that literacy originated as a means of information handling associated with the origins and early history of first states.[111] Thus, the origin of the state can be linked directly to the employment of the first major innovation in communication technology, unless one counts language, in global history.[112] This is not to say that literacy caused primary state-formation to occur, but rather that literacy coevolved with the formation of the first states.[113]

In all of these examples it is possible to argue that political (and geopolitical) transformations were associated with dramatically changed strategies of information processing and communication. Changes in the mode of information processing and communication not merely enabled these polities to operate efficiently, but actually permitted the existence of particular sorts of political form. Shifts in the informational possibilities open to polities enabled the emergence of new political forms, by overcoming previous limitations on their scale and organizational structure.

The geopolitical transformations described earlier in this paper, and associated with these "three ages" of world politics, can also be understood in this way. Each of these transformations altered the spatial organization of political activity. In this respect, informational limits constrained global geopolitics from the outset, but as these limits were overcome, new geopolitical forms could emerge. In the "age of the state" the potential for distanced communication—afforded by literacy—overcame the limitations imposed by demographic factors once and for all. Polities could now encompass ever-larger populations, and operate over much wider territories than previously. In effect, literacy removed demography as a motor for expansion.

This did not, of course, mean that states were less expansionist than chiefdoms. However, this expansionism was now derived from other factors than the "need to feed." Moreover, literacy also had other implications for geopolitics. Written descriptions of boundaries and treaties describing states' territorial rights and duties, gave an unprecedented fixity to frontiers.[114] The earliest certainly known political map is from (and contemporary with) the earliest state (Uruk), and there seems a clear association between pictorial mapping and the state. No chiefdom or kin-based polity is known to have mapped territorial borders.

Thus, literacy (and associated cartographic innovations) transformed geopolitics at the origins of the state. But the connection between state geopolitics and informational factors extends far beyond these origins. This is clearly illustrated by the relationship between the growth of printing, mass literacy, and news reporting in Europe and of the modern European state.[115] These afforded opportunities for the intensified growth of scientific knowledge, for the spread of new religious and political ideas and values, and for the mass-production of printed materials, not least maps, proclamations and other official documents. Later still, further intrastate geopolitical changes were associated with the growth of more efficient road and postal networks, as several scholars have noted.[116]

Even more striking, of course, is the association between communication technologies and the growth of global imperialism, a world economy and global news-reporting.[117] Plainly, worldwide empires (or the global economies with which they were associated) are inconceivable without worldwide communications systems, as exemplified by the histories of seafaring, railways, and telegraphy.[118]

Having seen this clear correlation between information processing, communication, and (geo-) political transformations in the past, let us return to the present. Currently, as many scholars have pointed out, a new "revolution" is underway in information-processing and communication.[119] So it seems logical to ask whether this heralds a new phase of political transformation, in which old limitations on political and geopolitical organization will be swept away.

The End of Anarchy?

The current "revolution" in information processing and communication might be said to have begun not with the computer, but with the origins of electronic communication and modern forms of long-distance transport.[120] The twentieth century has seen the growth of a whole range of new technologies of long-distance communication and travel: telegraphy, air-transport, automobiles, telephones, television, nuclear-powered seagoing vessels, space-flight, satellite relays, and—of course—computer-based communications.[121] No previous century has seen the introduction of so many new means of communication and this has been accompanied by a growth in new forms of information processing, most notably of course, through computing.

Consequently, the twentieth century has, by any historical measure, been characterized by a "revolution" in communications and information processing. This has vastly increased the rate of global interaction, as is demonstrable by the virtual elimination of transmission time for some types of information, the rapid increase in long-distance travel for work or leisure, the engagement of worldwide publics with "global issues" and the massive reduction in travel times in general.[122] The counterargument that these technologies and changes are unevenly distributed among the global population, seems to be ruled out by the fact the so too were all the previous changes discussed so far.

On theoretical grounds alone it is possible to make some suggestions regarding the probable impacts of this revolution on global geopolitics, using the macrodynamic approach already outlined. The expansive possibilities for most states at the end of the twentieth century are severely limited by the very prevalence of statehood, so any response to this "revolution" is unlikely to be in the form of a new phase of imperialism. The most likely options are the innovation of new tiers of information processing, increased differentiation, and/or the growth of cooperation between polities in coping with this "revolution" in information flows. We would also expect that the global change would be occurring at an ever-faster rate and global convergence in cultural and other terms increasing.

It hardly need be said that every one of these points is, at least arguably, well-evidenced in contemporary global politics. The growth of international institutions and of regional political, economic and security groupings seems consistent with an expectation of new organizational tiers of information-processing hierarchy above the state. The coexistence of globalizing and fragmenting political dynamics coincides well with potential differentiation within a worldwide system.[123] There seems some evidence too of an increasing willingness by state governments to cooperate in the face of global problems, while worldwide news and comments has led to the emergence transnational "public opinion" on some political subjects.[124] So too, the increasing rate of change is often noted by analysts of global politics and economics.[125] In these ways, therefore, this approach may offer support to those who see the current phase of world politics as one in which transnational and supranational organizations may play an enhanced role, and in which liberal democracy, free-market economics, and other "liberal" values may spread globally.

The potential consequences of such changes for global politics would be wide-ranging. But they are no less so than those which occurred in the only comparable communication revolution: that surrounding the origins of writing. If this last comparable phase of global history was associated with the shift from an "age of chiefdoms" to the "age of the state," then it can hardly be too extreme to see this as marking an end to the "age of the state."

However, this does not mean that we are likely to be about to see the end of states. The experience of previous political and geopolitical transformations (discussed earlier) suggests that we are unlikely to find the state redundant in the near future, rather than coexisting with whatever new political forms emerge from these transformations (such as regional—or global—tiers of governance). Nonetheless, it might render "international anarchy" (in the sense of a lack of formal political authority above that of the state) obsolete.[126]

Transnational interactions might give rise to transnational political organizations, just as territorial priorities gave rise to chiefdoms and states. In the same way as literacy disengaged population from political organization, so too might new forms of information processing and communication disengage the relationship between territory and political identity, or reconfigure this in new ways.[127] This "deterritorialization" might take any of various forms, perhaps the growth of wholly nonterritorial political organization, based on transnational communications and transnational communities.[128]

This assumes that global political innovation can keep pace with increased information-flows. If current global political innovations cannot keep pace with ever-greater information being transmitted at an ever-faster rate, then the world political consequences may be very bleak. Self-criticality might well emerge not only on the level of polities or regional political systems, as in the past, but rather on a global scale: the global system could itself become catastrophic. It hardly needs saying that what we have witnessed in terms of the collapse of states and empires so far in global history may be only small-scale catastrophes compared to the collapse of the global political system as a whole. Such collapse is historically unprecedented, but then so is the existence of the global system.

Moreover, any collapse may be all the more sudden and unexpected because of the rapid rates of information flow involved. Here, the "death of distance" inherent in transformed time: geographies of the global system well may constitute a "death of warning" also. We simply do not have the historical experience of a global system to gainsay this on the grounds that such dynamics are inconceivable in an entity of this sort. All we can do is look for indications that these processes are in action.

There might well be evidence that the global system is already under stress. Many scholars have commented on the way in which fragmentation and conflict seems to be intensifying at present, exactly as we might expect in a system undergoing "scalar stress." Current economic crises, increasing intrastate warfare, the growth of militant nationalism, and ethnic conflict since the end of the Cold War could all be interpreted in this way. The phenomenon of "turbulence"—betokening high levels of systemic instability—seems particularly worrying, as this might indeed suggest that systemic self-criticality has begun to emerge.[129]

The innovation of new modes or new tiers of world and regional governance, and other new forms of handling unprecedented information flows and interactions, are a possible way of ameliorating processes of scalar stress before global collapse occurs. Transnational communities and NGOs may also have a new role to play too, in a global system which places much more emphasis on nonstate entities and less on the territorial state.

If global collapse on these grounds is at all possible, then more effective transnationalism and global governance is not an utopian dream, but an urgent need. The time scale may be very short: systemic criticality may come on us with little warning.

If we are slow to act in this respect, it may be too late to avoid a political and economic calamity of unprecedented proportions. As it is, we may already be faced with a literal bifurcation between two historically unique options: the innovation of effective global governance or global collapse becoming a reality.

Notes

1. Defined broadly, geopolitics has had something of a revival both in geography and international relations in recent years. For examples of what is an extremely extensive literature, see: J. Painter, *Geography, Politics and Political Geography* (London: Arnold, 1995); P. J. Taylor, *Political Geography: World Economy, Nation-state and Locality*, 3rd

ed. (Harlow: Longman, 1993); A. Jarvis, "Societies, States and Geopolitics: Challenges from Historical Sociology," *Review of International Studies*, vol. 15, no. 3 (1989): 281–293; F. Kratochwil, "Of Systems, Boundaries and Territoriality: An Inquiry into the Formation of the State System," *World Politics*, vol. 39, no. 1 (1986): 27–52.

2. Samples of an extensive literature on this theme in anthropology and archaeology are: M. J. Casimir and A. Rao, eds., *Mobility and Territoriality: Social and Spatial Boundaries among Foragers, Fishers, Pastoralists and Peripatelics* (New York and Oxford: Berg, 1992); H. Donnan and T. M. Wilson, eds., *Border Approaches: Anthropological Perspectives on Frontiers* (Lanham, MD and London: University Press of America, 1994).

3. For an example of the centrality of statehood to recent geopolitical analysis, see Taylor, *Political Geography*.

4. K. R. Dark, *The Waves of Time* (London and New York: Pinter, 1998), chap. 5.

5. There is a vast scholarly literature on both kin-based polities and chiefdoms (mostly in anthropology and archaeology) but hardly any substantial discussion of these in IR—presumably because they have seemed "remote," "irrelevant," or "distant." Exceptions are found in the work of Yale Ferguson, Christopher Chase-Dunn, Stephen Sanderson, and in my own writing. For an IR paper in a celebrated collection of studies concerning chiefdoms, see Y. H. Ferguson, "Chiefdoms to City-States: The Greek Experience," in T. Earle, ed., *Chiefdoms: Power, Economy and Ideology* (Cambridge: Cambridge University Press, 1991), 169–192.

6. Dark, *The Waves of Time*, ch. 5.

7. Ibid.

8. Ibid.

9. Ibid.

10. Ibid.

11. The earliest state, Uruk, dates from the fourth millennium B.C. See Dark, *The Waves of Time*, chap. 5.

12. R. A. Dodgshon, *Society in Time and Space. A Geographical Perspective on Change* (Cambridge: Cambridge University Press, 1998), chap. 4.

13. K. Kosse, "The Evolution of Large, Complex, Groups," *Journal of Anthropological Archaeology*, vol. 14 (1993): 35–50.

14. For examples, E. Leacock and R. Lee, eds., *Politics and History in Band Societies* (Cambridge, Cambridge University Press, 1982); T. Ingold, D. Riches, and J. Woodburn, eds., *Hunter and Gatherers 1: History, Evolution and Social Change* (New York and Oxford: Berg, 1988).

15. C. Gamble, *Timewalkers* (Stroud: Alan Sutton, 1993).

16. In the sense of "the becoming worldwide of political activity."

17. For instance: N. Peterson, ed., *Tribes and Boundaries in Australia* (Canberra: Australian Institute of Aboriginal Studies, 1976).

18. For example: T. D. Price and J. A. Brown, eds., *Prehistoric Hunter-Gatherers: The Emergence of Cultural Complexity* (Orlando: Academic Press, 1985).

19. For a classic account, see: M. Godelier, *The Making of Big Men* (Cambridge: Cambridge University Press, 1986).

20. For example, see T. Earle, *How Chiefs Come to Power* (Stanford CA: Stanford University Press, 1997).

21. P. V. Kirch, *The Evolution of Polynesian Chiefdoms* (Cambridge: Cambridge University Press, 1989); D. Ó Cróinín, *Early Medieval Ireland 400–1200* (London: Longman, 1995).

22. Examples are discussed by Earle, *How Chiefs Came to Power.*

23. Ibid., esp. chaps. 3 and 4.

24. P. Heather, *The Huns* (Oxford: Oxford University Press, 1998); D. Morgan, *The Mongols* (Oxford: Oxford University Press, 1986).

25. Dark, *The Waves of Time*, chs. 3 and 5.

26. These public monuments are so commonly found as to have led to the development of a theory of "monumentality" in relation to chiefdoms: C. Renfrew, *Approaches to Social Archaeology* (Edinburgh: Edinburgh University Press, 1984), 130, 178–180.

27. For example, B. Wailes, "Irish Royal Sites in History and Archaeology," *Cambridge Medieval Celtic Studies*, vol. 3 (1982): 1–29.

28. For example, R. B. Warner, "The Archaeology of Early Historic Irish Kingship," in S. T. Driscoll and M. R. Nieke, eds., *Power and Politics in Early Medieval Britain and Ireland* (Edinburgh: Edinburgh University Press, 1988), 47–68.

29. Earle, *How Chiefs Come to Power*, chap. 4.

30. The issue of the relationship between world political change and the location and dynamics of urbanism, places of government, elite residences and other discrete political centers is another underexplored question in international relations theory. Here long-term approaches may again have much to offer the discipline.

31. Dark, *The Waves of Time*, chaps. 5, 6, and 7.

32. Dark, *The Waves of Time*, chaps. 5 and 6.

33. Dark, *The Waves of Time*, chap. 7.

34. Dark, *The Waves of Time*, chaps. 5, 6, and 7.

35. A point well illustrated by: Y. H. Ferguson and R. W. Mansbach, *Polities: Authority, Identities and Change* (Columbia S.C.: University of South Carolina Press, 1996).

36. By "global geopolitics," I mean the geopolitics worldwide, not carrying with this term the implication that the whole world is perceived as integrated into one geopolitical system at any given time.

37. I have in mind here the emergence of new general forms of spatial ordering, such as the transition from hunter-gatherer territories to chiefdoms, rather than such relatively minor shifts as localized border-adjustments in existing polities.

38. For example: S. E. van der Leeuw and J. McGlade, eds., *Time, Process and Structured Transformation in Archaeology* (London: Routledge, 1997).

39. For the relevant material to 1998: Dark, *The Waves of Time*, chaps. 2 and 4.

40. For example, F. E. Yates, ed., *Self-Organizing Systems* (New York, Plenum Press, 1987); I. Prigogine and I. Stengers, *Order Out of Chaos: Man's New Dialogue With Nature* (London: Heinemann, 1984).

41. P. W. Anderson, K. Arrow, and D. Pines, eds., *The Economy as an Evolving Complex System* (Redwood City PA: Addison-Wesley, 1988); P. M. Allen, "Models of Creativity: Towards a New Science of History," in van der Leeuw and McGlade, *Time, Process and Structured Transformation in Archaeology*, 39–56.

42. Dark, *The Waves of Time*, chap. 4.

43. Ibid.

44. For examples, see B. J. Loasby, "The Organization of Capabilities," *Journal of Economic Behaviour and Organization*, vol. 35 (1998), 139–160; G. Johnson, "Organizational Structure and Scalar Stress," in C. Renfrew, M. Rowlands and B. Segraves, eds., *Theory and Explanation in Archaeology* (New York, Academic Press, 1982): 389–421; K. Kosse, "Group Size and Societal Complexity: Thresholds in the Long-Term Memory," *Journal of Anthropological Archaeology*, vol. 9 (1990): 275–303.

45. M. Casson, *Information and Organization* (Oxford, Clarendon Press, 1997).

46. Johnson, "Organizational Structure."

47. While largely neglected in IR theory, communications have been a key focus of work in several other disciplines, such as: C. M. Cipolla, *Guns and Sails in the Early Phase of European Expansion 1400–1700* (London, Collins, 1965); S. Brunn and T. Leinbach, eds., *Collapsing Space and Time: Geographic Aspects of Communication and Information* (London: HarperCollins, 1991).

48. For a review see Dark, *The Waves of Time*, chap. 4; and Johnson, "Organizational Structure."

49. Dark, *The Waves of Time*, chap. 4; Kosse, "Group Size" and "The Evolution of Large, Complex Groups."

50. Johnson, "Organizational Structure."

51. Ibid.

52. Kosse, "The Evolution of Large, Complex Groups."

53. Johnson, "Organizational Structure."

54. Ibid.

55. Kosse, "Group Size"; Johnson, "Organizational Structure."

56. A. L. Stinchcombe, *Information and Organization* (Berkeley: University of California Press, 1990); Casson, *Information and Organization.*

57. Hierarchy has been the focus of a great amount of recent research in economics, organizational analysis and other disciplines. For examples: R. Radner, "Hierarchy: The Economics of Managing," *Journal of Economic Literature*, vol. 30 (1992), 1382–1415; M. C. Casson, "Why Are Firms Hierarchical?" *International Journal of the Economics of Business*, vol. 1, 47–57.

58. For example as Krishan Kumar notes, "All known societies practice some division of labour" (i.e., some differentiation of activities). (*Prophecy and Progress: The Sociology of Industrial and Post-Industrial Society*, 2nd ed. [Harmondsworth: Penguin, 1978], 83.)

59. There seems to have been no previous recognition of the effects of interactor cooperation on information processing.

60. Casson, *Information and Organization*; K. Kornwachs and K. Jacoby, eds., *Information: New Questions to a Multidisciplinary Concept* (Berlin: Akadamie-Verlag, 1996); Kosse, "Group Size."

61. Kosse, "Group Size" and "The Evolution of Large, Complex Groups"; Johnson, "Organizational Structure."

62. C. Renfrew and J. Cherry, eds., *Peer-Polity Interaction and Socio-Political Change* (Cambridge: Cambridge University Press, 1986); H. R. Erwin, "The Dynamics of Peer-Polities," in S. E. van der Leeuw and J. McGlade, *Time, Process and Structured Transformation in Archaeology*, 57–96.

63. Renfrew and Cherry, *Peer-Polity Interaction and Socio-Political Change.*

64. Dark, *The Waves of Time*, chap. 4.

65. Ibid.

66. Johnson, "Organizational Structure."

67. This makes the almost total neglect of this work in International Relations theory particularly surprising. For rare exceptions, see Dark, *The Waves of Time*, chap. 4.

68. M. Gell-Mann, *The Quark and the Jaguar: Adventures in the Simple and the Complex* (New York: Little, Brown, 1994); J. Horgan, "From Complexity to Perplexity," *Scientific American*, vol. 272, no. 6 (1995), 104–109; R. Lewin, *Complexity: Life at the Edge of Chaos* (New York: Dent, 1993); M. M. Waldrop, *Complexity: The Emerging Science at the Edge of Order and Chaos* (London: Viking, 1993).

69. S. Y. Auyang, *Foundations of Complex-System Theories: In Economics, Evolutionary Biology and Statistical Physics* (Cambridge: Cambridge University Press, 1998).

70. Dark, *The Waves of Time*, chap. 4.

71. Ibid.

72. Ibid.

73. M. Gell-Mann, "Complex Adaptive Systems," in G. D. Cowan, D. Pines, and D. Meltzer, eds., *Complexity: Metaphors, Models and Reality* (Reading Mass: Addison-Wesley, 1994), 17–45; P. M. Allen, "Evolution: Why the Whole Is Greater Than the Sum of the Parts," in W. Wolff, C.-J. Soeder, and F. R. Drepper, eds., *Ecodynamics: Contributions to Theoretical Ecology* (Berlin, Springer-Verlag, 1988), 2–30.

74. Lewin, *Complexity*; Gell-Mann, *The Quark*; Waldrop, *Complexity*.

75. This is illustrated by the existence of complex dynamics in economics: P. M. Allen, "Evolution, Innovation and Economics," in G. Dosi, C. Freeman, and R. Nelson, eds., *Technical Change and Economic Theory* (London: Pinter, 1998), 95–119; Anderson, Arrow and Pines, *The Economy as an Evolving Complex System*.

76. Clearly shown by work on urban evolution, using approaches combining complexity and agency: P. Allen and M. Sanglier, "Urban Evolution, Self-organization and Decision Making," *Environment and Planning*, A13 (1981), 169–183.

77. For examples: J. N. Rosenau, *Turbulence in World Politics* (London: Harvester Wheatsheaf, 1990). See also J. N. Rosenau, *Along the Domestic-Foreign Frontier: Exploring Governance in a Turbulent World* (Cambridge: Cambridge University Press, 1997).

78. J. Gleick, *Chaos: The Making of a New Science* (London: Heinemann, 1997).

79. Examples are given in J.-P. Eckman, "Roads to Turbulence in Dissipative Dynamical Systems," *Review of Modern Physics*, vol. 53 (1981): 643–654.

80. R. V. Jensen, "Classical Chaos," *American Scientist*, vol. 75 (1987): 168–181; D. Ruelle, *Chaotic Evolution and Strange Attractors* (Cambridge: Cambridge University Press, 1989).

81. S. A. Kauffman, "Antichaos and Adaptation," *Scientific American* (August 1991): 78–84;

82. S. A. Kauffman, *The Origins of Order: Self-Organization and Selection in Evolution* (New York: Oxford University Press, 1993); H. Haken, *Information and Self-Organization* (Berlin: Springer-Verlag, 1988).

83. Kauffman, *The Origins of Order.*

84. Ibid.; D. Ruelle, *Chance and Chaos* (Princeton: Princeton University Press, 1993).

85. For example, G. Silverberg, G. Dosi and L. Orsenigo, "Innovation, Diversity and Diffusion: A Self-Organization Model," *The Economics Journal*, vol. 98 (1988), 1032–1054. As in chaotic systems, although this need not lead to unprecedented uncertainty, as some political scientists seem to believe (See E. Ott, *Chaos in Dynamical Systems* [New York; Ruelle, 1991]).

86. N. Clark, F. Perez-Trejo, and P. Allen, *Evolutionary Dynamics and Sustainable Development* (London: Edward Elgar, 1995).

87. Demonstrated, for instance, by Kauffman, *The Origins of Order*, who nevertheless probably overstates the ability of Complexity alone to build sophisticated form.

88. J. Mingers, *Self-Producing Systems: Implications and Applications of Autopoiesis* (New York, Plenum Press, 1995).

89. Dark, *The Waves of Time,* chap. 4.

90. P. Bak and K. Chen, "Self-Organized Criticality," *Scientific American* (January 1991): 46–53; P. Bak, K. Chen, and M. Creutz, "Self-Organized Criticality in the 'Game of Life,'" *Nature*, no. 342 (1989): 780–782.

91. For examples: Lewin, *Complexity*; Gell-Mann, *The Quark*; Waldrop, *Complexity.*

92. For example, C. Brown, *Chaos and Catastrophe Theory* (Thousand Oaks CA, Sage, 1995).

93. R. V. Sole, S. C. Manruba, B. Luque, J. Delgado, and J. Bascompte, "Phase Transitions and Complex Systems," *Complexity*, vol. 1, no. 4 (1996): 13–26; B. A. Huberman and T. Hogg, "Complexity and Adaptation," *Physica* D42 (1990): 12–32.

94. S. J. Gould and N. Eldredge, "Punctuated Equilibrium Comes of Age," *Nature*, no. 366 (1993), 223–227.

95. M. H. Nitecki and D. V. Nitecki, eds., *History and Evolution* (Albany: State University of New York Press, 1992).

96. Dark, *The Waves of Time*, chap. 4. For examples of the application of aspects of nonlinear dynamics to IR, see R. Jervis, *System Effects: Complexity in Political and Social Life* (Princeton: Princeton University Press, 1997); L.-E. Cederman, *Emergent Actors in World Politics* (Princeton: Princeton University Press, 1997).

97. W. Holzmuller, *Information in Biological Systems* (Cambridge: Cambridge University Press, 1984).

98. For macrodynamics see Dark, *The Waves of Time*, chap. 4.

99. Kosse, "Group Size."

100. Ibid.

101. Ibid.

102. Dark, *The Waves of Time*, chap. 5

103. On war in nonstate settings: L. H. Keeley, *War Before Civilization: The Myth of the Peaceful Savage* (Oxford: Oxford University Press, 1996); J. Haas, ed., *The Anthropology of War* (Cambridge: Cambridge University Press, 1990).

104. Dark, *The Waves of Time*, chap. 5.

105. Ibid. See also W. Bernardini, "Transitions in Social Organization: A Predictive Model from Southwestern Archaeology," *Journal of Anthropological Archaeology*, vol. 15 (1996): 372–402.

106. Dark, *The Waves of Time*, chap. 5.

107. Ibid.

108. A. Gaur, *A History of Writing* (New York: Cross River Press, 1992).

109. P. T. Daniels and W. Bright, eds., *The World's Writing Systems* (Oxford: Oxford University Press, 1996).

110. H. Nissen, P. Damerow, and R. Englund, *Archaic Book-Keeping: Early Writing and Techniques of Economic Administration in the Ancient Near East* (Chicago: University of Chicago Press, 1993); Anon, *World Archaeology*, vol. 17 (1994) (special issue on early literacy).

111. N. Postgate, T. Wang, and T. Wilkinson, 1995, "The Evidence for Early Writing: Utilitarian or Ceremonial?," *Antiquity* vol. 69 (1995): 459–480.

112. Ibid.

113. See Dark, *The Waves of Time*, chap. 5 for a fuller discussion of this.

114. For instance, T. Campbell, *The Earliest Printed Maps 1472–1500* (London: British Library, 1987).

115. D. Buisseret, ed., *Monarchs, Ministers and Maps: The Emergence of Cartography as a Tool of Government in Early Modern Europe* (Chicago: University of Chicago Press, 1992); M. McLuhan, *The Gutenberg Galaxy: The Making of Typographic Man* (Toronto: University of Toronto Press, 1962).

116. M. Brayshay, P. Harrison, and B. Chalkley, "Knowledge, Nationhood and Governance: The Speed of the Royal Post in Early-Modern England," *Journal of Historical Geography*, vol. 24, no. 3 (1998): 265–288.

117. F. Lestringant, *Mapping the Renaissance World: The Geographical Imagination in the Age of Discovery* (Cambridge: Polity/Blackwell, 1994); H. Macedo, "Recognising the Unknown: Perceptions in the Age of European Expansion," *Portuguese Studies*, vol. 8 (1992): 130–136.

118. L. Kern, *The Culture of Time and Space 1880–1918* (Cambridge, Mass: Weidenfeld and Nicholson, 1983); D. R. Headrick, *The Tools of Empire: Technology and European Imperialism in the Nineteenth Century* (Oxford: Oxford University Press, 1981).

119. For example, L. M. Harasim, ed., *Global Networks: Computers and International Communication* (Cambridge, MA: MIT, 1993).

120. Kern, *Culture of Time and Space*; T. I. Williams, ed. *A Short History of Twentieth Century Technology c.1900 to c.1950* (Oxford: Clarendon Press, 1982); M. Castells, *The Information Age* (2 vols.) (Maldon, MA: Blackwell, 1996/97).

121. Williams, *Short History of Technology*; Castells, *The Information Age*.

122. S. Kirsch, "The incredible shrinking world? Technology and the Production of Space," *Environment and Planning D: Society and Space*, vol. 13 (1995): 529–555; T. Varis, 1985, *International Flow of Television Programmes* (Paris: Unesco, 1985).

123. S. Sassen, *Losing Control? Sovereignty in an Age of Globalization* (New York: Columbia University Press, 1996); S. Strange, 1996, *The Retreat of the State: The Diffusion of Power in the World Economy* (Cambridge: Cambridge University Press, 1996); K. Ohmae, *The End of the Nation State* (London: HarperCollins, 1995).

124. On the impact of the media on global politics, see D. Dayan and E. Katz, *Media Events: The Live Broadcasting of History* (Cambridge, MA: Harvard University Press, 1992); J. Neuman, *Lights, Camera, War: Is Media Technology Driving International Politics?* (New York: St. Martin's Press, 1996). For the emergence of shared norms and cooperative strategies in contemporary world politics, see: C. F. Sabel, "Studied Trust: Building New Forms of Cooperation in a Volatile Economy," *Human Relations*, vol. 46, no. 9 (1993): 1133–1170; J. G. Ruggie, *Constructing the World Polity* (London: Routledge, 1998).

125. L. Reynolds, "Fast Money: Global Markets Change the Investment Game," *Management Review*, vol. 81, no. 2 (1992): 60–61.

126. For some recent views of international anarchy, see: H. Milner, "The Assumption of Anarchy in International Relations Theory," *Review of International Studies*, vol. 17, no. 1 (1991): 67–85; B. Buzan and R. Little, "Reconceptualizing Anarchy: Structural Realism Meets World History," *European Journal of International Relations*, vol. 2, no. 4 (1996): 403–438.

127. R. Martin, "Stateless Monies, Global Financial Integration and National Economic Autonomy: The End of Geography?" in S. Corbridge, N. Thrift and R. Mar-

tin, eds., *Money, Power and Space* (Oxford, Blackwell, 1994), 253–278; M. R. Ward, "The Effect of the Internet on Political Institutions," *Industrial and Corporate Change*, vol. 5 (1996): 1127–1141.

128. It could be claimed this is already occurring in economic and cultural life: R. O'Brien, *Global Financial Integration: The End of Geography* (London, Pinter, 1991); K. Ohmae, *The Borderless World* (London: Fontana, 1990). An alternative might be regionalism: A. Hurrell, "Explaining the Resurgence of Regionalism in International Politics," *Review of International Studies*, vol. 21, no. 4 (1995): 331–358; M. Smith, "Regions and Regionalism," in B. White, R. Little, and M. Smith, eds., *Issues in World Politics* (Basingstoke and London: Macmillan, 1997), 69–89.

129. Rosenau, *Turbulence*, and *Along the Domestic-Foreign Frontier.*

CHAPTER 4

Remapping Political Space:
Issues and Nonissues in Analyzing Global Politics in the Twenty-First Century

Yale H. Ferguson
and
Richard W. Mansbach

Like the title voice-over of the television series *Star Trek*, both the concept of "political space" as a "frontier" and the exciting nature of contemporary global politics challenge us to go boldly where none of us has gone before. The end of the Cold War, present-day global/local trends, and the campaign against terrorism make much of traditional International Relations (IR) theory seem seriously outdated. Even those of us who have adopted nontraditional approaches are keenly aware of how rapidly things are moving and how little we really know. We sense both the startling new-ness of the current era and how much it resembles the past, not only the European epoch of the Westphalian state (put into proper perspective, as we shall discuss in due course), but also the vast stretches of human history going back to the earliest political forms. T. S. Eliot's opening lines in his *Four Quartets* capture the situation exactly and yet (paradoxically, as Eliot would appreciate) leave us to fill in the details: "Time present and time past / Are both perhaps present in time future, / And time future contained in time past."[1]

As we are all travelers, like it or not, in relatively uncharted political space, we thought it might be constructive to outline what *seem to us* to be the central issues and nonissues—that is, the core questions and also the red herrings—that we theorists need to address and avoid, respectively, when we venture forth. Let us emphasize at the outset that these questions are not strictly "academic." Practitioners may be uncomfortable with anything other than the familiar realist texts most of them studied in school, but they have *got* to admit greater complexity if they are to cope with the challenges they face every Monday at the office. Although some scholars are doing pioneering work, many more are insufficiently attuned to the tectonic shifts in contemporary global politics, because they are having so much fun and profit spinning out endless variations of the tired state-centric theories of yesteryear in major journals or playing rational choice and other games in their ivory towers. The most charitable assessment is that the field of "international relations" is not moribund because it is so diverse, but that very name for the field bespeaks a mainstream that is still tied to the past rather than a postinternational present and future.[2]

The Nonissues

Empiricism versus Relativism

In the post–World War II era many would-be social "scientists" preached the gospel that we can know nothing about X unless we can somehow quantify how much of X there is. IR theorists compiled and coded data at a feverish pace, and of course, since professional statisticians had so long been gathering statistics about states, the quantitative IR enterprise inevitably supported the realist map of the world. State boxes were ready-made repositories for numbers about population, military spending, and so on. What did the social sciences in general learn from the scientific revolution? In sum, very little, except in such fields as public opinion or voting behavior, where the numbers actually seemed to have some real connection to the likes of electoral outcomes or the degree of party cohesion in national legislatures.[3] Strict "science" in IR died a quiet albeit lingering death, and some of us actually thought we might soon be finished with equations . . . and then along came rational/strategic choice and second-generation game theory.

In the 1980s various other social scientists (*not* "scientists") started reading Nietzsche, Wittgenstein, Derridà, Foucault, and other relativists. Their gospel message was that language is inherently ambiguous and biases of all sorts enter into our choice of the problems we seek to study, the way we address them, and the conclusions we reach. Now most natural scientists would not find that sort of assertion particularly threatening, because they are keenly aware of the essential subjectivity of science, even that the famous scientific method rarely describes what happens in the process of discovery in a lab or anywhere else. But, of course, the relativist argument in the social sciences was intended to be a gauntlet flung directly in the face of "positivism" or "scientists," except that by then most card-carrying "scientists" had experienced a conversion to "softer" science or else retreated to their own quantitative panels at professional meetings where postmodernism was never mentioned. The game theorists and rational/strategic choice scholars—who by that time were experiencing a second coming—couldn't have cared less, because they *know* their cards are loaded, in fact, utterly dependent on initial assumptions.

The scholars who found the postmodernists most outrageous were those who thought they actually *were* discussing the "real world." What surprised them most was that postmodernism caught on big, not least in Europe, where scholars who had difficulty publishing in American journals or were searching for a European "voice" had been waiting to ambush the Yanks at the first good opportunity. Realists and other traditional scholars hated all that stuff about hermeneutics and "the other"? To top it all off, it was nearly impossible to read, which seemed particularly ironic coming from a group of intellectuals with roots in literary criticism. What the real-worlders missed was that the extreme relativists were engaged in games of a yet another sort, language games, with double entendres and other clever word-play. On the other hand, Habermasian, Wallersteinian world-systems, feminist, and "critical" theorists generally had their own more positive agendas. All theories rest on normative foundations, but theirs were and are overtly normative and reformist.

Now that we all have greater chronological perspective on some of these contests, allow us to sum up what we believe to be the facts:

1. The scientific revolution in IR was based on the wrong premises about science, started on the wrong foundation of realist theory, and therefore counted what it could find without much result. Does this mean gathering data is a useless enterprise? Certainly not, if reliable data is available and it can be put to the service of decent theory. Sometimes it *is* genuinely helpful to know how much of X we have.

   Having something useful to count depends initially on conceptual clarity and, of course, that is something that is particularly difficult to achieve in the field of global politics. Almost all our central concepts are so vague and controversial that we have to define them every time we use them: democracy, state, terrorism, power, and so on. Nor are rational/strategic choice and game theoretical models any more reliable, because they are inherently no more dependable than the (in our view) very dubious theoretical assumptions on which they are based. In the end, the proof is always in the pudding: How much of the world of politics do such theories convincingly describe and explain?

2. Is everything we "know" subjective, and even our choices of the puzzles we choose to address? At one level, yes of course. At another level, not everything goes or at least is equally convincing. Consider an example from literary criticism: the works of Ernest Hemingway. His most famous persona is the *macho* Hemingway, who chronicled heroism in the Spanish Civil War or matadors defying death in the bullring. Then there is the existential Hemingway familiar to college students who read about "A Clean Well-Lighted Place" and the

anguish of many key characters who are deeply suspicious that there is *nada* at the root of all. Most surprising is the androgynous Hemingway of the posthumous novel, *The Garden of Evil*, in which the main protagonists of both sexes continually switch roles. Other readers might mention his *verismo* journalism and travel accounts, or political activism including his actual participation in the Spanish Civil War and intelligence boat runs in the Caribbean during World War II. There are thus "several" Hemingways and perhaps more than have yet been "discovered," either by way of interpretation or because more manuscripts are still waiting in a vault somewhere. But the point here is that there are currently only a limited number of views of this major American author that can reasonably be admitted and serve as the basis for fruitful discussion. Someone might argue that Hemingway was a master of science fiction or a crusader for anticolonialism in Africa, and we would almost certainly remain unconvinced.

It is much the same with historical interpretation. What caused the collapse of classical Mayan civilization? Was it land exhaustion from overcropping? Lack of water compounded by drought? Other natural disasters such as pestilence or plagues of locusts? A revolt of peasants against their oppressors? Constant warfare among Mayan cities? There is some evidence for each of these interpretations or, most probably, more than one of them operating together. We can discuss these things and literally dig for further evidence. But there are not an infinite number of possibilities, and we continue to learn more about the Mayas year by year. Although one sensationalist scholar suggested that aliens helped inspire Mayan civilization, no one has maintained that aliens took them all away in spaceships.

Likewise the "causes" of the Cold War or its ultimate demise. Was the Cold War a realist struggle for power or an inevitable clash of two superpowers in a neorealist bipolar contest? Was it a war between two incompatible political and economic ideologies, that is, democracy and capitalism versus totalitarian socialism? How much was misperception on both sides? How much was the struggle a product of personalities like a paranoid Stalin? How much was dictated by national culture and history: Russians acting like Russians, Americans in their familiar moralistic expansionist mode? Once again, there are convincing arguments for these and other factors affecting outcomes alone or in various combinations.[4] We can and should go on combing the archives and interviewing participant observers, and no doubt—partly because of our competing theories—will never resolve some of the most important questions. But it is an interesting and useful debate with manageable parameters. No one is seriously suggesting that bears and eagles are natural enemies or that the entire Cold War experience was some sort of Islamic fundamentalist plot.

Agents, Structures, and Constructed Worlds

In the early days of the IR field, the so-called levels-of-analysis problem was a hot issue, not least because it reflected differences among different theoretical perspectives in a fledgling discipline. Realists saw a world of individual states as actors; others preferred to focus on individuals, especially any decision maker who might be regarded as a "great man"; and still others like neorealist Kenneth Waltz attributed the course of events to the basic power structure of the international system. Realists and neorealists dominated the field, but the levels-of-analysis "problem" itself was always greatly overrated. Nearly everybody knew perfectly well (whatever they admitted)—and Harold and Margaret Sprout wrote an early book[5] about it—that decision makers could not help but reflect influences from their environment. Also, leaders' behavior could sometimes be erratic, and they could misperceive what lay in the "objective national interest" of their countries. Even Morgenthau lamented that some decision makers, blinded by moral concerns or ideology, often failed to act like realists. Furthermore, the situation did tend to differ to some degree issue by issue and case by case. In one issue-area or case, structure seemed the most powerful influence; in another, personality; in another, a widely shared consensus as to national interest, and so on.

Oddly enough, however, IR theories did not start to accommodate deviations from dominant state-centric and neorealist modes in their theories until the 1980s, when the lessons of political psychologists like Robert Jervis[6] finally began to break through, postmodernism seemed to make subjectivity downright normal, and British sociologist Anthony Giddens's structuration theory[7] had an impact in certain U.S. intellectual circles that were not willing to embrace relativism with entirely open arms. The "agent/structure problem" was born, a sort of mutation of the old levels-of-analysis problem. Individual agent's perceptions of their environment including structures influence their actions, which in turn affect the environment/structures in which they are engaged, and then environment/structures in a giant feedback loop influence the perceptions and behavior of individual agents.

A central theoretical expression of agent/structure has been constructivist thought, which—it is important to recognize—has at least two distinct branches. One state-centric branch pioneered in the United States by Alexander Wendt[8] focuses on the way decision makers of states perceive their environments, which helps account for their actions and the nature of the international system. The environment is itself "objective," but readings of it may differ and have important consequences. He offers the example of the Aztec emperor Montezuma and Cortés: the Aztec initially thought the Spanish were gods, acted accordingly, and paid dearly for his misreading of the actual situation.[9] Note well, however, that in Wendtian constructivism, "anarchy" in the modern world is still what "states make of it,"[10] and other actors get very short shrift in his analysis. Also, "the state" as an actor remains ill-defined—Who or what *exactly* is doing the making? Finally, Wendt's observation that there is a potential for cooperation as well as conflict among states, harking back to Hedley Bull[11] in the late 1970s, is today commonsense for all but die-hard realists.

Another branch of constructivist thought has demonstrated that considering agents and structures in global politics need not result in limiting the field almost exclusively to states-as-actors. Friedrich Kratochwil,[12] Nicholas J. Onuf,[13] and others have spotlighted the "rules" that structure social relationships among a variety of actors and levels. On a related front, Thomas J. Biersteker and Cynthia Weber treat state sovereignty as a "social construct" whose "meaning is negotiated out of interactions within intersubjectively identifiable communities." In their view, "practices construct, reproduce, reconstruct, and deconstruct both state and sovereignty."[14]

When all is said and done, however, it seems to us that agent/structure is a nonissue, not because asking who are the agents and what are the structures is not an important question. Rather it is a nonissue because thus far it has given us a seriously incomplete and therefore misleading answer—that is, states and a society of states—or not much of any other answer at all. Asserting that agents "read" their environment and act accordingly, from which there also flow consequences, should be obvious. Only an IR field stunted from birth by realism could ever regard such a simplistic observation as much of a revelation! But, *specifically,* who or what *are* those agents and structures, and what patterns in global politics result?

Global politics shifts from issue to issue and even case to case: an agent (actor) in one issue or case may well be structure in the next, or largely irrelevant. For example, whether a particular group of banks (agent) extend loans to Russia may impact both the Russian economy (structure) and global financial markets (structure); in turn, the volatility of global financial markets (agent) may discourage depositors and investors (agents) from putting their money in banks with a high percentage of foreign loans (structure). At the same time, banks and financial markets have little or no impact on the development of regime rules to protect the whales, deforestation,[15] nuclear nonproliferation, and on and on. At the end of the day, it is fair to ask, what are the major and lesser issues in global politics, what types of actors/agents seem to be gaining and losing in the contests for influence around those issues, and what specific processes and background trends are shaping issues and outcomes? Constructivists have usefully reminded us of the subjective dimension of political space and the potential for order in anarchy, but they have either rested with the notion of a society of states or as yet eschewed the task of developing an alternative model that captures the full complexity of global politics.

Democracy and Peace

Perhaps no other single IR theory topic has lately occupied more pages in scholarly journals than the relationship between democracy and peace. Among all the theoretical "issues" we address, this is so insubstantial that it is hard to avoid the cynical conclusion that the debate owes mainly to a desperate effort by traditional security scholars and the quantitatively inclined to keep their pursuits alive in an era of declining interstate wars and skepticism about "science."

There are so many problems with the democracy/peace IR enterprise that it is difficult to know where to begin. The fundamental problem is the difficulty of defining "democracy," which each analyst does either in his or her own terms or ignores entirely by writing as if the meaning were self-evident. More important is the fact that, by any reasonable definition, the number of "democracies" that have existed in human history have been precious few—we have a *very* small *n* to work with—and most of the so-called democracies created in the wake of the Cold War's demise remain fledgling ones at best. The numbers of historical dictatorships or authoritarian regimes have been legion, and by no means all of them have been inclined to interstate wars, so it is safe to suggest that we might do equally well or better focusing our research on *that n*. For his part, Thomas Friedman has observed (only half facetiously) in his "Golden Arches Theory of Conflict Prevention" that countries with McDonald's restaurants have also refrained from interstate war.[16] Joanne Gowa's work suggests that democracies prior to 1914 were just as likely to engage one another in armed conflict as other states.[17] Patrick James and his research team have gone so far as to assert, persuasively, that the strongest numerical correlation is between peace and prosperity and the success of democracy, not democracy and an absence of interstate conflict.[18]

There is an additional matter here of priorities in theory-building: if not for the cynical reasons mentioned at the outset, why choose democracy and peace, of all topics, to investigate at this time? To be sure, there appears to be something of a worldwide trend toward greater popular participation in governments, relatively free elections, constitutionality, the development of legal systems, less arbitrary government, and so on. But there is also an apparent decline in interstate wars. (The War on Terrorism after the attack on the World Trade Center, strictly speaking, was not *interstate*.) That is exactly the point, insists the democracy/peace contingent, when one *n* (democracy) goes up the other (interstate war) goes down—is that not significant? How do we know? There was a "long peace" among great powers during the Cold War, and the worldwide democratic trend is so new that it seems almost impossible for it *already* to have had such a profound effect. Might the explanation for less interstate conflict not be, as Friedman suspects, the increasing extent and complexity of the global economy? Or the declining importance of territory? The rising cost in both human and material terms of warfare? How do we get away from the everything-else-being-equal dilemma? One way is to take a longer view, go back into history—of course, then we are back to the small number of historical democracies.

Most unfortunate of all is how the democracy/peace literature distracts us from far more significant questions, suggested in part by our comments about economic trends and the declining importance of territory. Indeed, much more pressing at the present time than interstate warfare is warfare *within* states that sometimes spills over borders into adjoining territory—"civil" (though often horrific) conflicts reflecting the forces of ethnicity, nonstate nationalism, religion, and/or tribalism. Another question, of course, on the democracy side of the equation, is what increasing popular participation means for government legitimacy? Will it lead to repeated constitutional crises or to a closer identity and involvement of citizens with their governments? Will better educated and skilled citizens demand more of their states, only to be frustrated with a growing recognition that states are simply ill-equipped to meet their needs for group pride and material welfare on any sort of sustained basis?

Globalization

Globalization is a different sort of nonissue from the ones we have been discussing. The problem here is not that the subject is unimportant or that there is controversy about it; it is that most of the heat about the novelty and degree of contemporary globalization seems to come from theorists talking past one another—that is, from conceptual confusion, rather than direct disagreement. In short, the ground for more consensus may well be available if the terms of the debate can be clarified. On the other hand, such an optimistic assessment may well underplay the extent to which the normative predispositions of the parties involved make them reluctant to do anything but muddy the waters. Convinced globalists confront those who have a personal stake in state-centric theories, a dislike for "big business," a concern that economic liberalization will threaten "progressive" labor and environmental policies, and a fear of a growing "democratic deficit" in transnational organization.

Globalization obviously has many important dimensions, including economic, military, migration of peoples, culture, environment, crime, terrorism, and (last but not least) governance. Suffice it here to focus on the economic dimension to illustrate the matter of conceptual confusion.

If we limit "economic globalization" to the growth of international trade and investment, as Paul Hirst[19] and others prefer, such a process (he observes) has indeed been going on, with fits and starts, for well over a century. Hirst, in fact, identifies three earlier sustained periods, 1870–1914, the end of World War II to 1973, and 1973–1979. So has nothing changed? Hirst acknowledges that direct merchandise trade has become much less significant as capital flows have increased, but he prefers to avoid asking whether today's vast speculative flows of currency are not truly unprecedented and does not address what impact they might have on state autonomy.

His only indirect counter is his observation that over 90 percent of FDI (foreign direct investment) still takes place between and among the rich countries, representing just over a quarter of the world's population. His point is twofold, first that much investment is not actually global but concentrated and, second, that as long as this is the case, the potential for the relatively small group of affected countries to design joint strategies for regulation remains high. He writes that "governance [is] possible, given the political will and a measure of international consensus."[20] That political will and consensus would clearly have to come as much or more from the private sector as from governments themselves. The history of SEC rules in the United States offers a precedent of that sort, although we should not underestimate the much greater challenge of creating rules among disparate state parties in a rapidly shifting global economic environment.

Variations abound on the theme that economic globalization can best be understood as a phenomenon that is actually somewhat narrower in scope than the entire world. Analysts rightly observe that much of the action in the global economy emanates from "world cities,"[21] particular bilateral relationships (like the historical ones between the U.S. and Canada, and the U.S. and Mexico), certain regions or subregions (NAFTA, the European Union and its subregions, the Pacific Rim, and so on), and networks that involve not only firms but also bureaucrats, professionals, and others.[22] Interestingly, those commentators who focus on globalization are often the first to "deconstruct" the global economy, while those who are keen to defend the continued primacy of states in global politics are usually reluctant to "deconstruct" either states themselves or the "state system." Presumably, the latter group fears to reveal the importance of nonstate actors, markets, and the like. We can argue about which patterns and actors are primary or dominant, but there is more room for mutual accommodation among these different perspectives than some of their proponents might admit.

The same may be said for yet another attack on the idea of economic globalization, the assertion that theorists have been prone to overestimate the extent to which large firms have really globalized, in terms of structure, management styles, and/or market strategies. Hirst, for instance, maintains that firms "are still multinational, not transnational; that is, they have a home base in one of the Triad [Europe, Japan, and North America] countries" and "are not footloose capital but are rooted in a major market in one of the three most prosperous regions of the world."[23] Paul N. Doremus et al. similarly insist that American firms remain essentially American; German firms, German; and Japanese firms, Japanese.[24]

Surely we can accept many of the foregoing observations about the global economy without losing sight of the fact (which some analysts want to do) that the contemporary situation *is* also dramatically new in some key respects. National economies *are* ever-more dependent on transnational and global forces; corporate leaders *are* designing transnational and sometimes global strategies; production and management structures *are* increasingly being integrated across vast stretches of the planet; e-commerce has gradually been transforming the marketplace; firms *are* pursuing an unprecedented number of transborder mergers, alliances, and networks; there *has* been a revolution in communications and information; and, despite the slowdown that began in mid-2001, the volume and pace of transactions *has* increased to an amazing degree in recent years.[25]

For Jan Aart Scholte, globalization is "the spread of 'supraterritorial' or 'transborder' relations." That definition enables him to come to a quite different conclusion than Hirst, even while accepting that relative levels of "cross-border trade, investment and migration a hundred years ago were roughly the same or higher than they are today." What Scholte finds most "distinctive" about contemporary globalization is that it involves "a fundamental transformation of human geography" in which "world affairs have acquired a (rapidly growing) global dimension alongside the territorial framework of old" that is being reflected in spheres such as telecommunications, marketing, and "transworld finance." As he reads it, "borders are not so much crossed as *transcended*."[26]

David Held et al. offer a similar conceptualization. As they explain it: "Globalization can best be understood as a process or set of processes rather than a singular condition" that does not necessarily reflect "a simple linear developmental logic," a prefiguration of "a world society or world community," or "global integration." What it does reflect is "the enmeshment of national and societal systems in wider global processes . . . complex webs and networks of relations between communities, states, international institutions, non-governmental organizations and multinational corporations which make up the global order." "Under conditions of globalization, 'local,' 'national,' or even 'continental' political, social, and economic space is re-formed such that it is no longer necessarily coterminous with established legal and territorial boundaries." The "exercise of power through the decisions, actions, or inactions, of agencies on one continent can have significant consequences for nations, communities and households on other continents." To be sure, they observe, "elites in the world's major metropolitan areas" have much more impact on global networks than do "subsistence farmers in Burundi."[27]

In sum, global politics and the global economy are not entirely old or new. They are dimensions of a world experiencing rapid change and even transformation, in some respects and not others. As a consequence, Jessica T. Mathews reminds us: "National governments are not simply losing autonomy in a globalizing economy. They are sharing powers—including political, social and security roles at the core of sovereignty—with businesses, with international organizations, and with a multitude of citizen groups."[28]

The Autonomy of Regimes

State-centric theorists have long had severe difficulties in coming to terms with the roles of formal international organizations and less-formal regimes, which have been steadily increasing in numbers since the late nineteenth century. Realist theorists tended to admire great-power organizations like the Concert of Europe but to associate those with wider ambitions like the League of Nations with Wilsonian so-called idealism. Both Hedley Bull[29] and liberal institutionalists like Robert Keohane[30] allow that international organizations are, in fact, a natural outgrowth of converging state interests to secure a greater measure of order in anarchy and the advancement of a limited number of shared goals. Others go a step further to suggest that various forms of institution building beyond the state are increasingly essential and inevitable, and result in organizations and regimes with considerable authority and independence. Predictably, much theoretical work has focused on one of the most interesting experiments, the European Union. How much autonomy and clout does the EU have apart from its members? To what extent do policy initiatives like the single currency stem from the interplay of state interests or from EU technocrats?

Although this discussion strikes us as slightly more intriguing on the face of it than the democracy/peace debate, in fact there is very little substance here either. To be blunt, it should be obvious that each organization and regime has its own character: some are paper organizations only, others merely reflect the current state of diplomatic bargaining among their members, and still others have built reputations and bureaucracies with considerable autonomy and influence. In multipurpose organizations like the EU, the situation tends to differ (like agents and structures) issue by issue (function by function). It is somewhat analogous to international law, where some norms are almost completely ignored and still others are effectively binding, because they are respected and observed by practically everyone. With a nod to the constructivists, engagement in international institutions almost inevitably affects participants. Governments and their representatives cannot help but do some learning; they are perhaps more likely to see matters from a wider point of view, although (depending on the issue) this may or may not be sufficient to elicit their support for additional cooperative initiatives—and some experiences may be so unpleasant that such support actually declines.

A more fundamental problem with a focus on international organizations and regimes is that it may not put them in the proper perspective, not only of states, but also of all the other polities that share the stage of global politics. Regions within Europe, world cities, networks, provincial and local governments, religious organizations, families, tribes, firms—these and others are also important, legitimate, and often substantially autonomous political actors within their respective realms of authority. Clearly, the primary reason for the traditional fascination with international institutions is that states are the main members. Why should this influence our research agenda? Is not governance in all its manifestations what we social scientists should be investigating, whatever the sources and degree of institutionalization involved? We will return to this subject shortly. Suffice it to say here that a recent very encouraging development in the study of regimes has regarded their increasing formal and informal engagement with a variety of networks and civil society.[31]

Curtain for the Westphalian State?

The last nonissue we need to address is a particular formulation of the common observation that states are under siege in the contemporary world: to wit, that states are no longer relevant and may soon disappear. Perhaps not surprisingly this absurd proposition is most often set up by present-day defenders of the state as a sort of straw person. It makes an easy target: state-centric theorists can show that there is much life in the old state yet, and thereby avoid addressing the *relative* decline of states in late-twentieth-century global politics.

Actually, the statist counteroffensive begins with a different sort of preemptive strike, an effort by some scholars like Stephen D. Krasner to suggest that those who continually notice that the state is not what it used to be, simply do not appreciate that realists and others have always known that the state was never an all-powerful monolith. Westphalia did not inaugurate a sovereign state that completely controlled all other political actors, nor did sovereignty ever mean absolute authority.[32] Agreed!—if not with the part about what realists have claimed, at least about the truth of the observation regarding the state. Charles Tilly,[33] Janice E. Thomson,[34] Hendryk Spruyt,[35] and others have conclusively demonstrated that the developments in Europe that lead to the sovereign state might well have taken an entirely different course and that the states that did emerge were highly tentative and fragile constructions from the start. Indeed, as we have argued and Rodney Hall details, the aristocratic "state" (and state system) of the ancien régime was far different from the later models associated with nationalism and popular sovereignty.[36] The same might be said for the modern welfare state.

Getting back to the line of reasoning that there is life in the old state yet, a variety of arguments have been offered, some of which are more persuasive than others.

Stable State Boundaries

One correct claim is that, with a few exceptions like the internal breakup of the Soviet Union, the territorial boundaries of states have recently been remarkably stable. "In the twentieth century, and especially since 1945," declare Robert H. Jackson and Mark W. Zacher, "states have not only come to a judgment that they should not murder each other, they have adopted the position that they should not maim each other—that is to say, they should not cut off pieces. Today states are more respectful of each other's independence and territory than they have ever been, or in a different terminology, they are more normatively committed to the territorial covenant."[37] A variety of factors, including the Cold War rivalry, paradoxically, strengthened the territorial covenant. Iraq's wars against Iran and Kuwait and the Ugandan-Rwandan-sponsored invasion of Zaire remind us that there are still those who do not accept it, but certainly the reaction of the international community to Sadam's aggression was swift and sure.[38] However, the most important reason for more stable boundaries, in our view, is a relatively simple one: For states—by contrast with restive minorities seeking self-determination or autonomy—the importance of territory in global politics has declined dramatically while the cost of war has risen. Unlike the 1991 Gulf War, the 2001 War on Terrorism responded to a horrific attack on the United States by a transnational terrorist network, rather than a state, and the subsequent military campaign was essentially a matter of supporting rival tribal groupings and warlords to oust the Taliban and apprehend Al-Queda leaders. The most relevant state boundary, that of Pakistan, proved to be a continuing problem because it was so porous.

State Capacity

A second argument is that the capacity at least of some states has actually grown.[39] Although the welfare state and national budgets—even military budgets, until the War on Terrorism—have been downsizing (in relative terms) in the older states, it is also true that many national budgets are still large by any measure and a few countries, especially in the developing world, are actually improving their public administration, education, and welfare services. Many governments continue to produce and enforce with reasonable efficiency rules about taxation, trade and foreign investment, health, public order, industrial safety, labor standards, affirmative action, environmental protection, and so on. Indeed, as market controls have been liberalized and more enterprises and social services have been privatized, some governments have tried to compensate by developing a new generation of regulations.[40] Moreover, mounting concern about terrorism has lead to a tightening of immigration and asylum policies, and increased law enforcement and intelligence-gathering.

Yet it is at least as important to recognize that there is, in fact, considerable ambivalence in many (most?) citizens' attitudes. On the one hand, there is an urgent need for government protection, better public services, and rules that will assure more fairness and justice in society. On the other hand, there is a pervasive and probably well founded doubt as to whether government can or will effectively provide much of what is required. Times when fears about physical security loom large, as after the World Trade Center attack, tend to strengthen states temporarily, while the perceived emergency lasts and governments appear to be dealing with it. But spikes in public opinion polls in favor of leaders in wartime should not obscure the recent history that tax revolt and privitization measures have been widespread phenomena. Likewise, nearly all politicians in power for any length of time have tended to fare dreadfully in public opinion polls. Despite the current limited "backlash" against "globalization," governments seem to have little capacity to protect citizens from globalizing shocks and most appear far more anxious to offer incentives and remove obstacles to having their national economies fully integrated into the global economic system. Most states appear to be more servants of the private sector than regulators when it comes to the global economy.

The "Asian state" is often cited as an exception to any generalization that states are weak. Quite apart from the current economic crisis, one difficulty with this assertion is that some states in Asia are hard to differentiate from their own private sector.[41] Singapore's government started out by identifying sectoral opportunities within the global economy for national and transnational firms, but somewhere along the line the private-sector tail started wagging the dog. As for Japan, Susan Strange maintained that that country's "exceptionalism" was substantially the result of postwar Western aid, technology, and dispensation to pursue closed-market policies.[42] That era is now over, and Japanese citizens themselves are less willing to make traditional sacrifices and believe that what is good for business, organized crime, and government bureaucrats is necessarily good for them. In China, it remains to be seen whether a strong state can long coexist with increasingly privatized firms and markets. Moreover, the national government may have grave problems controlling its own military and regional and local insubordination.

Until recently, economic success shielded Chinese and other Asian governments from too much citizen scrutiny and criticism. Then came Japan's severe economic difficulties and the financial crisis that struck Southeast and East Asia in 1997 and 1998. In state after state—Thailand, Indonesia, and South Korea—governments had to give way to the exigencies of global economic forces. Malaysia fought back by imposing restrictions but has now had to backtrack. Should the present worldwide economic slump persist, the pressures will surely mount.

Number of States

A third argument is that with the rise of numerous mininationalisms, the list of states is likely to grow longer rather than shorter. In remarkable doublethink fashion, defenders of the state thus transform a problem for their map of the world—the fact states may be disintegrating and boundaries therefore might be altered from the inside—into a virtue. States are begetting more states, up to several thousand if all the movements succeed. We are supposed to applaud this final triumph of the nation-state ideal. Such a world would be far from anything we know at present and is highly unlikely to come about in any event. Many "ethnic" groups "merely" want autonomy rather than full independence, which most would be unable to obtain even if they did want it. However, the demands and often violent behavior of such groups will doubtless continue to plague many existing states.

Interstate Cooperation

The last argument is that states are recovering many of their lost prerogatives by cooperating through international organizations and regimes, and using nongovernmental and international nongovernmental organizations as well—entities that do have the capacity to operate across sovereign boundaries. Doublethink continues: states simply cannot cope by themselves, so they are salvaging "their" authority partly by creating international institutions that "they" still control? In truth, states' outsourcing (rather like firms) to other polities are helping states to cope with some contemporary challenges. The results differ from issue to issue, as does the autonomy of the resulting transnational institutions (as we have discussed), and the eventual impact on citizen identities and loyalties remains to be seen.

We are back to the straw person. Georg Sørenson proposes that a more productive way of looking at some of the same matters is simply to ask—not whether states are "winning" or "losing" relative to other polities—rather how states are changing or adapting to new conditions.[43] We agree that the second is a useful question. However, considering that question by no means excludes the other, which is not only a fair question but also an important one. By contrast with the nonissue (whether states are likely to become extinct), we still can and should ask to what extent states are poorly equipped to cope with the demands imposed on them from above and below in what James N. Rosenau terms today's world of "turbulence" and "fragmegration"?[44] How are they faring relative to other polities—and why?

The traditional map of political space inhabited only by states has embodied a number of false assumptions. The legal independence derived from sovereignty—the recognition by other sovereign states that a new territorial polity should be admitted to the club[45]—is too often confused with genuine authority and autonomy.[46] A sovereign state may *assert* that outsiders *should* not intervene in its affairs, and that citizens *should* respect its legitimacy and obey its laws, but there is no guarantee that they will. Jorge Domínguez, for instance, writes of "a persistent fear" that haunts Latin America, "an obsession with failure." "Many still believe that economic success is ephemeral and that democracy's worst enemies are the politicians who claim to speak in its name."[47] Sovereign independence since World War II, as we have noted, has offered considerable protection against military aggression and boundary changes.[48] In many places, unfortunately, the result has been what Robert Jackson calls "negative sovereignty," that is, protection for corrupt regimes.[49]

Sovereignty makes it appear that states are homologous, disguising the more important fact that actual states have little in common *except* legal sovereignty. Today's list of nearly 200 states includes one superpower and a large number of entities that are scarcely viable. Some 87 states have fewer than 5,000,000 inhabitants, 58 have less than 2,500,000, and 35 fewer than 500,000.[50] Sovereign Nauru, for example, is a Pacific atoll of eight square miles, with 8,000 inhabitants, many of whom are rich from the sale of phosphates. When the atoll gets washed away or runs out of phosphates, that will be the last of Nauru. Or, consider the contrast between the prosperous city-state of Singapore and conflict-torn Afghanistan. Or the failed state of Sierra Leone, which features more than a dozen ethnic groups, repeated coups, brigands, and "sobels" (former soldiers), along with the Revolutionary United Front that engages in looting and diamond smuggling. In Sierra Leone as well as elsewhere in Africa, argues William Reno, illicit commercial networks help compensate for the loss of traditional patronage systems reinforced by aid from former colonial powers and Cold War rivals.[51] In many of these countries, the idea of sovereignty is turned on its head; instead of providing citizens with security from foreign aggression by guarding the country's borders, the "national" army is *the* source of insecurity for citizens who are desperate to flee across those very borders. On occasion "private" mercenaries such as the now-defunct South Africa–based Executive Outcomes (one of some ninety private armies operating in Africa) are employed to substitute for a national military or protect a government from its own army.

Perhaps the most common fallacy perpetuated at least by realists is that states can be treated as unitary actors. In fact, most states are usually rent by political faction and subject to intense bureaucratic infighting and interest-group politics, often with a transnational dimension. Unfortunately, there remains a tendency to anthropomorphize states, when almost inevitably the real "actors" or "agents" are either government subgroups, social subgroups, or both. If we wish to identify the actual sources of policies, we have to trace them back to individuals and groups within and outside the state.

Even the distinction between "within" and "outside" is gravely misleading. In its most distorting form, this distinction contrasts domestic "tranquillity" with international "anarchy." In many respects, the reverse is closer to the truth, as urban centers from Bogotá and Karachi to Washington, D.C. and Moscow are afflicted by organized crime, ethnic conflict, random terrorism, and anomic violence. By contrast, interstate wars (as we have noted) are rare, and formal and informal rules govern much of the transnational and international worlds. However much traditional IR theories may argue to the contrary, there is a great deal more order or "global governance" than anarchy, and much of that order is a direct consequence of governance by other actors than the state. Increasingly, such actors are dealing directly with one another, bypassing the state.[52]

Finally, the distinction between "public" and "private" that dominates political philosophy and international law is largely false, serving mainly as a prop to perpetuate sovereignty and (ironically) to shield the "private" sector from adequate scrutiny. Until the field of political economy finally gained steam in recent years, liberals and realists in political science both believed anything to do with business and finance belonged to management schools. Even in the United States, where the free market is a fundamental ideological tenet, "private" business interests have influenced public policy since the Republic was founded, and government, in turn, routinely looks to the knowledge and resources of the private sphere for public purposes.[53] The "public" good and the "national interest" have often been indistinguishable from the good of "private" interests. This is even more so in the case "Japan Inc." and "Singapore Inc.,"[54] and more generally, the "crony capitalism" that characterizes much of Asia. The deregulation of capital markets has highlighted the fact that the resources of private investors and firms have come to outstrip dramatically the resources of most national treasuries.

In sum, if the state-centric model of global politics has always been misleading, today it hopelessly distorts the world in which we live. All states must share authority and influence with other polities. Everywhere, governments are bewildered by the pace and impact of change, and this bewilderment intensifies factionalism and bureaucratic competition, often leading to government gridlock and inertia. In addition, as a result of education and greater access to information, citizens are less and less passive and are getting harder and harder to fool. They are also mobilizing themselves for political ends across cyberspace. As Strange observed: "Politicians everywhere talk as though they have the answers to economic and social problems, as if they really are in charge of their country's destiny. People no longer believe them."[55]

The Real Issues

Change

By contrast to all the nonissues we have discussed, our field's conception of "change"—and its reading of the degree to which we are and are not experiencing it in the contemporary world—*is* an issue worthy of the name. We will not dwell on that issue here, mainly because Kal Holsti and Jim Rosenau explore it so elegantly in their respective contributions to this volume (Holsti also addresses Rosenau's writings on this subject).

Allow us, then, merely to stress a few points. As Holsti suggests, change need not be discontinuous or, as he puts it, "replacement." It may only be an "addition" to present patterns, not necessarily obliterating all that has gone before. Change may also be "transformative," putting new wine in old bottles. Our own work has tended to highlight change both as addition and as transformation, and to suggest that the two are profoundly related. In our case studies of thousands of years of political history,[56] it was clearly evident to us that old political forms, identities, and loyalties rarely disappeared entirely. Rather, they tended to "nest" in successor polities, like an incubus, waiting for an appropriate moment to reassert themselves, to be "rediscovered" or "reinvented." As in our opening Eliot quotation, the past is deeply embedded in both present and future; the world, as we ourselves expressed it, is a "living museum." Yet the process is a highly dynamic and often unpredictable one. Again, depending on the issue or generally (although not necessarily without exception), "addition" usually results in, not "replacement," but "transformation." Tribes became electoral districts in classical Athens, and independent states in the United States became states in a confederal and then a federal union (backsliding violently during the Civil War). Today the relationship between the states of the United States and Washington is still being negotiated. In the present-day world context, similarly, sovereign states are gradually losing to or sharing—certainly not all—but some of their important traditional functions with other polities within, without, and transcending their borders. At the same time, we have noted, some states may actually be increasing their capacity in certain respects. We reiterate, it is fair to ask for a balance sheet: Which states, which respects, and what is the health of the state form—in all its manifestations—in the global system overall?

A second point harks back to our initial nonissue of empiricism versus relativism. Rosenau in his essay in this book observes that there seem to be different "temperaments" at work in theory, those who are predisposed to look for continuities and those who are inclined to emphasize the degree to which the present is different from the past. His is an uncharacteristically postmodern observation, albeit sound as far as it goes. We would argue, however, that such matters should and need not be so open-ended. Herein lies the critical importance of history, with all the subjectivity inevitably involved in its interpretation. At the end of the day, the present is the same and/or similar to the past in some respects and different in others. We need to stop excusing the excesses of apologists for the state, prophets of a globalized world, and so on. So *exactly* how *is* the present *both similar to the past and also different?* If all theorists were obliged to answer *both* questions and marshall evidence before writing anything else, we would soon have a substantive and constructive debate on the issue of change.

Governance

Barry Jones in his essay in this book insists that "governance is the issue." We heartily agree! In previous pages and our earlier work, we have consistently maintained that the state is only one of many "polities" that (generally, with variations issue by issue) layer, overlap, and interact—coexist, cooperate, and conflict. In our definition, "polities" are those entities with a measure of identity, hierarchy, and capacity to mobilize followers for political purposes (value satisfaction/relief from value deprivation). All polities are "authorities" within their "domain," that is, those persons, other resources, and issues over which they exercise "effective control or influence." As Rosenau remarks: "[T]he effectiveness of an authority structure lies not in its formal documents but in the readiness of those toward whom authority is directed to comply with the rules and policies promulgated by the authorities. Formal authority is vacuous if it does not evoke compliance, whereas informal authority . . . can be stable and effective if its exercise produces compliance."[57]

We have to depart slightly from Rosenau's formulation to acknowledge that a greater or lesser degree of coercion has played a role in establishing the capacity of polities since time immemorial. Yet it is far too easy to overestimate the degree to which coercion has been a factor in effective control. Compliance and even identity can under some circumstances be imposed, but loyalty is a different matter altogether. Loyalty is an exchange phenomenon and flows *only* to those polities that provide the requisite psychological and material rewards.

That brings us to what we would argue is one of the two central issues in the study of contemporary global politics: what polities control or significantly influence what issues in the world arena—and why. If we could somehow free our field from all the aimless discussion of the nonissues we have mentioned and focus on this question (and the one to follow), we might actually make some genuine theoretical headway. We urgently need numerous case studies of specific issues, the actors engaged in each, their relative influence, and analysis of the reasons for the patterns observed. Such a collective enterprise might provide some old-fashioned evidence (in the non-"science" sense) and take some of the "gas" out of the sweeping assertions that most of us in the field are wont to make.

Identities and Loyalties

Our final real issue is the implications of present-day changes, as well as continuities, for human identities and loyalties. Citizenship and nationality no longer define by themselves who we are and where our loyalties lie. The question of who is "inside" and who is "outside" the boundaries of civic and moral obligation is regaining an importance for political theory and global politics not seen since the birth and maturation of the Westphalian state.

A variety of features may serve as a basis for self-identity—race, religion, ideology, gender, profession, to name a few. As a result, an individual is to some extent both the same as and different from others. However, most identities are insufficiently stable or salient to provide clear political cues or durable boundaries between political communities. Any definition of self is multidimensional and fluid, and for each individual the ranking of identities will be slightly different. That hierarchy will change and new identities may be created as the significance attached to political relationships with others is altered. Thus, few Bosnians identified themselves by religion until Bosnian "Muslims" discovered a collective identity as a result of collective persecution. Just as the identities of subjects and, later, citizens were manipulated by kings and revolutionaries to strengthen the state, so today mullahs and nationalists manipulate identities to undermine the state.

By contrast to the linking of national and subject/citizen identities in the late eighteenth and nineteenth centuries, the last decades of the twentieth have witnessed their decoupling. State fragmentation and "neotribalism" are especially prevalent in the developing world, the Balkans, and along the Russian periphery. Identities and loyalties that colonial authorities and commissars repressed are resurfacing, often making a mockery of sovereign boundaries. In this sense, ethnic conflict is partly a problem of shifting identity boundaries in a state system constructed by Europeans in non-European settings. The governments of many of these states, far from being impartial arbiters of social conflicts or surrogates for a "national interest," represent the privileges of a tribal, family, regional, or military faction.

Unlike most of the developing world, the developed regions have become what Karl W. Deutsch called a "pluralistic security community" in which war appears almost inconceivable.[57] States in these regions are enmeshed in larger political and economic systems that limit their capacity to behave autonomously or protect citizens from spillover from those systems. Under such conditions, it is not surprising that local, national, regional, and other identities challenge citizenship for pride of place.

In sum, at the turn of the millennium, a central concern in global politics is the long-range impact of "the retreat of the state" on identities and loyalties. We have to face growing uncertainty as to where our allegiances should and will lie. Strange wrote: "In a world of multiple, diffused authority, each of us shares Pinocchio's problem: our individual consciences are our only guide."[58] Nevertheless, each of us is enmeshed in old identities and loyalties, and the future choices we make will not be entirely voluntary. Various authorities are bidding for our allegiance, and they are establishing their influence over us at the same time. When the opportunities arise, as they surely will in the contemporary fluid environment, will we ressurect or refurbish old identities and loyalties, or establish new ones? Our conceptions of ourselves and others will be continually changing, or sometimes will be ages old, and the task for us political scientists is to explain what the limited range of choices are, which are likely to prevail—and, again as always, why.

Notes

1. We note that Dicken closes the last section of his book on the "global shift" in the world economy with the same lines from Eliot. Peter Dicken, *Global Shift: Transforming the World Economy*, 3rd ed. (New York: Guilford, 1998).

2. See (including essays by both of the present authors) Heidi H. Hobbs, ed., *Pondering Postinternationalism: A Paradigm for the Twenty-First Century?* (Albany: State University of New York Press, 2000).

3. See Yale H. Ferguson and Richard W. Mansbach, *The Elusive Quest: Theory and International Politics* (Columbia, SC: University of South Carolina Press, 1988).

4. See Yale Ferguson and Rey Koslowski, "Culture, International Relations Theory, and Cold War History," in Odd Arne Westad, *Reviewing the Cold War: Approaches, Interpretations, Theory* (London: Frank Cass, 2000), 149–179.

5. Harold and Margaret Sprout, *The Ecological Perspective on Human Affairs with Special Reference to International Politics* (Princeton: Princeton University Press, 1965).

6. See Robert Jervis, *Perception and Misperception in International Politics* (Princeton: Princeton University Press, 1976).

7. See Anthony Giddens, *The Constitution of Society: Outline of the Theory of Structuration* (Berkeley: University of California Press, 1984).

8. For the most complete exposition of his views, see Alexander Wendt, *Social Theory of International Politics* (Cambridge: Cambridge University Press, 1999).

9. Ibid., 56.

10. Ibid., 241.

11. Hedley Bull, *The Anarchical Society: A Study of Order in World Politics* (New York: Columbia University Press, 1977).

12. Friedrich Kratochwil, *Rules, Norms, and Decisions: On the Conditions of Practical and Legal Reasoning in International Relations and Domestic Affairs* (Cambridge: Cambridge University Press, 1989).

13. See by Nicholas J. Onuf: *World of Our Making; Rules and Rule in Social Theory and International Relations* (Columbia: University of South Carolina Press, 1989); "Levels," *European Journal of International Relations*, vol. 1 (March 1995), 35–38; and Vendulka Kubálková, Nicholas Onuf, and Paul Kowert, eds., *International Relations in a Constructed World* (Armonk, NY: M. E. Sharpe, 1998).

14. Thomas J. Biersteker and Cynthia Weber, eds., "The Social Construction of State Sovereignty," in *State Sovereignty as a Social Construct* (Cambridge: Cambridge University Press, 1996), 11.

15. Cf. Ronnie D. Lipschutz with Judith Meyer, *Global Civil Society and Global Environmental Governance: The Politics of Nature from Place to Planet* (Albany: State University of New York Press, 1996), 250–252.

16. Thomas A. Friedman, *The Lexus and the Olive Tree: Understanding Globalization*, rev. ed. (New York: Anchor Books, 2000), chap. 12.

17. Joanne Gowa, *Ballots and Bullets: The Elusive Democratic Peace* (Princeton: Princeton University Press, 1999).

18. See the exchanges between the team of Patrick James, Eric Solberg, and Murray Wolfson, and the duo John R. O'Neal and Bruce Russett, in vols. 10 and 11 of *Defence and Peace Economics* (1999–2000).

19. Paul Hirst, "The Global Economy—Myths and Realities," *International Affairs*, vol. 73, no. 3 (July 1997), 409–425; and Paul Hirst and G. Thompson, *Globalization in Question: The International Economy and the Possibilities of Governance* (Cambridge, UK: Polity Press, 1996).

20. Hirst, "The Global Economy," 425.

21. Cf. Paul L. Knox and Peter J. Taylor, *World Cities in a World-System* (Cambridge: Cambridge University Press, 1995); and Saskia Sassen, *The Global City: New York, London, Tokyo* (Princeton: Princeton University Press, 1994).

22. For an exceptionally thoughtful and well-documented overview of different trends, see R. J. Barry Jones, *The World Turned Upside Down? Globalization and the Future of the State* (Manchester: Manchester University Press, 2000). See also, A. J. Scott, *Regions*

and the World Economy: The Coming Shape of Global Production, Competition, and Political Order (Oxford: Oxford University Press, 1998); and Kenichi Ohmae, *The End of the Nation-State: The Rise of Regional Economies* (New York: Free Press, 1995). On regions, cities, and networks in the EU, see Christer Jönsson, Sven Tägil, and Gunnar Törnqvist, *Organizing European Space* (London: Sage, 2000).

23. Hirst, "The Global Economy," 418.

24. Paul N. Doremus, William W. Keller, Louis W. Pauly, and Simon Reich, *The Myth of the Global Corporation* (Princeton: Princeton University Press, 1998).

25. In this and the sections that follow, we incorporate some of the arguments and language found in another essay of ours, "Global Politics at the Turn of the Millennium: Changing Bases of 'Us' and 'Them,'" *International Studies Review*, vol. 1, no. 2 (Summer 1999), 77–107.

26. Jan Aart Scholte, "Global Capitalism and the State," *International Affairs*, vol. 73, no. 3 (July 1997), 429–430, 432. See also by Schoulte, *Globalization: A Critical Introduction* (New York: Palgrave, 2000).

27. Held, McGrew, Goldblatt, and Perraton, *Global Transformations*, 27–28.

28. Jessica T. Mathews, "Power Shift," *Foreign Affairs*, vol. 76, no. 1 (January/February 1997), 50.

29. Bull, *The Anarchical Society*.

30. Cf. Robert O. Keohane, "International Institutions; Can Interdependence Work?" *Foreign Policy*, no. 110 (Spring 1998), 82–96.

31. See, for example, Mark W. Zacher and Brent A. Sutton, *Governing Global Networks: International Regimes for Transportation and Communications* (Cambridge, UK: Cambridge University Press, 1996); Jönsson, Tägil, and Törnqvist, *Organizing European Space;* Oran F. Young, *Governance in World Affairs* (Ithaca: Cornell University Press, 1999); and Robert O'Brien, et al., *Contesting Global Governance: Multilateral Economic Institutions and Global Social Movements* (Cambridge UK: Cambridge University Press, 2000).

32. Stephen D. Krasner, *Sovereignty: Organized Hypocrisy* (Princeton: Princeton University Press, 1999).

33. Charles Tilly, *The Formation of National States in Western Europe* (Princeton: Princeton University Press, 1975).

34. Janice E. Thomson, *Mercenaries, Pirates, and Sovereigns* (Princeton: Princeton University Press).

35. Hendrick Spruyt, *The Sovereign State and Its Competitors* (New York: Columbia University Press, 1994).

36. Rodney Bruce Hall, *National Collective Identity: Social Constructs and International Systems* (New York: Columbia University Press, 1999).

37. Robert H. Jackson and Mark W. Zacher, *The Territorial Covenant: International Society and the Stablization of Boundaries,* Working Paper no. 15, Vancouver, BC, Canada: Institute of International Relations, The University of British Columbia, 1997.

38. Also, at least in the case of oil-rich Kuwait, some remaining resolve on the part of the international community to defend boundaries militarily.

39. This argument and the two that follow are similar to the "three paradoxes" spotlighted by Strange (1996:4–7).

40. Cf. Stephen K. Vogel, *Freer Markets, More Rules: Regulatory Reform in Advanced Industrial Countries* (Ithaca: Cornell University Press, 1996); and Linda Weiss, *The Myth of the Powerless State* (Ithaca: Cornell University Press, 1998).

41. Cf. Eun Mee Kim, *Big Business, Strong State: Collusion and Conflict in South Korean Development, 1960–1990* (Albany: State University of New York Press, 1997).

42. Susan Strange, *The Retreat of the State: The Diffusion of Power in the World Economy* (Cambridge: Cambridge University Press, 1996), 6–7.

43. Georg Sørensen, "An Analysis of Contemporary Statehood: Consequences for Conflict and Cooperation," *Review of International Studies,* vol. 23, no. 3 (July 1997), 253–269.

44. Cf., by James N. Rosenau, *Turbulence in World Politics* (Princeton University Press, 1990); *Along the Domestic-Foreign Frontier: Exploring Governance in a Turbulent World* (Cambridge: Cambridge University Press, 1997); and his essay in this collection.

45. Oyvind Osterud, "The Narrow Gate: Entry to the Club of Sovereign States," *Review of International Studies,* vol. 23, no. 2 (April 1997), 167–184.

46. We agree with Alan James on this point. See *Alan James, Sovereign Statehood: The Basis of International Society* (London: Allen and Unwin, 1986).

47. Jorge Domínguez, "Latin America's Crisis of Representation," *Foreign Affairs,* vol. 76, no. 1 (January/February 1997), 101.

48. See Jackson and Zacher, *The Territorial Covenant* (1997).

49. Robert H. Jackson, *Quasi-States: Sovereignty, International Relations, and the Third World* (Cambridge: Cambridge University Press, 1990).

50. Statistics from *The Economist* 1998, an article based on the work of Harvard economist Alberto Alesina.

51. William Reno, "Privitizing War in Sierra Leone," *Current History,* vol. 96, 227–230.

52. Cf. Robert O'Brien, Anne Marie Goetz, Jan Aart Scholte, Marc Williams, *Contesting Global Governance: Multilateral Economic Institutions and Global Social Movements* (Cambridge: Cambridge University Press, 2000).

53. In recent years, for instance, the U.S. government has encouraged U.S. banks and corporations to assist Russia and other former communist states to make the transition to free-market democracies.

54. See Usha C. V. Haley, Linda Low, and Mun-Heng Toh, "Singapore Incorporated: Reinterpreting Singapore's Business Environments Through a Corporate Metaphor," *Management Decision*, vol. 34, 17–38.

55. Strange, *The Retreat of the State*, 3.

56. Yale H. Ferguson and Richard W. Mansbach, *Polities: Authority, Identities, and Change* (Columbia: University of South Carolina Press, 1996).

57. His essay in this collection, 260.

58. Karl W. Deutsch et al., *Political Community and the North Atlantic Area* (Princeton: Princeton University Press), 1957.

59. Strange, *The Retreat of the State*, 199.

PART II

Geographical Scale, Identity, and Relationships

CHAPTER 5

Political Power and Geographical Scale

John Agnew

The workings of political power are usually seen as a historical constant: witness Paul Ricoeur's remark that "power does not have much of a history."[1] At the same time, political power is overwhelmingly associated with the quintessential modern state. It is envisioned as pooled up in equivalent units of territorial sovereignty (at least for the so-called Great Powers) that exercise power throughout their territories and vie with one another to acquire more power beyond their current boundaries. In this paper I want to dispute both of these contentions. In the first place I want to historicize understanding of the workings of political power. By this I mean to claim that power does in fact have a history. In the second place, I claim that this history is revealed in the changing nature and spatiality of power. By this I mean that power is not fixed in given territorial units but changes both its character and spatial structure as different geographical scales (local, regional, national-state, world-regional, international and global) change their relationships to one another as the political practices of the global geopolitical order change.

I want to proceed by outlining three crucial assumptions of conventional views of the relationship between political power and geographical scale and by disputing their transcendental hold. The first assumption is that of the rigid territorial conception of the *spatiality of power*. A richer conception of the spatiality of power sees the state's territory as only one of a number of geographical scales at which power is operational. The particular importance of different geographical scales to the workings and impact of power changes historically in rhythm with the changing spatial structure of economic, cultural, and political activities. The second is the dyadic (person-person, person-state, state-state) definition of *the nature of power relationships*. This abstracts power from the sociological contexts in which it originates and operates into a set of isolated individual relationships at singular geographical scales. It also views power as solely a quantitative capacity of self-evident and preexisting entities: the ability of a person or a state to direct others or expand its range of influence despite resistance. The third, and final, is the homology that is drawn between individual persons and states such that *states are treated as if they are the moral equivalents to individual persons*. This both familiarizes the state and gives it a moral/political

115

status equivalent to that of a person. This assumption privileges the scale of the
territorial state by associating it with the character and moral agency of the
individual person, an intellectually powerful feature of Western political theory.
In medieval European political thought, however, the state did not have such
an exalted status. This points again to the historicity of the relationship between
political power and geographical scale. Before considering each of these contentions I want to say something about my understandings of political power
and geographical scale.

Defining "Political Power" and "Geographical Scale"

There are any number of learned treatises defining political and other
types of power. My purpose here is not to survey them. Rather, I want to suggest a workable definition that draws together existing currents of critical
thinking about power. These tend to focus on *either* instrumental *or* associational
conceptions of the capacity to influence the character, allocation, and distribution of collective goods (everything from public services to institutional structures, military and police activities, foreign and trade policies, and modes of
political participation). The former is the familiar capacity to make others do
one's will through direct action. The latter is more the power to do things by
acting in concert or using institutional mediation. This facilitative view of political power is the centerpiece of much recent innovative thinking in political
theory.[2] I would claim that each of the two views grasps a dimension of power
that the other lacks, even though we might find different words for what they
signify. The first is the ability to control, dominate, co-opt, seduce, and resent.
In other words this is a "negative" power. The second is the capacity to act,
resist, cooperate, and assent. In other words, this is a "positive" power. Taking
these two "sides" together, one might say that political power is the sum of all
resources and strategies involved in conflicts over collective goods in which
parties act with and on others to achieve binding outcomes. In practice, because
of the view that power is pervasive, the outcome of the application of power is
inherently unpredictable. No single party can monopolize political power. The
contemporary emphasis on the positive side of power, therefore, leads away
from the a priori association of outcomes with the possession of superior negative power.

Political power *in toto* (inclusive of both its negative and its positive sides)
is never exercised equally everywhere. Partly this is because power does "pool
up" in centers as a result of the concentration of resources and the ascription
and secondment of power to higher levels in power hierarchies by people at
lower levels. But it is also because the "transmission" of power across space
involves practices by others that lead to its transformation as it moves from

place to place. So, in the first place power is exercised from sites that vary in their geographical reach. These ranges can be referred to as geographical scales that extend from the body through the locality to the region, state territory, world-region, and globe. Sometimes power flows in sequence from scale to another. At other times it short circuits one or more scales. Thus, today we often speak of localities or regions interacting directly with a global economy without the national scale mediation that once dominated such relationships. In the second place, the labels used to identify scales are social and intellectual constructs rather than existing "out there," so to speak. Though they suggest an independence of one another, almost discrete "slices" of reality, in practice each scale implies the existence and impact of the others, by definition.[3] The order of listing also indicates the implicit relative valuation of each in any particular account that makes use of that listing. Third, and finally, it is not the separate scales so much as the differential interaction between them that determines the constitution and effects of political power. The balance between processes operating from sites over different geographical ranges determines the ways in which power works and is deployed. It is to understanding the consequences for political power of shifts in the balance of processes operating at different geographical scales that this paper is devoted.[4]

Historical Spatialities of Political Power

In much modern political theory political power has been narrowly defined as the ability to make others do something you (person, state) desire and, at least from the nineteenth century, it has been increasingly associated with territorial states. The spatiality of power, however, need not be invariably reduced to state territoriality. At least four models of the spatiality of power can be identified, each of which has dominated in different epochs of geopolitical order. Each of these models is closely associated with a particular set of political-economic and technological conditions.[5] The dominant spatiality of power has changed, therefore, as material conditions and dominant modes of understanding of them have changed. This approach to the historicity of spatiality implies that both material forces and intellectual perspectives or representations interact to produce the spatiality of power predominant within a given historical era.[6] But each also has a synchronic validity in the sense that political power in any epoch can never be totally reduced to any one of them. Rather, in a sense equivalent to Karl Polanyi's discussion[7] of market society in terms of the emergence of market exchange at the expense of reciprocity and redistribution as principles of economic integration, as one model comes to predominate, others are not so much eclipsed as placed into subordinate or emerging roles. The models offer, then, not only a way of historicizing political power but also

of accounting for the complexity of the spatiality of power during any particular historical epoch (Figure 5.1).

The first model is that of an "ensemble of worlds." In this model human
groups live in separate cultural areas or civilizations with limited communication and interaction between them. The nodes here are "civilizations." Each
area has a sense of a profound difference beyond its own boundaries without
any conception of the particular character of the others. Communal forms of
social construction take place within a territorial setting of permanent settlement with flows of migrants and seasonal movements but with fuzzy exterior
boundaries. Time is cyclical or seasonal with dynasties and seasons replacing
one another in natural sequence. Political power is largely internally oriented
and directed toward dynastic maintenance and internal order. Its spatiality rests
on a strongly physical conception of space as distance to be overcome or circulation to be managed.

The second model is that of a "field of forces." The nodes here are states.
This is the geopolitical model of states as rigidly defined territorial units in
which each state can gain power only at the expense of others and each has
total control over its own territory. It is akin to a field of forces in mechanics
in which the states exert force on one another and the outcome of the
mechanical contest depends on the populations and resources each can bring
to bear. Success also depends on creating blocs of allies or clients and identifying spatial points of weakness and vulnerability in the situation of one's
adversaries. All of the attributes of politics, such as rights, representation, legitimacy, and citizenship, are restricted to the territories of individual states. The
presumption is that the realm of geopolitics is beyond such concerns. Force
and the potential use of force rule supreme beyond state boundaries. Time is
ordered on a rational global basis so the trains can run on time, workers can
get to work on time, and military forces can coordinate their activities. The
dominant spatiality, therefore, is that of state-territoriality, in which political
boundaries provide the containers for the majority of social, economic, and
political activities.

Third on the list of models is that of the "hierarchical network." The
nodes here are city-regions. The spatial structure in which they are embedded
is a world-economy of geographical cores, peripheries, and semiperipheries
linked together by flows of goods, people, and investment. Transactions based
largely on market exchange produce patterns of uneven development as flows
move wealth through networks of trade and communication producing
regional concentrations of relative wealth and poverty. At the local scale, particularly that of urban centers, hinterlands are drawn into connection with a
larger world that has become progressively more planetary in geographical
scope over the past 500 years. Political power is a function of whereabouts in
the hierarchy of sites from global centers to rural peripheries a place is located.

Figure 5.1
Spatialities of Power

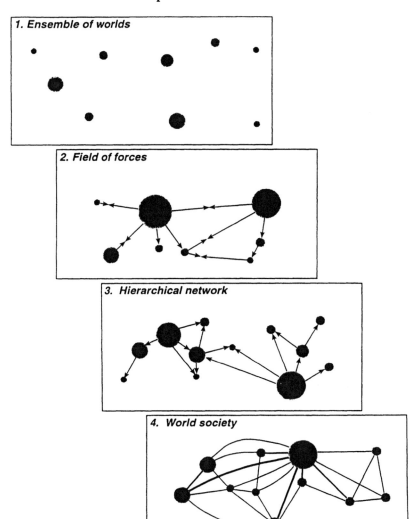

1. Ensemble of worlds

2. Field of forces

3. Hierarchical network

4. World society

Based on Durand et al., 1992: 18.

Time is that which is organized by the geographical scope and temporal rhythm of financial and economic transactions. The spatiality is that of spatial networks joining together a hierarchy of nodes and areas that are connected by flows of people, goods, capital, and information. Today, such networks are particularly important in linking together the city-regions that constitute the nodes around which the global economy is increasingly organized.

The fourth, and final, model is that of the "integrated world society." The nodes here are social groupings. This model conforms to the humanistic ideal of a world in which cultural community, political identity, and economic integration are all structured at a global scale. But it also reflects the increased perception of common global problems (such as environmental ones) that do not respect state borders, the futility of armed interstate conflict in the presence of nuclear weapons and the advantages of defense over offense in modern warfare, and the growth of an international "public opinion." This model privileges global scale communication based on networks among multiple actors that are relatively unhierarchical and more or less dense depending on the volition of actors themselves. The sproutlike character of these connections leads some to see them as (in a term popularized by Deleuze) somewhat like the "rhizomes" of certain plants that spread by casting out shoots in multiple but unpredictable directions. Time and space are both defined by the spontaneous and reciprocal timing and spacing of human activities. Real and virtual space become indistinguishable. This model obviously has a strong utopian element to it but does also reflect some emergent properties of the more interconnected world that is presently in construction.

In the contemporary world there is evidence for the effective copresence of each of these models with the former territorial models somewhat in eclipse and the latter network models somewhat in resurgence after a 100-year period in which the field of forces model was preeminent (if hardly exclusive). If the trend toward regional separatism portends a fragmentation that can reinforce the field of forces model as new states emerge then economic globalization and global cultural unification work to reinforce the hierarchical network and integrated world society models. At the same time movement toward political-economic unification (as in the European Union) and the development of cultural movements with a strong territorial element (as with Islamic integralist movements) tend to create pressures for the reassertion of an ensemble of worlds.

Historically, however, there has been a movement from one to another model as a hegemonic or directing element. In this spirit a theoretical scheme can be suggested in which, first of all, the ensemble of worlds model slowly gave way to the field of forces model around 1500 A.D. (Figure 5.2). As this was establishing its dominance, the hierarchical network began its rise in and around the framework provided by the state system. Under European colonial-

Figure 5.2
Diachronics of Spatialities of Power

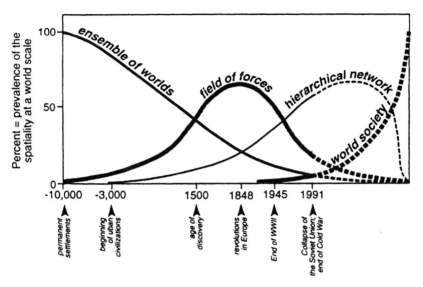

Based on Durand et al., 1992: 18.

ism, the part of the world in which states recognized one another as legitimate actors was divorced from the regions in which such status was denied.[8] Since 1945 the hierarchical-network model has become more and more central to the distribution of political power. With the end of the Cold War, which had produced an important reinstatement of the field of forces model, the hierarchical network model is in the ascendancy with signs of the beginning of a trend towards an integrated world-society model. But this is as yet very much in its infancy.

This framework is, of course, only suggestive of long-term tendencies. What it does provide is a sense of the historical spatiality of political power, associated in different epochs with different dominant modes of spatiality. From this point of view, the state-territorial scale is only one among a number of geographical scales that are implicated in the organization and expression of political power. In each of the four models different relationships between geographical scales are highlighted: from the world-regional and local scales in the ensemble of worlds model, through the state-territorial and global scales of the field of forces model, to the complex core-periphery and global-local connections of the hierarchical network and integrated world-society models. What is clear is that the state-territorial conception of power is not a transcendental feature of modern human history but, rather, a historically contingent feature of the relationship between geographical scales in the definition and concentration of political practices.

The Geosociology of Power Relationships

Political power manifests itself in its effects, in the ability to produce an effect through the application of certain capacities and resources.[9] This typically leads to an emphasis on its quantitative possession by self-evident, preexisting actors, usually individual persons or states, that apply power against one another. This narrow definition of political power has undergone considerable challenge in recent years.[10] In particular, various notions of structural power or metapower have been invented to account for the indirect effects of power, the impersonal effects of power, or both in addition to or in counterpoint to the traditional idea of power as the *direct* action of one individual or state on another.[11] By this extension, the concept of power can now serve to account for the emergence of collectivized and higher-order systems of authority (e.g., regimes), governance (e.g., international institutions) and nonstate transnationalism (e.g., transnational firms, epistemic communities and issue-networks) that regulate or provide the rules for the relations between the unit-actors in the system of structural power.[12] This kind of power analysis moves the understanding of power relationships "upscale," so to speak, beyond the dyadic conception characteristic of conventional political and international-relations theories. But it is still lacking a thorough grounding in the social-geographical conditions for the creation and operation of power relationships. I endeavor to provide something of that here.

In the first place, neither personhood nor statehood is pregiven. Rather, they are both types of subjective identity established in the midst of the workings of power relationships. We should start with the flow of events and actions in social and political life out of which contingent identities as either persons or states are formed. Such identities emerge (1) to gain a footing or control in an uncertain world; (2) where goals or intentions are defined by presuming the intentions of others; (3) in which errors in interpretation and judgment feed back into identity; and (4) biographies or histories are told and written to clean-up the identity and make it self-evident. These are the steps to "personhood" identified by Harrison White in his social theory of identity.[13] In this construction, personhood develops out of identity struggles for control in a mix of social networks in which putative persons are enveloped from childhood. White's main point in connection with the analysis of power relationships is that "stable identities are difficult to build; they are achieved only in some social contexts, *they are not pre-given analytic foci*" (my emphasis).[14] Similarly, statehood is the outcome of struggles for control, not a preexisting basis on which such struggles are built.[15] A larger, geographically encompassing social world is required for identities as states to develop. States become centers of power as identities are defined in networks of relationships that vary in their geographical density (from localized to globalized) and the degree to which network links lead to mutual or asymmetric gains for actors. This is how a hierarchy of states develops.

In other words, and to paraphrase Richard Ashley,[16] a state is not ontologically prior to a set of interstate relations. A state is defined and recognized as such only within a set of relationships that establish rules for what is and what is not a "state." The power of states, therefore, is never the outcome of action at a single geographical scale, that of individual territorial states, but also of necessary social rules working at a broader geographical scale.[17] This argument about the social construction of statehood, however, does not entail a parallel claim to the moral equivalence between it and personhood (see the next section). Harrison White's argument is analogical, not homological to the case of statehood.

Second, power in networks of subjectivity emerges as a mix of quantitative capacity or conventional power over *and* power in the sense of the ability to bind others into networks of assent. It is this latter power that terms such as "structural power" point toward. In this understanding, however, it is not the ability of a single actor (such as a hegemon) to create assent that is privileged, that would likely be the indirect result of direct power, but rather *the strength of association between actors based on shared norms and values.* This would include, but not be restricted to, the writing of agendas, the silencing of certain options and other modes of "mobilization of bias." It necessarily covers, therefore, the "rules of the game" among actors to which structural power draws attention. Historically, these rules among modern territorial states have emphasized "hard" or coercive power. Today, some commentators argue, they involve the much more pervasive use of "soft" or co-optational power in which assent has become more significant than coercion.[18] This reflects the emergence of a world in which diffuse economic transactions are more vital to the constitution of political power than are the means of military coercion. But, by definition, even coercion requires the application of commonly accepted rules of conduct concerning its purposes and limits that all involved had at least to tacitly or subconsciously acknowledge.

Third, and finally, the social networks in which quantitative and discursive power relationships are *embedded* have historically defined geographical settings. In nineteenth- and early twentieth-century Western industrial society, for example, networks were confined within rigidly bounded state-territorial, imperial and world-regional settings. Jeremy Bentham's understanding of the power of the regulatory gaze exerted through state bureaucracies exemplifies the epoch, as Michel Foucault has famously claimed. A rigid territorial core-periphery model ruled the spatiality of power. In Timothy Luke's terms: "relatively clear relational-spatial distinctions of social status, cultural preeminence, and political authority develop[ed] in line with a print-bound, panoptical space in traditional industrial societies or industrializing agricultural societies."[19] In other words, raw material-manufacturing linkages within territorial empires, print-based media of communication and centralized state apparatuses produced a territorialized set of relationships between local nodes of networks with denser connectivity within state boundaries and more attenuated links across the globe.

In contemporary "informational society," however, the spatial-temporal character of power relationships is being transformed. As Luke expresses this trend: "With the growing hegemony of transnational corporate capital, the means of information become the critical force in modern modes of production. A new politics of image, in which the authoritative allocation of values and sanctions turns on the coding and decoding of widely circulating images by politicized 'issue groups,' arises alongside and above the interest-group politics of industrial society. Contesting these mythologies can expose some of the contradictions and hidden dimensions of image-driven power. But, on the whole, the endless streams of mythological images in turn bring together the flow of elite control, mass acceptance, and individual consent in a new informational social formation—the 'society of the spectacle.'"[20] This is a deterritorialized network system in which nodes are widely scattered around the world, although more densely connected within and between Europe, North America, and East Asia, though still constrained by the territorial structures of power inherited from the earlier epoch.[21] The geographical embeddedness of power relationships today, therefore, signifies something different from what was the case in the past in terms of the relative balance between territorial and geographical-network elements and the geographical scope conditions (broadly, from national-international to local-global) under which power relationships are produced.

Problematizing the Moral Geography of State-Based Political Power

Exalting the state as the singular font of power has involved equating the state with the apparent autonomous identity of the individual person. This is not to say that there is no analogy between the *social construction* of personhood and that of statehood. Indeed, this was precisely the point I have been arguing. Rather, it is to deny the atomized understanding of both states and persons that conventional approaches to personal and state agency entail. Not only is this a desocialized view of the person or state, implying an essentially transcendental persona making itself, it also turns sovereign states into naturalized abstract individuals that can then be inscribed with the moral authority of their own personhood. Modern statehood is thus underwritten by modern individualism. A moral argument about the equating of the autonomy of the individual person with that of the state is masked by the *natural* claim that is made on behalf of the state as an *equivalent* individual. The appeal of this strategy has been twofold and reflects a powerful aspect of the modern social construction of statehood. First, it allows, as Thomas Hobbes was perhaps the first to note, identification of a historical "state of nature" in which a set of primitive individuals, liberated from social conditions, can compare their natural condition with that offered by a specific set of social-political conditions associated with statehood.[22] Actual power relationships can thus be ascribed to the need for security, wealth, or both in a world that is not the independent creation of any single individual.[23] The separation and isolation of individuals (persons, states) thus produces a logical case for a pooling of power in the hands of a single sovereign. It is now what can be called the Standard Social Science Model in which a "ruleless" state of nature is assumed from which socially disciplined individuals emerge by means of social and state conditioning.[24]

Second, the unrelenting suspicion and hostility with which human individuals regard one another in Hobbes's state of nature, yet also, and paradoxically, the humanistic tendency to raise the self-aggrandizing individual onto an intellectual and moral pedestal in much Western thought (drawing from Adam Smith), underpin the projection of the qualities of personhood *onto* statehood. At one and the same time the state embodies the two sides of the modern moral coin. The state represents (*pace* Hobbes) the territorial solution to human aggression and fear of untimely death among a discrete group of persons, displacing aggression into the realm of interstate relations. The state is also constructed as a primitive individual such as a person with unique abilities, particularly its ability to specialize within a division of labor (*pace* Smith), which potentially offers a way of maximizing output and thereby increasing the wealth and satisfaction of all. These two moves, the one political and addressing human aggression and the other economic and addressing human acquisitiveness, boost the state into a position of historical preeminence in relation to the distribution of power irrespective of their empirical veracity.

Yet, even though acknowledging the powerful influence of this equating of the state and the individual person on actual practices of statehood down the years, there are ways in which its contemporary adequacy can be questioned on empirical as much as theoretical grounds. One is to point to the lack of unity in the making of foreign policy by states. This involves pointing out the distinctive positions adopted by different sectoral and geographical interests within states.[25] Different social and economic groups, lower-tier governments and sectional lobbies all bring different identities and interests to bear that under certain circumstances can burst into "civil wars" or immobilize state institutions. Second, statehood is the result of mutual recognition among states[26] and not the result of "isolated states" achieving statehood separately and then engaging with one another as abstract individuals, in the sense of thoroughly autonomous persons.[27] The importance of the Treaty of Westphalia, for example, lay in its legitimation of the emerging territorial states as neutral centers of public power imposing order on warring religious factions.[28]

Another less frequently chosen route to pointing out the empirical contingency of statehood as thought of as morally equivalent to personhood is to argue historically by referring to the social-moral position of statehood in medieval political thought, thereby demonstrating through its difference with modern conceptions the historical contingency of the mode of thought we now tend to project backward and forward in history. The state as a unitary actor akin to a modern person is the product of the determinative social conditions of European modernity. This point is worthy of further comment. As Monahan has noted, medieval writings offer a good opportunity to "address our own questions to the past so that it can teach us."[29]

Long before Hobbes, medieval European political thought had arrived at a quite different interpretation of statehood than the one that the later masters such as Hobbes were to offer. Though obviously more complex than I give credit for here, medieval thought tended to work down from an ideal of human unity within a God-ruled Universe to a "horizontal" world in which an "antique-modern" conception of the state as a centralizing and territorializing power (drawing from the ancients and some contemporary trends toward monarchical absolutism) vied with multiple loyalties to spiritual and temporal authorities and overlapping jurisdictions as the dominant normative standard for judging political rule.[30] What is clear, however, at least from the classic account of Gierke,[31] is that initially the state had no separate personality. Only the "visible wielders" of power or a "Ruler-personality" were recognized as having authority.[32] People were merely the collective sum of all persons, not a collective entity in its own right.[33] As a result, "the path to the idea of 'State-sovereignty' was barred for medieval theory."[34] Indeed, for many years there was widespread acceptance of the idea of a hierarchy of communities with specified purposes and overlapping spatial jurisdictions which was only slowly replaced by that of "a theoretical concentration of right and power in the highest and widest group on the one hand and the individual man, on the other, at the cost of all intermediate groups."[35]

Conclusion

In this paper I have tried to identify the three main ways in which political power has been made historically constant by associating it with the state-territorial scale of geographical resolution. I have then countered each of these by pointing to their historical-geographical contingency: (1) the trap of a constant spatiality of political power, that of state-territoriality in a field of forces model of political power; (2) the dyadic conception of power as involving persons or states as ontologically preexisting units in bilateral relations at a single geographical scale; and (3) the state as a unitary and singular actor having a moral status equivalent to that of the individual person in Western thought. During periods of seeming political-geographical stability, such as reigned during the Cold War, "geography," in the form of rigid assumptions about the character of spatiality, hides history, particularly the history of power, from us. During periods of great change such as we have been living through over the past twenty years our awareness of geography returns as we experience a world in which "all that is solid melts into air." The main moral of the paper is clear: to understand the working of political power requires understanding its geography. Its geography is a function of historical change in the combinations of material and representational processes operating across different geographical scales. Power does indeed have a history. But it is one that can *only* be understood through its changing geography.

Notes

1. P. Ricoeur, *Lectures on Ideology and Utopia* (New York: Free Press, 1986), 198.

2. See, for example, J. Allen, "Spatial Assemblages of Power: From Domination to Empowerment," in D. Massey et al., eds., *Human Geography Today* (Cambridge: Polity Press, 1998), 173–193.

3. R. Howitt, "Scale as Relation: Musical Metaphors of Geographical Scale," *Area*, vol. 30 (1998): 49–58.

4. For more detailed discussions of geographical scale relevant to political power, see, for example, R. Howitt, "A World in a Grain of Sand: Towards a Reconceptualization of Geographical Scale," *Australian Geographer*, vol. 24 (1993): 33–44; and J. A. Agnew, "The Dramaturgy of Horizons: Geographical Scale in the 'Reconstruction of Italy' by the New Italian Political Parties, 1992–95," *Political Geography*, vol. 16 (1997): 99–121.

5. M.-F. Durand et al., *Le Monde, Espaces et Systèmes* (Paris: Presses de la Fondation Nationale des Sciences Politiques and Dalloz, 1992); and J. Lévy, *Europe: Une Géographie* (Paris: Hachette, 1997).

6. See J. A. Agnew and S. Corbridge, *Mastering Space: Hegemony, Territory and International Political Economy* (London: Routledge, 1995): 15–23.

7. K. Polanyi, *The Great Transformation* (Boston: Beacon Press, 1944).

8. R. L. Doty, *Imperial Encounters: The Politics of Representation in North-South Relations* (Minneapolis: University of Minnesota Press, 1996), 44.

9. For example, R. A. Dahl, "Power," in D. Sills, ed., *International Encyclopedia of the Social Sciences*, vol. 12 (1968): 405–415; and M. Weber, *Economy and Society*, ed. by G. Roth and C. Wittich (Berkeley and Los Angeles: University of California Press), chap. 10.

10. See, for example, J. Gaventa, *Power and Powerlessness: Quiescence and Rebellion in an Appalachian Valley* (Oxford: Clarendon Press, 1980); S. Lukes, ed., *Power* (New York: New York University Press, 1986); P. Morriss, *Power: A Philosophical Analysis* (Manchester, England: Manchester University Press, 1987); and S. Guzzini, "Structural Power: The Limits of Neorealist Power Analysis," *International Organization*, vol. 47, no. 2 (Summer 1993): 447–478.

11. See, for example, Guzzini, "Structural Power."

12. See, for example, S. D. Krasner, "Regimes and the Limits of Realism: Regimes as Autonomous Variables," *International Organization*, vol. 36, no. 2 (Spring 1982): 497–510; J. A. Rosenau, *The Study of Global Interdependence: Essays on the Transnationalization of World Affairs* (London: Pinter, 1980); S. Gill and D. Law, "Global Hegemony and the Structural Power of Capital," *International Studies Quarterly*, vol. 33, no. 4 (December 1989): 475–499; P. M. Haas, ed., "Knowledge, Power and International Policy Coordination," *International Organization*, vol. 46, no. 1 (Winter 1992): 1–390; and K. Sikkink, "Human Rights, Principled Issue-Networks, and Sovereignty in Latin America," *International Organization*, vol. 47, no. 3 (Summer 1993): 411–441.

13. H. White, *Identity and Control: A Structural Theory of Social Action* (Princeton: Princeton University Press, 1992).

14. Ibid., 201.

15. T. Biersteker and C. Weber, eds., *State Sovereignty as a Social Construct* (Cambridge: Cambridge University Press, 1996).

16. R. K. Ashley, "The Poverty of Neorealism," *International Organization*, vol. 38 (1984): 240.

17. For example, A. Wendt, "Anarchy Is What States Make of It: The Social Construction of Power Politics," *International Organization*, vol. 46, no. 2 (Spring 1992): 391–425; more generally, see H. B. Mokros, ed., *Interaction and Identity* (New Brunswick, NJ: Transaction Books, 1996).

18. For example, J. Nye, "The Changing Nature of World Power," *Political Science Quarterly*, vol. 105, no. 2 (Summer 1990): 177–192.

19. T. W. Luke, *Screens of Power: Ideology, Domination, and Resistance in Informational Society* (Urbana, IL: University of Illinois Press, 1989), 47.

20. Ibid., 51.

21. See, for example, D. W. Harvey, *The Condition of Postmodernity* (Oxford: Blackwell, 1989); M. Castells, *The Rise of the Network Society* (Oxford: Blackwell, 1996); and A. J. Scott, *Regions and the World Economy: The Coming Shape of Global Production, Competition, and Political Order* (Oxford: Oxford University Press, 1998).

22. N. Inayatullah and M. Rupert, "Hobbes, Smith, and the Problem of Mixed Ontologies in Neorealist IPE," in S. Rosow et al., eds., *The Global Economy as Political Space* (Boulder, CO: Lynne Rienner, 1994), 89–120; N. Jacobson, "The Strange Case of the Hobbesian Man," *Representations*, vol. 63 (1998): 1–12; and Q. Skinner, "Hobbes and the Purely Artificial Person of the State," *Journal of Political Philosophy*, vol. 7 (1999): 1–29.

23. D. Held, *Democracy and the Global Order: From the Modern State to Cosmopolitan Governance* (Stanford, CA: Stanford University Press, 1995), 38.

24. See, for example, J. Buchanan and G. Tullock, *The Calculus of Consent* (Ann Arbor: University of Michigan Press, 1965); J. Rawls, *A Theory of Justice* (Cambridge, MA: Belknap Press of Harvard University Press, 1971); R. Nozick, *Anarchy, State, and Utopia* (New York: Basic Books, 1974); and C. R. Sunstein, *The Partial Constitution* (Cambridge, MA: Harvard University Press, 1993).

25. For example, P. Trubowitz, *Defining the National Interest: Conflict and Change in American Foreign Policy* (Chicago: University of Chicago Press, 1998).

26. Biersteker and Weber, *State Sovereignty as a Social Construct*; and P. Hirst, *From Statism to Pluralism* (London: UCL Press, 1997).

27. S. Lukes, *Individualism* (New York: Harper and Row, 1973), 46–47, 76–77, 99.

28. R. Koselleck, *Critique and Crisis: Enlightenment and the Pathogenesis of Modern Society* (Oxford: Berg, 1988); and Hirst, *From Statism to Pluralism*, 216–235.

29. A. P. Monahan, *From Personal Duties Towards Personal Rights: Late Medieval and Early Modern Political Thought, 1300–1600* (Montréal: McGill-Queen's University Press, 1994), 8.

30. See, for example, C. J. Nderman and K. L. Forhan, eds., *Medieval Political Theory—A Reader: The Quest for the Body Politics, 1100–1400* (London: Routledge, 1993).

31. O. Gierke, *Political Theories of the Middle Age*, trans. by F. W. Maitland (Cambridge: Cambridge University Press, 1924).

32. Ibid., 70–71.

33. Ibid., 72.

34. Ibid., 73.

35. Ibid., 87.

CHAPTER 6

Mapping Global/Local Spaces

Robert Latham

"International," "transnational," or "global" interactions involve a broad array of activities and practices, ranging from the transmission of ideas and commodities to the signing of treaties and the deployment of armies. Identifying structures within the variety of international and global interactions is not an easy task. We can point to organizational ensembles like the UN or institutional configurations like an international financial regime. But we do not have any way to evaluate claims as to whether these or other entities are basic structures that shape the global realm.

Thinking about political life at the level of the state, in contrast, is girded by a baseline recognition of some common features—there are forms of demarcated territory, functional administration, organized systems of coercion, and political claims involving citizenship. The lack of parallel constructions at the global or international levels is often explained by an abiding commitment to the state as the central political form that impoverished the other levels. Thickness at one level, so it goes, yields thinness at others.[1]

As scholars like Barrington Moore have underscored, states have had powerfully organized constituencies vying to shape their contours and purposes. However diffuse in comparison, the shaping of international and global life has also involved powerful pressures, from merchants pursuing trade routes and statesmen organizing world war to the myriad purveyors of predominant norms and practices, imperial and liberal. Thus, we end up with a global realm that is thin, fluid, and lacking an accountable center, and yet in its diffusion is rich with varied forms, political projects, and discourses.[2]

But the existence of obstacles to identifying structure for this realm has not deterred theorists from this task. Efforts have not been limited to the Wallersteinian capitalist world systems perspective. John Meyer, who also claims to be working from a world systems perspective, has posited the existence of a world polity to describe the ensemble of knowledge and norms circulating

This is a shorter version of a paper originally published in Thomas Callaghy, Ronald Kassimir, and Robert Latham, eds., *Intervention and Transnationalism in Africa: Global-Local Networks of Power* (Cambridge, UK: Cambridge University Press, 2001).

131

among elites in state capitals and international bureaucracies about how to organize states and societies.[3] Robert Cox has suggested that we may be in the early stages of the formation of an "international state" that can govern fields of political, social, and economic relations on an international basis.[4] And Susan Strange contends there are four fundamental international structures of power (organized around security, production, finance, and knowledge) that affect political and social life across the planet.[5]

In these approaches a configuration of power and institutions is identified as an essential structure of governance, shaping the seasons and tides of international and transnational relations. These configurations entail specialized sets of functions operating at the international level (constituting nation-states in Meyer's case, shaping political and economic relations in Cox and Strange's case). The underlying attitude from which these structures are proffered is decidedly top-down, perched at the heights of planetary existence.

The purpose of this chapter is not to contest one or more of these types of structures or offer yet one more of my own.[6] My strategy is not to start by differentiating international configurations of institutions and power per se, nor by first analyzing how interactions such as international communications are generated by one type of institutional form or another (a regime, an alliance, or a hegemony). Instead, I want to focus on a structure of differences in the nature of interactions occurring across boundaries.

I will begin by distinguishing basic dimensions within which interactions occur across human spaces: namely, international arenas, translocal networks, and transterritorial deployments. This structure allows us to do more than distinguish forms of transboundary interactions. It also helps us make substantive arguments about configurations of power involving intersections of global and local forces. To illustrate this possibility, I will explore one dimension in detail, transterritorial deployments (and consider the other dimensions in reference to this one). Transterritorial deployments are associated with interactions that are often considered interventions, broadly conceived. That is, intervention understood to include not just humanitarian aid, international development work, or military incursions, however important these are, but also imperialism, international economic advisory teams, and the economic penetration of merchants and capitalist practices. As should become clear, however, the range of issues and dynamics surrounding transterritorial deployments move far beyond the intellectual and political legacy surrounding the term intervention.

Transterritorial deployments are hinges joining global and local forces around the exercise of responsibility, the assertion of rights, and, the pursuit of political projects across boundaries. I will argue that the limited possibilities available for how social entities can encounter one another across, boundaries shape these hinges in decisive ways.

Dimensions of Transboundary Interaction

There are three options that individuals, groups, and institutions in one place (e.g., a city or headquarters) have for interacting with agents in another place to, for example, communicate, act in concert, or exchange with them. They can convoke in some common arena; they can transmit something from one point to another; or they can dispatch or deploy themselves or a representative from their place to another place. Convocation, transmission, and deployment are the genetic logics of interaction of three basic dimensions to international and global life.

The first dimension, associated with the mode of convoking and convening, has actually been the most long-standing object of study in the field of International Relations. It is composed of those myriad international arenas where, for instance, states meet to hammer out treaties, conventions, war settlements, alliances, regimes, and where nongovernmental organizations (NGOs) attempt to influence those activities and define new ones by public lobbying and advocacy campaigns. In these arenas intangible social forms and practices such as international law or worldwide conventions share the characteristic of populating a sort of spaceless "international realm" that is everywhere and nowhere. It is here that international norms are articulated and disseminated in the documents and discourse of the UN and its officials and diplomats, and in the reports, campaigns and statements of activists.

This dimension can be thought of as "international" exactly because it rests, more than anything, on the recognition by actors and audiences that there is between different states and societies, of which they are a part, various points of convening. Arenas in this way exist in the interstices between different states and societies. Also, arenas typically form around issues bearing directly on the activity of states, although the actors involved are often not state representatives themselves. And there is not one but many international arenas as defined by the set of actors joined in some public common field, the constellation of issues around which they are joined, and the audience witnessing the "business" conducted. Together, these many arenas overlap and intersect to constitute what is often perceived to be an international realm.

Diplomatic conventions and meetings, NGO forums, and international court proceedings are examples of activities in arenas.[7] But arenas are not merely international public events. They can persist as long as there are actors, issues, discourses, and an audience. For an arena to form there need not be a literal coming together in a face-to-face encounter. All that is necessary is some common forum where practices and discourses have immediate and direct amplification beyond the point from which they are produced.[8]

It is not just local conditions that that can shape discourses, norms, and practices in international arenas. Networks of various forms that populate the pages of this volume are often crucial actors in the politics of arenas. These networks transmit values across political boundaries and social spaces. Since the 1960s and 1970s they have received increasingly concentrated attention in a variety of disciplines. While network activity can surely shape activities in international arenas—and become relevant to decisions and discussions in them—it remains a fundamentally different dimension of interaction. With an international arena there is a formal or informal joining of actors—state and nonstate—constituting part of a sort of bounded international public sphere that is populated by the principles, language, and practices that are unique to that sphere. What may be called "translocal networks" rest on the transmission of one form of capital or another (political, symbolic, informational, financial, etc.) from one node (populated by individuals or organizations, including those of a state) in one place to another node and place. The point is that the constituents of these networks remain emplaced in their various local contexts, propelling flows of symbols and materials to one another from those positions.[9]

Of course, an international arena can be shot through with networks and can, if one likes, be identified itself as one large network or web of networks. Likewise, networks can be viewed as types of arenas as celebrants of virtual communities like to point out. This is, however, a reductive claim that fails to acknowledge the distinct public character of international arenas (space where not only diplomats convene, but where things like international law and universal declarations are written, ratified, coded, and stored). Translocal networks stand out from arenas as specialized pathways of flows of messages, knowledge, and goods from one "place" to another along a channel or trajectory that is not open to the view of a public.

Indeed, the relationship between networks and arenas is more than a matter of how comparatively narrow networks shape the arguments and regulative contours of public arenas (or how a "network of networks" can publicize an issue through its accumulative reach)—compare Keck and Sikkink.[10] From the other direction, the discourses of international arenas can enter the more narrow, exclusive circuits of networks defined by circumscribed memberships according to claims to professionalism (e.g., NGOs), privilege (e.g., financial access), and faith (e.g., religious "brotherhoods").

The diversity of activities pursued by the variety of institutions and individuals that populate networks and arenas is on its face seemingly overwhelming. Moreover, the boundaries between networks and arenas are often not self-evident, especially when the network exchanges of an organization like Greenpeace can spill over into an arena as an ever wider circle is exposed to its activities and information. An organization can operate in both networks and arenas, and they face fundamental strategic and tactical choices as to which dimension of interaction they will pursue. One way to move toward mapping differences in the nature, range, and impact of activities across networks and arenas is to identify how widely amplified activities and practices are. Internationally circulating publications or press releases are far more widely amplified than the internal memorandums of a given network.

Besides arenas and networks there is a third dimension that is associated with the logic of dispatch and it is populated by what can be called, "transterritorial deployments." This dimension has received no real explicit theoretical attention—and yet activity in it is relatively easily recognized and historically prevalent. A transterritorial deployment is an installation in a local context of agents from outside that context. The place from which they are deployed is typically some kind or organizational platform (e.g., the headquarters of an international agency like UNHCR, a TNC, or even the capital of a western state). However much they may intersect with them, these platforms are relatively autonomous from the forums of international arenas, driven by self-articulated organizational imperatives, projects, and practices concerned with the activities toward which they are deployed.[11]

I will focus in this chapter on this third dimension of interaction, transterritorial deployments, for reasons described above and because it is arguably the least understood of the three, despite its historical prevalence. To the extent that I will explore the first two below, it will be a function of my concern with the third dimension.

It should be obvious that the manifestations of these three dimensions of interaction in history and contemporary international and global life are extensive. But ultimately, these are heuristic distinctions, which certainly do not subsume the many issues, discourses, phenomena, and projects that permeate that international history and life (such as colonialism, liberal order, war, and the environment). What such distinctions do is specify modes of interaction that are entailed by these broad social forms.[12]

Transterritorial Deployments

I am using the word "transterritorial" to describe the movement of an entity across the boundaries of a territory from some external place, where the entity retains in that territory its identity as external.[13] That entity could be an invading army, a scientific expedition, a charitable aid organization, or a group of technocratic international financial institution advisors.

Crucial to an entity's status as external is its organic links back to a point of reference outside of a territory. Deployment entails the purposeful forward placement of a unit, division, or representative of an organization or institution in some local context, such that the entity deployed stands as a component of that deploying organization (which I labeled above a platform). An army sent into a territory from some command center is a prime example. But so is a team of World Bank experts or the field operations of the Red Cross.

Transterritorial deployments are by definition specialized in relation to any local social order they enter since they rest on the forward placement of a defined and delimited organization from outside. In other words, they move along relatively narrow bands of intervention or engagement with local order. An organization, individual, or institution could never carry with it the range of culture, politics, and social relations that are encountered in a given locale. The most extreme form of this external movement is extraterritorial, where the deployed organizational form (e.g., military or consular) carries its own culture, laws, and juridical authority. Armies conveniently carry their own system of order on their backs in the shape of strict hierarchies and circumscribed missions. They also are unlikely to be dependent on local security forces. Despite being relatively self-contained they cannot help confronting the problem of local order if for nothing else than they so often disrupt the orders that fall in their pathway. An army's presence in a place forces it to confront, reluctantly or not, the question of postconflict order.

If deployments are (in principle) limited, then how are the boundaries of their specialization enacted "on the ground" and defined or identified by planners, practitioners, and local recipients of the deployment? This is really a question about the scope of the involvement of the organization deployed—how much of political and social life "on the ground" is drawn up into its purview and range of responsibility.

Another dimension that is basic to the identity of a transterritorial deployment (TD) is its *status* as temporary or permanent. What distinguishes a military occupation in formal terms from a colonization or political incorporation is its status as temporary. This is not a mere function of duration since how long a deployment lasts is often quite variable. However, once it does last for an indefinite period of time, permanent status becomes difficult to deny, as in the Israeli occupation of Palestine.

Status, like scope, has a bearing on the question of responsibility for local order. Both together serve as markers for what an outside agent thinks it has a right to do in some place. With temporary status there is no acknowledgment that what is deployed is there to be the ultimate and lasting authority over a local order (which is a claim the state makes within its territory). It is another basis for keeping a deployment along narrow, delimited channels within a local context. Whether something is recognized as permanent or temporary will likely change the terms of interaction between transterritorial and local actors. For example, in calculating whether it is worth cooperating with an international aid effort, local actors need not do so when they know that withdrawal is near at hand. This is understood to be part of the logic of interaction between Somali warlords and international intervenors in the early 1990s.

Although the variety of deployed forms that can operate across social or political boundaries is considerable, the dimensions of scope and status allow us to begin to map out some differences and help us identify where transterritoriality begins and ends:

	Narrow	Wide
Permanent	Extraterratorial offices; colonial religions missions; mercantile enterprises; TNCs; consuls; and diplomatic missions	Organs of a state or annexation
S T A T U S	Humanitarian operations; exploratory expedition; military campaign; trading	Occupation forces; Trusteeship administrators; and UN transition
authorities		
	post; arms merchants; fact-finding missions; financial advisory teams; and development projects	
Temporary		
	Narrow	*Wide*

SCOPE

At one extreme are deployments so narrow and temporary that their direct, immediate imprint on a social space is questionable (such as explorations). On the opposite end of the continuum are phenomena that are permanent and broad. Even if political forms such as colonial states and annexations are initiated and maintained through organs deployed from a metropole or state capital, these are really not classifiable as transterritorial deployments. That is, whatever the original scope and states of a deployment, once moves toward annexation, political incorporation, or state-formation emerge the external quality of deployments evaporates: the move from a military occupation (temporary but likely to be relatively broad) to the permanent claims of a colonial regime to order a social space implies an internalization of the conquerer's presence within the territory in question.

(Decolonization can be understood as exactly the attempt to externalize colonial regimes.)

But we also have to be careful about assuming all imperialisms were broad in scope. Dutch imperial strategy only drew up into its net what was essential to profitable commercial relations.[14] Territorial responsibility was avoided where possible in the pursuit of "secure retreats" for merchants.[15] With time this changed as the scope of activity widened (especially with settlers following on the foot of merchants and explorers in the South of Africa or the East Indies). Even with the acquisition of colonies in the Americas they were generally treated by the Dutch "as if they were mere factories or estates."[16]

In general, a given form of deployment, such a trusteeship, can change its status and scope, especially from temporary to permanent and from narrow to wide (or exhibit more than one type of status or scope). This implies that across the various types of deployments—ranging across differences in scope and status—there are sometimes significant connections. In the historical development of various imperial relations, there was often a starting point where missionaries, merchant adventurers, or soldiers were deployed along narrow channels of relations. In time the scope of these penetrations expanded along with a clear definition of permanent status, leading to full-fledged colonization.

Why and how these transformations occur is among the more interesting sets of questions associated with transterritorial deployments. With the exception of the Spanish in the Americas, formal and outright acquisition of relatively large aggregations land and peoples was not the typical process of colonial development. Not only was there sometimes explicit interest in expanding only through strategic points and key monopolies (the Dutch minimal approach), but the initial penetrations into Africa and elsewhere were often undertaken by mercantile companies that sought to contain their scope of responsibility (in social, political, and territorial terms) to that which was judged profitable. Narrowly defined scope to serve privately defined purposes was often not a viable basis to build a self-sustaining presence even along a coast, prompting aid from and often acquisition by states from home.

Quite often, one transterritorial deployment can invite in another, typically to bolster or advance its position in some locale. Missionaries were not immune from inviting in European armies in Africa in the name of order and security. These invitations often ended in the establishment of protectorates, which in turn transformed into formal colonies. Even though missions, traders, and explorers or adventurers may be forms of microdeployments, their activities have often forced the question of what kind of relationship their home states have to a penetrated place, and thereby changes in status and scope.[17]

It should not be assumed that the only type of relevant transformation of a deployment is toward permanent and broad forms associated with colonialism. A deployment such a church mission, a transnational oil corporation installation, or an international NGO office can also become a node in a translocal network. The organizational form in this case is no longer simply an external entity: a mission becomes a diocese and a TNC unit becomes a "national" firm.

Finally, with the delegitimation of colonialism in the second half of the twentieth century, the most likely fate for a transterritorial deployment is not some transformation to a permanent and broad political form but some sort of termination. Rather than render TDs irrelevant, we have entered an age when it seems that narrow and temporary deployments are proliferating in form, if not also number, perhaps for no other reason than there are no longer direct connections to the sheaths of more broad or permanent transboundary political engagements.[18]

Situational Power

In contrast to international arenas, which rest on the expansive possibilities of widely amplified discourses and practices, transterritorial deployments are defined by limits. It might even be legitimate to say that the more limited a deployment (the more narrow its scope and provisional its status), the more transterritorial it is. The most transterritorial of deployments, in principle, would draw hardly any the social and political life occurring in a territory into its web of relations. But even the lightest of deployments can affect life considerably within the locale it enters. Once we move away from the realm of abstraction, it becomes plain that the scope of most deployments lie somewhere between the widest and narrowest possible.

If TDs are generally defined by their limits in scope and status, then why are they so closely linked with some of the most excessive exercises of power in human history? It is natural to look to uneven capabilities associated with technology, social organization, and wealth.[19] While certainly this is part of the answer, it cannot be the whole story, especially since quite often deployments (limited by their very nature) were out-manned and out-resourced by the political forms they encountered (such as other empires or states). I think there is something uniquely powerful about the narrowness of deployments that works to their advantage in local contexts. This form of power does not require the formation of a hegemonic position. But it is also a particularly vulnerable form of power.

The relationship between limits and power is usually viewed in terms of constraints, those imposed on someone or something by power (or power understood as the construction and imposition of constraints that shape outcomes).[20] What I have in mind is different: how constraints shape the agencies producing such limits.[21] The constraints I am interested in are those of the limited mission of a UN led aid effort, the minimal engagement of a TNC with problems of local governance, the lack of public authority of an international NGO, or the disregard for existing political relations in a locale by a mercantile company. Transterritorial deployments, being narrow in character, define a delimited range of concerns and interactions within which they will be engaged. That delimited range can be thought of as a "situation." It might be a refugee crisis, a famine, an ethnic conflict, a security threat, or an opportunity to extract primary resources. Power first operates in the emergence of a bounded definition of a situation—a crisis, conflict, or opportunity. The power—understood as shaping outcomes—comes from the keeping out of other issues—those associated with the broader political and social implications of a situation.[22] With a boundary, a TD is able to locate a range of operation: thus, the constraints may open the way to capability within a narrow channel of practices and discourses.

In the last couple of decades, inspired by leftist critiques and Foucault, we have become used to thinking of power outside of the classic Weberian "power over another's choices" as a matter of having power over or within the structures that constitute social existence. The more constitutive capacity, the more power. Situational power, in contrast, is a power within which this constitutional role is delimited: it refracts people, discourses, and resources into a contained situation, by coding them and bringing them into a delimited, temporary space, ranging from the refugee camp to the makeshift factory. This is not power that can be hegemonic. That is, it is quite different from the intensive power over and extensive power within society and social space as described by Michael Mann.[23] It is the power not to have to take on the responsibility entailed by these powers over and within society. It is the power to enter and withdraw relatively flexibly from situations. The SWAT team analogy, as drawn by one UNHCR spokesman to describe the agency's growing emergency relief operations, is quite apt.[24]

The relationship between situational power and flexibility is interesting. Flexibility has often been thought of as flowing from the strength and depth of an institution—its ability to adapt to changing circumstances without decaying.[25] But when it comes to TD's, flexibility should be seen as a function of constraint and narrowness. It reflects an ability to move along narrow channels without being overly constrained by the broader social and political environment in a local context. We are familiar these days with this relationship because of its economic manifestations, however much they may be exaggerated. Capital is "footloose" and production is flexibly configured. When deployments that start out transterritorial become deeply embedded in their social contexts—evident most typically in the assumption of responsibility for constituting forms of social and existence—they lose this quality. In the least, a deployment loses some latitude over movement and withdrawal. This happens, for example, when a trading post becomes a seat of colonial administration.[26]

What does it mean to have a lot or a little situational power? Being powerful in this context means maximum flexibility, containedness, the ability to remain highly specialized to channel flows of resources, meanings, and bodies in and out of a "situation" according to its defined logic. The ideal level of this power is perhaps only approached by TNCs in free trade zones around the world or investment houses channeling capital in and out of markets. But even such supposedly "footloose" actors are quite dependent on and vulnerable to the regulatory and constitutive actions of states within which they operate. All TDs are vulnerable to pressures and "manipulation" by local forces or powerful states in the international arena (just as those local forces remain vulnerable to manipulation by TDs). One pointed example is the use of UNHCR refugee camps as safety and concentration zones by rebel or counterrebel forces in central Africa, or as sources of cheap labor for local enterprises.

From one angle it may seem contradictory to posit a form of power so closely tied to vulnerability. But the point is that self-contained forms of power abdicate to varying degrees responsibility for organizing and securing their external environments. They therefore remain subject to organization by—and threats from—others. When the Portuguese built their seaborne empire mostly on the control of key points (factories, trading posts, and bases) they assembled a remarkable web of power that was, however, highly vulnerable to manipulation and capture by others exactly because of its minimal presence in various places. Indeed, quite often factories and forts were established through negotiation with local powers rather than force. Likewise, today a great many humanitarian deployments rest on "negotiated access" or the promise of "peace corridors" for their operation.

The relationship between TDs and local forces does not unfold in a vacuum. There are various relevant networks and arenas to which local actors can be a part. Access to these networks and arenas can change their relationship to TDs. When, for example, UNDP deploys a field team to a district, it not only interacts with "locals" but with some locals who are part of regional or translocal networks exchanging information about development with international NGOs that in turn can be applied in negotiations with UNDP. The point is that the local must always be understood to be a juncture point between all three dimensions.[27] The problem is that the politics of those junctures rarely unfold on equal terms, as capacities to shape images in arenas or the terms and currency of exchange have been historically uneven.

Local Governance, Supralocal Rule, and the State

The question of power has taken us close to what lies at the heart of TDs: their interface with actors and forces in the places they are present. Deployed entities can traverse territory to approach some particular place within it (a town or state capital). The key here is the way that what is deployed intersects with a specific range of what is "happening on the ground."

Intersections of this sort can be viewed most easily in geographical terms (the village, town, or district). But we should not overlook the question of whether the space of intersection is not a geographical but a functional one. In this case a deployment engages with some specialized and delimited range of political and social functions within a territory. For example, when an IFI advisory unit is deployed to a state capital to help shape national policy, it typically does not confront the range of communities in that city or territory or the problems governance associated with them, but a narrow range of technical specialists.

Whether the locality is functional or geographical, the local can be conceived as the "range of the everyday" for a group or collectivity. A town is many things, but is distinguishable as a space to move about in and conduct one's business for members of that collectivity. The same could be said for, on one end, a city (the range is more expansive) and, on the other end, a rural district. This range is not just about the intersubjective experience of members of that collectivity. It is also about what political structures govern the everyday, whether they are municipal executives or chiefs. In functional terms, the range of the quotidian "business" within the purview of a set of experts or a given governmental department.

Since TDs are narrow in scope and often temporary in status they are unlikely to be very good candidates as constitutors of the terms of local social existence, even if they sought to be so. There is, of course, order constituted within the relatively self-contained spaces of a deployment. An example is a refugee camp. These camps do not typically change their status and become a permanent part of the geographical landscape. They can be viewed as an ordered social space for its population of refugees, since quite a lot of effort goes into governing a camp's internal domain. But refugee camps are hardly able to be cordoned-off from the contexts they are installed in. They are usually installed in some identifiable *and recognized* locale, whether it is on the outskirts of a town or in a district or region. It is telling that a great deal of UNHCR effort goes into negotiating with local authorities or "local power groups"[28] the terms of the establishment of a camp (especially security and access).

True to their forms as TDs, UNHCR field operations have had severely limited capacity to directly shape local order and have found themselves, as mentioned above, quite often subject to penetration from outside forces, including militias. It is their situational power that allows them to construct a refugee domain in a local context—and an order within it—without being hegemonic over the local context itself.[29] Their presence affects that local context, but does not order it.

But again, a consideration of the relationship between TDs and locales cannot proceed as though these two forms directly intersect on their own terms. There is also the question of what fields of order—emanating from the outside with wider geographical reach—can lay claim to a locale and what type of relationship a relevant TD has to those fields. (I am using the term *order* here to denote some form of bounded political association rather than to denote an arrangement or system of relations as is typically meant by terms such as "international order.")

The two master fields are the state and empire. It is not possible to think seriously about the relationship between local life and nonlocal forces without making processes of state-formation, colonial or not, central. Whether a TD is a direct component of such processes depends on the platforms from which it is deployed. For instance, when specialized agencies and international organizations such as the UNDP become involved in projects of postconflict reconstruction they likely become directly linked to state-making processes.

Constituting an order of this sort entails making claims of responsibility, on a supralocal basis, over one or more locales. These locales can aggregate into a contiguous territory as in the case of a state or a land-based empire, or remain relatively isolated and dispersed islands of incorporation and colonization within other geographical spaces (the seaborne fort and outpost based-empire—e.g., early Dutch model). The pursuit of supralocal claims over locales is something that—in the history of social science theory—rulers do, whether they are imperial metropoles or just state institutions in national capitals.[30] How and why supralocal claims are made depends on the types of political projects rulers are caught up in: the type of state-formation or empire-building being pursued.

Supralocal rule emerges when an ensemble of institutions and agents, organized hierarchically and coordinated around some common identity, can project itself into a set of geographical and social spaces. In this sense, rulers are often quite capable of constituting platforms for deployments as the history of imperialism makes clear.[31] Expeditions to explore and map spaces, to develop trade monopolies, and to convert to a religion are pointed examples. Whatever the initial motives of encounter, in principle, a supralocal ruler has a choice as to whether a deployment will entail claims over a local to incorporation within the wider order it rules over or not. The possibility of choice becomes robust when a given project, like an imperialist one, by its nature more or less maps what the relationship between a ruler and an encountered locale should become.[32]

The project of a supralocal rule that perhaps offers the least latitude over relations with locales is the construction of national territory. States can adopt two basic attitudes toward geographical spaces and the locales within them. One attitude is that of territorial incorporation. Obviously, incorporation can involve internal territorialization (adding national territory) or external incorporation (adding colonies). Both entail claims to embed locales in wider

supralocal orders. The second attitude is the development of some external relationship, short of incorporation and that can be labeled interventionary. The
interventionist approach of a state depends on TDs sent from platforms floated
by the state (e.g., in the U.S. case the Pentagon and its Southern Command).
Interventionary deployments by states typically are transterritorial and do not
involve taking responsibility for local order or embedding a local in a wider
order, however much such interventions impact local life. The activities of
USAID stand out as exactly this type of intervention.

Scope and status may also be relevant to the way states operate within
their own formal territories. Certainly we know that in the long history of
European state formation there have been some very narrow deployments (e.g.,
taxes, courts, and sheriffs) relative to the twentieth-century experience in the
west with the comprehensively ordering state (or as Foucault would have it, the
"governing" state).[33] For me, there is a lot at stake in this question. And those
stakes are not just about the sometimes noted potential parallels between the
history of European state formation and the development of states in regions
like Africa. Rather, they are about viewing such parallels in terms of internal
and external patterns of formation, moving to the point that taking the separation of the internal and external for granted as a starting point of analysis
ought to be questioned.[34]

This turn of view is especially relevant for a region like Africa, where
supralocal rule is considered weak—barely able to penetrate national territory
to govern and construct an order. And, so it goes, those who cannot penetrate
are condemned to being penetrated. This perspective rests on the assumption
that states in the west enjoy a monopoly over the terms of penetration within
their national territories (and that they would enjoy this monopoly even without the "sovereignty game"[35] operating in an international arena—or without
being the key forces constituting the game). UNHCR does not set up refugee
camps in western Europe or north America. Yet we know that western national
territories are viewed as being notably vulnerable to transborder networks of
intrafirm trade, currency transactions, capital movements, and so on. And while
they still may monopolize the terms of transterritorial deployments, they do
not monopolize the terms of network penetration via nodes that emerge
within national borders reaching out across international space.[36] When we
consider some of the local implications—the formation of "global cities" somewhat disarticulated from national centers and territories and local claims to
some autonomy against state centers within wider configurations of order like
the European Union—we also need to loosen the internal/external dichotomy
for the west.

It may be—somewhat ironic—that the ability of locales to order and
integrate themselves into translocal webs of networks or broad systems of transborder order decreases the pressure on rulers to have to do the ordering them-

selves (providing there does not emerge any untenable costly conflict between the ruler's interest and those external networks and orders or challenges to national territorial claims). This point has a parallel in the long history of empires founded on forms of indirect rule, where it was in the interests of metropoles to let locales govern locally so that the imperial power would not have to take responsibility itself for governance all the way down. The precarious balance suggested by this prospect may be leaving states with far greater latitude over when, where, and how they might intervene in local contexts.

Conclusion

This chapter began as an exercise in trying to unpack what we mean by international or even global. From that simple initial task a rather disturbing side to international interaction was focused on: the narrow, circumscribed, and temporary character that dominates much of it, especially those parts that are labeled humanitarian.[37] While this may leave more latitude for those seeking to maintain or constitute local forms of existence, that freedom unfolds in spaces sometimes penetrated by unsettling forces, from camps to rebel militias.

Political theorist John Dunn points to the "perils" posed by the "temporary empire" of humanitarian military intervention when they come close to the assumption of "the responsibilities of dominion" without a developed understanding of the aims and reasons for intervention.[38] This condition exists because today the relatively robust array of interventionary deployments available to the international community outflanks the development of political projects to guide them. The age of imperialism, differently, allowed for a uniquely powerful reconciliation of unfortunately robust transboundary political projects (empires) with self-contained and self-defined limits of responsibility for the life that was reached into. In contrast to Dunn, we ought to be troubled by interventions where little, if any, responsibility is assumed (a pattern all easily imitated by states in relation to their "nations"). The problem is the history of all of the twentieth century teaches us that we ought to be suspicious of general calls for more responsibility: Responsibility for whom and on what terms?

Clearly, formulaic prescriptions for lodging responsibility in one place or level or another (local, national, international) need to be tempered by a recognition that concepts of responsibility should flow, rather, from the substance of a given political project. In this respect it matters who the actors involved are. The long historical precedent of private actors serving as central players in deployments of all forms (from mercantile to humanitarian) is hard to overlook. Through private charters and missions the flow of moral purpose and public authority across boundaries is contained (although, as the above discussion about transformation mentioned, hardly forever).

Ultimately, we may need to look more closely at the history of capitalism to see the extent to which it has depended on narrow, penetrating deployments, the containment of responsibility, and the flexibility of temporary entries and exits across the fabric of local contexts around the world. We may then need to ask not only whether this contrasts with the far broader and deeper forms of responsibility and penetration associated with capitalist systems of industrial production, but also to what degree narrow and temporary relations apply to states and forms of political and social intervention around the world.[39]

Notes

1. Traditional and nontraditional approaches to international relations share this observation. For traditionalists it is the international anarchy flowing from a plurality of states that limits the international. For critical theorists or poststructuralists it is a form of modernity wherein the political is contained in the state form.

2. The extent to which the relatively limited dimensions of collective claim-making constitute an important difference is an issue that is beyond the scope of this essay. Standing out as notable exceptions are movements to end European colonization, South African apartheid, and to limit weapons in Europe.

3. John Meyer, "The World Polity and the Authority of the Nation-State," in *Institutional Structure*, George Thomas et al., eds. *Institutional Structure* (Newbury Park, CA: Sage, 1987), 41–70.

4. Robert Cox, *Production, Power, and World Order* (New York: Columbia University Press, 1987).

5. Susan Strange, *States and Markets* (London: Pinter Publishers, 1988).

6. I believe there are many structures of governance operating coterminously and that we lack the theory to understand how they interact and intersect. I have explored this issue in Robert Latham, *The Liberal Moment* (New York: Columbia University Press, 1997). See also the project of Haywood Alker, Tahir Amin, Thomas Biersteker, and Takashi Inoguchi, *The Dialectics of World Order* (1998, unpublished manuscript).

7. By public I do not mean to imply that all the activities carried out in an international arena are accessible or open to general view (as they are not, for example, in "private diplomacy"), but only that at least there is a "public" to which the business of the arena is directed.

8. It is for this reason that the media and its coverage of international news is so central to international arenas. In the mid-1880s, in his famous *Gemeinschaft and Gesellschaft*, Ferdinand Tönnies wrote about the media as an organ of public opinion that it "is comparable and, in some respects, superior to the material power which the states possess through their armies. their treasuries, and their bureaucratic civil service. Unlike

those, the press is not confined within natural borders . . . it is definitely international, thus comparable to the power of a permanent or temporary alliance of states. It can, therefore, be conceived as its ultimate aim to abolish the multiplicity of states and sub-stitute for it a single world republic, coextensive with the world market, which would be ruled by thinkers, scholars, and writers and could dispense with means of coercion other than those of a psychological nature." (Ferdinand Tönnies, *Gemeinschaft and Gesellschaft* [Ann Arbor: University of Michigan Press, 1957], 221.)

9. Translocal networks are a distinct species of the wider network genus. If translocal networks are on one end of a hypothetical continuum, then on the other end are networks based on "elective affinity," composed of nodes in close, everyday proxim-ity to one another (such as a network of support among immigrants in an urban neigh-borhood).

10. Cf. Margaret Keck and Kathryn Sikkink, *Activists Beyond Borders: Advocacy Net-works in International Politics* (Ithaca: Cornell University Press, 1998).

11. The reader might want to argue that a given system of deployment is noth-ing but a network. However, in the way I am using the term *network* here this makes no sense, as we shall see, because what is unique about deployments is the connection of that which is deployed (e.g., a temporary field office) and the organizational platform from which it is deployed (e.g., and international agency headquarters), rather than its more autonomous links to nodes situated in other local or national contexts.

12. Whether or not we validate globalization as a legitimate phenomenon in its own right, its unfolding is typically understood either as an intensification of the busi-ness of international arenas or the activities of transborder networks (capitalistic, dias-poric, or "mediatique"). For two different views on this intensification, see Robert Keo-hane, "Hobbes's Dilemma and Institutional Change in World Politics: Sovereignty in International Society," in *Whose World Order: Uneven Globalization and the End of the Cold War*, eds., Hans-Henrik Holm and Georg Sørensen (Boulder: Westview Press, 1995); and Arjun Appaduri, "Disjuncture and Difference in the Global Cultural Economy." *Public Culture* 2 (2) (1990), 1–24. While Appaduri has a relatively expansive five-fold differen-tiated model of the globalization process stressing increased network activities, Keohane, working within the perspective of U.S. IR theory, sees it straightforwardly as "the inten-sification of transnational as well as interstate relations" (Keohane, "Hobbes Dilemma and Institutional Change in International Politics," 165).

13. By using the term *transterritorial* in this specialized way I am clearly distanc-ing myself from the more common use of it to describe all the interactions and institu-tions that are not rooted in territorially bounded organization. Ruggie sees these inter-actions as anchored in "non territorial functional space." (John D. Ruggie, "Territoriality and Beyond: Problematizing Modernity in International Relations." *International Orga-nization* 47 [1] [1993]: 139–74.) 1 am arguing that such interactions and institutions appear in all of the three dimensions outlined above (the international arena, the translo-cal network, and the deployment). I am saving the term *transterritorial* for the last dimen-sion because the movement of an entity across territory is what distinguishes it from the "non territorial" arena. In contrast, what is distinctive about the transborder network is

the rootedness of its nodes in territorial organization, from which capital (monetary or informational) can thereupon be transmitted across borders or territory if you like.

14. Fernand Braudel, *Civilization and Capitalism*,Vol. III, *The Perspective of the World* (New York: Harper & Row, 1984), 202; compare also Giovanni Arrighi, *The Long Twentieth Century* (New York:Verso), 201.

15. D. K. Fieldhouse, *The Colonial Empires* (New York: Dell Publishing, 1966), 50–51.

16. Ibid., 52.

17. Cf. Ibid., 84–85, 97, 179; and Michael Doyle, *Empires* (Princeton: Princeton University Press. 1986), 179.

18. The attempt to resurrect something like the occupation model to organize and authorize broader-based UN led interventions is outlined in Jarat Chopra, "The Space of Peace-Maintenance," *Political Geography* 15 (3–4), 335–57.

19. Daniel R. Headrick, *The Tools of Empire: Technology and European Imperialism in the Nineteenth Century* (Oxford: Oxford University Press, 1981).

20. Compare Steven Lukes, *Power: A Radical View* (London: Macmillan, 1974).

21. An abstract discussion of power as negativity more broadly is in Torben Bech Dyrburg, *The Circular Structure of Power* (New York:Verso, 1997), 133–37.

22. In one example of an explicit recognition of how important situational power has become to an agency like the UNHCR, and how it displaces broader political approaches, a recent anonymous staff member contrasted "situational approaches" to those that focused on the politics of an entire region by engaging "with regional institutions such as OAS, OSCE, OAU, and CIS in order to address asylum practices and forced migration patterns on a regional basis." (Anonymous, "The UNHCR Note on International Protection You Won't See," *International Journal of Refugee Law* 9 [2] [1997]: 267–73.)

23. Michael Mann, "The Autonomous Power of the State: Its Origins, Mechanisms and Results," *Archives Europeennes de Sociologie* 25 (1984): 185–213.

24. Cited in Mikhael Barutciski, "The Reinforcement of Non-Admission Policies and the Subversion of UNHCR," *International Journal of Refugee Law* 8 (1/2) (1996): 49–110.

25. Samuel Huntington, *Political Order in Changing Societies* (New Haven: Yale University Press, 1968), 13–17.

26. The Huntingtonian notion of adaptability and situational flexibility are related, in that what gives a thick institution the ability to flexibly adapt is its capacity to set boundaries around past, outdated practices, around too many demands on those and current ones, and so on. In effect, within its world it narrows and rechannels itself.

27. This juncture is one of two ways that intersections can occur between the dimensions. The other is from within one of the dimensions. For example, representa-

tives of a group of states convening in the international arena can be recipients of information or money from networks whether they are lobbying NGOs or corporate contributors. In general, in order for an intersection to take place there needs to be some kind of a "space" (or more accurately point in space) that serves as the juncture point. A local context, where there is likely to be a mixing of actors and institutions operating in the different dimensions (often any given actor can operate in all three dimensions), is especially propitious for such intersections.

28. John Kirby, et al., "UNHCR's Cross Border Operation in Somalia: The Value of Quick Impact Projects for Refugee Resettlement," *Journal of Refugee Studies* 10 (2) (1997), 182.

29. It can be argued that ultimately there is no single force that is responsible for constituting local or any other form of order (and that it is always a matter of multiple forces and actors). I am quite sympathetic to that view and argue for it elsewhere regarding sovereignty—see Robert Latham, "Social Sovereignty," *Theory, Culture, and Society* 17 (4): 1–18. However, my concern is not with any one actor, institution, or configuration of forces constituting order. Rather, it is with the relationship between a field of order constituted—meanings, codes, legitimate practices—and a set of agents establishing or maintaining that field. My argument is that a TD can contribute to a part of such a field of order through its presence and the domain it works within or creates, but it need not be one of the forces directly constituting the general fabric of order in a given locale. For example, while UNHCR may constitute a refugee camp that shapes order near a small city, it does not constitute the municipal order (even though that order rests on a varied array of actors and institutions in government, the economy, and society).

30. The term *supralocal rule* is being used instead of political center. The term, *political or societal center* (cf. Edward Shils, *Center and Periphery* [Chicago: University of Chicago Press, 1975]), has been with us for some time and is not without problems. Most of all, the concept, as an ideal type, automatically accords the status of center to a configuration of agency like a state in relation to some typically formal social field like a territory and its inhabitants, when this status may be in the least questionable. Of course, problems with the power and status of centers vis-à-vis a territory was exactly what theorists like Edward Shils were concerned with. But in the intellectual spirit of modernization theory, they allow an idealized theoretical vision of centrality per se to guide their analysis (challenged by dependency theories' peripheralization of centers). Note that the concept is also wholly internalistic, with no suggestion of dynamics between internal and external forces (however much the impact of colonialism was recognized in modernization theory). The point is not to throw out terms like center, or even related ones like core and metropole since they usefully suggest structures of hierarchy. But we need to qualify and contextualize our use of such terms by recognizing, on the one hand, that the status of centrality is is function of a political project rather than being an inherent condition and, on the other hand, that there are internal and external dimensions to the boundaries or social spaces a center applies to that also are a function of a political project. Supralocal rule supplies an analytical vantage point from which to make those qualifications.

31. The interesting question is what kind of field of power comprises contemporary international organizational deployments, NGO networks, and international arena activities. So far the catchall phrase for it is either international order or more recently "global governance."

32. This does not preclude arguments over whether a locale is to be subject to colonization (leading, when answered in the negative, to potentially informal imperialistic relations).

33. Likewise, a national sphere is laced with networks, some of which reach out beyond national borders. And it is not so far fetched to imagine that a nation-state is composed in part by a overlapping set of national arenas, which have many of the characteristics of international arenas.

34. Cf. Jean-François Bayart, *The State in Africa: The Politics of the Belly* (New York: Longman Publishing, 1993), 20–32.

35. Robert Jackson, *Quasi-States: Sovereignty, International Relations and the Third World* (Cambridge: Cambridge University Press, 1990).

36. We could view these networks as operating at the behest of the state as informal charters (arguing that they could be shut down at any time by western states that construct the space for them—see Latham, "States, Globalization, and Social Sovereignty"). This would require some very complicated and confusing counterfactual reasoning that is likely to exaggerate the import of the observation that western states have been complicit in the construction of these networks and underplay the observation that states are quite dependent on them and unable to maneuver in the web of interests involved in their operation.

37. Alex de Waal, *Famine Crimes* (Bloomington: Indiana University Press, 1997).

38. John Dunn, "The Dilemma of Humanitarian Intervention." *Government and Opposition* 29 (2) (1994), 248–261.

39. It may be misleading to assume historical dichotomies between broad and narrow forms of engagement and responsibility (the latter we now associate with neoliberalism).

CHAPTER 7

Cartographies of Loathing and Desire: The Bharatiya Janata Party, the Bomb, and the Political Spaces of Hindu Nationalism

Stuart Corbridge

"Many of us have persuaded ourselves that the nuclear tests at Pokhran mark the triumph of Shakti, the primordial energy, the resplendent Mother Goddess. I fear, however, that it is quite another figure who ranges the skies above Pokhran and Chagai: the sinister figure of Ashvatthama, his eyes bloodshot, his hands covered with gore, his hair swept back to reveal the gleaming snake-jewel set in his head."[1]

When India exploded three nuclear devices in the Rajasthan desert on May 11, 1998, it announced a new role for itself in international affairs.[2] This was very much the intention of the Bharatiya Janata Party (BJP)-led government which ordered the tests. The BJP used the tests to challenge the monopoly powers enjoyed by the nuclear "club of five," and to strengthen its position within the lower (or people's) House of the Indian Parliament, the Lok Sabha. (The Hindu nationalist BJP was able to form a minority government in New Delhi in March 1998 with the support of various regionalist parties. It secured a stronger position for itself after the thirteenth Lok Sabha elections in September–October 1999). The gauntlet which the BJP threw down to Pakistan was predictably taken up by India's western neighbor, and support for the BJP's line on nuclear testing became a litmus test of Indian patriotism in the Lok Sabha debates that followed Pakistan's own weapons tests.[3] The Congress Party, for so long the "natural" party of government in postcolonial India, was now forced to sing from the BJP's songbook. The party of Nehruvian secularism had apparently lost out to a new political force that imagined India anew, and through the lens of a militarized Hindu nationalism.

This article has been adapted from a previously published paper, "'The Militarization of all Hindudom'? The Bharatiya Party, the Bomb and the Political Spaces of Hindu Nationalism," *Economy and Society*, 28 (7): 222–255. (Copyright held by Taylor and Francis [Routledge].)

But what does this new India look like, and to whom and on what terms? In this paper I first discuss the means by which the BJP and its allies in the Sangh parivar[4] have sought to reinvent India as *Bharat* (the Hindi word for India), or as Hindustan, an ancient country whose boundaries are set by fixed geographical features and whose rivers and landscapes are indicative of the mythological unity of India as "Hindudom." I also discuss the gendered rituals of pilgrimage and spatial representation that allow Hindu nationalists to position Mother India (*Bharat Mata*) as a geographic entity under threat from Islam, and in need of the protective armies of Lord Rama, the [now] very masculine incarnation of Vishnu whose birthplace is Ayodhya in eastern Uttar Pradesh. I then consider how and why these representations of India's domestic spaces are used by the BJP and its allies to fashion a new conception of India as a Great Power. I also review the problems that the BJP must face in seeking to make its accounts of the political spaces of India hegemonic at home, let alone abroad. The BJP came to power in the late-1990s as much because of its repudiation of hard-line Hindu nationalism after the 1996 elections as because of its ideology of Hindutva.[5] Hindu nationalism is also challenged by an ideology of secularism that has struck deeper roots in India than some critics allow, and by a rainbow coalition of popular movements that disavow the dirigiste projects of Nehruvian modernity and militant Hinduism. I conclude the paper with some brief reflections on this theme.

Inventing and Reinventing India: From Nehru to Vajpayee

Nationalist historians are not alone in seeing the period from 1947 until 1964, the year of Nehru's death, as a golden age of economic growth and social cohesion in modern India. Following a long period of arrested development and British misrule, the India that was fashioned by Nehru and the Constituent Assembly of India (1946–1949) promised a new age of democratization, secular reason, and socialist economic development. The rise of the BJP is often understood, and judged, against this uncritical account of the high modernist years of Nehruvian socialism and secularism.

There is some basis for this contrast between the invention of a "modern India" under Prime Minister Nehru and the rather different (if still "modernizing") ambitions of Prime Minister Vajpayee and the BJP. The governments of Pandit Nehru were indeed committed to an ideology of development wherein the economy would be directed in large part by the state and for the "greater good," and they promoted secularism as one of the founding mythologies of the postcolonial state. Nehru himself imagined that purposive government actions to rid the country of untouchability and casteism, together with a political creed that aimed to keep religion out of India's political life (while guaranteeing the private spaces of all religions), would in time, when coupled with the extension of mass education and universal suffrage, create modern men and women who would think of themselves as Indians first and foremost, and not as Tamilians or Yadavs.

More recently, however, following the apparent failure of some parts of the "Nehruvian project," several critics have advanced the view that Nehru's account of Indian modernity was at odds with popular understandings of Indian realities and Indian futures. Sudipta Kaviraj has argued "that if Indian politics becomes genuinely democratic in the sense of coming into line with what the majority of ordinary Indians would consider reasonable, it will become less democratic in the sense of conforming to the principles of a secular, democratic state acceptable to the early nationalist elite. What seems to have begun in Indian politics is a conflict over intelligibility, a writing of the political world that is more fundamental than traditional ideological disputes."[6]

Kaviraj is not advancing this argument in order to support the BJP's claim that Nehru took Bharat away from its religious moorings. (The Sangh parivar has long argued that Nehru imposed on India a "pseudosecularism" that pampered the country's religious minorities (notably the Muslims), and turned its back on the "authentic" religious traditions of Hindudom). He is rather concerned to challenge the paternalistic and high modernist ambitions of the postcolonial state. But arguments of this ilk serve to remind us that Nehru's vision of a modern, industrial India was not shared by all parts of the nationalist movement in India. Gandhi, of course, was strongly opposed to what he saw as the evils of industrial modernity And Gandhi's killer, Nathuram Godse, articulated yet another view of India when he declared at his trial that: "I firmly believed that the teachings of absolute *ahimsa* [nonviolence] as advocated by Gandhiji would ultimately result in the emasculation of the Hindu community and thus make the community incapable of resisting the aggression or inroads of other communities, especially the Muslims."[7]

The word *emasculation* was well chosen. Godse was an articulate Brahmin from Maharashtra and a lapsed member of the Hindu nationalist Rashtriya Swayarrisevak Sangh (RSS), to this day the central organization in the Sangh parivar. The India that Godse wished to see built after Independence was a strongly masculine India, an India which would develop a military- industrial capability that would befit its status as a great civilization. Godse's vision of India was thus the vision of the Sangh and the Hindu Mahasabha, an organization that was founded in 1907 in Punjab and organized on an all–India basis from 1915. And the leader of the Mahasabha, and very much the father of Hindu nationalism in twentieth–century India, was Veer Savarkar, the author of *Essentials of Hindutva* and the forgotten man of India's Freedom Struggle.[8] It was Savarkar, and not Nehru, who Gandhi had in mind when he wrote his anti-modern manifesto for India, *Hind Swaraj*.[9] And it was Savarkar, intriguingly, and perhaps even fatefully, who argued for an atomic India. As Lise McKean puts it: "As necessary elements of militarization, Savarkar encouraged Hindus to support science, technology, and industrialization; he condemned Mahatma Gandhi's opposition to industrialization. In Savarkar's plan for India's industrialization, 'science would lead all material progress and would annihilate superstition.'[10] In a speech to high school students in 1953 Savarkar exhorted the audience to bring 'the secret and science of the atom bomb to India and make it a mighty nation.'[11] This was in line with his demand for Hindu nationalists to "Hinduise all politics and [to] militarise all Hindudom."

There are grounds, then, both for distinguishing strongly between the modernizing visions of Nehru and of the Hindu nationalists, and for suggesting that the rise of the latter might be accounted for, in some part at least, by the failings or even the hubris of the former. This, of course, is the line that the BJP has sought to prosecute. And it is significant that many of the Sangh parivar's arguments have been directed toward an account of the political spaces of pre- and postcolonial India. The India Nehru wished to see built was an orderly and legible political space (a point well made by the commission given to Le Corbusier for the construction of Chandigarh), and it was to be produced according to Western designs and technologies. Nehru referred to the dams that made up the Damodar Valley Scheme as "the temples of modern India." Reason was would replace Religion as the Godhead in a modernizing India.[12] The political spaces that have marked the BJP's rise to power, by contrast, and which have been created by this rise to power, depart radically from this high modernist vision. At the heart of the BJP's imaginary in the late 1980s and early 1990s was the pilgrimage center of Ayodhya, the birthplace of Lord Rama, the seventh incarnation of the god Vishnu. The BJP-VHP mobilized support for its "new map of India" around the issue of the Babari Masjid, a mosque that was built in Ayodhya in 1528 by a general of Babar, the founder of the Mughal dynasty. The mosque replaced, it is said, "an even more ancient Hindu temple to the god Rama, which had occupied the spot from the eleventh century A.D. The temple commemorated the place where Rama, the god-hero of the great epic poem the Ramayana, had been born. After destroying the temple, the general built his mosque, using carved pillars that had been taken, the story goes, from the temple ruins."[13]

The British recognized that the mosque/temple issue was a sensitive one, and following their annexation of the region in 1856 they "decided to put a railing around the mosque and to raise a platform outside on which Hindus could worship, while Muslims were allowed to continue their prayers inside."[14] This arrangement continued until independence in 1947, when the government of India ringed off the complex from both communities. Hindus and Muslims continued to claim the site as their own in the decades that followed, but it was not until October 1984 that a comparatively new member of the

Sangh family, the Vishwa Hindu Parishad (VHP), led an "Ayodhya procession" across north India and brought the matter to national attention. The VHP then restated its demand for the lock on "Rama's birthplace" to be removed, and from 1986 it joined with the BJP to press home its demands. Communal riots broke out across north India in the wake of the VHP's campaign. The Ayodhya issue gained further momentum in 1990 when many Hindus were forced to leave the Vale of Kashmir. The BJP played the anti-Muslim card in response to the Kashmir uprising, and it gained further support from high-caste Indians opposed to the pro-reservations agenda of the National Front government (1989–1991). When the BJP gained power in Uttar Pradesh in the Assembly elections of 1991, the VHP was given the green light for further mobilizations around the Babari Masjid. On December 6–7, 1992, a rally in Ayodhya organized by the BJP and VHP degenerated into a savage attack on the mosque and resulted in its demolition. The BJP-VHP had made the point they always intended to make, and secular India was briefly in tatters.

The events of December 1992 are well known even outside India. What is less well known is that the attack on the Babari Masjid was part of a wider attempt to imagine and reclaim an undivided India—*Akhand Bharat*—for "Hindudom." Ayodhya was at the center of this imagining in more ways than one. In crudely geographical terms, Ayodhya occupies a position midway between "the Indus and the Seas" [the Bay of Bengal], a west-east axis that was naturalized by Savarkar and that for many Hindu nationalists has become the true measure of India's width. (This definition of India's west-east axis makes demands on present-day Pakistan and Bangladesh, a point I will come back to in section III.)[15] Ayodhya also stands in the plain of the sacred Ganges, which in turn sits to the south of the Himalayas. The mountain chain is the abode of many Hindu gods, including Lord Shiva. According to Hindu mythology, the Ganga is the most sacred of a number of a sacred rivers in India (others would include the Jamuna, Cauveri, Godavari, and Narmada), and it flows to earth near the pilgrimage center of Hardwar from the matted locks of Shiva himself.[16]

But Ayodhya's significance for Hindu nationalism is not only geometrical. Ayodhya is the birthplace of Lord Rama, who has recently been made into a particularly male and martial (kingly) incarnation of Vishnu. The *Ramayana* tells the story of Rama's epic battles with Ravana, the demon-king of Lanka, to rescue his wife, Sita, and regain his throne in Ayodhya. When an adaptation of the *Ramayana* was screened on Indian television in 1987 and 1988, an audience of eighty million was able to watch a martial epic brought to life by teams of well-muscled actors and special effects merchants. Many more followed the story on videocassette. The Hinduism that was on offer here was the Hinduism that Savarkar set out to trumpet in the 1920s. This was not the effete or androgynistic Hinduism of Shiva or Mahatma Gandhi (a religion of nonviolence and spiritual contemplation),[17] but a Hinduism that could defend the timeless glories of Indian civilization. This is why Ayodhya became so vital to BJP-VHP politics. By confronting Islam in Ayodhya, the BJP-VHP could present itself as the savior of Mother India: a Mother that had been raped by the Muslims and the British (the "two invasions" referred to by Hindu nationalists), and whose honor could only be restored by men and women who resisted "the emasculation of the Hindu Community."

This cult of the male or the masculine informs many aspects of Hindu nationalism. It is evident, for example, in the way in which some ideologues of Hindu nationalism have sought to define the male bodies that can be entrusted with the defense of the Motherland. Just as the (female) body of the nation has to be made pure by driving out the foreign bodies of Islam and the British Raj (including "bodies" like the Taj Mahal and the Victoria Memorial in Calcutta according to the most extreme hit-lists), so also should the male body be made resolute against the sins of the flesh. In parts of north India the rise of Hindu nationalism has coincided with a renewed interest in wrestling.[18] It has also coincided with an attack on degenerate Westernism, whether in the form of Western cinema or Western attachments to beef. According to the VHP ideologue, Shastri: "As a form of entertainment, cinema is a great enemy of modern society. It is full of obscene, erotic, and indecent images which enter the sub-conscious, lie dormant, and then result in night-emission."[19] The traditional Hindu fear of the loss of semen, of male strength, is also highlighted by Shivananda, who maintains that: "The more a person conserves his semen, the greater will be his stature and vitality. His energy, ardour, intellect, competence, capacity for work, wisdom, success and godliness will begin to manifest themselves, and he will be able to profit from a long life. . . . To tell the truth, semen is elixir."[20]

It is at this point that the concerns of modern-day Hindu nationalists connect back to the Mahatma, another Hindu who lived for a while as a *brahmacharyi* (celibate). But Hindu nationalism has problems with Gandhi, as we have seen. Another way of reading the story of the "elixir of semen" is in terms of the body politics of fascism (which is just how the state of Pakistan renders Hindu nationalism). Hindu nationalism's obsession with male bodily strength and purity calls to mind the cult of the Aryan male in Hitler's Germany. And with it goes the typical paraphernalia of militarism or even fascism: the cult of the uniformed and disciplined sevak (volunteer), in the case of the khaki-clad RSS; the cult of the charismatic leader (Lal Krishnan Advani posing as Rama); and of deliberate attacks on the bodies of the Other (most obviously the dirty and ill-disciplined body of the Muslim male, who is said to be outbreeding the Hindu in northern India).[21]

In all of these ways, and at each of these spatial scales (from the corporeal body, to the household, to the city, to the region, to the nation), the political geography of India was being imagined anew, contested and partly rewritten by the sponsors of Hindu nationalism in the late 1980s and 1990s. India was being re-presented as Hindustan or as Hindudom, an ancient country whose natural borders ran from the Indus to the Eastern Sea, and from the Himalayas (including Kashmir of course) to Kanyakumari.[22] India was a country that only made sense, and that attained its unity, in terms of the cosmology and civilization of Hinduism. At the center of this great civilization was Ayodhya and Banaras (or Kashi, the City of Light). What these cities have in common, along with Hardwar and Mathura in north India, Dwarka in the west, Ujjain in the center, and Kanti at India's southern tip, is the capacity to grant Hindu pilgrims release from the cycle of rebirth should they chance to die there. (Some Sanskritic texts maintain that escape from the cycle of reincarnation will be enjoyed only by those Hindus who die with their lower body immersed in the waters of the Ganges at Banaras. According to Hindu lore, Banaras is the city that Shiva built in honor of the cosmogonic austerities of Vishnu, who called the world into existence at Kashi.)[23]

It is this mythological unity of India that Hindu nationalists have sought to place before India's electors. In addition, then, to leading the campaign to free Rama's birthplace from "Muslim overlordship," the BJP-VHP has twice led processions around India with the aim of mapping in public the Hinduized nature of Indian territory. The first of these processions took place in 1983 and was successful in bringing the VHP-BJP to national prominence in India. The *Ekatmatayajna*, or "All-India Sacrifice for Unity," was based around three large and well-organized Yatras, or processions, which traversed the country in the last quarter of 1983.[24] A first Yatra left Hardwar on November 16 and processed southward across India until it reached Kanyakumari on December 20 (see Figure 7.1). A second Yatra was inaugurated by the King of Nepal, in Kathmandu, on October 26 and reached the pilgrimage center of Rameshwaram in the southern State of Tamil Nadu on December 16. A third Yatra left Gangasagar in eastern India on November 15 and reached the Shiva temple at Somanatha in Gujarat on December 17. Up to sixty million people took part in these Yatras, and in the fifty or more minor processions that plugged into them. It is significant, too, that each of the major Yatras crossed in Nagpur, a city that is in the middle of peninsular India and is the headquarters of the Hindu nationalist RSS. This crossing would have called to mind, for many Hindus, the sacred space of Prayag (Allahabad) in northern India, a city that lies at the confluence of three holy rivers and that every twelve years hosts a great religious fair (the *kumbh mela*).

The idea of pilgrimage is deeply engrained in the Hindu religion. It is said that a "good Hindu" should visit the four temples that beckon to India's "cardinal points"—the *dhamas* of Puri in the east, Rameshwaram in the south, Dwarka in the west and Badrinath in the north.[25] A temple chariot resides in each of these great centers of pilgrimage, and the VHP-BJP took care to front their Yatras with

Figure 7.1
1983 Ekatmatayajna: Stylized Routes of Three Yatras

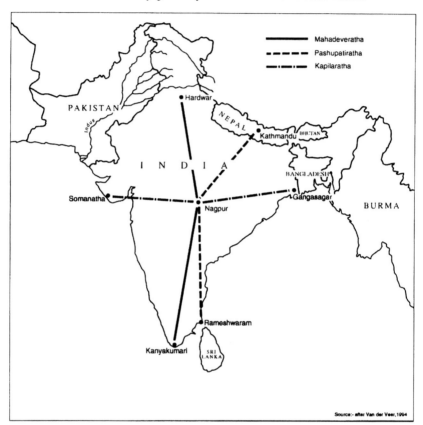

trucks bedecked in the style of these chariots. The three main Yatras were named
after their chariots—as Mahadeveratha, Pashupatiratha, and Kapilaratha—and the
imagery of the temple chariot was blended with the "militant symbolism of the
war chariot of Arjuna in the *Bhagavad Gita*," a text that speaks of the "duty of the
warrior to fight when war is inevitable."[26] At the head of each chariot/(truck)
stood Advani or another Hindu nationalist leader. Advani would sometimes pose
as Arjuna (the archer), and his chariot carried an image of Bharat Mata, the
Mother India figure who stood in need of male protection. Finally, each chariot
carried an enormous waterpot (*kalasha*) filled with water from the Ganges, along
with other pots of water from locally sacred rivers. A delegation from Burma took
care to bring water from the Irrawaddi, and there was even "sacred water" from

Pakistan, Bangladesh, and Mauritius. As one VHP leader put it at the time: "[All this] proved that Nepal, Bhutan and Burma may be politically separate from Bharat but the cultural soul of all these countries is one within."[27]

The BJP organized a second Yatra in June 1997, shortly after it had been "evicted" from power in New Delhi and shortly before the celebrations planned to celebrate fifty years of modern/(secular?) India. This time Advani took charge of a *Swarna Jayanti Rath Yatra*, or political pilgrimage, the route of which called to mind the history of Hindu nationalist politics as much as it did Hindu cosmology. The Yatra began in Mumbai (Bombay as was), a city which was in thrall to the Shiv Sena, the BJP's ally in Maharashtra. It then processed to the southern tip of India before turning north to Chennai (Madras as was), and thence (for some) by air to Port Blair in the Andaman Islands (see Figure 7.2). Veer Savarkar was held prisoner by the British in the Andamans from 1910 until 1922, and the pilgrims aimed to reach Port Blair on May 28, Savarkar's birthdate. After returning to Chennai, the Yatra moved northward and westward across India to Porbander in Gujarat, the birthplace of Mahatma Gandhi (a provocative or conciliatory gesture, this). The Yatra was then routed eastward through Rajasthan, Madhya Pradesh, Orissa, Bihar, and West Bengal, before it wound its way to Delhi via Uttar Pradesh, Himachel Pradesh, Jammu and Kashmir, and Punjab. The Yatra aimed to reach Delhi on July 10. Yatra participants celebrated the birthdate of Dr. S. P. Mookerjee (the founder of the Jana Sangh) in Jammu on July 6 and his Martyrdom Day in Calcutta on June 23.

The *Swarna Jayanti Rath Yatra* was not a success on the scale of the *Ekatmatayajna*, but it did help to consolidate an imaginative geography of Hindustan that departed radically from more conventional mappings of South Asia. "Nationalism," as Van der Veer reminds us, "is a selective, homogenizing discourse that tends to demarcate social boundaries sharply and to narrow down the diversity and ambiguity of everyday life."[28] This is very much the case with Hindu nationalism, which entertains Muslims in India only as "Muslim Hindus," and finds little room for the religious borrowings that one finds in Sufism or various devotional cults.[29] The Hindu nationalism that has emerged in India under the auspices of the BJP and VHP, and with a good deal of funding from Indian big business and the Hindu diaspora, poses a threat to India's Muslim population, the second largest such population in the world. It maps India in exclusively Hindu terms, through rituals of migration and pilgrimage and a litany of sacred sites and rivers. It is a cartography of loathing and desire, in roughly equal parts.[30]

The BJP, The Bomb and the "Militarization of all Hindudom"

The ideological father of modern Hindu nationalism, Veer Savarkar, demanded that Hindu nationalism should "Hinduise all politics and militarise

Figure 7.2
LK Advani's "Swarna Jayanti Rath Yatra" May 18–July 10, 1997

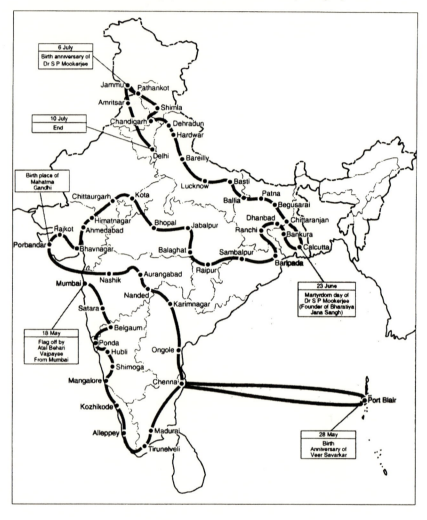

all Hindudom." The project of Hinduizing India's politics is now well advanced, but what of the demand for the militarization of Hindudom?

The rise of Hindu nationalism in India raises questions about India's ambitions in the South Asian region, and these questions were brought into focus when the BJP came to power in New Delhi in March 1998. They were thrown into sharper relief by the nuclear explosions carried out at Pokhran on

May 11. The BJP had promised in its manifesto for the 1998 elections that it would resume a process of nuclear testing that was begun by the Congress Party under Mrs. Gandhi in 1974. But it gave no hint that the tests would follow so swiftly on its inauguration. We know now that the tests on May 11 were ordered as soon as the BJP came to power. It is also believed that the first three men to know about the tests were Atul Behari Vajpayee, Lal Krishnan Advani, and Professor Rajendra Singh, an RSS officer; India's Finance and Defence Ministers were informed after this last-named individual.[31] Shortly after coming to power, the BJP also reopened the debate on the proper use of the site of the demolished mosque in Ayodhya. In respect of Kashmir, much as expected, the BJP maintained the hawkish stance it had developed in opposition.[32] The BJP has long opposed the constitutional arrangement (Article 370) which provides for a measure of autonomy in Kashmir, and it went to great lengths at the June 5, 1998 meeting of the P5 countries in Geneva to persuade Russia, the United States, China, France, and Britain not to mention Kashmir in their joint statement. The BJP has also boosted India's military presence along the Line of Control in Kashmir, and in the eyes of Pakistan it has made threatening noises about the status of Azad [Free] Kashmir.

The "eyes of Pakistan" matter very much to this story, of course. The Indian weapons tests encouraged Pakistan to make six tests of its own, sparking fears of an arms race in South Asia.[33] Several commentators in Pakistan have expressed the view that India is keen on a regional arms race. Given the parlous state of the Pakistan economy in terms of debt-export ratios and a persistent current account deficit, it is possible that the increased costs of defense spending will bite more harshly in Pakistan than in India. Some commentators have gone further than this. Right-wing religious parties in Pakistan maintain that a fascist BJP is making plans with Zionists in Israel for an attack on Pakistan. Such an attack would not only rid the region of an "Islamic bomb," it would also prepare the way for the "reunification" of India. Reunification is said to be the main goal of the BJP, and it is a goal that is informed by the ideology of Hindutva and the teachings of Savarkar. Pakistan, so this argument goes, is not recognized as a legitimate state by the BJP. It is regarded as a quasistate that was carved out of true and eternal India by India's enemies: the occupying British and the once imperial Muslims.[34]

It is not hard to see where these arguments come from. Notwithstanding the fact that the army in Pakistan has its own reasons for playing up tensions on the Indo-Pak border (and was duly rewarded with a budget hike in June 1998),[35] and notwithstanding the fact that Pakistani intelligence officers are widely suspected of planting bombs in India, it remains true that BJP rhetoric about the natural boundaries of Hindustan are a source of concern in Pakistan. Mahatma Gandhi, it will be recalled, was killed by Nathuram Godse for "agreeing" to the Partition of (British) India in 1947. More recently, Hindu

nationalists in present-day India have been at pains to describe the political
spaces of South Asia in terms of an assumed cultural unity (the idea of Hindutva). From the Indus to the Seas, "Bharat-India" is the sacred land of Hindudom, within which other religions are welcomed only to the extent that their
adherents behave as Muslim-Hindus, or Sikh-Hindus or Christian-Hindus.[36]
The public space of Bharat-India is Hindu, even where the private space of
households might be non-Hindu.

The BJP-VHP has advertised its own sense of the unity of (Greater)
India on several occasions. The organization of the *Ekatmatayajna* in 1983 is
especially revealing in this respect. The leadership of the VHP-BJP started one
of the Yatras in Kathmandu (in Hindu Nepal), and it took care to process
around India with contributions of holy water from the Indus (in modern-day
Pakistan), as well as from the Irrawaddi (Burma), Meghna (Bangladesh), and the
Mahaweli Ganga (Sri Lanka). The BJP leadership has also reminded India's voters that Jainism, Sikhism, and Buddhism emerged from within the fold of Hinduism, and that the Buddha is counted by many Hindus as the ninth incarnation (*avatara*) of Vishnu.[37]

Yet it would be wrong to equate the BJP's rhetoric on the "natural"
boundaries of Bharat too directly with Zhironovsky's demands for a Greater
Russia. I say this for two reasons, the first of which relates to the BJP and the
bomb, and the second of which relates to the position of the BJP within the
landscapes of Indian politics.

Consider, first, the "militarization of Hindudom." It is important to draw
a distinction between the ideology of Hindu nationalism and the practical politics of the BJP government in New Delhi. The May 1998 tests were surely
intended to provoke Pakistan, possibly with a view to India renegotiating its
position on Kashmir. They were also, or so it was claimed, a response to Pakistan's testing, in April 1998, of an Intermediate Range Ballistic Missile
(IRBM) "capable of carrying nuclear warheads as deep as 1,000 miles into
Indian territory."[38] In a letter to President Clinton, Prime Minister VaJpayee
made reference to Pakistan's IRBM tests, and defended the tests at Pokhran as
a way of dramatizing "the country's security concerns before an international
audience."[39] The tests were also described by the Defence Minister, George
Fernandes, as a warning to China, India's main rival in Asia and the one LID
country to have inflicted a military defeat on Independent India (in 1962).[40]
India has long been concerned about a possible sharing of nuclear knowledge
between China and Pakistan.

But it would be difficult to argue on this basis that India has designs on
the territory of Pakistan (except in Kashmir); indeed, provoking Pakistan into
nuclear tests of its own was always likely to make war with Pakistan more dangerous for India, not less dangerous. In addition, I have yet to see it argued that
the BJP has designs on Bangladesh or any other country in the South Asian

region. India has good relations with Bangladesh, and it is unlikely that this will change much under a BJP government. Bengal may be part of the Hindu nationalist imaginary of "Bharat-India," but Bangladesh is not under threat from the BJP in New Delhi. What does concern the BJP is the influx of Bengali migrants into India, but this is largely because it sees these migrants as a vote-bank for the Congress party.[41]

The truth is that Bangladesh offers no threat to the BJP or to India. The main threat that faced the BJP in 1998 came from its own coalition partners in the minority government in power in New Delhi. In the General Election of 1998 the BJP took just 179 seats (from 543). The BJP was able to survive its first vote of confidence only because its principal rival, the Congress party (142 seats), chose not to vote against the new government.[42] Against this background, the BJP's bomb should be seen as the BJP's bomb in a double sense. The nuclear tests of 1998 were authorized *by and for* the BJP: the BJP went ahead with them so quickly because it wanted to consolidate its position in the Lok Sabha. This strategy worked very well in the short run. In the aftermath of the Pokhran tests, and even more so in the aftermath of the Pakistani tests, the BJP enjoyed a massive surge of support in India.[43] The press in New Delhi wrote glowingly of India's "Great Power" status, and tributes were offered up to India's scientists. Scorn was also poured on the protestations of the existing nuclear powers; protestations that were variously denounced as "cant" or "hypocrisy" or as evidence of a "new imperialism." Meanwhile, in Parliament, few MPs dared to challenge the BJP's decision to carry out the weapons tests. To the contrary, MPs from the Congress Party and what remained of the United Front fell over themselves to claim the bomb as their own. Indira and Rajiv Gandhi—even Gujral—were vaunted as the true progenitors of nuclear India.

The fact that India's nuclear bombs were exploded for party-political rather than ideological reasons does not make the situation in South Asia any less serious. If anything, the danger of a nuclear exchange across the Indo-Pak border was heightened by the BJP's calculations of short-run political advantage, as the proxy war in Kashmir in 1999 so clearly demonstrated. In the longer run, however, the BJP's bomb may come to be seen as a sign of the party's weakness, and perhaps even of the limits of Hindu nationalism. There is already opposition to the bomb in India, albeit on a small scale.[44] More especially, there were signs in the summer of 1998 that the euphoria that the bomb unleashed in India was wearing off. Other questions were forcing themselves back onto the agenda. Secular questions; questions of national interest in a more conventional sense. The press began to worry about the possibility of the United States and European sanctions on India, and questions were asked about the economic costs of a nuclear arms race in South Asia.[45] More prosaically, but just as seriously, the leader of the BJP's principal coalition partner, the AIADMK, waited for barely more than one month after the Indian tests before threatening to pull down the BJP government. Here, sadly (or happily), one finds the ugly truth about Indian politics in the late-1990s. The ostensibly "ideological" government that ruled in New Delhi in May 1998 was kept in power (or not) by the quixotic figure of Madam Jayalalitha, the leader of the ALADMK and a woman once put in jail in Tamil Nadu for looting the State's coffers. Even after its election victory in 1999 the BJP was dependent on the support of its allies, including, more notably this time, the Telegu Desam Party from Andhra Pradesh (another State at a remove from the "cowbelt" States of the Hindi heartland).

Conclusion

I have suggested that Hindu nationalists are involved in an imaginative remapping of Bharat-India, and that the Hindu nationalism of Savarkar and the Sangh Parivar does indeed make a series of exclusionary claims about the political spaces of present-day India; it also makes inclusionary claims about the political spaces of Greater India. At the same time, I have sought to argue that these remappings are far from secure, and that as many Indians voted for the BJP in the 1998 and 1999 elections in spite of its ideology of Hindutva as because of it.

The politics of Hindu nationalism reflects this ambivalence on the part of India's voters. There is, to be sure, a constituency in India for a hard-line Hindu nationalism which might seek to "Hinduise all politics and militarise all Hindudom." This constituency is to the fore in the VHP, and it is well represented in the RSS and Shiva and Sena. But this constituency is offset for the moment by a "moderate" tendency within the BJP that is concerned to consolidate power in a democratic polity. This tendency has to respond to the concerns of an Indian electorate that has proved unwilling to give up what remains of the secular state in India. It also has to compete for votes with various casteist political parties or social movements that reject the high-caste underpinnings of the Sangh. It is to be hoped that Hindu nationalism can be contained by these agencies and pressures. The poor in South Asia have nothing to gain from "the militarization of all Hindudom."[46]

Notes

1. Ranjit Hoskote in *The Times of India*, June 6, 1998. Ashvatthama's tale forms part of the *Mahabharata*: "He was a hero who went wrong. . . . Possessed by hatred, he abandoned the way of right action and nearly destroyed the earth with his deadly weapons" (ibid.). Pokhran is in Rajasthan, India; Chagai is in Baluchistan, Pakistan (the main Pakistan test site).

2. Two more devices were exploded on May 13, 1998. Although India exploded an atomic bomb in 1974, the May 1998 tests were significant for the testing of a thermonuclear device. The Movement in India for Nuclear Disarmament (MIND) suggests that "the 1998 tests are connected to a programme of weaponisation of bombs of different sizes and yields. They suggest that India is even thinking of producing battlefield nuclear weapons like nuclear-tipped artillery shells, etc. This raises the chances of their being used, leading to dangerous nuclearisation of conventional military exchanges, possibly triggering a full-scale nuclear exchange." http://www.mnet.fr/aiindex/mindfl.html; posted on or before June 17, 1998. It should be noted that some Western scientists have questioned whether India was successful in testing a thermonuclear (or H-bomb) device on May 11, 1998. See also I. Abraham, *The Making of the Indian Atomic Bomb: Science, Secrecy and the Postcolonial State* (London: Zed).

3. Pakistan exploded six nuclear devices on May 28 and 30, 1998; five in the Chagai hills on May 28, and one in the Kharan desert (also in northwest Baluchistan) on May 30.

4. The Sangh family consists, principally, of the Rashtriya Swayamsevak Sangh (RSS), the BJP (itself a successor to the Jana Sangh), the Vishwa Hindu Parishad (VHP), and Bajrang Dal. Its close ally in Maharashtra is Shiv Sena. On the Sangh Parivar, see W. Anderson and S. Dalme, *The Brotherhood in Saffron: The Rashtriya Swayamsevak Sangh and Hindu Revivalism* (New Delhi: Vistaar, 1987). See also Thomas Blom Hansen, *The Saffron Wave: Democracy and Hindu Nationalism in Modern India* (Princeton: Princeton University Press, 1999), and Christophe Jaffrelot, *The Hindu Nationalist Movement and Indian Politics: 1925 to the 1990s* (New Delhi: Viking, 1996).

5. The meanings of Hindutva continue to be contested by the BJP and its critics: see *The Hindu*, June 30, 1998, which reports the Union Home Minister, Advani, as saying that "The word 'Hindutva' had been misinterpreted, resulting in total distortion of its meaning and spirit." Advani now wishes to maintain that Hindutva signals nothing more than the Hindu culture that underpins secular (that is, pluralist) India. Others would interpret it as a more assertively pro-Hindu (and anti-Muslim) ideology which seeks to claim Hindustan for Hindu Indians. That is how it is understood here.

6. Sudipta Kaviraj, "On state, society and discourse in India," in J. Manor (ed.) *Rethinking Third World Politics* (Harlow: Longman, 1991).

7. Quoted in Van der Veer, *Religious Nationalisms: Hindus and Muslims in India* (Berkeley: University of California Press, 1994), p. 96.

8. *Essentials of Hindutva* was written in 1922 when Savarkar was in jail in Ratnagiri. In this text, Savarkar defines Hindutva as that which "embraces all the departments thought and activity of the whole being of our Hindu race"—Veer Savarkar, *Samagra Savarkar Wangmaya: Writings of Swatantrya V. D. Savarkar, Volume 6* (Poona: Maharashtra Prantik Hindusabha, 1964), p. 3. Savarkar talks about Hindus sharing a common blood and culture, and he proclaims "Rama as the founder of a new political institution, the *chakravartin*, or world conqueror-ruler. Rama's return to Ayodhya after his diplomatic

and martial successes in the south and in Lanka marks the birth of a Hindu nation" (after Lise McKean, *Divine Enterprise: Gurus and the Hindu Nationalist Movement*, Chicago: University of Chicago Press, 1996), p. 80.

9. First published in 1908 and published again in 1997 in the series of *Cambridge Texts in Modern Politics*. In his fine introduction to the 1997 edition, Anthony Parel writes: "It is difficult to estimate the extent of Savarkar's role in the formulation of the philosophy of *Hind Swaraj*: D. Keer, the biographer of both Gandhi and Savarkar, goes so far as to claim that it was written in response to Savarkar. This is clearly an exaggeration, but there is definitely some truth in it. However that may be, during the later decades the ideological gap between the, two only widened. Savarkar, who in his London days was a supporter of Hindu-Muslim unity [but an advocate of industrial strength: SC], later changed his attitude towards the Muslims and propounded the intensely anti-Muslim ideology of hindutva. Not surprisingly, it was one of Savarkar's militant supporters who turned out to be Gandhi's assassin" (Parel in M. K. Gandhi, M. K., *Hind Swaraj and Other Writings*, Cambridge: Cambridge University Press, 1997) pp. xxvii–xxviii.

10. McKean, 1996: 89, quoting D. Keer, *Veer Savarkar* (Bombay: Popular Prakashan, 1966) p. 84, and echoing Nehru in this regard.

11. McKean, "Divine Enterprise," p. 89.

12. This argument after Ronald Inden, "Embodying God: from imperial progresses to national progresses in India," *Economy and Society* 24 (1995): 245–278.

13. Van der Veer, "Religious Nationalisms": p. 2.

14. Ibid.

15. Savarkar described the formation of Hindudom as follows: "By an admirable process of assimilation, elimination and consolidation, political, racial and cultural, they [the Aryans] welded all other non-Aryan peoples whom they came in contact with or conflict with through this process of their expansion in this land from the Indus to the Eastern sea and from the Himalayas to the Southern sea into a national unity"—Veer Savarkar, *Hindu Rashtra Darshan* (Bombay: Khare, 1949), p. 38.

16. To be precise, the Ganges "rises in the western Himalayas at Gangotri. It flows southwards out of the mountains, and enters the plains at Hardwar," T. Blurton, *Hindu Art* (London: British Museum, 1992), p. 100. Blurton (pp. 101–102) explains the mythological link between Shiva's matted locks and the Ganga.

17. Shiva takes many forms, of course, including as the creator/destroyer figure of Hindu mythology. In Shiva's many personae we find the unity of opposites that Westerners sometimes look for in "Eastern" thought: of male and female, good and evil, night and day, ascetic and family man, and so on.

18. See Joseph Alter, *The Wrestler's Body: Identity and Ideology in North India* (Berkeley: University of California Press, 1992).

19. Quoted at p. 49 in Joseph Alter, "Celibacy, sexuality and the transformation of gender into nationalism in north India," *Journal of Asian Studies* 53 (1994): 45–66.

20. Ibid.

21. The uniform of the RSS is khaki shorts, white shirt, and black cap. On Hindu fears of the untamed Muslim body (the fear of differential population growth as between Hindu and Muslim communities in north India), see R. Jeffery and P. Jeffery, *Population, Gender and Politics: Demographic Change in Rural North India* (Cambridge: Cambridge University Press, 1997), chap. 6. On the BJP and local cultures of violence in Western UP, see Paul Brass, *Theft of an Idol: Text and Context in the Representation of Collective Violence* (Princeton: Princeton University Press, 1997).

22. See also McKean: "In a rebuttal to a statement by Jinnah concerning Pakistan, Savarkar described the [furious) process whereby the Hindu people came to constitute the nation and polity he names Hindudom: 'During the course of the last 5,000 years of its continuous growth and consolidation, this gigantic Octopus of Hindudom has clutched and crushed within the formidable grips of its mighty arms a number of Shakasthans, Hunsthans; the Marathas swallowed and gulped down your very Empire entirely and altogether before it knew what was happening'"—quoted in McKean, "*Divine Enterprise,*" p. 80. I am pleased to signal my debt to Lise McKean's excellent account of Savarkar and the ideological bases of the Sangh Parivar.

23. For a brilliant account, see Jonathan Parry, *Death in Banaras* (Cambridge: Cambridge University Press, 1994).

24. The Ekatmatyajna was not a freestanding pilgrimage: it was followed up, in 1984, by a VHP-organized procession from Janakpur, the birthplace of Rama's wife Sita, to Ayodhya. In 1985 an image of Lord Rama imprisoned in a cage was paraded around India in another attempt to raise support for the "liberation" of Ayodhya. For a more wide-ranging account of Hindu nationalist processions through the 1980s, see J. Assayag "Ritual action or political reaction? The invention of Hindu nationalist processions in India during the 1990s," *South Asia Research* 18 (1998).

25. On pilgrimage and Hinduism, see Ann Grodzins Gold, *Fruitful Journeys: The Ways of Rajasthani Pilgrims* (Berkeley: University of California Press, 1988). On India's sacred geographies, see Diane Eck, "India's tirthas: crossings in sacred geography," *History of Religions* 22 (1981): 323–344, and David Sopher (ed.), *An Exploration of India: Geographic Perspectives on Society and Culture* (Ithaca: Cornell University Press, 1980).

26. Van der Veer, "Religious nationalisms," p. 125.

27. Quoted in van der Veer, ibid: p. 126; the description of the *Ekatmatyajna* is indebted to van der Veer at pp. 124–126.

28. Ibid., p. 105.

29. Hinduism should be understood as a diverse and sometimes unruly set of religious practices, some of which, at least, are not inconsistent with the worldviews of Islam or Christianity. Many "Hindus" in rural and urban India partake of religious festivals that cut across these too-neat borders. Sufism in Kashmir, and some of the *baul* cults in Bengal, are each suggestive of cross-cultural "religious" fertilizations. For a useful introduction to Hinduism, see G. Flood, *An Introduction to Hinduism* (Cambridge: Cambridge University Press, 1996).

30. On the connexions between cartography, anxiety and the "body politics in India," see Sankaran Krishna, "Cartographic anxiety: mapping the body politic in India," chap. 6, in J. Agnew (ed.), *Political Geography: A Reader* (London: Edward Arnold, 1997). "The prevalence of cartographic themes in political discourse can be seen in the following spectacle. During the Republic Day celebrations in January 1992, the Bharatiya Janata Party (BJP) leader, Murli Manohar Joshi, embarked on what was described as an Ekat Yatra (literally, Unity Pilgrimage: note the religious metaphor), planned to begin at the southern tip of India and to end in a grand flag-hoisting ceremony in Srinigar, the capital of Kashmir, in the north. When it appeared that the yatra would be delayed, if not aborted. by avalanches and bad weather, the nation was exhorted by the BJP's leaders to draw an outline map of India in the soil nearest them and plant the Indian tricolor on the spot representing Srinigar" (1997: 84). 1 am grateful to John Agnew for drawing this reference to my attention, and for his comments on an early draft of this paper. Krishna's paper is also notable for his emphasis on the violence that attends the production of the Indo-Pak border in Kashmir (and borders more generally). He notes that: "Since April 1984 [his paper was first published in 1994 in *Alternatives*], the two sides have lost well over two thousand soldiers, 97 percent of them killed by the 'weather and the terrain'" (ibid.: 85).

31. The Defence Minister, George Fernandes, was quoted in *India Today* as saying: "Nuclear weaponry is not a priority area for me. Nevertheless, we will keep the option open" (March 30, 1998: 13, international edition). The magazine described Fernandes as a "loose cannon."

32. *India Today* (international edition), June 1, 1998 and July 6, 1998 (and see cover stories).

33. The international edition of *India Today* led on Pakistan's nuclear tests ("Bang for Bang") on June 8, 1998. There is little information yet on Pakistani opposition to the Pakistan bomb, though the Web Page of South Asians Against Nukes (http://www.mnet.fr/aiindex/NoNukes.html) did post a story on June 17, 1998 about the "deep distress" registered in Lahore by the Women's Action Forum (WAF). Significantly, the WAF "holds the Western nuclear powers responsible for the current situation in South Asia, as they have consistently followed the dual policy of keeping their own arsenals intact while urging restraint on others."

34. To repeat: Hindudom describes a sacred land (*punya bhumi*), over which the Hindus ostensibly wish to "restore" a *Ram Rajya* (the golden age of Hindu mythology).

35. *The Hindu* newspaper of June 13, 1998 reports an 8.2 percent hike in Pakistani defense spending.

36. Ashutosh Varshney comments on the assimilationist rhetoric of Hindu nationalism in a fine review essay: A. Varshney "Battling the past, forging a future? Ayodhya and beyond," chap. 1, in P. Oldenburg (ed.), *India Briefing* 1993 (Boulder: Westview, 1993). He notes that Advani, "once argued that because the term 'Hindu' described the nation, Muslims could be called Muslim Hindus; Sikhs, Sikh Hindus; and Christians, Christian Hindus"—p. 31 quoting an interview that Advani gave to the magazine *Sunday* (Calcutta), July 22, 1990. Quite what Muslims would make of this construction, Advani does not say.

37. Hinduism, Buddhism, Jainism, and Sikhism were each born in India; Islam and Christianity, Hindu nationalists wish to underline, were not. The Holy Lands of Muslims, Jews, and Christians lie elsewhere. Muslims, Christians, and Jews can profess allegiance to Hindudom only after a process of assimilation (or a process of denial).

38. P. Mishra, "A New, Nuclear India?" *New York Review of Books* (June 25: 55–64), p. 55.

39. Ibid. Mishra also notes that the Indian tests represented a further bid by India for a permanent seat in the UN's Security Council.

40. The international edition of *India Today* led on May 18, 1998 with a story entitled "George in the China Shop."

41. For an early but still useful review, see S. Baruah, "Immigration, ethnic conflict and political turmoil—Assam, 1979–1985," *Asian Survey* XXVI: 1184–1206.

42. The international edition of *India Today* is a reasonable guide to some aspects of the political weather in India. Its cover stories of March 16, 1998 and March 30, referred to, respectively: A. B. *Vajpayee: Crown of Thorns and Vajpayee Government: Perilously Yours.*

43. Mishra refers to a postpoll approval rating for the BJP of 91 percent among "the urban middle class, the BJP's prime constituency"—Mishra, "A New": p. 55.

44. CNN's New Delhi Bureau reported that, on Saturday, May 16, 1998, "300 anti-nuclear protestors marched through New Delhi, joined by members of India's poor low castes, who complained that the government shouldn't be spending money on nuclear weapons when people are starving and dying in the streets" (http://cnn.com/WORLD/asiapcf). The antinuclear protest movement(s) in South Asia can usefully be followed at the web page set up in mid-May 1998 by *South Asians Against Nukes*—http://www.mnet.fr/aiindex/NoNukes.html.

45. On the sanctions issue, see the editorial in *The Times of India*, June 20, 1998 ("Life After Sanctions"); see also the piece by Ramesh Chandran in the same newspaper on May 29, 1998: "US Sanctions will 'Sting' India for a Long Time: Official."

46. It is worth recalling that the fiscal crisis of the Indian state in the late 1980s and early 1990s—a crisis that precipitated the "liberal" reforms of 1991—was occasioned in no small part by India's high and rising spending on defense in the second half of the 1980s.

PART III

Globalizing Trends in the World Economy

CHAPTER 8

A New Cross-Border Field for Public and Private Actors

Saskia Sassen

The new geography of power confronting states today entails a far more differentiated process than notions of an overall decline in the significance of the state suggest. And it entails a more transformative process of the state than the notion of a simple loss of power suggests. We are seeing a repositioning of the state in a broader field of power and a reconfiguring of the work of states. This broader field of power is partly constituted through the formation of a new private institutional order linked to the global economy, but also through the growing importance of a variety of other institutional orders, from the new roles of the international network of NGOs to the international human rights regime. As for the work of states, it has had many incarnations over the centuries. These epochal shifts contributed to lend specificity to the substantive rationality of the state—raison d'etat. Each of these transformations has had significant consequences. Today, I argue, the work of states has once again undergone a deep transformation producing its own specific notions of the state's substantive rationality, or more simply answers to the question "Why do we need states?"

We are seeing the emergence of a mostly, but not exclusively, private institutional order whose strategic agents are not the national governments of leading countries but a variety of nonstate actors. One of its marking features is its capacity to privatize what was heretofore public and to denationalize what were once national capacities and policy agendas. This capacity to privatize and denationalize entails specific transformations of the national state, more precisely of some of its components. Further, this new institutional order also has normative authority—a new normativity that is not embedded in what has been and to some extent remains the master normativity of modern times, raison d'etat. This

This essay is based on the author's "Denationalized State Agendas and Privatised Norm-Making." Inaugural Lecture, Division of Social Sciences, University of Chicago, April 28, 1999. On File with author. It is part of a larger research project to be published as Saskia Sassen, *Denationalization: Economy and Polity in a Global Digital Age* (Princeton: Princeton University Press, 2003).

173

new normativity comes from the world of private power yet installs itself in the public realm and in so doing contributes to denationalize what had historically been constructed as national state agendas, notably the Keynesian agenda.

My argument here is not that we are seeing the end of states but, rather, first, that states are not the only or the most important strategic agents in the new configuration and, second, that states, including dominant states, have undergone profound transformations in the sense that some state agencies begin to function as the institutional home for the operation of powerful dynamics that denationalize national frameworks for policy and resource allocation. This, then, raises a question about what is national in several of the key institutional components of states linked to the implementation and regulation of economic globalization.

These transformations inside the state are partial and incipient but strategic and the new privatized institutional order being formed to govern key aspects of the global economy is also partial and incipient but strategic. Both of these have the capacity to alter the substantive agendas, the scope and the exclusivity of state authority and the interstate system, today still the crucial organizational architecture for cross-border operations.

The State and Globalization

The structural foundations for my argument lie in the current forms of economic globalization. I conceptualize the latter as a key dynamic in the formation of a transnational system of power that is to a considerable extent disembedded from the formal interstate system yet needs states in very specific ways because it partly inhabits national economies. Thus, economic globalization does not only have to do with crossing geographic borders, as in international investment and trade.[1] It also has to do with the relocation of national public governance functions to transnational private arenas and with the development inside national states—through legislative acts, court rulings, executive orders—of the mechanisms necessary to accommodate the rights of global capital in what are still national territories under the exclusive control of their states, thereby denationalizing several highly specialized national institutional orders.[2]

One of the roles of the state vis-à-vis today's global economy, unlike earlier phases of the world economy, has been to negotiate the intersection of national law and foreign actors—whether firms, markets, or supranational organizations. This condition makes the current phase distinctive in a number of ways. We have, on the one hand, the existence of an enormously elaborate body of law developed in good measure over the last hundred years that secures the exclusive territorial authority of national states to an extent not seen in earlier centuries, and on the other hand, the considerable institutionalizing, especially in the 1990s, of the "rights" of nonnational firms, cross-border transactions, and supranational organizations. This sets up the conditions for a necessary engagement by national states in the process of globalization.[4]

The emergent, often imposed, consensus in the community of states to further globalization has created a set of specific obligations on participating states.[3] The state remains as the ultimate guarantor of the "rights" of global capital, that is, the protection of contracts and property rights. Thus the state has incorporated the global project of its own shrinking role in regulating economic transactions.[4] Firms operating transnationally want to ensure the functions traditionally exercised by the state in the national realm of the economy, notably guaranteeing property rights and contracts. The state here can be conceived of as representing a technical administrative capacity that cannot be replicated at this time by any other institutional arrangement; furthermore, this is a capacity backed by military power, with global power in the case of some states.

This guarantee of the rights of capital is embedded in a certain type of state, a certain conception of the rights of capital, and a certain type of international legal regime: it is largely embedded in the state of the most developed and most powerful countries in the world, in western notions of contract and property rights, and in a new legal regime aimed at furthering economic globalization.[5] The United States as the hegemonic power of this period has led/forced other states to adopt these obligations toward global capital—and, in so doing, contributed to strengthen the forces that can challenge its power.[6] The state continues to play a crucial, though no longer exclusive, role in the production of legality around new forms of economic activity, but increasingly this role has fed the power of a new emerging structure.

Denationalized State Agendas and Privatized Norm-Making

We generally use terms such as "*deregulation,*" *financial* and *trade liberalization,* and *privatization,* to describe the outcome of this negotiation.[7] The problem with such terms is that they only capture the withdrawal of the state from regulating its economy. They do not register all the ways in which the state participates in setting up the new frameworks through which globalization is furthered; nor do they capture the associated transformations inside the state.[8]

We can illustrate this using the case of central banks. These are national institutions, concerned with national matters, implementing policies for their national economies. Yet today, over the last decade, they have become the institutional home within the national state for policies that are necessary to futher the development of a global capital market, and indeed, more generally, a global economic system.[9] The new conditionality of the global economic system—the conditions that need to be met in order for a country to become integrated into the global capital market—contain as one key element the autonomy of central banks so that they may institute a certain kind of monetary policy. In most countries of the world the central bank has tended to be under the influence of the executive or of local oligarchies. Securing central bank autonomy certainly cleaned up a lot of corruption. But it has also been the vehicle for one set of accommodations on the part of national states to the requirements of the global capital market. From the perspective of research this entails the need to decode what is national about that particular set of activities of central banks.

At the level of theorization, it means detecting and conceptualizing a specific set of operations that take place within national institutional settings but are geared to nonnational or transnational agendas where once they were geared to national agendas. I conceptualize this as denationalization—denationalization of specific, typically highly specialized, state institutional orders and of state agendas.[10]

There is a set of strategic dynamics and institutional tranformations at work here. They may incorporate a small number of state agencies and units within departments, a small number of legislative initiatives and of executive orders, and yet have the power to institute a new normativity at the heart of the state; this is especially so because these strategic sectors are operating in complex interactions with private, transnational, powerful, actors. Much of the institutional apparatus of the state remains basically unchanged. The inertia of bureaucratic organizations, which creates its own version of path dependence, makes an enormous contribution to continuity.

Further, the new types of cross-border collaborations among specialized government agencies concerned with a growing range of issues is another aspect of this participation by the state in the implementation of a global economic system. For instance, the growing interactions among antitrust regulators of a large number of countries in the last three or four years, a period of reinvigorated antitrust activities in the context of economic globalization, has contributed to a growing convergence in antitrust regulations of countries with very diverse competition laws.[11] This convergence around specific antitrust issues frequently exists in an ocean of enormous differences among these countries in all kinds of laws and regulations about the economy. It is then a very partial and specialized type of convergence among regulators of different countries who often begin to share more than they may with colleagues back home in the larger bureaucracies within which they work. Yet another instance is the growth in transactions among central bankers, necessary in the context of the global capital market. While central bankers have long interacted with each other across borders, we can clearly identify a new phase in the last ten years. I would think that another example would be the institutional and legal framework necessary for the operation of the cross-border commodity chains identified by Gereffi.[12]

One outcome of these various trends is the emergence of a strategic field of operations that represents a partial disembedding of specific state operations from the broader institutional world of the state geared exclusively to national agendas. It is a fairly rarified field of cross-border transactions among government agencies and business sectors aimed at addressing the new conditions produced and demanded by economic globalization. In positing this I am rejecting the prevalent notion in much of the literature on globalization that the realm of the national and the realm of the global are two mutually exclusive zones. Globalization is partly endogenous to the national and is in this regard produced through a dynamic of denationalizing what had been constructed as the national. And it is partly embedded in the national, for example, global cities, and in this regard requires that the state reregulate specific aspects of its role in the national.

This is a field of transactions that are strategic, cut across-borders, and entail specific interactions with private actors. They do not entail the state as such, as in international treaties, but rather consist of the operations and policies of specific subcomponents of the state—whether legislative initiatives or some of the agendas pursued by central banks, for instance. They cut across borders in that they concern the operations of firms and markets operating globally and hence produce a certain convergence at the level of national regulations and law in the creation of the requisite conditions for globalization. By saying that they entail specific interactions with private actors I mean that it is not simply about interstate transactions, or a subfield of the interstate system. On the contrary it is a field of transactions partly embedded in the interstate system and partly in a new, increasingly institutionalized cross-border space of private agents/actors.

It is in this fairly rarefied field of transactions, partly disembedded from the broader institutional world of the state, that what I call denationalized state agendas get defined and enacted. This field of transactions represents then an unbundling of whatever the condition of state bundling preceding the current period, the current period being one that is fully in swing for the case of the United States by the mid-1980s. This unbundling is also one element in the broader dynamic of a changed relation between sovereignty and national territory—a subject I began to work on in my book *Losing Control*.

But for all of this to happen, it took a broader normative transformation in matters concerning the substantive rationality of the state, matters concerning raison d'etat. In good part this normative transformation is enacted outside the state and originates outside the interstate system. Further, there is a multiplicity of private agents, some minor, some not so minor, that ensure and execute this new normative order.

This transformation has to do with the normative weight gained by the logic of the global capital market in setting criteria for key national economic policies.[13] In the multiple negotiations between national states and global economic actors we can see a new normativity that attaches to the logic of the capital market and that is succeeding in imposing itself on important aspects of national economic policy making, though, as has been said often, some states are more sovereign than others in these matters. Some of the more familiar elements are the new importance attached to the autonomy of central banks, antiinflation policies, exchange rate parity and the variety of items usually referred to as "IMF conditionality." In this new normative order, certain claims emerge as legitimate, others are delegitimated—(generally matters concerned with the well-being of people at large).

I try to capture this normative transformation in the notion of a privatizing of certain capacities for making norms that we have associated with the state, at least in our recent history. This brings with it strengthened possibilities of norm-making in the interests of the few rather than the majority—which in itself is not novel, except in its further and sharper restricting of who might benefit.

A New Institutional Zone of Private Agents

While central, the role of the state in producing the legal encasements for economic operations is no longer what it was in earlier periods. Economic globalization has been accompanied by the creation of new legal regimes and legal practices and the expansion and renovation of some older forms that bypass national legal systems. This is evident in the rising importance of international commercial arbitration and the variety of institutions which fulfill rating and advisory functions that have become essential for the operation of the global economy.[14]

One aspect of this question concerns the particular forms of legal innovation that have been produced and within which much of globalization is encased and, further, how these innovations interact with the state, or more specifically, with the sovereignty of the state. These legal innovations and changes are often summarized under the notion of "deregulation" and taken as somewhat of a given. In much social science, deregulation is another name for the declining significance of the state. There is, it seems to me, a more specific process contained in these legal changes, one that along with the reconfiguration of space may signal a more fundamental transformation in the matter of sovereignty, pointing to new contents and new locations for that particular systemic property we call sovereignty.

The emerging privatized institutional framework to govern the global economy has possibly major implications for the exclusive authority of the modern national state over its territory, that is, its exclusive territoriality. There is a new set of intermediary strategic agents that contribute to the management and coordination of the global economy. They are largely, though not exclusively, private. And they have absorbed some of the international functions carried out by states in the recent past, for instance in the predominantly protectionist regimes of the post–World War II decades through which governments governed international trade.

For instance, over the past twenty years, international commercial arbitration has been transformed and institutionalized as the leading contractual method for the resolution of transnational commercial disputes.[15] In a major study on international commercial arbitration,[16] Dezalay and Garth conclude that it is a delocalized and decentralized market for the administration of international commercial disputes, connected by more or less powerful institutions and individuals who are both competitive and complementary.[17] Another instance of a private regulatory system is represented by debt security or bond rating agencies which have come to play an increasingly important role in the global economy.[18] Ten years ago Moody's and Standard and Poor had no analysts outside the United States; by 1999 they each had well over a thousand.[19]

Private firms in international finance, in accounting and law, the new private standards for international accounting and financial reporting, and supranational organizations such as WTO, all play strategic non-government-centered governance functions. The events following the Mexico crisis provide us with some interesting insights about these firms' role in changing the conditions for financial operation, about the ways in which national states participated, and the formation of a new institutionalized intermediary space.

J. P. Morgan worked with Goldman Sachs and Chemical Bank to develop several innovative deals that brought back investors to Mexico's markets.[20] Further, in July 1996, an enormous 6U.S.$billion five-year deal that offered investors a Mexican floating rate note or syndicated loan—backed by oil receivables from the state oil monopoly PEMEX—was twice oversubscribed. It became somewhat of a model for asset-backed deals from Latin America, especially oil-rich Venezuela and Ecuador. Key to the high demand was that the structure had been designed to capture investment-grade ratings from S&P and Moody's (it got BBB- and Baa3). This was the first Mexican deal with an investment grade. The intermediaries worked with the Mexican government, but on their terms—this was not a government to government deal. This secured acceptability in the new institutionalized privatised intermediary space for cross-border transactions—evidenced by the high level of oversubscription and the high ratings. And it allowed the financial markets to grow on what had been a crisis.

After the Mexico crisis and before the first signs of the Asian crisis, we see a large number of very innovative deals that contribute to further expand the volumes in the financial markets and to incorporate new sources of profit, that is, debts for sale.[21] Typically these deals involved novel concepts of how to sell debt and what could be a saleable debt. Often the financial services firms structuring these deals also implement minor changes in depository systems to bring them more in line with international standards. The aggressive innovating and selling on the world market of what had hitherto been thought to be too illiquid and too risky for such a sale has further contributed to expand and strengthen the institutionalization of this intermediary space for cross-border transactions operating partly outside the interstate system. The new intermediaries have done the strategic work, a kind of "activism" toward ensuring growth in their industry and to overcome the potentially devastating effects of financial crises on the industry as a whole and on the whole notion of integrated global financial markets.

Finally, the growing importance and formalization of what is now generally referred to as private authority is yet another component of the new privatized institutional order through which the global economy is governed and organized.[22] One important component of this development is the emergence of self-regulation in economic sectors dominated by a limited number of firms. It indicates the extent to which the global economic system needs governance and regulation, though of a different sort from that associated with the older normativity of the Keynesian state.[23]

These and other such transnational institutions and regimes do raise important and difficult questions about the relation between the state and economic globalization. As Rosenau has noted, because so many processes are transnational, governments increasingly are not competent to address some of the major issues confronting our societies; this is not the end of sovereignty, but rather an alteration in the "exclusivity and scope" of the competence of governments.[24]

A New Spatiality: The Cross-Border Network of Global Cities

There is, further, a question about the spaces of the global economy and how this in turn interacts with national sovereignty. As I have argued at length elsewhere, the spaces of economic globalization are partly embedded in what has historically been constructed as national territory, yet they constitute a spatiality that is distinct from that of the national. Much of the work of the state I described above as the formation of denationalized government agendas and much of what the private legal regimes are about has to do precisely with the fact of the institutional and locational embeddedness of economic globalization in national settings and the need to negotiate this embeddedness of global actors in national settings while at the same time the processes constitutive of globalization produce a distinct spatiality.[25]

In what follows I want to describe briefly the logic of this locational embeddedness because it is part of the spatiality of the global economy. Here I confine myself to a brief description of how the leading economic sectors and command functions of the global economy wind up embedded in these national settings. This institutional and locational embeddedness of globalization represents a deepening of the institutional base of economic globalization and a greater complexity because what we might still think of as the national institutional order and as national territory is actually becoming imbricated with the global.

The geographic dispersal of factories, offices, and service outlets that has marked the expansion of the global economy has taken place as part of integrated corporate systems. When dispersal occurs as part of such systems, particularly ones with centralized top-level control, there is also a growth in central functions. My argument is that the more globalized firms become, the more their central functions grow—in importance, in complexity, in number of transactions.[26] What matters to the analysis here is the dynamic that connects the dispersal of economic activities with the ongoing weight and often growth of central functions. In terms of the territorial state and globalization this means that an interpretation of the impact of globalization as creating a space economy that extends beyond the regulatory capacity of a single state, is only half the story; the other half is that these central functions are disproportionately concentrated in the national territories of the highly developed countries.

By central functions I do not only mean top-level headquarters; I am referring to all the top-level financial, legal, accounting, managerial, executive, and planning functions necessary to run a corporate organization operating in more than one country, and increasingly in several countries. These central functions are partly embedded in headquarters, but also in good part in what has been called the corporate services complex, that is, the network of financial, legal, accounting, advertising, and other corporate services firms that handle the complexities of operating in more than one national legal system, national accounting system, advertising culture, and so on and do so under conditions of rapid innovations in all these fields.[27] Such services have become so specialized and complex, that headquarters increasingly buy them from specialized firms rather than producing them in-house. I have conceptualized this as a networked specialized service sector of firms producing central functions for the management and coordination of global economic systems, and as marking the specific production function of global cities. This networked specialized service sector is disproportionately concentrated in the major cities of the highly developed countries.[28] This concentration of functions represents a strategic factor in the organization of the global economy.

One argument I am making here is that it is important to unbundle analytically the fact of strategic functions for the global economy or for global

operation, and the overall corporate economy of a country.[29] They are not completely overlapping worlds; many components of a country's corporate economy have little to do with globalization and, conversely, many "national" corporate sectors have become deeply globalized in their orientation and have
little resemblance to their erstwhile national-market orientation. For the purposes of many kinds of inquiry this distinction may not matter; for the purposes
of understanding the global economy, it does.

Another instance today of this negotiation between a transnational
process or dynamic and a national territory is that of the global financial markets. These transactions are partly embedded in telecommunications systems
that make possible the instantaneous transmission of money/information
around the globe. Much attention has gone to this feature. But the other half
of the story is the extent to which the global financial markets are located in
particular cities in the highly developed countries; indeed, the degrees of concentration are unexpectedly high.[30] The topography of activities in many of the
global industries such as finance actually weaves in and out of digital space; and
when it moves out of digital space and hits the ground it does so in massive
concentrations of very material resources, from infrastructure to buildings.

The drive to secure the institutional and legal transformations discussed
in the preceding sections is in good part explained by the necessary embeddedness of the most strategic functions of global firms and markets in national
institutional settings; and this holds even for firms operating largely in electronic markets. Operating a worldwide network of factories, offices and service
outlets, and implementing global financial markets, required not only cross-
border institutional frameworks, but also major and minor legal innovations in
national legal systems.

Conclusion

Strategic spaces for economic globalization had to be produced, both in
terms of the practices of corporate actors and the requisite infrastructure (i.e.,
global cities), and in terms of the work of the state in producing or legitimating new legal regimes. The outcome is an emergent new spatiotemporal order
that has considerable governance capabilities and structural power. While par-
tially embedded in national institutional settings it is distinct from these. One
way of conceiving of it is as a denationalized order. Because it is partly installed
in national settings, its identification requires a decoding of what is national in
the national. The social sciences are not well equiped for this task given a strong
state-centric approach to theory and research.

From the angle of my research I would posit that we can list at least the
following consequences for the state, the interstate system, and international

law. First, the fact of a growth in cross-border activities and global actors operating outside the formal interstate system, affects the competence and scope of
states and of international law. Second, the fact that this domain is increasingly
being institutionalized and subjected to the development of private governance
mechanisms, affects the exclusivity of state authority and of international law.
Third, the fact of growing normative powers in this private domain affects the
normative power of international law. Fourth, the state's participation in the
reregulation of its role in the economy and the incipient denationalization of
particular institutional components of the state necessary to accommodate
some of the new policies linked to globalization, transform key aspects of the
state, and in so doing alter the organizational architecture for the interstate system and for international law.

This institutional order contributes to strengthen the advantages of certain types of economic and political actors and to weaken those of others. It is
extremely partial rather than universal, but strategic in that it has undue influence over wide areas of the broader institutional world and the world of lived
experience yet is not fully accountable to formal democratic political systems.
This new institutional spatiotemporal order I am identifying here exists partly
inside and partly outside the state and the interstate system and cannot be
thought of as a primarily geographic entity but rather needs to be conceived
in spatial terms, where space is itself productive of the new dynamics of power
and control as well as produced by these. Space is not a mere container or tabula rasa. Moving from territorial organizations such as the modern state to spatial orders is no easy analytic task and what I briefly presented here is but a
mere set of elements.

Notes

1. Several critical scholars have examined features of cross-border dynamics that
operate outside the interstate system and involve a far broader range of actors than the
crossborder private institutional order I describe here. See Yale H. Ferguson and Richard
W. Mansbach, *Polities: Authorities, Identities, and Change* (Columbia, SC: University of
South Carolina Press, 1996); James N. Rosenau, "Governance, Order, and Change in
World Politics," in Rosenau and E. O. Czempiel, eds., *Governance without Government:
Order and Change in World Politics* (Cambridge, UK: Cambridge University Press, 1992),
1–29;.and Richard Falk, *Explorations at the Edge of Time: The Prospects for World Order*
(Philadelphia: Temple University Press, 1992).

2. There is a critical scholarship that has dealt with the ambiguities of sovereignty and the interstate system but from the perspective of international relations and
using very different vocabularies. See particularly R. B. J. Walker, *Inside/Outside: Interna-*

tional Relations as Political Theory (Cambridge: Cambridge University Press, 1993); and Weber, C., *Writing Sovereignty* (Cambridge: Cambridge University Press, 1996).

3. P. G. Cerny, *The Changing Architecture of Politics* (London and Newsbury, CA: Sage, 1990); and P. G. Cerny, "Structuring the Political Arena: Public Goods, States and Governance in a Globalizing World," in Ronen Palan, ed., *Global Political Economy: Contemporary Theories* (London: Routledge, 2000), 21–35.

4. See Robert Cox, *Production, Power, and World Order: Social Forces in the Making of History* (New York: Columbia University Press, 1987); Leo Panitch, "Rethinking the Role of the State in an Era of Globalization," in James Mittelman, ed., *Globalization: Critical Reflections, International Political Economy Yearbook*, Vol. 9 (Boulder, CO: Lynne Rienner Publishers, 1996); Stephen Gill, "The Emerging World Order and European Change," in Ralph Milliband and Leo Panitch, eds., *New World Order? The Socialist Register* (London: Merlin,1992), 157–196; and Saskia Sassen, *Losing Control? Sovereignty in an Age of Globalization*. The 1995 Columbia University Leonard Hastings Schoff Memorial Lectures (New York: Columbia University Press, 1996).

5. This dominance assumes many forms and does not only affect poorer and weaker countries. France, for instance, ranks among the top providers of information services and industrial engineering services in Europe and has a strong though not outstanding position in financial and insurance services. But it has found itself at an increasing disadvantage in legal and accounting services because Anglo-American law dominates in international transactions. Foreign firms with offices in Paris dominate the servicing of the legal needs of firms, whether French or foreign, operating out of France. (For an analysis that captures the early stages of this development, see Jean Francois Carrez, *Le developpement des fonctions tertiares internationales a Paris et dans les metropoles regionales*. Rapport au Premier Ministre. [Paris: La Documentation Francaise, 1991].) Similarly, Anglo-American law is increasingly dominant in international commercial arbitration, an institution grounded in continental traditions of jurisprudence, particularly French and Swiss. (See Yves Dezalay and Bryant Garth, *Dealing in Virtue. International Commercial Arbitration and the Construction of a Transnational Legal Order.* [Chicago: The University of Chicago Press, 1996]).

6. See Arrighi's analysis of this type of dynamic: Giovanni Arrighi, *The Long Twentieth Century. Money, Power, and the Origins of Our Times.* (London:Verso, 1994); and for a debate around this notion, see Diana E. Davis, ed., "Chaos and Governance," in *Political Power and Social Theory*,Vol. 13, Part IV: Scholarly Controversy (Stamford, CT: JAI Press, 1999).

7. The changed condition of the state is often explained in terms of a decrease in regulatory capacities resulting from some of the basic policies associated with economic globalization: deregulation of a broad range of markets, economic sectors and national borders, and privatization of public sector firms. Many scholars coming at the subject from a variety of angles would agree, even as they might use other concepts, that something important has changed in the condition of state authority. See, for example, Eric Hobsbawm, *The Age of Extremes:A History of the World, 1914–1991* (New York:Vintage, 1994); Charles Tilly, "Globalization Threaten's Labor Rights," *International Labor and*

Working-Class History, vol. 47 (1995): 1–23; and Robert Jessop, "Reflections on Globalization and Its Illogics," in Kris Olds, Peter Dicken, Philip F. Kelly, Lilly Kong, and Henry Wai-Chung Yeung, eds., *Globalization and the Asian Pacific: Contested Territories* (London: Routledge, 1999), 19–38. See also various chapters in each of the following collections to get a cross-section of perspectives in English-language literature: Mittelman, *Globalization*; Olds, et al., *Globalization and the Asian Pacific*; David Smith, D. Solinger, and S. Topik, eds., *States and Sovereignty in the Global Economy* (London: Routledge, 1999); and Andrew Calabrese and Jean-Claude Burgelman, *Communication, Citizenship, and Social Policy: Rethinking the Limits of the Welfare State* (Lanham, MD: Rowman & Littlefield, 1999).

8. For important contributions to the latter perspective, see Sol Picciotto and Ruth Mayne, *Regulating International Business: Beyond Liberalization*. (London: Macmillan, in association with OXFAM, 1999); and Thomas J. Biersteker, Rodney Bruce Hall, and Craig N. Murphy, eds., *Private Authority and Global Governance* (Cambridge: Cambridge University Press, 2002).

9. Sassen, *Losing Control?* chaps. 1 and 2.

10. In my current research (Sassen, *Denationalization*) I am extricating a whole series of legislative items and executive orders from their enframing as "national" government acts and reframing them as incipient "denationalizing" acts. They can be read as accommodations on the part of the national state and as its active participation in producing the conditions for economic globalization. This is a history of micro-interventions, often minute transformations in our regulatory or legal frameworks that facilitated the extension of cross-border operations of U.S. firms and markets. This is clearly not a new history, not for the United States or for other Western former imperial powers. Yet, I argue, we can identify a new phase, one which has very specific instantiations of this broader feature. I am trying to distinguish this from older notions of the state as a tool for capital, comprador bourgeoisies, or neocolonialism. One of the first of these new types of measures, and perhaps one of the best known, are the tariff items passed to facilitate the internationalization of manufacturing, which exempted firms from import duties on the value added of reimported components assembled or manufactured in offshore plants. I date this microhistory of legislative and executive interventions to the late 1960s, with a full crystallization of various measures facilitating the global operations of U.S. firms and the globalization of markets in the 1980s, and work continuing vigorously in the 1990s. The Foreign Investment Act of 1976, the implementation of International Banking Facilities in 1981, the various deregulations and liberalizations of the financial sector in the 1980s, and so on, are but the best known landmarks in this microhistory.

11. Brian Portnoy, "Constructing Competition: The Political Foundations of Alliance Capitalism." Ph.D. dissertation, Department of Political Science, University of Chicago, 1999.

12. Gary Gereffi, "Global Production Systems and Third World Development." In Barbara Stallings, ed., *Global Change, Regional Response: The New International Context of Development* (New York: Cambridge University Press, 1995), 100–142. See generally the

work by Slaughter on transgovernmental networks. See Anne-Marie Slaughter, "The Real New World Order," *Foreign Affairs* 183 (Sept.–Oct.). Also Max Castro, *Free Markets, Open Societies, Closed Borders?* (Berkeley, CA: University of California Press, 2001).

13. Sassen, *Losing Control?*, chap. 2.

14. See Yves Dezalay and Bryant Garth, *Dealing in Virtue. International Commercial Arbitration and the Construction of a Transnational Legal Order;* Jeswald Salacuse, *Making Global Deals: Negotiating in the International Marketplace* (Boston: Houghton Mifflin, 1991); Timothy J. Sinclair, "Passing Judgement: Credit Rating Processes as Regulatory Mechanisms of Governance in the Emerging World Order." *Review of International Political Economy*, vol. 1, no. 1 (Spring, 1994): 133–159; and Sylvia Maxfield, *Gatekeepers of Growth* (Princeton: Princeton University Press, 1997).

15. Today international business contracts, for example, the sale of goods, joint ventures, construction projects, or distributorships, typically call for arbitration in the event of a dispute arising from the contractual arrangement. The main reason given today for this choice is that it allows each party to avoid being forced to submit to the courts of the other. Also important is the secrecy of the process. Such arbitration can be "institutional" and follow the rules of institutions such as the International Chamber of Commerce in Paris, the American Arbitration Association, the London Court of International Commercial Arbitration, and many others. Or it can be "ad hoc," often following the rules of the UN Commission on International Trade Law (UNCITRAL). The arbitrators are private individuals selected by the parties; usually there are three arbitrators. They act as private judges, holding hearings and issuing judgments.

16. Dezalay and Garth, *Dealing in Virtue.*

17. See also Salacuse, *Making Global Deals.*

18. Sinclair, "Passing Judgement"; Maxfield, *Gatekeepers of Growth.*

19. Saskia Sassen, *The Global City,* 2nd ed. (Princeton, NJ: Princeton University Press, 2001).

20. The U.S.$40 billion emergency loan package from the IMF and the U.S. government and the hiring of Wall Street's top firms to refurbish its image and find ways to bring it back into the market, helped Mexico "solve" its financial crisis. With J. P. Morgan as its financial adviser the Mexican government worked with Goldman Sachs and Chemical Bank to come up with several innovative deals. Goldman organized a U.S.$1.75 billion Mexican sovereign deal in which the firm was able to persuade investors in May 1996 to swap Mexican Brady bonds collateralized with U.S. Treasury bonds (Mexican Bradys were a component of almost any emerging market portfolio until the 1994 crisis) for a thirty-year naked Mexican risk. This is in my reading quite a testimony to the aggressive innovations that characterize the financial markets and to the importance of a whole new subculture in international finance that facilitates the circulation, that is, sale, of these instruments.

21. For a more detailed account of these deals, see Sassen 2001, *The Global City: Part One,* and chapter 7.

22. See, for example, Biersteker, Hall, and Murphy, eds., *Private Authority and Global Governance*; Claire A. Cutler, Virginia Haufler, and Tony Porter, eds., *Private Authority in International Affairs* (Albany: SUNY Press, 1999); and Rodney Bruce Hall, "Private Authority in the Changing Structure of Global Governance." Presented at the workshop on "Private Authority and Interantional Order," Thomas J. Watson Institute for International Studies, Brown University, February 12–13, 1999.

23. Sassen, *Losing Control?*, chap. 2.

24. There is a wider systemic process here that needs to be distinguished from the effects of globalization. There is a worldwide and apparently growing distrust of governments and bureaucracies. Shapiro finds that this has contributed to the emergence of certain commonalities in law, notably the growing importance of constitutional individual rights that protect the individual from the state and other organizations. (Martin Shapiro, "The Globalization of Law," *Indiana Journal of Global Legal Studies*, vol. 1 [Fall, 1993]: 37–64.) The particular hallmark of American constitutionalism is constitutional judicial review, which now has also emerged endogenously in Germany and Italy, and to some extent even in France (where there now is an active constitutional court and a constitutional bill of rights). The Court of Justice of the EU has evolved into a constitutional court with human rights jurisdiction (which entailed that constitutions and rights had to come about in Europe). (Sassen, *Losing Control?* chapters 2 and 3). Some of the intellectual technology that Foucault noted governments have and allow them to control, i.e., governmentality, are now shifted to nonstate institutions. For a critique of the general notion of governance and liberal order, see Robert Latham, *The Liberal Moment: Modernity, Security, and the Making of Postwar International Order* (New York: Columbia University Press, 1997).

25. For an excellent examination of the question of space in this context, see Neil Brenner, "Global Cities, Glocal States: Global City Formation and State Territorial Restructuring in Contemporary Europe," *Review of International Political Economy*, vol. 5, no. 2 (1998): 1–37. For a theorized account of the spatialities and temporalities of the global, see Saskia Sassen, "Spatialities and Temporalities of the Global," *Public Culture*, vol. 12, no. 1 (Millenium Issue on Globalization, 2000).

26. This process of corporate integration should not be confused with vertical integration as conventionally defined. Gereffi's elaboration of Polany's commodity chains and Porter's value added chains also illustrate the difference between corporate integration at a world scale and vertical integration as conventionally defined.

27. See, e.g., Paul L. Knox and Peter J. Taylor, eds., *World Cities in a World-System* (Cambridge, UK: Cambridge University Press, 1995); Edna Bonacich, Lucie Cheng, Norma Chinchilla, Nora Hamilton, and Paul Ong, eds., *Global Production: The Apparel Industry in the Pacific Rim* (Philadelphia: Temple University Press, 1994); and F. Moulaert and A. J. Scott, *Cities, Enterprises and Society on the Eve of the 21st Century* (London and New York: Pinter, 1997).

28. See also John Allen, Doreen Massey, and Michael Pryke, eds., *Unsettling Cities* (London: Routledge, 1999); and Keil, Hitz, Ronneberger, Lehrer, Wolff, Schmid, eds., *Capitales Fatales* (Zurich: Rotpunkt Verlag, 1995).

29. These global control and command functions are partly embedded in national corporate structures but also constitute a distinct corporate subsector. This subsector can be conceived of as part of a network that connects global cities across the globe. In this sense, global cities are different from the old capitals of erstwhile empires, in that they are a function of crossborder networks rather than simply the most powerful city of an empire. There is, in my conceptualization, no such entity as a single global city as there could be a single capital of an empire; the category global city only makes sense as a component of a global network of strategic sites.

30. Sassen, *The Global City*.

CHAPTER 9

Finance in Politics:
An Epilogue to *Mad Money*

Susan Strange

Although analysts readily admit that international trade and investment have important implications for the distribution of wealth and
power among nations, no similar agreement exists regarding the significance of the international monetary system. [1]

So Bob Gilpin began the fourth chapter of *The Political Economy of International Relations*, titled "International Monetary Matters." He went on to say,

"A well-functioning monetary system is the crucial nexus of the international economy . . . a prerequisite for a prosperous world economy. . . . Money
and financial flows now dwarf trade flows and have become the most crucial
links among national economies. The efficiency and stability of the international monetary system, therefore, are major factors in the international
political economy." [2]

That was written more than a decade ago, in 1986. Gilpin argued that the
enhanced role of the international monetary system constituted "a virtual revolution in world politics." It was a revolution that almost no one else in international relations or even the international studies business recognized or wrote
about. A deafening silence followed Gilpin's clarion call. [3] One reason could
have been that he did not distinguish clearly between the "International monetary system" that governed exchange rates between national currencies, and
the "international financial system" that governed the creation, access to and
trade in credit. Indeed, only five out of more than fifty pages of the chapter
focus on what I have called the "financial structures" of political economy.
Since the public debate since the middle 1960s, and consequently the bulk of
the academic writing by economists and others, concentrated on the currency
and exchange rate issues and not on the organisation and management of
credit, it was hardly surprising that those five revolutionary pages got overlooked both by students and by Gilpin's colleagues in international relations. [4]

189

A glaring example of this bias was the earlier and influential work of Keohane and Nye, *Power and Interdependence*.[5] Although their comparative study of U.S.-Canadian and U.S.-Australian relations claimed it was focused on the two issue areas of money and oceans, the definition of the money issue area was not only state-centric to a degree but also narrowly confined to currency and exchange rate questions. There was nothing there about capital flows, nor about the informal "regime" governing the allocation of transnational credit.)

All the same, twelve years is a long time for a challenging pronouncement by an acknowledged leader in an academic discipline like Gilpin to go unremarked. How can we explain this long neglect; this long and deafening silence?

The answer seems to me to lie in the basic assumptions underlying the study of international relations, and in the related problematic that defines the discipline. The basic assumption is that world politics—international relations—are conceptually different from national/domestic politics, and must therefore be studied separately, preferable in separate departments of universities, or in separate courses of study. The assumption is taken directly from the international lawyers who early on argued that international law was different from municipal law in that it was not sustained by established political authority and stable institutions of juridical responsibility. It was fluid where municipal law was much more static. Much of it was "customary" law. The judgments of international courts, unlike those of national courts, could not always be enforced. If this was not the result of a state of anarchy in world politics, it was certainly the result of the lack of an overarching political authority sustaining international law.

Today, it is true, this sharp distinction between international law and domestic law, and, correspondingly, between international politics (including foreign policies) and domestic politics is being widely questioned.[6] The evidence of overlap and of reciprocal influence is abundant. What is still generally lacking is any explanatory theory for why this has happened; coining unlovely terms like *fragmegration* is no substitute for theory.[7]

Even more important in explaining the long neglect of the politics of the international financial system in the IR literature is the central problematic accepted by the great majority of contemporary scholars engaged in studying and teaching international relations/world politics. This central problematic is the prevalence of violent conflict and war between states. The historical background to this choice is important; the coincidence of mass slaughter in two world wars and an academic interest in questions of war and peace highlighted the importance of studying world politics. It also favored the realists of the 1930s[8] and the 1950s[9] (John Herz, Hans Morgenthau, and—most of all perhaps, Ken Waltz) over the idealists of the 1920s.[10]

Search the booklists of standard IR courses today and the absence of any discussion at all of international finance, how it works and is managed or mismanaged is striking. Check out the most used texts—Holsti,[11] Waltz,[12]

Maghoori and Romberg,[13] Aron,[14] Claude,[15] and Bull.[16] You will find in some of these texts appended chapters on transnational corporations, environmental and ethical issues, adding secondary actors to the cast-list of the state-centric system. You will not find analysis of the role of credit in the politics of the world market economy nor even of the politics of international financial relations.

Or search the extensive literature now devoted to theories of international relations. There is nothing there about the international financial structure and how it may affect the power and wealth of states. Yet there is the prime example of Japan, once perceived as the leader of a third economic bloc, challenging both the United States and Europe for leadership. What else but international finance accounts for the different perceptions of 1998: Japan as the weak link in the world market economy, dependent on support from the United States, its recovery from deep financial disorder delayed by its own political institutions. In recent months, I have searched this IR theory literature in vain for the slightest hint of concern about finance. There is none.[17]

Even the neogramscians and other critical theorists who are not usually inhibited when it comes to criticising the capitalist system have had astonishingly little to say about the role of finance, and financial policy, in deciding the who benefits? question at the heart of international political economy.

If the myopia of international relations theorists is derived from their obsession with the problematic of war and peace and conflict between states, the equal myopia of Western political theorists is derived from a similar obsession with values of political liberalism. Their current literature focusses a great deal on the nature, extent and promotion of democracy and liberty. Look in vain for any consideration of the structural power in democratic states based on the financial system which—as Polanyi clearly perceived[18]—could directly affect both the international political system—the gold standard—and the relative influence of social classes over domestic politics.

Other social scientists share the general myopia. David Landes, an historian of repute whose recent book, *The Wealth and Poverty of Nations*,[19] made a comparative historical study of societies and their success or failure in adopting or discovering new technologies. Much of the detail is fascinating. But the key question of how innovations were financed, and whether access to credit was a deciding factor is totally overlooked. And a social theorist, Francis Fukuyama, identified the key variable in societies as the level of trust developed between its members.[20] High-trust societies owed their advantage to social capital developed over time. Low-trust societies; lacking such social capital were conversely handicapped. But he too fails to ask whether the society did or did not develop the trust in the value and stability of money necessary between buyers and sellers, debtors and creditors.

The neglect is the more astonishing because it is contradicted by the everyday experiences of people. What is it that causes most conflict at every level of social interaction, from the family, to the village and the local sports club, up to the management of the city, the state, or international organizations? It is the control of money—whether cash or credit. Who gets to spend it and under what constraints. Is it you or I, wives ask, who manages the housekeeping budget, or who signs for the social security check? In the sports club, is it the members, or the club secretary and other paid employees, who decide between alternative uses of the funds? In national governments, it is Finance ministries that try to control the spending of other departments, and thus to determine the hierarchies within the national bureaucracy. It is they who govern if anyone does the raising of revenue, the state's access to other peoples' money by borrowing, and the discharge of debts. International institutions too experience their sharpest clashes over finance—whence it comes and where it goes.

Are these not all highly political issues? Why then are writers on international politics or national politics so perversely oblivious to them? The answer, as I have suggested elsewhere, is to be found in their narrow and constricting understanding of what constitutes politics, and of how and by whom power is exercised within society.[21] If you start from the assumption that politics is what politicians do, and that corporate politics or university politics don't count, you draw a restrictive line around the questions to be asked and investigated. Similarly, if you start from the assumption that power resides in resources, and overlook the kind of power derived from regimes or structures of political economy, you again draw a restrictive line around the questions to be asked and the methodology to be used in answering them. The conceptual wall that was built to define the study of international relations has become a prison wall putting key questions like the politics of the financial system off-limits in the study of international politics.

This is precisely what Kal Holsti has done in a brave attempt to get to grips with the problematic of change in the international system.[22] By defining that system as the way in which states relate to each other and conduct their business, he is unable to explain change, although he concedes that we live today in an era of profound change without having discovered a new way of seeing the world. He agrees with Ruggie that there is no consensus on what constitutes change, nor how to identify it.[23]

Peter Dombrowski is a writer who asserts the contrary: that there is a consensus. He concludes a long and exhaustive survey of the literature by writing, "researchers have reached a consensus on a number of key questions emerging from the increasing importance of international finance within the global economy."[24] One is that though capital mobility has greatly increased since the late 1960s, price and regulatory differentials still separate national financial markets. Second, the extent of regulatory or policy coordination between states "has been more limited than might be expected," so that despite liberalisation and deregulation, significant regulatory differences remain. Lastly, there is "some agreement" he finds, on the origins and management of financial crises, the relationship between states and financial markets, the role of finance in economic development and the interaction of financial markets and regulatory change. And the growing literature on international finance, he notes, is cumulative. That is, it slowly adds to our understanding of what is going on and why.

In fact, there is in reality wide *disagreement* on every one of these points. Some believe financial crises—the 1997 Asian crises, for example—were self-inflicted by incompetent and short-sighted national governments; others blame the external factors and actors which brought hot money flooding in and setting off financial bubbles that were bound to burst. Equally, there is disagreement on how such crises should be managed; whether rescue lifeboats are necessary because otherwise the repercussions of say, Indonesian bank failures will spread the contagion throughout the region and possibly to the whole world market economy. And while the IMF and most liberal economists see capital mobility in the system as enhancing competition and therefore efficiency, others argue that it has not been in the interest of developing countries. They would point to the two or three Asian countries that escaped the worst of the turmoil—China, Taiwan, and South Korea and find a common factor in their maintenance of exchange controls over financial transactions with the rest of the world.[25]

Hardly surprising, therefore, that the "lessons" Dombrowski draws from his wide-ranging survey are equally dubious. First, he says the state is not in retreat. "Even though globalized financial markets now appear beyond the control of individual states, states have not declined in significance." They have just changed their role to a more permissive one and changed the way they operate in the financial system. That seems to me to be a retreat before the power of markets and financial operators. And if ever there was a description of the structural power of beliefs and ideas in political economy, this is surely it. It was not the power of the United States or the IMF that persuaded France or Germany to privatize, to deregulate and to liberalize their financial markets. It was structural change in the world market economy, the imperative of competition for market shares and underlying change in the knowledge structure, reflected then in the power of the financial structure.

Students will find Dombrowski's bibliography useful, even though it is heavily weighted toward economists and U.S.-published books and journals and toward the international monetary system rather than the financial system. Non-Americans—Phil Cerny, Geoffrey Underhill, Stuart Corbridge, and Susan Strange—however, get credit for their work. Randall Germain's recent seminal book should be added, precisely because it deals in historical perspective with the relations of state authority and financial markets.[26] These works suggest that the neglect of finance noted earlier has been more marked in the U.S. literature on international political economy than in the European. Perhaps the prevailing ideology of liberal economics in America has something to do with this?

In short, both of Dombrowski's conclusions are complete rubbish. There is no consensus and no clear cumulative lessons to be drawn from the work surveyed about the power of states and other authorities in relation to financial markets.

Keynes, Baqehot, and Soros

The most amazing omission in all this is the work of John Maynard Keynes. After all, it was Keynes who developed the only coherent, rigorous, and influential theory concerning the conduct of financial markets. His *General Theory* influenced generations of economists, and still does despite the counterinfluence of Friedman and Hayek.[27] In fact, the *General Theory* is more of a sociological theory than a purely economic one, even though it argues in economic terms and draws on empirical economic data. Keynes's target was not capitalism per se; it was the capitalists who ran the system. When financial markets collapsed and profits fell, these capitalists lost their nerve. They lost their "animal spirits" as Keynes put it. They went, suddenly and disruptingly, from illogical optimism to deepest pessimistic gloom. Drunken sailors one minute; terrified rabbits the next. Market opportunities beckoned, but were ignored. The only remedy for the real economy was state intervention to restore demand and therefore economic growth.

Keynes's work had popular appeal partly because it drew on homely analogies familiar to most of his readers. He explained the illogical behaviour of the markets by drawing an analogy with the competitions run by newspapers in the 1930s to build circulation. Readers were shown pictures of pretty girls. They were asked to pick the prettiest. But the winner was not the best objective judge of beauty or sex appeal. Nor was it the entry closest to others' judgment of the prettiest. Rather, it was the entry reflecting what other entrants thought other entrants would put down. This, Keynes said, was how financial markets behaved. They did not respond to objective truths, nor to prevailing opinions about objective truth. They reacted to perceptions of how others perceived the likely behavior of the markets.[28]

A nearly forgotten elaboration of Keynes's analysis was the work of Hyman Minsky in his "Financial Instability Hypothesis," written in the 1930s, reprinted in 1982 and rediscovered after the 1987 stockmarket collapse.

> Prices of capital assets depend on current views of future profits flows and the current subjective view placed upon the insurance embodied in money or quick cash; these current views depend upon the expectations that are held about the future development of the economy.[29]

A source which surely influenced Keynes's thinking but is also ignored in Dombrowski's survey is that of Walter Bagehot, the long-time editor of *The Economist* before the first world war and author of *Lombard Street*.[30] Bagehot closely observed the relations between state authority, as exercised over banks in the City of London chiefly by the Bank of England and the House of Commons. His comments on the fall of Overend Gurney in the aftermath of the American Civil War and the reasons why the Bank of England allowed it to fall highlight the very similar difficult choices faced by regulators today—including the Federal Reserve, the European central banks or the Bank of Japan. To let a big bank fail threatens to destabilize the entire financial market; to rescue it, enhances the moral hazard problem, encouraging others to think they can pursue profit at the expense of security.

Bagehot's judgments were not always the conventional ones. These were that the swift rescue of Barings in 1890 was necessary because Barings was not insolvent but merely illiquid and its failure would have had major repercussions for the City and the whole world system of credit. Overend Gurney, however was simply insolvent. It had lent too much and unwisely—even dishonestly and there was no way it could have met its commitments. But while not dissenting from this fundamental point, Bagehot thought there was a bit more to the two cases than met the eye. Baring's Argentine partners had been callously abandoned, sacrificed to City interests, and the rescue had well served the latter's interest by reinforcing the existing structures of power in London and increasing the Bank of England's control over the joint stock banks. Allowing Overend Gurney to go down too was not a simple case of exercising regulatory discipline over a bad bank. Overend Gurney was an inconvenient competitor for commercial business important to the Bank of England; letting it fail while supporting the rest of the system was not simply an impartial regulatory act. In both cases, therefore, motivations were mixed; preferences multiple and complex.[31]

Finally, I would direct Dombrowski's myopic vision to the contribution of George Soros. Like Bagehot, Soros is no professional academic but an observer of—and a successful player—in the financial market game. But his analysis of *why* financial markets behave as they do is actually more profound and radical than Keynes's explanation. Soros claims that it is derived from his studying with Karl Popper at the LSE in the 1950s; I would say it is much more based on direct personal experience and reflection.

The basic concept he calls the "reflexive principle."[32] This is what fundamentally distinguishes natural from social science. In (most) natural science, theory is based on objective observation of the subject matter, which remains unaware and unmoved by the research. The behavior of variable stars is a good example. But in social science, in Soros's estimation, a reflexive principle is at work, whereby the object of the research—financial markets, say—reacts to the opinions expressed by researchers and other observers; while, conversely, the researchers react to the behaviour of the markets. This cannot be properly described as objective science. An aspiration to scientific objectivity, or at least impartiality between vested interests may still be desirable and achievable. But a truly scientific result is not. Good-bye, social science, and the scientific study of society, national or international. Welcome, the necessary and welcome practice of multidisciplinary social studies including international studies.

The Implicit Theories in Mad Money

Having briefly justified my preferred sources for the study of international finance, it is time to explain why I think of *Casino Capitalism,* supplemented by *Mad Money,* as containing within them important contributions to the neglected role of credit and finance in the international political economy. They are rather more than analytical surveys of change in the world's system. Perhaps they are a bit like those children's comic-book puzzles in which the reader had to try to find the cat, the rabbit, the fox, and the dog hidden in the foliage of a forest scene. A quick glance may not reveal them. But they are still there for the careful observer.

Some of the theoretical implications of both books are already apparent in *Casino Capitalism.*[33] *Mad Money,*[34] which takes the story on from the mid-1980s, asks the questions what changed and what was still the same?, and in answering adds further theoretical implications and conclusions. One important one is that both political theory and economic theory have ignored the power of technological change—and have impoverished and crippled all of social science in doing so. In international political economy, the omission is particularly disabling, for technological change, more than anything else, has driven change in the structures of power.[35] It has certainly changed the financial structure, as explained in chapter 2 of *Mad Money).* And it has changed the production structure by shifting power over trade and production from governments to firms. Because it is firms—including financial enterprises—who have developed the new technologies, the knowledge structure (as described in *States and Markets*[36]) has also been changed. In the postwar decades and for much of the Cold War, technology was led and directed by states . By the 1990s, it was led and directed from the private sector—Microsoft, for example. Important for theory here is the tendency of technological change to accelerate, and to spread more easily over economic and political space.

You will not find much about the technology factor either in political theory nor economic theory. Both tend to take it for granted and to ignore the dynamism that produces ripples of change throughout the world economy. What there is, comes from observers of science policy[37] and from totally new directions. For example, John de la Mothe and Gilles Paquet both of Universite d' Ottawa are editing a new series, published by Pinter, showing how science and technology are shaping the world economy. Business schools and policy analysts are more aware of this than conventional social scientists.

The other thing that has changed from the earlier period is the involvement of organized crime in the international financial system. Of course, there have always been criminals active in financial markets,[38] some of them respected pillars of society. Organized crime is different. Large, rich transnational networks flushed with profits from the international trade in drugs, arms, and illegal immigrants emerged during the 1980s as big players in international finance. Their operations were the basis for a boom in the business of money laundering—the conversion of dirty money derived from crime into untraceable, legitimate investment funds. Because organized crime has developed from mafias, especially the United States and Italian mafias, it has not functioned like other economic enterprises. Secrecy between its members has protected it from state authority.[39] The obligation not to bear witness against fellow members—the principle of *omerta*—protected the Sicilians against prosecution until in 1993 the Italian law was changed, making membership a criminal offense.[40]

The theoretical implication of the closer links between finance and crime, however, go deeper, into the structures of power in the international political economy. *Mad Money* identifies three structural features that not only allowed but encouraged these links. One was the strong demand for hallucinatory drugs in the rich countries. Second was the ready supply from poor ones—Colombia, Burma, Afghanistan. In the 1960s and 1970s, the developed countries had steadfastly refused UNCTAD pleas to apply the principles of agricultural support and protection that they used at home to support and protect export crops produced by developing countries poor returns for coffee, tobacco, sugar, and so on compared with high returns from growing cannabis and opium and processing the material for the eager market. And third was the amazingly permissive market for transnational banking services, including the laundering of dirty money. *Mad Money* argues that the ideational sources of the permissiveness lie in the ambivalence of capitalist systems toward the "learned professions." This permissiveness allowed bankers and accountants to share with priests the privileges of client confidentiality. Banks and tax havens have exploited this privilege, and in doing so have punched a big hole in the governance system of international finance.

Nor was it the only one. A major change, noted in *Mad Money,* has been the change in the role of banks, and the diffusion of financial service business to all sorts of new players. The business of banking used to be what was called intermediation—that is the bank intermediated profitably between the wish of savers to lend money profitably and the interest of borrowers to make use of OPM (other people's money). Their profit was the price difference to the savers and the borrowers. Liberalization of financial markets going back to the

Eurodollar story in the 1960s, increased competition between banks and cut profit margins. (Liberal economic theory fell into the error that competition necessarily lowered prices to the customer. Not so in banking; it induced bankers to take bigger risks[41]).

The policy implications of this change are far-reaching. They have been denied by conventional writers. Ethan Kapstein, for example, wrote in the mid-199Os that the system was secure because it was regulated both at the national level by central banks and other regulatory bodies, and at the international level by cooperative accords reached through the Bank for International Settlements in Basle, and the International Monetary Fund in Washington.[42] But subsequent research has revealed the fallacies in this comfortable belt-and-braces analysis.[43] Globalization of finance has poked big holes in national regulatory systems and bankers and others have not been slow to use them. Everywhere, these systems have been eroded to the point where they no longer deter nor control.[44] As for the international accords, the evidence again suggests that they are no longer effective. The BIS in 1996 abandoned its efforts to impose common capital-loan ratios on banks worldwide, deciding to leave the consequent risk-management to the banks themselves to take care of.[45]

The theoretical implications are even more far-reaching. Economic and social theories of regulation make the assumption that regulation has a clear purpose—to reduce pollution for example, or to protect consumers against monopoly pricing—and that the market and its operators to be regulated are clearly defined.[46] These assumptions no longer hold for financial services. Where banking used to be clearly defined and its essence was intermediation of OPM, so that the banker was not himself risking capital, the present competitive market for financial services, in which banks compete with nonbanks, and in which they are tempted to bet their own as well as their clients' money, is poorly defined. That, essentially, is why the Basle rules were abandoned and the prudential role left to the managers of banks themselves.

States' Role in Globalization

Perhaps least obvious of the theoretical implications of the two studies are those concerning the role of states in the liberating the forces of globalization. A lot of the literature on globalization has presented the power of states as being under threat from the forces of the market. The alternative view, tenaciously held by realists in IR and some economists, is that the erosion of state power has been exaggerated and that the changes encapsulated in the term *globalization* have not been nearly so great as the opposing school asserts.

Although it was never explicitly stated, the resolution of this important disagreement lies in the attention given in both my books to decisions and nondecisions. They are picked out for their longer-term effects on the structures of the world economy. *Casino Capitalism* chose just five decisions or nondecisions that seemed to have contributed to the heightened volatility in financial and other markets that was the leitmotiv of the whole study. They were, first, the refusal of Europeans to accept more equal burden-sharing with the Americans for the costs of Western defense and particularly NATO. Second and third were the rich countries' refusal to undertake redistributive UN aid, and the decision to opt for case-by-case, ad hoc treatment of sovereign debt.[47] Fourth, was the failure to make and keep rules about subsidized export credits; and fifth was the British Labour government's decision to reopen the City of London for international financial business.

These were all early postwar decisions. I added five more critical political choices taken in the later period 1971–1985. Briefly, these were the U.S. withdrawal from foreign exchange markets in the mid-1970s; the cynical pantomime (as I called it) of continued discussion on international monetary reform in the 1960s; American refusal after the oil-price rise in 1973 to negotiate with the oil-producing states; and the stonewalling strategy chosen by Washington to deal with the French-led Conference on International Economic Co-operation (CIEC) in 1974. The only positive key decision was the U.S. response to bank failures—the Franklin National Bank and Bankhaus Herstatt, both in 1974.

Note that all these key decisions were decisions of state policy-makers—mainly but not all, American. That was also true of the key decisions picked out as important in *Mad Money*. In 1987, the stockmarket crash in October of that year might have led the U.S. authorities to reimpose stricter rules on share dealing, insider trading, entry conditions, and so forth. It did not. The light stayed green for deregulation and liberalization not just in the United States but in competing markets in London, Europe, Tokyo, and the markets emerging in the developing world. Second, in 1988, there was a positive decision on the regulation of banks. The Bank for International Settlements (BIS), led by the United States and supported by Britain, adopted to 8:1 capital-assets ratio. Third, came the decisions following the fall of the Berlin Wall and the collapse of the Soviet rule in central Europe. Germany unilaterally decided to reunite east with west Germany but all the other decisions were negative. Fourth, was the reversal in 1996 of the Basel Accord on capital-assets ratios, already referred to. Fifth, was the response of the United States, the IMF, and the Group of Ten to the turmoil in Asian currency and investment markets in the summer and autumn of 1997. Even when it meant rescuing insolvent banks in Mexico or in Asia, the security of the system took precedence in policy making over the principles of bank regulation.

In a nutshell, it was the governments of states—especially that of the United States—that decided in favor of deregulation and globalization. Sometimes pushed by market forces, they still had freedom of choice, and by and large opted to give way, rather than resist. If this caused problems for them later, it was their own doing, their choice.

We are back, therefore, with the old International Relations question of the national interest. Looking after national interests is the responsibility of national governments. But who decides what policies are in the national interest? History gives us many examples of states choosing policies supposedly in the national interest, but which in fact were chosen to serve the interests of social, political, or economic elites, and burdened society in general with high costs and risks that could hardly be avoided. What we have to ask, therefore, is whether, and how far, the decisions and nondecisions taken by the United States were really in the long-term interests of the American people or whether, and how far, they served the vested interests of Wall Street and big business.

This is not a new question. History has many examples of national policies serving special interests. The British government decision in the mid-nineteenth century, after the Indian Mutiny, to take over government from the East India Company might be one example. This clearly served the interests of British traders in India, opened new career possibilities in the army and civil service for the younger sons of an expanding British middle class and added imperial glamor to the monarchy—"the brightest jewel in the imperial crown." But the longer-run consequences for the British economy and society generally were negative. The British education system was shaped to produce young colonial administrators, rather than the technologically trained industrial managers produced in Germany.[48] The Indian tail came to wag the British dog, despite the subordination of Indian trade and production to British interests and the extraction of gold to finance persistent payments deficits.[49]

A comparable case would be the French decision to annex Algeria and to use it as a cheap way of rewarding underpaid French army veterans with land taken from the locals—a policy first practised systematically by the Romans. Although special state and economic interests benefited, the end result was the creation of the "pieds noirs"—the settlers who bitterly resisted de Gaulle's decision to give Algeria its independence, cutting the material and human losses to French society.

Another might be the American decision, first taken by Kennedy, to intervene with "military advisers" in Vietnam. Military and ideological interests were given priority in the name of containment and the U.S. national interest in resisting communism. But the cost and the involvement escalated under Johnson to the point where American society, seeing no national interest worth pursuing, turned against the Vietnam War.

And a more recent one might be Chancellor Kohl's unilateral decision on German unification after 1989. His decision found widespread popular support. But was it really in the long-term national interest of west German citizens? It was certainly very costly for west German taxpayers, particularly when Kohl insisted against the advice of the central bank on an exchange rate of 1:1 between west and east German currencies. And who benefited? German (and some foreign) companies who were given protection and generous state subsidies to expand in the new Lander; a miscellany of administrators, employed east German workers, west German academics, and others who climbed on the unification bandwagon. History and sentiment assured popular support. But was it really a rational choice?

One could go back through history collecting more of the same: the British rejection of autonomy for the American colonies, the Spanish and Portuguese invasions of south America in search of gold and silver, and many, many more. Moreover, ideas and ideologies—"manifest destiny," "the white man's burden," "la mission civilisatrice," "the final triumph of socialism worldwide"— have often served to veil the conflict between special and national interests. In the period covered by *Mad Money*, the concealing ideology has been that of liberal economics and specifically, monetarism and supply-side economic logic. The failures of Soviet planning and the successes of U.S. capitalism carried the message to the developing countries and then to the ex-socialist ones.

American Decline?

It is hardly necessary, in view of the record since the mid 1980s, to reiterate the point that the power of the United States, far from declining as conventional American thinking had it in the 1980s, is greater than ever, and that there is growing asymmetry between the structural power of U.S. decision-making over the world economy (and especially the financial system) and that of other states has greatly increased. The United States is more powerful; they are less powerful. *The Retreat of the State*, therefore, is imposed on most national societies, but is self-imposed on U.S. society. Joseph Nye's notion of the "soft power" of the United States in the world is not wrong, but still distorts the truth, which is that there is nothing very soft about the way U.S. administrations can take unilateral decisions affecting others, military or monetary, with immunity.[50] Most of such decisions, we have seen, have enhanced the power of market forces, increasing volatility and uncertainty. But some have also been consciously system-preserving, imposing reregulation rather than deregulation, and undertaking new costs and responsibilities in the interests of global financial stability rather than simply the shorter-term interests of the U.S. economy and its taxpayers.

This ambiguity in U.S. policies toward the international financial system—permissive in some directions, reregulatory in others—reflects in miniature the continuing but ill-founded controversy over globalization. Is it real or a myth? The clear conclusion to be drawn from the evidence in *Mad Money* is that globalization is real. It can be exaggerated, but change there undoubtedly has been. State power, on the other hand, still exists and can be—and has been—used to limit the local consequences of globalization. The erosion of national controls over banks and nonbanks,[51] however, shows that this state power is increasingly shared with markets, enterprises and nonstate authorities.[52]

But the evidence also shows the wide diversity of experience—for states and governments, for enterprises and for social classes. The theoretical implication is clear: the search for general theories is a vain one. Social scientists—and especially economists—have always hoped to find such general theories—theories of economic growth and development, theories of the business cycle, theories of the firm, theories of inflation. A recent study in international political economy by Jonathan Nitzan has explained why such hopes were always vain and exposed the hollowness of theoretical pretensions in economics.[53] Nitzan argues that economists always left the power of capital out the picture. It could not be accommodated in the logic of liberal economics; and no agreed definition of what constituted capital was therefore possible among economists. Without an agreed definition, no general theory could be found. Nitzan, interestingly, draws inspiration from Thorstein Veblen and Lewis Mumford, arguing that the power of capital is not a constant. Rather, the differential power of capital (DPK) and variations in the rate of differential accumulation (DA) help explain the widening rich-poor gap in incomes and the progressively higher returns in the United States to financial business than to manufacturing or agriculture.

In their vain search for general theories, social scientists have for a long time put great faith in the value of quantitative data. The more, the better. Both *Casino Capitalism* and *Mad Money* poured cold water on such hopes. The earlier work introduced the concept of the "areas of significant ignorance" developing in international finance. As capital became more and more mobile across national jurisdictions, regulatory authorities had less and less reliable information about behavior in financial markets and about the effectiveness—or otherwise—of government fiscal and monetary interventions. The evidence in *Mad Money* strongly suggests that the areas of significant ignorance are even more extensive today than they were in the mid-1980s.

Bad Theory Misleads Policy

To sum up, the description of change in international finance does not merely show there is very little good theory to discover. It shows that there is a lot of bad theory out there that continues to dominate research agendas and

teaching practices. Students should be warned against these bad theories. They
may choose to disregard the warnings for career reasons, or they may cling to
them in desperation as drowning men clutch at straws. In the United States
especially, researchers are told that you must find an hypothesis and proceed to
test it against the available data. This imperative derives from Karl Popper who
defined a theory as a proposition that could be falsified.[54] The alternative
approach to research—generally ignored in contemporary social science—was
that of Feyerabend. In *Against Method*,[55] this eccentric writer argued that all you
needed for research was a good question. Forget theory. Ibn Khaldun in North
Africa in the fourteenth century would have agreed. His question was, simply,
"Why and how are things as they are?"

Two examples of bad theory, leading to counterproductive policy decisions were, first, the theories of declining U.S. power just mentioned; and, second, theories of the beneficent effects of capital mobility.

Belief in the decline of U.S. power dominated American thinking in the
1970s and 1980s. Paul Kennedy's *Rise and Fall of the Great Powers*[56] and a number of other works promoted the idea that hegemonic power in the international system was fated to be temporary, either because of military overcom-
mitment[57] or because of the economic burdens of maintaining stability in the
world trade and finance. Events reinforced academic interpretation: the Americans were shocked by the oil-price rise engineered by OPEC, by the fall of the
Shah of Iran, by the depreciation of the dollar, and the loss of export and manufacturing production share to Japan.

But the policies adopted in accord with the theory were often—not
always—counterproductive and contrary to U.S. long-term interests. "Strategic" trade policies designed to promote U.S. exports and protect U.S. industry
from Asian competition meant adopting bullying tactics—as in the Super 301
programme—not only toward Japan but generally to Europeans, Latin Americans, and other allies. The Cold War had suppressed resentment. When it ended,
the legitimacy of U.S. structural power was damaged.

The other example of bad theory leading to counterproductive policy is
much more controversial. The theory plays a central role in liberal economics.
It holds that the market economy requires the free, unobstructed movement of
capital to achieve the efficient allocation of resources, from which all will benefit. In the last decade, country after country has appeared to subscribe to that
belief by opening its economy to foreign capital. They did so not only because
many of their policy makers came to accept liberal economic theory, but pragmatically to gain and hold market share with the help of foreign firms who
brought access to capital, new technology and access to rich-country markets.[58]
And they did not always distinguish between opening up to foreign investors
in long-term production and foreign investors looking for short-term speculative gains.

The most coherent, radical attack on the theory is to be found in a recent fifty-page UNDP monograph by the British economist John Eatwell. He challenges the validity of every theoretical claim made for the liberalization of capital as being contrary to the experience of countries that have obediently liberalized.[59] The clear conclusion is that theory has led to bad policy. First, he says, theory argues that markets will efficiently allocate capital from capital rich-economies to capital-poor ones. In fact, capital moves in the opposite direction, from poor countries to rich ones. Second, liberalization in theory would lower costs to borrowers. In fact, the borrowers have paid and the lenders have profited. Third, the theory praised the market for discovering derivatives and other devices for moderating risk. But in fact, the growth of derivatives has created new systemic risks unforeseen in theory. Fourth, the more efficient allocation of capital and other resources predicted by theory should have resulted in faster growth and more investment. It has not. Fifth and last, theory promised that the discipline of market forces would force states into policies that would promote both growth and stability. It has not done so.

Eatwell points out that none of these theoretical claims were reflected in the Bretton Woods agreement to maintain fixed exchange rates between national currencies. That was conditional on national currencies becoming by the late 1950s freely convertible with each other for current account transactions, not for transactions on the capital account. Thus, it was assumed states would keep exchange controls over capital coming in, and going out of the country. American financial and business interests, however, had other ideas. They sought freedom to produce and sell goods in Europe, and did not want exchange controls to stop them. The result was a revision of Bretton Woods rules to allow convertibility—and therefore IMF help—for countries (like Britain) with problems arising on the capital account as well as on the current account.[60]

By comparing the theoretical claims with actual experience over the last two or three decades, Eatwell arrives at the conclusion that the theory, far from producing greater efficiency and stability in the world economy, has resulted in policies that greatly increased its fragility. That fragility, he suggests, is manifest in four ways. The liquidity crises—as in Asia—actually cut GNP, lose jobs, and choke food supplies. Second, higher risks in the market sectors increases the bias toward short-term responses rather than productive long-term ones. Third, increased risks to states produces a deflationary bias in policy making. And fourth, market operators aware of the fragility of local currencies and markets, press for greater ease of exit—flexibility, which in effect relieves them of the costs of their own risk-taking.

The two examples are enough to reiterate Robert Cox's point that theory is always *for* someone. U.S. decline suited interests that wanted U.S. power to be used to open Japan's domestic markets to American competition. Liberal economic theories about the beneficent effects of financial liberalization for developing as well as developed economies suited Wall Street and its associated financial elites.

The Asian story also reinforces the contention that the pursuit of a general theory is futile. The only common feature in Asia in 1997 was the fatal combination of external pressures on Asian states to liberalize too fast and the weakness of state regulation and supervision of banks. Beyond that, the experience of China and Taiwan was quite different from that of Indonesia or Thailand. Explanatory theory should say why this was.

Eatwell concludes by asking the So What? question: If liberal theory has misled policy makers, what is to be done to save the international financial system from the consequences? It is a question neither economists nor other social scientists should ignore. They have a social responsibility—the price of academic freedom—to enlighten, to explain, and to prescribe if they can. Yet, although expectations of a bear market in shares, even of an ensuing decade of world recession, have grown, there has been a curious absence of serious academic discussion of measures that might be taken, even now, to avert or to moderate the downturn. Yet a number of proposals have been made, independently of others. Some, like the Tobin tax on foreign exchange transactions, have been debated. Others, like Soros's idea of a voluntary insurance fund for international banks, have not. Such free and open discussion can only be arranged by academics—national and international officials and market operators both have too many interests and prejudices to protect. And although academic debate by itself rarely changes the basic ideas—whether pro-market or pro-state—that at any time dominate the knowledge structure, academic debate when it takes place against a background of growing disillusion, of doubt and uncertainty can act as a catalyst to action.

Notes

1. Gilpin, Robert, *The Political Economy of International Relations* (Princeton, NJ: Princeton University Press, 1987), p. 118.

2. Gilpin, *Political Economy of International Relations*, p. 118.

3. My own work (Strange, Susan, *Casino Capitalism* [Oxford: Basil Blackwell 1986, reprinted 1997—Manchester University Press]) came out after Gilpin's big textbook. It evolved from earlier work on the pound sterling, S. Strange, *Sterling and British Policy* (London: Oxford University Press, 1971) and on international monetary and financial history in the 1960s (Strange, S., International Monetary Relations, vol. 2 of Schonfield, A., *International Economic Relations of the Western World 1959–71* [Oxford: Oxford University Press, 1976]). Its basic assumptions were the same as Gilpin's. And it suggested some prototheoretical hypotheses about the causes and consequences of Gilpin's "virtual revolution."

4. Gilpin, *Politial Economy of International Relations*, pp. 118–123.

5. Keohane, R. O. and Nye, J. S., *Power and Interdependence: World Politics in Transition* (Boston: Little, Brown, 1977).

6. Keohane and Milner (1996), *Internationalization and Domestic Politics* (Cambridge: Cambridge University Press); and Rosenau, James N., *Along the Domestic-Foreign Frontier: Exploring Governance in a Turbulent World* (Cambridge: Cambridge University Press, 1997).

7. Rosenau, J. N., *Along the Domestic-Foreign Frontier* (Cambridge: Cambridge University Press, 1997).

8. Carr, E. H., *The Twenty Years' Crisis, 1919–1939: An Introduction to the Study of International Relations* (London: Macmillan, 1939); Schwarzenberger, G., *Power Politics: A Study of World Society* (New York: F. A. Praeger, 1941); and Schumann, F., *International Politics* (New York: McGraw-Hill, 1933), among others.

9. Herz, J. H. *Political Realism and Political Idealism* (Chicago: Chicago University Press, 1951); Morgenthau, H. J. (1954) *Politics among Nations: The Struggle for Power and Peace* (New York: Knopf, 1948); and, most particularly, Waltz, K. N., *Man, the State and War* (New York: Columbia University Press, 1959).

10. Waltz's first and in the long run most influential work, *Man, the State and War* (1959) posed the basic question whether wars were caused by human nature, by the character of states claiming territorial sovereignty or by the system of states that ensured competition between them for power and wealth. As Waltz concluded, "war will be perpetually associated with the existence of separate sovereign states . . . there exists no consistent reliable process of reconciling the conflict of interest that inevitable arise among similar units in conditions of anarchy" (Waltz, 1959; p. 238). His later book, *Theory of International Politics* (1979) did not alter his basic realist assumptions, nor his essentially state-centric conception of world politics. (See his 1993 interview by Fred Halliday and Justin Rosenberg, *Review of International Studies*, July 1998; pp. 371–386.)

11. Holsti, K. J., *International Politics: A Framework for Analysis* (Englewood Cliffs, NJ: Prentice-Hall, 1967).

12. Waltz, Kenneth, *Theory of International Politics* (Reading: Addison-Wesley, 1979).

13. Maghoori, Ray and Romberg, Bennet (eds.), *Globalism versus Realism: International Relations' Third Great Debate* (Boulder, CO: Westview Press, 1982).

14. Aron, Raymond (trans. R. Howard & A. Baker), *Peace and War: A Theory of International Politics* (New York: Praeger, 1968).

15. Claude, Inis, L., *Power and International Relations* (New York: Random House, 1962).

16. Bull, Hedley, *The Anarchical Society* (London: Macmillan, 1977).

17. See, for example, Dyer, H. C., and Mangasarian, Loen (eds.), *The Study of International Relations; The State of the Art* (London: Macmillan, 1989); Smith, S. (ed.), *International Relations; British and American Perspectives* (Oxford: Blackwell, 1985); Smith, S. and Booth, K. (eds.), *International Relations Theory Today* (Cambridge: Polity, 1995); Smith, S., Booth, K., and Zalewski, M. (eds.) (1996) *International Theory; Positivism and Beyond* (Cambridge: Cambridge University Press, 1995); Groom, J. and Light, M. (eds.), *Contemporary International Relations: A Guide to Theory* (London: Pinter, 1994); Brown, C., *International Relations Theory: New Normative Approaches* (Hemel Hempstead: Harvester, 1992); Knutsen, T., *A History of International Relations Theory* (Manchester: Manchester University Press, 1992); Guzzini, S., *Realism in International Relations and International Political Economy* London, Routledge, 1998).

18. Polanyi, Karl, *The Great Transformation: The Political and Economic Origins of Our Time* (Boston: Beacon Press, 1957).

19. Landes, D., *The Wealth and Poverty of Nations* (London: Little, Brown, 1998).

20. Fukuyama, Francis, *Trust: The Social Virtues and the Creation of Prosperity* (London: Hamish Hamilton, 1995).

21. Strange, Susan, *The Retreat of the State: the Diffusion of Power in the World Economy* (Cambridge: Cambridge University Press, 1996), chaps. 2 and 3.

22. Holsti, K. (1998) "*The Problem of Change in International Relations Theory*," draft paper for the ISA-ECPR conference, Vienna, September 1998.

23. Holsti (1998); and Ruggie, J., "Territoriality and Beyond: Problematising Modernity in International Relations" *International Organization,* vol. 47, no. 4 (1993): 139–174.

24. Dombrowski, P., "Haute Finance and High Theory; Recent Scholarship on Global Financial Relations." *Mershon International Studies Review,* vol. 42, supplement 1 (1998): 1–28.

25. For the Asian perspective on the crisis, see Richard Higgott, "The Asian Economic Crisis: A Study in the Politics of Resentment." *Centre for the Study of Globalization and Regionalization Working Paper* 02/98, University of Warwick, March 1998.

26. Germain, R. (1997) *The International Organisation of Credit: States and Global Finance in the World Economy,* Cambridge University Press.

27. Keynes, J. M. (1936), *General Theory of Employment, Interest and Money* (London: Macmillan, 1936)

28. This was explained in *Casino Capitalism,* which also discusses the criticism of the Oxford economist, S. H. Frankel and the connection with Georg Simmel's philosophical analysis of the role of money in society (Strange, Susan, *Casino Capitalism* [Manchester: Manchester University Press, 2nd ed., 1997], p. 133 and following). The previous chapter had also referred to the seminal work of Frank Knight in distinguishing between actuarial risks that could be calculated and business risks which were, essentially, bets in the dark which often resulted in loss rather than profit to the entrepreneur.

29. Minsky, H., *Can it Happen Again? Essays on Instability and Finance* (Armonk, NY: M. E. Sharpe. 1982), p. 8.

30. Bagehot, W., *Lombard Street* (London, 1873).

31. See Cain, P. and Hopkin, A. (1993) *British Imperialism: Innovation and Expansion*, vol. 1, 1688–1914 (New York: Longman, 1993), pp. 153–160, on which I have drawn heavily for this paragraph. Their study of the changing role of the City of London in British domestic and foreign policy, and the emergence of what they call the "gentlemanly capitalists" in London as the driving force behind British imperialism is a fine exercise in multidisciplinary international political economy based on detailed and perceptive use of historical material.

32. Soros, G. (1987, 1994) *The Alchemy of Finance: Reading the Mind of the Market* (London: Wiley, 1997), esp. chap. 1.

33. Strange, S., *Casino Capitalism* (Oxford, Basil Blackwell, 1986) (Manchester: Manchester University Press, 1997).

34. Strange, S. *Mad Money* (Manchester: Manchester University Press, 1998).

35. Stopford J. and Strange, S., *Rival States, Rival Firms: Competition for World Market Shares* (Cambridge: Cambridge University Press, 1991).

36. Strange, Susan, *States and Markets: An Introduction to International Politics* (London: Pinter Publishers, 1988).

37. Freeman, C., "Networks of Innovators, A Synthesis of Research Issues," *Research Policy*, vol. 20, no. 5 (1991): 499–514; Pavitt, K. L. R. and Soete, L., "International Differences in Economic Growth and the International Location of Innovation," in H. Giersch (ed.) *Emerging Technologies: Consequences for Economic Growth, Structural Change and Employment* (Tubingen: J. C. B. Mohr, 1982).

38. Strange, Susan, *Mad Money* (Manchester: Manchester University Press, 1998).

39. Paoli, L, *The Pledge of Secrecy: Culture, Structure and Action of Mafia Associations*, unpublished Ph.D. thesis, European University Institute, Florence.

40. Strange, *Mad Money*, p. 128.

41. Strange, *Mad Money*, chap. 8.

42. Kapstein, Ethan B., *Governing the Global Economy: International Finance and the State* (Cambridge, MA: Harvard University Press, 1994).

43. Strange, *Mad Money*, chap. 9.

44. Story, J. and Walter, I., *Political Economy of financial integration in Europe; The Battle of the Systems* (Manchester University Press, 1997).

45. Strange, *Mad Money*, chap. 9.

46. Majone, G., "The Rise of the Regulatory State in Europe," *West European Politics*, vol. 17, no. 3 (1994): 77–101.

47. Strange, *Casino Capitalism*, pp. 31–58; and Strange, *Mad Money*, pp. 5–6.

48. Barnett, Correlli, *The Audit of Power: The Illusion and Reality of Britain as a Great Nation* (London: Macmillan, 1986); and Zinkin, Maurice, *Britain and India* (London: Chatto and Windus, 1964).

49. Kenwood A. G. and Loughheed, A. L., *The Growth of the International Economy, 1820–1980* (London: George Allen and Unwin, 2nd ed., 1983); and de Cecco, M. *Money and Empire: The International Gold Standard, 1890–1914* (Oxford: Blackwell, 1974).

50. Nye, J., *Bound to Lead: The Changing Nature of American Power* (New York: Basic Books, 1990).

51. Strange, *Mad Money*, chap. 8.

52. Strange, Susan, *The Retreat of the State: The Diffusion of Power in the World economy* (Cambridge: Cambridge University Press, 1996).

53. Nitzan, J. (1998). "Differential Accumulation: Towards a New Political Economy of capital." *Review of International Poitical Economy*, vol. **5**, no. 2 (1998): 169–216.

54. Popper, Karl, *Objective Knowledge* (Oxford: Oxford University Press, 1972).

55. Feyerabend, P., *Against Method* (London: NLB, 1975 and 1988).

56. Kennedy, Paul, *The Rise and Fall of the Great Powers: Economic Change and Military Conflict from 1500 to 2000* (New York: Random House, 1988).

57. Kenney, *The Rise and Fall of the Great Power*; Calleo, David, Calleo, David, *The Imperious Economy* (Cambridge, MA: Harvard University Press, 1982).

58. Stopford and Strange, *Rival States, Rival Firms* . . .

59. Eatwell, J. (1996) "International Financial Liberalisation; the Impact on World Development," *United Nations Office of Development Studies. UNDP*, reprinted from 1996 working paper.

60. Strange, Susan, "International Monetary Relations," in Schonfield, A. (ed.), *International Economic Relations in the Western World 1959–1971*, vol. 2 (Oxford: Oxford University Press, 1976).

CHAPTER 10

Offshore and the Institutional Environment of Globalization

Ronen Palan

Metaphors are central to the process of concept formation in the sciences. They work, writes David Bloor, by "transferring the associated ideas and implications of the secondary to the primary system." Considering the pervasiveness of metaphors, it is not surprising to find that a *spatial* metaphor such as globalization is generating great interest concepts of space and time. David Harvey[1] caught the mood of an era by identifying a direct link between globalization and subjective transformations in perceptions of the concepts of time and space, or as he puts it, time-space compression. Similarly, Gianni Vattimo[2] attaches great importance to communication technologies bombarding the subject with a "cacophony of truths" beaming from every corner of the globe, destabilizing not only our beliefs in our own "truth," but also in the possibility of holding on to some stable notion of truth.

The problem, however, as David Bloor warns, that "the very act of conjoining concepts in a metaphor can produce subtle alterations in the meanings of both the concepts brought together."[3] Far from serving as neutral heuristic tools, metaphors often actively, if subtly, invade and inform perceptions of objects, inanimate or social, that appear to be "out there." For example, as a metaphor, globalization evokes images of the dislocation of the "local," the familiar; implying that the kind of social relationships that have evolved initially within the confines of a face-to-face communities, and that have then been adapted to the imagined community of the nation state, are no longer sustainable. Thus, in the slide from a spatial metaphor to an analytical concept, the conjoining of globalization with space imparts a particular "self-evident" quality to the statement that "the capitalist economy has become progressively more disembedded, in the sense of more abstract and more abstracted."[4] Globalization, therefore, is strongly associated with what Shapiro calls, "derealization."[5] Finance, in particular, is often pressed in the service of this "space-less" virtual-world argument, presented as it were, as a cyberspatial event, economically. Normatively if not physically segregated from the striated territorial spaces of the state, finance had become the paradigm of imaginary spaces.[6] Such a view is a misunderstanding. As Saskia Sassen has demonstrated, finance is very much embedded in the sociology of leading cities.

In my own writings,[7] I have stressed the importance attached to a variety of juridical "infrastructures" provided by a diversity of cities and states including the so-called spontaneous offshore financial centers of London and Hong Kong, the specialized International Banking Facilities of New York, Tokyo, and Singapore and the plethora of tax havens that surround all the major as well as minor trading centers in the world.

A cardinal assumption of the new geography is that social life takes place in "constructed" spaces, hermeneutics, or "meaningful" spaces. Artifacts, designed products and topographical entities are socially laden images representing as much as construing social relationships. Thus, Kathleen Kirby chides: "Our customary bias is to assume that mapping comes to an object—space— that is already formed and needs only to be perceived."[8] She quotes Edmundo O'Gorman who says that in examining the history of exploration, we need to "focus historical events in the light of an ontological perspectives, i.e., as a process producing historical entities instead of a process as is usually assumed, which takes for granted the being of such entities as something logically prior to it.[9] But if constructed spaces are the subject of growing interest, it is still surprising to find how little is written about the *spaces of globalization*—the concrete juridiopolitical structures that support and sustain a globalizing economy.

Assuming, then, that "space is not simply there" but in fact an historical and social construction, what are then proper spaces of globalization? How do they come about? And equally important: *When did they come about?* Can we simply assume that the juridicopolitical spaces of globalization spontaneously emerged as by-products of the processes of internationalization of capital? In this chapter I discuss only one, albeit an important aspect of this question, centering in particular on the history of the construction of the political-legal spaces of globalization. My argument is grounded in the so-called institutionalist perspective, namely, I start from the proposition that economic transactions are juridical relations conducted between legally defined "actors" operating within a legally defined environment. As Pashukanis observes: "In as much as the wealth of capitalist society appears as 'an immense collection of commodities,' so this society itself appears as an endless chain of legal relations."[10] The space of modern capitalism, or globalization, overlays, therefore, an *existing* global juridical infrastructure supporting this "endless chain of legal relations." Thus, the market is not simply "embedded" in social relationships—a trivial point as Braudel argued in his polemics against Polanyi,[11] but in fact, as Sol Picciotto notes, market relationships "cannot exist without state regulation, since the state is essential to the creation and guaranteeing of the property rights that are traded."[12] Internationalization of capital has, and could only have been, advanced on some *already existing* globalized infrastructure of standardized set of laws (historically) sanctioned by the state. How and when such a global juridical infrastructure had emerged?

In describing the processes that have laid the foundations of a global juridical infrastructure, I find Nigel Thrift's idea of "practical capitalism" particularly useful. Thrift raises doubts about the centrality of political economy as conventionally understood and stresses that "capitalist business is based on a notion of 'theory' that is of a different order from more formal theory; it is based on problematizing and redefining political space rather than on a succession of scholarly theories."[13] During the late nineteenth century, a period that proved to be of critical importance to our discussion, the pragmatic suggestions of law and of policy makers, apparently oblivious to the enormity of their task, produced the juridical principles that have, in the event, laid down the framework for the modern juridical space of globalization.

The Past, The Future, and Theories of Institutional Change

Ruccio, Resnick, and Wolf complain that most of the established approaches to globalization are grounded in a "kind of 'economism' according to which the capitalist economy is considered to be a self-regulated space whose dynamic is given by its inherent laws of competition, accumulation of capital, or similar essentialist forces."[14] Against that mode of conceptualization, they argue that we should begin theorize the very "unity of the economic space."[15] Paradoxically, theories that have contributed to the neglect of the conceptual and theoretical issues pertaining to spaces of economic activities rose to dominance precisely during the period of the laying down of the juridical infrastructure of what had become later, the global market. Thus, in mainstream economic literature space (or political economy in general) had become a nonissue toward the end of the nineteenth century or around the time when the marginalist school in economics rose to prominence. The marginalists began to conceptualize market in the abstract, as price mechanism and resource allocation mechanism.[16] Their contribution notwithstanding, the locality of markets and their relationship to the social environment was kept, as a result, away from the "cutting edge" economic thought.

An opposing trend in economic theory can be traced back to the founders of modern evolutionary thought, Thortein Veblen and John Commons. Their followers within neoclassical economics have begun to explore the significance of such "exogenous" forces such as the legal cost of transactions and market efficiency. Thus, Ronald Coase urged economists to treat the market as a social institution, the function of which is to facilitate exchange. When economists speak of market structure, he said, they refer "to such things as the number of firms, product differentiation and the like; the influence of the social institutions which facilitate exchange being completely ignored."[17] Coase's institutionalism thus places the emphasis on the concept of the institution and the institutional environment of transaction. Similarly, Davis and North define the institutional environment as "the set of fundamental political, social and legal ground rules that establish the basis for production, exchange, and distribution."[18] Davis and North, however, places the emphasis on the relationship between a static environment, viewed as consisting of sets of "fundamental rules," and how these rules (or the environment) impact on the firm. Marxist and evolutionary writers, in contrast, dig deeper asking how the institutional environment that facilitates exchange is itself undergoing change—a question that is at the core of critical political economy.

While institutionalists and new institutionalists recognize the social, political, and legal aspect of the market, they still treat questions relating to the changing nature of society, politics, and contract as exogenous. New Institutionalists, for instance, possess an internally coherent if skewed theory of the state founded on concepts such as rent seeking and maximizing, but they do not have a theory of the changing structure of the state. Similarly, Gary Becker[19] may have some interesting things to say about the institutions of marriage and the family, but he has no theory of the changing nature of marriage and the family. Oliver Williamson[20] certainly has a theory which explains different managerial tactics and strategies of the firm, he has no theory that questions the very nature of the firm.

On the whole, adherence to a strong variant of historicism by the critical wing of political economy has ensured greater interest in the problem of change. A tacit operating assumption of this tradition had been, however, that change takes place within the boundaries of the state. In this context, Wallerstein's[21] theory of the world economy appeared as a radical departure from anything that went before it. But, as Regis Debray[22] once remarked, whatever is left untheorized, comes later to haunt; the void, the assumed, if untheorized, spatial context, has proved to be the Achilles' heel of such critical theories.

In fact, as Pashukanis reminds us, long before the advent of "institutionalism," Marxists worked on the premise that economic relations of exchange are simultaneously legal relations of contracts of purchase and sale. In the Marxist tradition, however, the problem of the dual character of relations of exchange is raised and promptly ignored. The significance of the juridical realm is acknowledged, and juridical relationships were relegated to a secondary role as part of a derived "superstructure" of capitalist accumulation. Similarly, while the juridical infrastructure of capitalism is well understood, the spatial context of these discussions remains unclear: To what extent capitalism necessitates the state or the state system? What is the relationship between the abstract forces of capital and concrete capitalism? If there is such a thing as a "capitalist law," how does such law evolve, adapt, and develop within a politically fragmented system? If the assumed spatial context is the state, then what are the forces that have contributed to the universalization of such capitalist law? In other words, what is the relationships between "the chain of legal relations" which now span the entire globe and sovereignty?

These theoretical problems have not been resolved, but to the merit of evolutionary institutionalists they have made some gains in thinking about the complexity of systemic and yet nondetermined societal change. Evolutionary economics tends to represent change as *pragmatic* and path-dependent. In this it tends to draw on Peirce's pragmatism, a theory that asserts that individuals judge knowledge by how useful it is in defining the situation they enter. The more they can apply it to what they encounter, the more they come to believe it.[23] In fact, the relationship between philosophical pragmatism and historical sociology goes deep. Pragmatist philosophy certainly played an important role in John Commons's thought. Moreover, while conventional historical sociology tends to emphasize how the past shapes the present, asserting that actors operate within existing institutional environment that prescribe and proscribe their behavior, pragmatism helps us recognize that, not only the past but also the future actors participate in shaping the present. While the institutional environment constrains response, actors behave largely on the basis of estimations and predictions of future events. We see this most clearly with the case of the value of capital, which is nothing but the capitalization of estimates of future earning.[24] The same is true about every aspect of institutional change—policies and decisions are framed largely on the basis of an anticipated future.

The present therefore consists of an interesting interplay of past and future, in which an anticipated future already determines to a considerable extent the nature of the present. But since the future is unknown, anticipation and prediction about the future are guided by those institutions whose job it is to respond to the future. Change therefore is not only path-dependent, but takes place in a ways that places a premium on individual and institutional knowledge and perception. In other words, social reality is actively "constructed." Following this line of reasoning, we may argue that the growing integration of the market within the context of a state system has created a series of problems, and these problems generate a series of attempted solutions. Attempted solutions were produced within an institutional context, the law in our case, so that general principles such as state sovereignty and other principles of the law were left (or appeared) unchallenged. At the same time, solutions were discussed and debated within the context of estimate of the likely future impact of both change and the laws that are being devised. The juridical spaces of globalization were created, according to this theory, as practical solutions and hence, I would argue, we need to examine a plurality of solutions and a plurality of spaces, which tend to be multifaceted and somewhat inconsistent.

The Law and the State

It is clear from the above that capitalist society is a society regulated by law: it is a society that can operate only within the context of a system of rules (historically) backed by the powers of the state. The law, however, does not only regulate the act of exchange, it also regulates the parties to an exchange, which it defines as subjects in possession of certain rights and duties. In addition, the law defines the environment of exchange. Since the law represents itself as self-sufficient or "autopoietic" system.[25] The three elements are mutually constitutive: the environment or "context" in which exchange takes place constitutes the subject and the nature of the contract and vice versa. This is not to say that exchange cannot take place outside a system of rules and law, but that such forms of exchange are more vulnerable to disruption.

The basic legal principles that regulate capitalist society evolved during the medieval ages in the adoption and application of Roman law, combined with Canon law, the law of commerce, and natural law.[26] These are complex and sometime inconsistent overlapping systems of rules that developed forms of legal relationships designed to accommodate and further commerce. Following in the footsteps of Fustel de Coulange, Barret-Kriegel stresses the religious and civil dimension to Roman law. The hegemony of religious rites had the effect not only of linking jurisprudence with religious rites but also to root the law in the family, and close it in space.[27] The modern state adopted many of these principles, but they underwent a number of important modifications. Tigar[28] emphasizes in particular the following provisions inherited from Roman law:

1. The establishment of procedures for the enforcement of claims (the nexus). In the first place, contracts were legally binding agreements provided the parties followed a complex set of rituals. But in time the ritual has been abandoned, but contracts remain procedural documents validated by rules that are defined by the state.
2. The recognition of executory contracts, which are contracts to do a thing in the future. Executory contracts underlie all modern commercial transactions. The validation of executory contracts removed the need for an immediate, face-to-face exchange of goods and services. It created a supplementary market specializing in promises for future action;
3. The universalization of Roman law by extending it to non-Romans. This provision opened the door for potentially indefinite spatial expansion of contractual relationships. At the same time it established the principle of the locality of the contract, which must remain "located" in a particular system of rules and therefore under

the jurisdictions of the courts. Contracts have to be anchored, therefore, within a territorially specific rule-binding system of law.
4. The law of corporation, which permitted the pooling of interests and recognizing corporations as "fictitious artificial persons," entitled to buy, sell, and enforce their claims in the courts.

The rise of capitalism required some additional developments, for commodity exchange presupposes the twin concepts of the "sovereign individual" and capitalist private property. Most important, capitalist market relationships are predicated on the assumption of conflict of (free) will. Hence in capitalism, the capitalist state places itself as regulator and mediator of these conflicts. Nicos Poulantzas describes this as the problematic of the modern capitalist state that has managed to present itself as the "embodiment of the general will." How did the state interpolated itself as the embodiment of the general will and the source of law? It was during the period of the rise of the absolutist state that the centralized state makes its appearance as the "source of all 'political' power inside a territorial-national domain."[29] In fact, both Poulantzas and Schnapper emphasize the importance of the nation, as "political legitimacy was no longer founded on dynastic and religious traditions, but instead on the principle of the sovereignty of the peoples."[30] As Juridical expression, sovereignty began to express during this period "the exclusive, unique institutionalized and strictly public dominance over a territorial national ensemble and the effective exercise of central power without the extra-political restrictions of juridical or moral order which characterize the feudal state."[31] The sovereign people then are presented as the ultimate source of rights and duties and hence of the law.

The modern state, in other words, "requires" a concomitant conception of the individual as juridicopolitical persons in possession of some freedoms. At the same time, the modern conception of the individual constitutes, as is constituted by, the modern state; it can only be sustained within a particular conception of the state. Since state, citizen and corporation are defined by the same set of rules and norms, and are subordinated to the same ultimate logic, there must be an ultimate reference point outside the law: the lawgiver. Traditionally, this external point of reference was God, who, symbolically if not literally gave humanity his laws at the foot of Mount Sinai. In absolutist political theory, the prince, the sovereign, upheld God's laws. To the skeptical mind, however, the referent point could be principles of "natural" rights that are universal and unchanging. Following the French revolution, God was unceremoniously removed from the picture, and an abstraction, the "people" became the reference point to the law. Hence, as Poulantzas brilliantly describes, the concept of "society," which in modern parlance is not very different from the nation, serves as the hidden normative foundation of modern legal order.

The mythical origins of the law cannot mask the more immanent implications, placing the state as the crucial "messenger" between a constitutive absence of social closure and politics. The state (or sovereignty) becomes then a foundational basis for the law[32] and the individual is defined as a juridico-political person subject of certain freedoms. These freedoms are now presented as if they were provided by the state (whereas historically they were extracted from the state); as a result the state as viewed juridically as the sovereign law-"giver" of these freedoms. Similarly, the state sanctions the laws of civil and economic incorporation. Since the state is the lawgiver within a territory, it follows logically that it must recognize, and in turn be recognized by other states as lawgivers. In other words, the foundational assumption on which "domestic" or "municipal" law rests, namely, that the state sanctions individuals and civil and economic corporations, the fiction of the state as the "lord of the manor," requires concomitant recognition by the state, of similar rights to other states.

We can see now how the internationalization of capital forces a dilemma. If the state and/or sovereignty is removed, then the rights and duties of individuals and corporations becomes unclear. Indeed, considering that firms are legal fictions, their very existence is in peril. Can an IBM exist outside the framework of state's law? Some lawyers may argue that it can. But can an IBM or a General Motors tolerate such lack of clarity? Can they continue with their program of international investment without the guarantees provided by state law? I doubt it. There is, therefore, a powerful incentive in operation to maintain sovereignty as a universalizing code of the international order also during a period of globalization.

The Internationalization of Capital and State Law

An increasingly integrated global market operating within the context of a state system contains, therefore, its own peculiar set of contradictions. These contradictions are nothing new. In fact, many of the problems and the solutions (or attempted solutions) discussed today under the banner of globalization first came into prominence in the late nineteenth century. During that time, contradictions were felt in particular between, on the one hand, the continuing process of state formation on the basis of a national form, and on the other hand, the emergence of the modern multinational enterprises as European and American companies began branching abroad from the 1880s onward (although in most American firms waited until the end of the first world war before they began expanding oversees).[33] Faced by the new phenomena of the multinational firm, governments of the then advanced industrialized countries, particularly the United States and the British Empire, have adopted two broad principles, which they have treated as nonnegotiable. The first was the principle of exclusive sovereignty, or the sovereign's exclusive right to write the law in its territory. This robust conception of sovereignty evolved really only in the nineteenth century, and not in the seventeenth century as IR scholarship seem to suggest. The second principle enshrined the rights of business to internationalize. These governments conceived of their role as helping rather then hindering the processes that were leading to the internationalization of business.

Solutions to the contradictions inherent in such formulae had therefore to be of a tactical nature: They had to be negotiated in a pragmatic manner in ways that do not violate any of these two principles. The basic solution derives from the recognition that the concept of sovereignty and sovereign equality is at the very heart of modern international order. For, contrary to expectations, on the whole a particularistic political order has proved itself to be a sound basis for the extension of an international order in ways that were conducive to the trade, investment and the movement of capital. In other words, if sovereignty, or localized order, is the very foundation of that international order, transnational political-legal and social order of capitalism had to be in some important sense, "international" in character. The emergent transnational order consisted, therefore, at its core, of a patchwork of state-based orders which combined together at its apex by a thick web of bilateral and multilateral agreements.

This patchwork of "international" law evolved, first and foremost, through the principle tool took the form of "municipal" legislation on foreign affairs and law of treaties. The law developed gradually as states declared the manner by which they proposed to treat foreigners. To this, a second layer was then added, constructed through a host of bilateral treaties that aimed at harmonization the laws and treatment of aliens. At this stage, the universality of international law was not assumed and treaties frequently discussed the extent to which international law was applicable outside Western Christendom.[34]

Treaties of commerce became then, the most important species of international conventions. The turning point was the Franco-English treaty of commerce of 1860 (often called the Cobden treaty), which became the model for a numerous commercial treaties producing what Nussbaum[35] calls an "international bill of rights." Under such treaties, nationals of signatory power were granted personal and property protection in the other country, free sojourn, admission to trade and industry, including the right of permanent establishment protection from discriminatory treatment in taxation and similar imposts, free access to courts, freedom of ownership, and exemption from military service.[36] Many of these treaties were supported by stock clauses such as the "national treatment clause" that promised to the nationals of other country the same rights, in certain respects, as those enjoyed by the nationals of the promising country. In addition, a number of treaties were signed for mutual assistance in the enforcement of the law among governments and "among courts of civilized nations."[37] The most important, perhaps, was the establishment by treaty of uniform principle in the "choice of law," a principle that is central to the emergence of the offshore economy.[38]

National (municipal) law, supported by a host of bilateral and multilateral agreements was the backbone of the new transnational forms of governance. But the web of municipal and multilateral agreements proved insufficient, and during the same period the basis for the resurgence of nonstate law began to emerge. As Robé notes, as "[s]tate lawyers have found great difficulty in agreeing and formulating amongst themselves rules which apply to international commerce they preferred to leave the initiative to traders themselves."[39] This has had the effect of the growth of a hotly disputed branch of private international law, the *lex mercatoria*. Prior to the emergence of the modern state, international trade occurred within a self-regulating framework of customary law free from government interference. This private customary law of international trade was known as the law merchant or *lex mercatoria*. It was not law in the modern sense, but a voluntary code of conduct created, adjudicated, and enforced cooperatively among members of the international merchant community. The merchant judges relied on their knowledge of commercial custom and on their familiarity with the evolving needs of commerce to resolve disputes. The law merchant was then incorporated into national law during the seventeenth to the twentieth century.

National law proved, however, too cumbersome and frankly too expensive to serve the need of ordinary international business transactions. As a result a whole new set of international courts of arbitration have emerged, effectively, resuscitating the old *lex mercatoria*. By now international commercial arbitration is the preferred method that the commercial practice and there are at least seventy-five arbitration institutions throughout the world.[40] The *lex mercatoria* regulates, therefore, the bulk of international business. The relationship between this branch of the law and the state is a matter of dispute, but particularly interesting from our perspective is to see how a combination of sovereign-based law and nonsovereign law have emerged to deal with the contradictions.

The pragmatic manner by which the spaces of globalization were constructed produced in addition a fourth solution, founded on the more robust concept of sovereignty of the nineteenth century, as exclusive the right to write the law, has emerged. Here a growing number of states have taken advantage of their exclusive rights to write the law to establish juridical enclaves in which they voluntarily withheld some or all of their regulations. Such enclaves emerged initially in the more regulated aspects of international business: finance, insurance, and shipping. In finance a number of states, beginning with Switzerland, began to innovate by establishing the numbered account and, in accordance with the "national principle clause" (mentioned above) extended the courtesy to nationals of others countries. In doing so, they have opened their doors to a flood of "hot money" escaping regulation, taxation, or political instability. Tax havens, as these states known, proved to be a particularly popular method of economic development. Diamond and Diamond[41] estimate that there are by now sixty-two tax havens in the world (not including an additional ten failed havens), in which about half of the global stock of money either goes through or resides in. Tax havens have branched out into other forms of "offshore" activities, including export processing zones, ship and airline registration, offshore casinos, and offshore pornography.

In time offshore was transformed into a new type of an integrated juridical space, supported and sanctioned by states. Offshore may appear to be outside of state sovereignty, but it is not; it is in fact a juridical realm that can persist only as long as the principle of the exclusive sovereign right persists. Offshore is the nearest realm to the simpleminded concept of globalization as a fully integrated global market. In that sense offshore is the quintessential global market, and yet contrary to globalists, it is a juridical space that operates within the context of a particularistic political system. Offshore is in addition of great economic significance. It is estimated that over 80 percent of international financial transactions take place in the offshore financial markets; the export processing zones currently employ over twenty-seven million people worldwide, and international shipping is dominated by flags of convenience.

Conclusion

The globalization debate has by and large ignored the fact that economic interactions, of whatever spatial dimension, are legal relationships conducted between legally defined units operating within a legally defined environment. Traditionally, the juridical environment of economic transactions was the state. The state placed itself as the foundation of the rights of citizenship and the right of incorporation. It follows that transnational capitalist order has so far been, fundamentally an international order. The question, therefore, is how an international state system accommodates and sustains increasingly integrated global market.

This chapter argues that the new juridical spaces that support globalization were created pragmatically, as solutions to perceived problems. More often the not, there is no one preferred solution, but a myriad of solutions that operate somehow in unison to create a complex, multifaceted, and often inconsistent set of juridical spaces. These juridical spaces were constructed fundamentally on the principles of sovereignty, so that state law, supported by bilateral and multilateral agreements, formed the backbone of a new international juridical order. In that sense we may say that at its core, globalization is founded on an "international" juridical order. Meanwhile, the contradictions between the increasing integration of the markets within the context of a state system has produced two additional sets of juridical realms, each as it were, follows one pole of the contradictions to its logical conclusion. On the one hand, internationalization of capital is accompanied by the growth of a myriad of conventions, rules, and norms that need not rely on the state; so that capital is creating its own laws of commerce independent of the state. On the other hand, the concept of sovereign right is taken to its logical conclusion, paradoxically giving birth to a new lightly regulated global space for market operators.

These different juridical spaces are related and yet find themselves in a competitive situation. Ultimately, they all are founded on the concept of sovereignty. Even the *lex mercatoria* relies on the consent of states, and indeed, as many scholars argue, on the powers of the state. For if cases cannot be resolved within the arbitration courts, plaintiffs may still threaten to make use of state courts. At the same time, there is little doubt that both the *lex mercatoria* and offshore are competing with, and as such nibbling into the very legitimacy of state law and sovereignty. The result is that municipal laws and multilateral agreements have tended to take into account the possibilities of alternative venues and generally have produced a more "business friendly" set of rules.

Notes

1. D. Harvey, *The Condition of Post-Modernity: An Enquiry into the Origins of Cultural Change* (Oxford: Basil Blackwell, 1989).

2. G. Vattimo, *The Transparent Society* (Oxford: Polity Press, 1992).

3. D. C. Bloor, "Are Philosophers Averse to Science?" in D. O. Edge and J. N. Wolfe, eds., *Meaning and Control: Essays in Social Aspects of Science and Technology* (London: Tavistock, 1973), 12–13.

4. N. Thrift, "Virtual Capitalism: The Globalisation of Reflexive Business Knowledge," in J. G. Carrier and M. Daniel, eds. *Virtualism: A New Political Economy* (Oxford and New York: Berg, 1998), 162.

5. M. J. Shapiro, *Violent Cartographies: Mapping Cultures of War* (Minneapolis: Minnesota University Press, 1997).

6. M. Prykes and J. Allen, "Monetized Time-Space: Derivatives: Money's 'New Imagning,'" *Economy and Society*, vol. 29, no. 2 (2000), 264–284.

7. R. Palan, "Trying to Have Your Cake and Eating It: How and Why the State System Has Created Offshore," *International Studies Quarterly*, vol. 42 (1998), 625–644; and R. Palan, "Offshore and the Structural Enablement of Sovereignty," in M. Hampton and J. P. Abbott, eds., *Offshore Finance Centres and Tax Havens: The Rise of Global Capital* (Basingstoke: Macmillan, 1998).

8. K. Kirby, *Indifferent Boundaries: Spatial Concepts of Human Subjectivity* (London: The Guilford Press, 1996), 47.

9. Ibid.

10. E. B. Pashukanis, *Law and Marxism* (London: Pluto Press, 1983), 85.

11. F. Braudel, *Civilization and Capitalism Fifteenth–Eighteenth Century* (New York: Harper & Row, 1979).

12. S. Picciotto, *International Business Taxation* (London: Weindenfeld and Nicolson, 1992), 80.

13. Thrift, "Virtual Capitalism," 164.

14. D. Ruccio, S. Resnick, and R. Wolf, "Class Beyond the Nation-State," *Review of Radical Political Economics*, vol. 22, no. 1 (1990): 15.

15. Ibid.

16. R. Swedberg, "Markets as Social Structures," in N. Smelser and R. Swedberg, eds., *The Handbook of Economic Sociology* (Princeton, NJ: Princeton University Press, 1994), 259.

17. R. H. Coase, *The Firm, the Market and the Law* (Chicago: Chicago University Press, 1998), 8.

18. L. Davis and D. C. North, *Institutional Change and American Economic Growth* (Cambridge: Cambridge University Press, 1971), 6.

19. G. Becker, *The Economic Approach to Human Behavior* (Chicago: University of Chicago Press, 1976).

20. O. Williamson, *Markets and Hierarchies: Analysis and Antitrust Implications* (The Free Press: New York, 1975).

21. I. Wallerstein, *The Modern World-System, Vol. I. Capitalist Agriculture and the Origins of the European World-Economy in the Sixteenth Century* (New York: Academic Press, 1974).

22. R. Debray, *Critique of Political Reason* (London: Verso, 1981).

23. J. M. Charon, *Symbolic Interactionism: An Introduction, an Interpretation, an Integration* (New York: Simon & Schuster, 1988), 29.

24. J. Nitzan, "Differential Accumulation: Towards a New Political Economy of Capital," *Review of International Political Economy*, vol. 5, no. 2 (1998): 169–216.

25. G. Teubner, *Law as an Autopoietic System* (Oxford: Blackwell, 1993).

26. M. E. Tigar, *Law and the Rise of Capitalism* (New York: Monthly Review Press, 1977).

27. Barret-Kriegel, *Les Chemins de l'Etat* (Paris: Calman-Lévy, 1986), 23.

28. Tigar, *Law and the Rise of Capitalism*.

29. N. Poulantzas, *Political Power and Social Classes* (London:Verso, 1973); and see also B. Badie, *Un Monde sans Souveraineté: Les États entre Ruse et Responsabilité* (Paris: Fayard, 1999).

30. D. Schnapper, *Community of Citizens: On the Modern Idea of Nationality* (New Brunswick and London:: Transaction, 1998), 3.

31. Poulantzas, *Political Power,* 162.

32. H. Kelsen, *General Theory of Law and the State* (Cambridge, MA: Harvard University Press, 1945).

33. A. D. Chandler, *Scale and Scope: The Dynamics of Industrial Capitalism* (Cambridge, MA: The Belknap Press of Harvard University Press, 1990), 157–161.

34. W. C. Jenks, *The Common Law of Mankind* (London: Stevens & Sons, 1958), 29.

35. A. Nussbaum, *A Concise History of the Law of Nations* (New York: The Macmillan Press, 1961), 203.

36. Ibid., 204.

37. Ibid., 212.

38. R. Palan, "Offshore and the Structural Enablement of Sovereignty."

39. J-P Robé, "Multinational Enterprises: the Constitution of a Pluralist Legal Order," in G. Teubner, ed., *Global Law Without a State* (Aldershot: Darthmouth, 1997), 50.

40. M. T. Medwig, "The New Law Merchant: Legal Rethoric and Commerical Reality," *Law and Policy in International Business*, vol. 24, no. 2 (1992): 589–616.

41. W. and D. Diamond, *Tax Havens of the World* (New York: Matthew Bender Books, 1998).

PART IV

Shifting Patterns of Governance

CHAPTER 11

Governance and the Challenges of Changing Political Space

R. J. Barry Jones

The idea of a world of changing, and increasingly complex, political space opens a cornucopia of new possibilities and novel insights. However, changes of significance in structures and patterns of political space generate serious intellectual challenges and practical problems. Handling this range of issues in an orderly manner requires a disciplined approach to the notion of political space; possible current change changes in such space; and any difficulties created by such changes.

The first important point to stress is that in the world of practical politics neither possibilities nor needs automatically generate outcomes. That is to say, the possibilities of new patterns of human association and structures of collective governance created by such new factors as ubiquitous information technologies or mass long-distance transportation do not necessarily lead to the emergence of new patterns of political association or public governance: they merely create the possibility. Neither does the emergence of new needs and problems within the human condition guarantee the emergence of appropriate structures of public governance: mismatches are, and have been, far too common in the responses of human collectivities to even the most pressing of problems and requirements.

Governance is the Issue

Political space remains and extremely abstract and elusive concept until its primary substance is identified. Political space of any substantive significance involves far more than mere arenas within which individuals and groups can chat about issue of common concern or interest. Significant political space(s) concerns the management of issues that are of concern to various collectivities of human beings.

The term *governance* has come to represent the activities that take place within, or are definitive of, significant political space(s). However, governance, like many fashionable concepts, has now come to be used in a variety of ways—

at least six according to a recent review by Rod Rhodes in *Political Studies.*[1] A usable definition of governance has, however, been provided by the Commission on Global Governance:

> Governance is the sum of the many ways individuals and institutions, public and private, manage their common affairs. It is a continuing process through which conflicting or diverse interests may be accommodated and co-operative action may be taken. It includes formal institutions and regimes empowered to enforce compliance, as well as informal arrangements that people and institutions either have agreed to or perceive to be in their interest.[2]

Such a definition of governance suggests one, fairly conventional, approach to the identifying the prevailing patterns of political space in terms of its "supply side." Thus political space can be characterized in terms of the actual patterns of provision of governance in areas of widespread interest and salience: the institutions and arrangements that have been established or are being adopted currently in the face of changing conditions. This, however, covers merely one aspect of new political spaces, for political space can also be analyzed in terms of established, or emergent, patterns of requirement for governance: the "demand side" of the analytical equation.

The analysis of political space(s) in terms of needs or requirements runs into serious dangers of fallacious functionalism. It may, however, be invaluable in facilitating an orderly comparison of the relationships, and possible gaps, between "supply" and "demand" in contemporary patterns and processes of governance. The complexity of developments within the contemporary international (global) political economy suggests the likely existence, and possible growth, of substantial gaps between provision of and needs for effective governance. It also highlights the importance of the distinction between public governance and private governance and, in consequence, between formal and informal governance.

Public governance is the conventional subject matter of political science. It is that form of governance that serves an identifiable population across a range of issues of general concern and for which aggregation into political programs is feasible and desirable. Private governance, in contrast, is that generated by and for a specific group of actors and concerned with a restricted range of self-interested issues. Formal governance—based upon laws, constitutions or treaties—can also be differentiated, analytically at least, from informal modes—based upon understandings, mutual accommodations, tacit agreements, etc. Both distinctions may, of course, be less sharp in the empirical world as the British Constitution demonstrates in respect of state-level public governance.

A matrix of four polar types of governance arises from the public-private and formal-informal distinctions, as on Figure 11.1:

Figure 11.1
Modes of Governance (with Examples)

	public	private
formal	*Parliament/ Congress*	*Stock Exchange*
informal	*The "Power Elite"*	*Informal Price Setting Cartels*

The distinctions thus drawn encourage attention to the differential impact of changes in the International Political Economy on public and private governance. If many of the propositions associated with the stronger interpretations of the globalization thesis are true, then public governance is being increasingly challenged, while the domain of private governance is, potentially at least, expanding.

The Current Complexity

The governance of the public realm has always been a complex matter: far more complex the many textbook descriptions of political systems have often suggested. The apparent primacy of the modern state is both a recent phenomenon and a condition that has rarely been unchallenged. History reveals a complex and changeable pattern of political structures.[3] The modern state has also been challenged by the persistence of alternative authorities, like the Catholic Church, or by the emergence of new, transnational ideologies, like international socialism, and antistatist political centers, such as the Soviet Union in its early years.[4] Moreover, the variety of states, by size, strength, and general capability, has been so great as to throw doubt on the viability of a simple concept of the state.[5] Despite all such qualifications, the state has emerged as one of the most potent forces, for good and ill, within the modern world system: orchestrating constructive public enterprizes of an unmatched scope while also unleashing armed conflict on an unprecedented scale.

A recent challenge to the centrality of the state has, however, been posed by a number of new conditions and developments.[6] Such factors operate on both the "supply" and "demand" sides of the political space equation. On the "supply" side, recent technological advances have created novel opportunities for human association and collective action that facilitate, and even encourage, the reconfiguration of the "spaces" within, and across, which effective governance can be undertaken. On the "demand" side, developments within the global system appear to create new pressures for new patterns of political response and new structures and process through which to orchestrate those responses.

Arguments about the new "supply" side of global governance emphasize a number of technologies of undeniable potency. Rapid international travel is now available to an ever-wider proportion of the human population. Satellite television has now added its weight to earlier media of international auditory and visual communication. New means of information gathering, processing, and communication have unleashed an information revolution and, most significantly, through the Internet, wholly new means interpersonal communication on a worldwide basis. The information society[7] is thus a novel phenomenon of considerable, although as yet indeterminate, significance. None of these new conditions on their own, however, demonstrate the existence of new structures, patterns, or processes of global governance: offering merely possibilities rather than established achievements. Discriminating analysis still requires the identification of the actual institutions of governance and an assessment of their potency relative to longer-established structures and institutions.

Arguments on the "demand" side of global governance parallel, and partly overlap with, those on the "supply side." The key developments here are the increasing internationalization—or globalization—of economic activity[8] and the parallel growth of pressure on the natural environment.[9] The world is certainly witnessing a period of growth in the scope and scale of international business: of trade levels (Table 11.1);[10] levels of overseas investment;[11] the growth of Transnational Corporations;[12] (see Table 11.2 on the growth of British ODI between 1970 and 1988) and, most significantly, the integration of the world's financial system (Tables 11.3 and 11.4, on currency trading and cross-border share trading, respectively).[13]

Table 11.1
Ratio of Merchandise Trade to GDP at Current Prices
(Exports and Imports Combined)

	1913	1950	1973	1996
France	35.4	21.2	29.0	34.6
Germany	35.1	20.1	35.2	41.0
Japan	31.4	16.9	18.3	15.5
Netherlands	103.6	70.2	80.1	84.4
UK	44.7	36.0	39.3	47.0
United States	11.2	7.0	10.5	19.0

Sources: P. Hirst and G. Thompson, *Globalization in Question* (Cambridge: Polity Press, 1996), Table 2.5 for 1913, 1950, and 1973; and World Development Report, 1995 (Oxford University Press, for the World Bank), World Bank, World Development Indicators 1998 (CD ROM) (New York: World Bank) for 1996 figures.

Such developments have a wide range of effects. The well-being of many national economies is increasingly dependent on the wider world economy— as markets for exports and as the source of critical imports and as the source of revenue from investment. Increasing proportions of some economies are also owned and operated by nonnationals. The integrated world financial system, is also now of critical importance as a source of financial flows and, hence, of financial and economic stability for a significant number of economies. The day-to-day management of many aspects of the international economic and

Table 11.2
British Foreign Direct Investment
1975–1996

Year	FDI US$s (millions)
1975	3,319
1985	5,476
1995	22,504
1996	32,347

Source: World Development Indicators, 1998 (CD ROM) (New York: World Bank, 1998).

Table 11.3
Daily Trading in International Currency Markets
(US$ Billions)

1986	1989	1992	1995
207	620	880	1,100

Source: L. Bryan and D. Farrell, Market Unbound: Unleashing Global Capitalism (New York: John Wiley and Sons, 1996), p. 26.

Table 11.4
Cross–Border Sales and Purchases of Stocks and Shares
(US$ Billions)

1980	1982	1984	1986	1988	1990	1992	1994
93	96	155	378	517	616	789	1,523

Source: L. Bryan and D. Farrell, Market Unbound: Unleashing Global Capitalism (New York: John Wiley and Sons, 1996), p. 34.

financial system is, in consequence, undertaken by an increasingly complex set of public and private agencies.

Under such circumstances, then, the increasing complexity of the pattern of contemporary "political" space is a function of three critical components:

1. the challenges to conventional, largely state-level, public governance posed by the forces and developments conventionally associated with increased internationalization and globalization;
2. the range, persistence, and possible proliferation, of what Ferguson and Mansbach have called "nested polities";[14]
3. the proliferation of private associations that have been encouraged by the technical bases of contemporary internationalization and globalization; many of which enter, or shade into, the domain of private governance OR issue-specific approaches to public governance.

Combining these two facets of contemporary political space together presents a picture of considerable complexity and potential uncertainty. The complexities and uncertainties of this picture, in turn, underpin a sense that political space is now open to, or undergoing, radical reconstruction.

Establishing a handle on the problematic of evolving political space thus requires a clear view of the conditions that have generated, and that may be necessary for, the apparent complexity of the current situation. However, it is equally important to redefine the problems, competencies, and resources, arising at, or required by, governance in different domains and at different levels of human association, if the implications of new conditions and complexities are to be identified effectively.

The Functions of Public Governance

It is appropriate at this stage of the discussion to review the basic functions of public governance, other than the general notion that participation in political debate and decision is an intrinsically enhancing activity. This review does not, it should be reemphasized, imply any functionalist teleology—that human needs generate appropriate, or even optimal, behavioral or institutional adaptations in the short and medium term. Too much of human history has a distinctly dysfunctional flavor for that to be a readily acceptable view of change in human affairs.

Governance—both public and private—is addressed to two primary areas of functional need: collective goods and externalities.

Collective goods are those arrangements that are desired by the membership of any collectivity; and which, once provided, may be difficult to deny to any members of that collectivity—nonexcludability.[15] Such collective goods may also manifest the characteristics of jointedness—that is, they require the contributions of resources by all, or at least most, of the members of the collectivity to bring them into being; and lumpiness—that is, that there are critical levels of resourcing, supply, or both—below which suboptimal levels of provision will be experienced.

Externalities are, in effect, a special case of collective goods, which are of particular significance to agencies of public governance and which may also be to agencies of private governance. Externalities are effects generated as a side effect, possibly unanticipated and unintended, of any kind of activity. Such externalities may be negative—such as in the generation of pollution by a manufacturing process—or positive—as in the case of creating a pool of skilled labor that can become available to the wider society by a firm that undertakes high levels of training for its workforce. A particular form of eternality that is often generated by the operation of the free market is that of *market failures*, where the unrestricted functioning of a market economy generates unfortunate effects, including the emergence of distorting monopolies or oligopolies, constitute special cases of the collective goods and externalities that confront agencies of public governance.

The problem of such externalities is that the associated costs or benefits do not translate themselves into costs or benefits for the firm, or other actor, that is creating them. Such an actor can avoid external costs: external benefits, equally, do not bring direct rewards for the generating firm or actor. There may, therefore, be no direct incentive for adopting practices that avoid the external costs or to encourage developments that will produce external benefits.

Agencies of public governance, have to exist to deal with such externalities—both negative and positive—when they arise or are likely to arise.

There is also a third function of governance, which is primarily of concern to agencies of public governance and which is critical to the current debate about changes in the international political economy, political space, and governance:

Minority Needs

Minority needs, of many kinds, are generally those needs that are last suitable to satisfaction through market mechanisms, unless the members of the minority possess considerable personal resources. Such minority needs include the medical requirements of those who suffer from rare ailments; those who suffer from severe behavioral disorders; those who live in areas with greater than average threats to stability and personal security; or those who are disproportionately unfortunate in their current, or continuing, experience of economic or personal life. The definitive features of such minorities is that their needs and wants—current or continuing—will not be met by a market-based mechanism of supply—for the costs would be disproportionate and/or the price would be beyond the means of the members of the minority in question. Such needs and wants may also be beyond the means in terms of time, personnel and physical resources of local communities.

The range of potential minorities is far wider and more unpredictable than might commonly be supposed. Even the wealthy and well-favored may suddenly find that a major stock-exchange crash, a collapse of a financial institution, or a financial fraud can leave them in potential penury and acute need of statelike institutions to ensure restitution, where available, or support, where compensation is not feasible.

In the face of a wide range of actual and potential minority requirements, agencies of public governance act as an agency of insurance and supply, in which the means of effective supply are secured from the wider community. Securing appropriate means from the wider community, in turn, requires the aggregation of actual or potential minority needs into a wider agenda, or principled program, that warrants practical concern for such minorities—on the basis of *moral principles*—that it is right to meet such minority needs; and/or *prudential principles*—that individuals will never know when they may find themselves as members of one or other needy minority. The combination of facilitative and restorative functions on issues of worldwide concern is thus definitive of public governance at the international or global level.

The central issue for contemporary political space, then, concern both the patterns and sources of critical collective goods, externalities and minority needs, and their match with prevailing, or emergent, patterns of governance. To some observers, contemporary globalization has two primary implications for governance. The first is that state-level public governance is undermined by the effects of an ever-more integrated trade system and by the constraints on conventional fiscal and monetary policy exercised by mobile capital. The second major effect is the increased sway of private governance within the global political economy and its effective replacement of traditional institutions of public governance within many issue-areas. The extent, and implications, of such private governance, however, requires the most careful examination

Meeting Needs: Public Versus Private in the Provision of General Governance

Private Global Governance

The range and variety of private governance within the global political economy is far more extensive than is commonly appreciated. The more formal instances of such governance are often sanctioned explicitly by governments, individually or severally. Stock exchanges are often regulated by approved, but essentially private authorities and have participated in the arrangements that have now been established for equity trading across state frontiers. Private authorities have also been permitted, or even encouraged, for the self-regulation of industries in a number of industrial economies. Negotiations on common global standards in such areas as accountancy and banking may then involve representatives of both private regulative authorities and public (i.e., governmentally based) regulators. Standards of service or manufacture may also be established by agencies established by industries, rather than by governments.

Marketing arrangements are another realm within which extensive private governance is to be found, often with the quiescence, or tacit approval, of public authorities other than their positive encouragement. Joint ticketing arrangements among airlines reinforce cartelization tendencies within air transport, as have "liner conferences" within maritime shipping. Major transnational business operators are particularly well-placed to participate in issue-specific areas of governance. They are often in a position to dominate the production, distribution, and supply of some goods or services. They may also be well placed for the kinds of strategic agreements with similar enterprises that regulates specific markets.

Monopolies or tight oligopolies provide ready conditions for self-interested governance within the markets in which they arise. Such governance can encompass the prices and conditions under which goods and services are provide and can even dictate the rate at which technical innovations are allowed to filter through to the market.

The proliferating influence of internationally organized criminal organizations provides another, and even more insidious, form of private governance that challenges public authority and has a complex association with other instances of private governance. Many local economies and societies are more effectively under the sway of criminal, or quasi-criminal, agencies than of public authorities. Globally, control of the sources, supply routes, and outlets of a range of formally illegal commodities—from proscribed drugs to counterfeit aircraft parts—is wholly in the hands of criminal organizations acting alone or in concert with others.

Private governance within the new global political economy thus exhibits serious shortcomings. Arrangements for private governance are generally partial in their purview, being governed by the particular interests and concerns of the actors that contribute to such arrangements. They are also limited in the means through which governance can be effected. The resources for policing and physical coercion that are available to private agencies remain limited: by the costs and difficulties of their mobilization; and, of no little significance, by the constraints imposed in the past by states on the ability of nonstate actors to develop and deploy policing and military capabilities.[16] Finally, private governance lacks a popular warrant: private purposes undermine general legitimacy; and the dominance of special interests obstruct democratic principles and practices. Institutions and arrangements for private governance within the global political economy are thus unlikely to be able to serve the general interest with either effectiveness or legitimacy.

The institutions of private global governance are also, it is also important to note, largely based in the advanced industrial economies and based on firms and representatives from the advanced industrial economies. The biases inherent in private governance are thus compounded in the case of private governance within the contemporary global domain.

Public Global Governance

Public governance, for all its practical failings, is focused on the general interest of the public(s) being served. The need to address collective goods and critical externalities has lain at the heart of public governance from the outset. The development of ever-more complex patterns of economic and social life has generated a steadily widening range of pertinent collective goods and externalities and, hence, the widening of the domain of public governance. The pattern throughout the last five, or more, centuries has been that of the consolidation of the capabilities of states, their increasing monopolization of the means of violence and peaceful policing, and their acquisition of a growing proportion of the resources generated within the societies that they serve.

The existing pattern of states is historically contingent: contemporary states are not necessarily the only mode of organization capable of delivering necessary collective goods; and the current identities of states is by no means inevitable or durable. However, where states have been effective at generating the desired collective goods and addressing the critical externalities that affect their societies, their pivotal position has had two general consequences. First, they have represented their populations' needs and aspirations on the wider (international) stage. Second, well-established states have defined the scope and capabilities for action available to subordinate institutions—local governments, regional authorities, and lower-level "states" in the case of federal polities. Threats from outside or inside have commonly been met by forceful responses by states: the outcome, and thereby the future configuration of states, being a matter of the relative military capabilities of the warring actors and the effectiveness with which such resources are deployed. Some states have been consolidated by such struggles: Germany in the case of the "external" war with France in 1870–1871; the United States of America in the case of her own Civil War of 1861–1865. Other states have collapses and been reconfigured into a series of successor states by armed challenges, as the recent case of the former Yugoslavia has vividly demonstrated. Significantly, however, new states that emerge from the debris of previous, larger, states attempt, as far as possible, to construct themselves as conventional states: with a monopoly of legitimate means of coercion; a new currency; a domestic bureaucracy and diplomatic service; and, most significantly, a clearly defined territorial sovereignty.

States thus remain the primary agencies for generating collective goods and dealing with common externalities for territorially defined political communities. They also remain the primary members of most of the agencies that seek to deal with similar matters at a global level, configuring global public governance into a realm of intergovernmental management and regulation. Current conditions and developments, however, continue to exert a considerable influence on the forms and prospects of public global governance.

Public Global Governance: Patterns and Roles

Public governance at the state level focuses on security from external threat, internal disorder, and personal disadvantage; on the health and vitality of the economic and industrial system; and on a range of associated purposes and conditions. Given the variation of size, capability, and general effectiveness of contemporary states, it is difficult to identify any good reason for the pivotal role of these institutions other than the claims to ultimate formal sovereignty that they are able to maintain: of a unique capacity to mobilize communities and resources for the provision of desired, and often necessary, collective goods. Subordinate groupings lack either the resources or the authority to generate the full range of collective goods that characterize the contemporary state. Higher levels of human organization (with the partial, although controversial, exception of the European Union) have thus far been prevented from securing the supply of such collective goods by the problems of coordination on an extensive scale; persisting intercultural suspicions and hostilities; and, of no little significance, the powerful legacy of the statism that has become embedded within contemporary political culture.[17]

Public governance in the global sphere thus remains a matter primarily of hegemonic influence[18] and varied patterns of intergovernmentalism,[19] much of which has assumed regimelike characteristics. Much of the postwar growth of intergovernmental arrangements reflected the influence of the United States. The prewar League of Nations war reshaped into the postwar United Nations: a club of states that sanctified intergovernmentalism, through the enshrinement of the rights of sovereign states and, which acknowledged the dominant role of the major power through the permanent membership of the Security Council.[20] The fraternal institutions of the International Monetary Fund and the International Bank for Reconstruction were also constructed under U.S. direction. The

General Agreement on Tariffs and Trade was then employed, under U.S. encouragement, to form the basis of an intergovernmental forum for trade negotiations
and progressive liberalization of the world economy.[21]

The dominant role of the U.S. postwar economic governance in the
postwar noncommunist world was paralleled by her major influence in the
politicomilitary sphere: formally through treaty-based organizations like the
North Atlantic Treaty Organization and the ANZUS pact, and military action
under the auspices of the UN in Korea; informally, but no less dramatically,
through a worldwide military presence on land, sea, and in the air and in a
range of interventions in countries and regions with disfavored regimes and
political affiliations.

For many observers, the postwar military and economic hegemony of the
United States went hand-in-hand with the sculpting of a pattern of intergovernmental associations that accorded with U.S. views and that suited the interests of the United States and its major allies in the Western states and the leading sectors of business: a situation that has given encouragement to those
disposed to view the world through quasi-Marxist, Neo-Gramscian lenses.[22]
Many of these intergovernmental organizations then appeared to develop a life
of their own and to consolidate into self-sustaining "regimes." The empirical
variety of such regimes, their ultimate durability and their role as building
blocks of a new international system of governance in the aftermath of the possible decline of U.S. hegemony, are all matters of debate and dispute.[23]

What is clear, however, is that many contemporary regimes remain fundamentally intergovernmental, composed of representatives of the governments
of a wide variety of political systems. Moreover, until recently the democratic
credentials of participating states were of little concern within such regimes and
probably remain little more than a secondary issue when major issues of concern to the leading members are at stake. The formal representation of nongovernmental organizations has also been patchy, slow to develop and generally
stopped short of participation in central decision-making. Democracy has not,
therefore, been at the fore of postwar intergovernmentalism. Intergovernmentalism also ensures that democratic representation in such areas of international
decision-making could never be more than indirect (i.e., via the representatives
of governments, albeit democratically elected). A "club" of intergovernmental
"clubs," or regimes, is probably the best that can be hoped of from such a developmental trajectory.

The dangers facing intergovernmental governance continue to be those
of disruption by ideological or "cultural" differences; divergent economic interests; or the general temptations of "free riding." Any or all of these three sources
of division could sunder even the best-founded and long-lived intergovernmental organizations. Global governance thus remains poised delicately
between a potentially expanding realm of private governance and a dense, but

often fragile, structure of intergovernmental public governance. Popular democratic representation is largely (possibly necessarily) absent from the former; tenuous, and rarely more than indirect, in the case of the latter.

Consequences: Globalization, Complexity, and Chaos

Contemporary conditions are reinforcing the impression of the increasing complexity of the problems confronting humanity and the associated patterns of response, particularly in the realm of public governance. Such appearances contribute to the perceived need to reconceptualize political space. Such novelties do not, however, minimize the continuing problems of matching the agencies of public governance, and the resources and capabilities that they can deploy, to the contemporary range of problems and pressures.

The overwhelming danger is that patterns of public governance fail to correspond to the patterns of pressing problems and needs. Such a mismatch is by no means the only source of political and popular instability in history, but it is a major potential source of such difficulties. The populations of weak, or weakening, states can find themselves incapable of effective action at levels of organization appropriate to the problems being confronted and may, in particular, become prey to predatory forces from within, or outside, their territorial communities. For many of the world's population, then, globalization is a phenomenon to be experienced as passive objects rather than to participate in as active agents.

The dissolution of political orders, whether they be modern states or older forms of polity and governance is generally a turbulent process. With the exception of conquest from outside or such orchestrated successions as postwar decolonization, fully formed agencies of governance been rarely been available to step into the place vacated by a previously dominant agency of government—tribal structure, feudal state, empire, or whatever. The protracted character of such post-collapse turbulence is a function both of the mismatch of capabilities to requirements and the linked problem of predation. The possession, or lack, of military capabilities or those of forceful policing, have clearly been significant to such processes and experiences. Such capabilities have, in turn, carried strong implications for resources—particularly those required for the generation and maintenance of military forces and policing structures.

Overall, political space—patterns of public governance and human political identity—are shaped by the intersection of means, including force, and requirements. Such a proposition does not entail that there are universally valid, or contextually perfect, configurations of political space. The compliance of the many has often been compelled by the strong few; minorities have even more frequently been compelled to bend to the dictates of the many. Identity, itself, has often be shaped by protracted programs involving forceful religious conversion, institutional manipulation and linguistic homogenization. Human requirements can often be met through a variety of agencies at a number of levels of human conduct. The political space that has been shaped can often be directed toward meeting a variety of requirements, in such a way as to sustain the positions of those who have managed to occupy pivotal positions within the relevant political order. Most significantly, the polities for which people can be persuaded to kill and, if necessary, to die can be altered over time—often being transferred from prior polities to new, overarching polities such as the contemporary state, or by transterritorial ideologies that become persuasive with changing circumstances.

The continuing issue, however, is whether the prevailing patterns of public governance—their dominant polities and central authorities—will prove sufficient to meet the most pressing problems of the contemporary world; such collective goods and externalities as:

- the regulation of transnational actors, from transnational corporations to international drug smugglers;
- global environmental protection and preservation;
- the management or prevention of intersocietal conflicts.

States for all their variety of forms, sizes, and capabilities, have been the central actors in these areas of concern throughout the bulk of the twentieth century. They have also played a central role in a range of social provisions, the regulation of markets domestically and in the generation of policies for economic and industrial development.[24] The future might be shaped in one, or some combination, of a number of directions:

- an increasingly complex form of the current situation, with an increasing number of variety of "nested" polities;
- fragmentation of existing patterns of interstate association and many established states into more local polities;
- fusion among existing states and/or more attractive regional polities into:
  - regional quasistates;
  - a new global polity

The problem is to relate global-level governance requirements to these possible configurations of political space. It is difficult to identify many "nested" polities, at the substate level, that are likely to contribute much to the solution of global-level problems. However, the very fragmentation of the world political system into self-regarding states has often undermined collaborative efforts to deal with global level problems effectively. Regional fusion, in its turn, is an agenda that is fraught with problems and passions, as the tortured progress of the European Union has often demonstrated. The emergence of an effective new global form of governance is, however, probably the most problematical of projects—requiring the simultaneous dissolution of sovereignties, intercultural tensions and free-rider problems simultaneously on a vast scale.

Complexity is, itself, not a particular worry as we contemplate public governance in the twenty-first century. The worries come, rather, with the prospect that states will further weaken, or even dissolve as effective central agencies, without the prior, or simultaneous, emergence alternative agencies of public governance to deal with a wide range of human requirements, at societal as well as global levels. The collapse of states in particular, or of political orders in general, has rarely, if ever, been a peaceful process. The erosion of state capabilities in the face of the pressures of contemporary globalization conjures up a vision of collapsing domestic socioeconomic stability, and the political order on which has rested,[25] and the looming danger of intra- and intersocietal conflict.[26]

Structures of purely private governance will be unable to fill the governance gap created by any dissolution of established authorities. Their partial purposes will inhibit a genuine approach to a wide range of pressing collective issues. Their capacity for policing is constrained by material limitations and, most important, by an absence of legitimacy. The capacity of institutions of private governance for enforcement will rarely extend beyond the recruitment of relatively small bodies of mercenaries: the mass recruitment of volunteer or conscripted armies will be well beyond their means. Attempts at genuinely public governance by such constrained agencies would resemble far more the rule of self-interested oligarchies and plutocracies of the pre- and early modern eras, than the democratic governance of recent times.

Policing and enforcement capabilities remain critical issues for the future of global governance and the development of political space(s). Effective governance is impossible without such capabilities in any but the most utopian of societies. Current changes pose some threat to the policing and enforcement capabilities of established states and their intergovernmental institutions, without guaranteeing that new public institutions (political structures) will emerge with sufficient capabilities to deal with the challenges that now confront the global system. Institutions of private governance that might seek to step, or that might be thrust, into the governance gap will suffer, chronically, from their partiality of purpose, limited capabilities, and general lack of legitimacy.

It is possible, of course, that the advance of globalization, and its possible implications, have been exaggerated, will prove ephemeral, or both. There are certainly serious suspicions that the contemporary fashion for globalization reflects a range of special interests—economic, political, and intellectual.[27] Globalization has certainly been part of the agenda of corporate management to shift the relative rewards of industrial capitalism from workers to owners and managers, as the rise in the level of corporate profits as a percentage of the corporate wage bill within the United States from 12 percent in 1982 to 23 percent in 1997–1998 suggests.[28]

A world of declining state-based public governance and of growing, but ultimately limited and illegitimate, private governance may thus be the consequence of any advance of globalization and the substantive reality of greater complexity in political space. New political space(s) may thus be an arena of ultimately unsustainable complexity: a complexity composed not merely of new and variable patterns of governance, but also of highly variable capacities for effective action in the face of advancing (and encroaching) internationalization or globalization. History may be not so much at an end within the new world of globalization and complex political space(s) as about to lurch onto new, and eminently hazardous, paths.

Notes

1. R. A. W. Rhodes, "The New Governance: Governing without Government," *Political Studies*, vol. 44, no. 4 (September 1996): 652–667.

2. Commission on Global Governance, *Our Global Neighbourhood: The Report of the Commission on Global Governance* (Oxford: Oxford University Press, 1995), p. 2.

3. Y. H. Ferguson and R. W. Mansbach, *Polities: Authority, Identities and Change* (Columbia, SC: University of South Carolina Press, 1996).

4. On the nature and fate of which see David Armstrong, *Revolution and World Order: The Revolutionary State in International Society* (Oxford: Clarendon Press, 1992).

5. For a general discussion of the substantial inequalities that are obscured by the formal equality of states see Robert W. Tucker, *The Inequality of Nations* (New York: Basic Books, 1973).

6. Many of these are summarized in the other contributions to this panel/volume. See, in particular, the contributions by Ferguson and Mansbach, and by Rosenau.

7. Manuel Castells, *The Informational City: Information Technology, Economic Restructuring, and the Urban-Regional Process*, Oxford: Basil Blackwell, 1989.

8. On the nature and extent of internationalization, globalization, or both, see P. Hirst and G. Thompson, *Globalization in Question* (Cambridge: Polity Press, 1996); and R. J. Barry Jones, *Globalization and Interdependence in the International Political Economy: Rhetoric and Reality* (London: Pinter publishers, 1995).

9. For a wide review of the environmental issue in international relations see John Vogler and Mark F. Imber (eds.). *The Environment and International Relations* (London: Routledge, 1996).

10. For a detailed discussion of which, see J. Perraton, D. Godlblatt, D. Held, and A. McGrew, "The Globalization of Economic Activity," *New Political Economy*, vol. 2, no. 2. (July 1997): ???

11. See, especially, Hirst and Thompson, *Globalization in Question, op. cit.*, chap. 3.

12. See, especially, Hirst and Thompson, *Globalization in Question, op. cit.*, chap. 4; and see also "*Debate*: Transnational Corporations," *New Political Economy*, vol. 3, no. 2 (July 1998): 279–300 (contributions by Ankie Hoogvelt; John H. Dunning; Leslie Sklair; Andrew Walter; Ricardo Petrella; and David Bailey, George Harte, and Roger Sugden).

13. See L. Bryan and D. Farrell, *Market Unbound: Unleashing Global Capitalism* (New York: John Wiley and Sons, 1996), esp. chap. 2.

14. Ferguson and Mansbach, *Polities: op cit.*

15. For a further discussion of collective action and collective goods see N. Frohlich and J.A. Oppenheimer, *Modern Political Economy* (Englewood Cliffs, NJ: Prentice-Hall, 1978), chaps. 2, 3, and 4.

16. See some of the discussions in the special section of the journal Environment and Planning A, vol. 28, no. 11 (November 1996), especially those by R. J. Barry Jones, "Social Science, globalization and the problem of the state," pp. 1948–1953 and Michael Mann, "Neither nation-state nor globalism," pp. 1960–1964.

17. See R. J. Barry Jones, *Globalisation and Interdependence, op. cit.*, p. 4; and the discussions in the Special section of *Environment and Planning A*, November 1996, *op. cit.*

18. See R. O. Keohane, *After Hegemony: Cooperation and Discord in the World Political Economy* (Princeton, NJ: Princeton University Press, 1984).

19. See A. Movavcsik, "Negotiating the Single European Act: National Interests and Conventional Statecraft in the European Community"; *International Organization*, vol. 45, no. 1 (1991): 19–56.; A. Moravcsik, 'Preferences and Power in the European Community: A Liberal Intergovernmentalist Approach," *Journal of Common Market Studies*, vol. 31, no. 4 (December 1993): 473–524.

20. R. J. Barry Jones, "The United Nations and the International Political System," in D. Bourantonis and J. Wiener (eds.), *The United Nations in the New World Order: The World Organization at Fifty* (London: Macmillan, 1995), pp. 19–40.

21. J. E. Spero, *The Politics of International Economic Relations* (London: George Allen and Unwin [3rd ed.] 1985), esp. chap. 1.

22. See Gill and Law, *The Global Political Economy, op. cit.*

23. S. Strange, "Cave! Hic Dragones: A Critique of Regime Analysis," *International Organization*, vol. 36 (1982): 479–496 (reprinted in S. D. Krasner, *International Regimes* (Ithaca: Cornell University Press, 1983); V. Rittberger, with P. Meyer (eds.), *Regime Theory and International Relations* (Oxford: Clarendon Press, 1993). Keohane, *After Hegemony, op. cit.*

24. See, in particular, R. J. Barry Jones, *Conflict and Control in the World Economy: Contemporary Economic Realism and Neo-Mercantilism* (Brighton: Harverster/Wheatsheaf, 1986); and L. Weiss and J. A. Hobson, *States and Economic Development: A Comparative Historical Analysis* (Cambridge: Polity Press, 1995); and R. Palan and J. Abbott, with P. Deans, *State Strategies in the Global Political Economy* (London: Pinter Publishers, 1996).

25. See John Gerrard Ruggie, "At Home Abroad, Abroad at Home: International Liberalisation and Domestic Stability in the New World Economy," *Millennium: Journal of International Studies*, vol. 24, no. 3 (Winter 1994): 507–526; R. J. Barry Jones, "Globalization versus Community," *New Political Economy*, vol. 2, no. 1 (March 1997): 39–51.

26. For the classic account of earlier manifestations of such effects, see Karl Polanyi, *The Great Transformation: The Political and Economic Origins of Our Time* (Boston: Beacon Press, 1957).

27. See the discussions in R. Germain, *Globalization and Its Critics* (London: Macmillan, 2000, especially the chapter by R. J. Barry Jones, "The Globalization Debate in Perspective."

28. See the article "The Fat Cats Keep Getting Fatter," *The Financial Times*, 1/2 August 1998, p. 9.

CHAPTER 12

Club Identity and Collective Action: Overlapping Interests in an Evolving World System

Mark A. Boyer

Clubs, polities, socially constructed identities, and even international institutions. Each of these terms implies something about the ways actors within a system organize themselves in their efforts to achieve collectively desirable goals. Over the past decade in the field of international relations, much time has been spent discussing how each of these concepts and others fit within the traditional constructs of international relations theory and particularly how they relate to what has often been termed the defining concept of the study of our field: anarchy. But what is lacking in the work to date is an attempt to take all of these concepts together and determine how the divergent theoretical approaches complement one another in their challenges to realist thinking.

In particular, this essay focuses on integrating club theory—and public goods theory more generally—into the rich genre of studies in recent years that have helped us understand better the ways actors organize themselves in international political affairs. These works include among others Rosenau and his focus on the bifurcation of world politics and its implications for global interactions in the years ahead;[1] the work of Ferguson and Mansbach that advanced the concept of polities and how shifting and overlapping political identities within, across, and between national states affect the types of interactions in the contemporary world system;[2] the work of Wendt that has helped redefine the notion of political identity as a social construct that changes through interaction throughout the world system;[3] and the work of Buzan, Jones, and Little and Milner that has more clearly defined the effects of anarchy on global political relations.[4]

At a substantive level, the conceptual work contained in this essay is part of a larger project focusing on the prospects for the pursuit of global order and progress in a posthegemonic world.[5] Using a public goods framework to analyze the ways states have adapted to the decline in American power and how they work to pursue order and progress in a variety of issue areas, we have found that neither the dire predictions of the hegemonic stability theorists nor the more rosy predictions of those focusing on the positive impact of globalization are satisfactory for understanding the prospects for order and progress in the years ahead. Rather, we have found that multiple, variable, and cross-cutting international political clubs have for the moment staved off the worst predictions, but have also not assured the institutionalization of cooperation for the future quite yet.

Pushing Public Goods Theory
Beyond Its Narrow Interpretation

The theory of clubs is a variant of public goods theory and has been applied as an analytical framework to a variety of substantive issues throughout the field of international relations. Most notably in recent years, club theory, and public goods theory more generally, has been used to study the dynamics of alliance burden-sharing and the management of international environmental affairs.[6]

To begin, pure public goods are defined as joint and nonexcludable. Jointness means that consumption of a public good by one individual does not diminish the amount of the good available for consumption by another individual. Nonexcludability refers to the inability of producers of a public good to exclude those not paying for the production of the public good from consuming it. Once it is provided for one member of a collective, it is provided for all members, regardless of payment or lack thereof.

The basic dilemma that arises for public good provision is the familiar free-rider problem as laid out in Mancur Olson's classic work *The Logic of Collective Action*.[7] Because a member of a collective can consume the public good without diminishing the amount available for consumption by others and because the others in the collective cannot exclude an individual from consuming the good, members of the collective will free ride on the public good provision of others and thus try to receive the good for free. The strong version of the free-rider problem posits that no one in the collective will contribute to the production of the good—all making the same free-rider calculation—with nothing produced. The weak version holds that the good will be produced at a suboptimal level, as some members may not contribute at all and others may contribute less than they should for the good to be optimally produced, as they assume others will take up their slack.

Hegemonic stability theorists like Gilpin and even Cold War stability theorists like Mearsheimer point to the impact that a single actor or very small group of actors has had on the maintenance of peace and stability throughout the world political economic and political military subsystems during the post–World War II system.[8] Without those hegemonic forces and the power they wield in a variety of forums throughout the world, international cooperation toward the production of a variety of public goods aimed at cultivating order and progress will deteriorate.

But when one moves beyond the world of theory and attempts to place theoretical constructs into the real world, one quickly sees that *pure public goods*—and thus the strong free-rider problem suggested by Olson—do not exist in the real world. All of the goods focused on by international relations scholars and practitioners as exhibiting the characteristics of a public good are more accurately viewed as goods that exhibit some degree of impurity, either through some degree of nonjointness or excludability or both. As a result, the potential for free-riding is generally less pervasive, though still in evidence at times, than is posited by Olson's original models. Though each factor could be laid out in long essay form at least, the following brief discussion will suffice here to highlight the forces that in many instances can enhance the production of impure public goods throughout the world community:

1. *The production of private goods or joint products.* In many instances the production of private goods as by-products of public good production increases the amount a given actor will contribute to the production of a particular good. In the example of NATO burden-sharing, Sandler and his coauthors cited above have shown that conventional forces yield higher levels of private benefits to producers than do the production of nuclear weapons. For reasons of limits to force mobility and the geographic limits of force coverage, conventional weapons deployed in one country provide the deploying country with higher levels of privately consumable defense than those conventional forces provide to others in the collective. Thus, the state where the weapons are deployed has an incentive to spend on conventional weapons, because that state is consuming more of the benefits than the alliance neighbor.

2. The traditional public goods construction is parallel to an n-person prisoner's dilemma game, where two players are destined to arrive at a suboptimal outcome because of the structure of the payoffs in the game and also because the players are unable to communicate with one another during the playing of the game and thus are unable to coordinate strategy and solve the problem of the prisoner's dilemma.[9] But when communication is added to the mix of transnational decision-making processes, even when the payoffs are constructed in the same way as in the traditional prisoner's dilemma, the chance of cooperation and optimal resolution is much more likely. Clearly, the maintenance of open and active lines of communication between international actors is an integral part of contemporary world affairs. Such avenues for communication

include consultations at international organizations, the links maintained by embassies and consulates around the world, and even through the communication revolution taking place in cyberspace.

3. The assumption of an insufficient ability to cooperate in a world of egoistic actors also ignores the impact of commonly held values and goals among the actors of international collective. As Lumsdaine has shown in his work on the foreign aid programs of the advanced industrialized societies since World War II, a sense of collective interest in the pursuit of foreign aid programs helped to maintain those programs and also provided an element of coherence in them that simple unilateral programs would not have possessed.[10] In addition the work of Nau, Nye, Kagan, and Ikenberry and Kupchan have emphasized the degree to which the values of the hegemonic power became internalized in many other actors in the system during the Cold War era and also provided the kind of leadership and cohesive force needed for the stability of the system over the longer term.[11] As a result, the goals, policies, and approaches to world affairs, though possibly not the direct result of hegemonic leadership or control, possess an element of commonly held values that reinforce the structures in the system that promoted cooperation during the era of more obvious hegemonic dominance.

4. The simple public goods construct also creates its framework and hypotheses by examining only the provision of a single public good in isolation from the potential production of other public goods. As all observers of politics know, the interconnections among issues and actors that we now commonly refer to as interdependence provide fertile ground for the potential for trading of contributions toward the production of public and private goods across issues and actors. One can also add in the forces toward cooperation produced when different actors produce some goods better than others, and opportunities for gains in efficiency can be obtained through specialization by actors in the production of certain goods.[12]

As these ideas suggest, we can begin to chip away at the extreme pessimism of the original public goods model by accounting for additional pieces of international reality that are not part of that model.

And related to point 4 above, a last concept—the fact that the production of club goods are generally considered in isolation from one another—is also worth discussing. In almost all of the public goods literature, clubs and the goods they provide for club members are examined in the context of a single club and not how clubs overlap and interact throughout international relations. This point is particularly important in contemporary politics where interdependence of both actors and issues has reached such a level that it makes discreet consideration of actor policy choices almost impossible. Moreover, as Milner argues, interdependence is at least as fundamental to our understanding of contemporary international relations as is anarchy itself.[13] It has become a piece of pedagogical conventional wisdom in our field that the choices one actor makes are conditioned and constrained by the nature of the issues involved and also by the potentially countervailing actions taken by other actors involved in same policy drama.

From a club perspective, this conceptual problem becomes even more acute when accounting for the fact that contemporary international relations clubs may well exhibit cross-cutting and overlapping memberships. The question that arises, then, is what implications does this have for the provision of club goods when actors belong to multiple clubs relevant to varying issues with a similar core of actors present across the clubs? This question is the centerpiece of our discussion in the next section.

Integrating Public Goods Theory
Into the Discipline's State of the Art

Public goods theory assumes that the decisions made by international actors about whether or not to contribute to the production of public goods are the result of independent marketlike forces in the global political-economic market. But what is missing in this set of motivating factors is a notion of what forces are at work prompting actors to have common interests and goals and possibly to work toward the common achievement of those interests and goals. Wendt's work comes the closest of any in the field in trying to make a link between rational choice/public goods approaches to explaining cooperation and constructivist approaches that help us understand how individuals and their transnational aggregations define their identities in political space. Wendt argues that the ability to overcome the collective action problems defined by Olson's original work depends in large part on whether or not social identities generate more narrowly defined "self-interests" or more broadly defined "collective interests" among the actors involved in a particular collective action situation.[14] But where Wendt's argument falls short is in making the link between his argument and the commonality of interest that exists in club goods situations.

When we begin to think about the reasons why a member of a collective might want to contribute to the provision of a collectively desired good at levels higher than those posited by the seminal thinkers of the field, the central issue is what motivates an actor to contribute. As conceptualized by public goods theory, the conflict between short-term, self-interest is perceived as running counter to pursuit of the collective good: Why contribute if you can free-ride on others?

But this interpretation of actor interest and motivation assumes that the actor's identity is narrowly conceptualized and does not include elements of interest that may go beyond pure self-interest. In a state-centric world, this means that states define their interests only along the lines of nation-state identity and that anything that moves beyond that state-level construct is irrational. Buzan points out, however, that such a narrow notion of identity in modern international relations is rooted in a "nineteenth century view of exclusive nationalisms."[15] As a result, when beginning to think about the possibilities of a global society, one does not have to discard national identity, but rather must recognize that individuals, and by extension the states they comprise, can have multiple identities that may be compatible with one another in their pursuit of action throughout the world system. At some points, such identities may also be incompatible, but Buzan's point makes clear that the assumed conflict between self-interest and collective interest posed in the public goods problem need not always holds true.

In addition, the traditional assumption of narrow self-interest that is at the heart of calculations made in pure public goods theory is rooted in the assumption of anarchy. By assuming that actors operate in an environment dominated by self-help and ultimate authority for the state, many public goods theorists then speculate that cooperation, when it does occur, will only be short-lived. But as Milner argues, using anarchy as the defining construct for international relations downplays the impact of domestic politics on transnational decision-making (and thus the impact of socially constructed identities and the desired public goods associated with those identities) and needlessly ignores the impact of well-accepted norms of behavior and action in the system and emergent institutions linked to those norms.[16]

This point becomes even more important when we extend the concept to the realm of club theory and begin to think about the ways states, and other actors that participate in international clubs, possess identities that are sometimes state-based and at other times subsumed under the auspices of the pursuit of club-relevant goods. For example, those who think pessimistically about the future of cooperation in a posthegemonic world often point to the level of trade conflict that has developed between the United States and Japan as evidence to support their case.

From the direction of club-based identity, however, one can also argue that the core values that now exist between the advanced industrialized countries and institutionalized in such forums at the G-7/G-8 meetings, APEC, and even NATO bear witness to a club of industrialized states. Members of this club possess many common values, share many common interests, and pursue many common goals. The institutional forums themselves aid in identifying these commonalities on a recurrent basis and also in providing an opportunity to plan common and hopefully coordinated strategies for coping with various global challenges.

The reason the issue of a club-based identity is important to understanding the prospects for cooperation in a global society is that even public goods theorists acknowledge that when exclusion is possible, there is an increased tendency for members of the club to contribute to the production of the good. Put simply, if nonpayers can be excluded from consumption, then it is more likely that they will pay for the good.

Clubs in global political affairs also can develop an identity that at times transcends the individual national identities represented by the club members. In some instances, national preferences may be subordinate to the preferences of the collective, while in others the national preferences will be the dominant features evident across club decisions. Nonetheless, clubs are formed in the pursuit of some common goal, which in turn helps define the identity of that club. Without that identifying goal or goals, the club would have little reason to form or continue to exist over the longer term. And just as Wendt suggests that state identities change as a result of interaction among states in the world system, club identities change as new policy challenges are faced, new members are added to the club, and norms of interaction are established and recrafted as the club adapts to change in the system and among the constituent groups.[17]

Our understanding of club identity becomes even more complex when recognizing that membership in global political clubs can change and may exhibit a level of overlap with other clubs, both in terms of members and in terms of the goals pursued and identities held by the clubs. In a way, this increasing complexity moves our understanding of club activity and collective action beyond the linear pursuit of an individual club's desired public goods toward a multidimensional examination of the ways club issues (goods) and memberships change, overlap, and interact in the pursuit of multiple goods by diverse and varied transnational actors.

This "layering and overlapping" of club memberships—to borrow a term put forth by Ferguson and Mansbach—and the issue foci of clubs produces a situation where the potential for satisfaction of club goals is quite directly dependent upon what other clubs are doing in pursuit of their own distinct goals.[18] In some situations, goals held across clubs may be at odds with each other, such as in the case of antagonistic alliance relationships, while in other cases, club efforts may be complementary, such as when regional trading blocs cooperate to preserve global free trade norms and procedures.

Table 12.1 provides an illustration of the overlapping and cross-cutting nature of one set of contemporary international clubs by laying out a portion of the milieu of organizations that exist among the advanced industrialized

Table 12.1
Memberships of Overlapping International Clubs

Group of Seven/Eight/Nine (7 member states with Russia and a European Commission President included in annual meetings)	European Union (15 member states)
Canada	Austria, Belgium,
France	Denmark, Finland,
Germany	France, Germany,
Italy	Greece, Ireland,
Japan	Italy, Luxembourg,
United Kingdom	Netherlands, Portugal,
United States	Spain, Sweden,
(Russia, European Union)	United Kingdom

NATO (16 member states with three new members approved)	NAFTA (3 member states)
Belgium, Canada,	Canada
Denmark, France,	Mexico
Germany, Greece,	United States
Iceland, Italy,	
Luxembourg, Netherlands,	
Norway, Portugal	
Spain, Turkey,	
United Kingdom, United States	
(Czech Republic, Hungary, Poland)	

OECD (29 member states)	APEC (17 member states with international organization observers; also 3 new members joining)
Australia, Austria, Belgium,	Australia, Brunei,
Canada, Czech Republic, Denmark,	Canada, Chile,
Finland, France, Germany,	China, Indonesia,
Greece, Hungary, Iceland,	Japan, South Korea,
Ireland, Italy, Japan,	Malaysia, Mexico,
South Korea, Luxembourg, Mexico,	New Zealand, Papua New Guinea,
Netherlands, New Zealand, Norway,	Philippines, Singapore,
Poland, Portugal, Spain,	Taiwan, Thailand,
Sweden, Switzerland, Turkey,	United States
United Kingdom, United States	(South Pacific Forum, ASEAN, Pacific Economic Cooperation Council)
	(new members: Peru, Russia, Vietnam)

countries. What this table illustrates is the web of relationships that center on the participation of the G-7 countries throughout the world. Arguably the most politically and economically powerful group of states in the world, these states are the de facto leaders of all five other organizations shown in the table. The identity that each has as a member of the G-7 and the role it plays in pursuing common political and economic goals in the world through this club links it to other clubs that pursue similar though not identical sets of interests. In addition, each of the other five groups exhibits a clear hierarchical dimension at least in economic terms, as a portion of the membership of the club can be considered less developed countries. This hierarchy can then serve the purpose of inculcating a similar set of economic goals and thus possibly a "G-7–type" economic identity. This authority does not mean, however, that those occupying lower levels in the hierarchy cannot impact the higher-ups. As was clear from the recent series of Asian financial crises, each of these clubs is affected by the trials and tribulations of the others, no matter where the disruptions occur.[19]

But while this table serves to illustrate the surface interconnections of the various Western-based clubs, it does little to help us understand the impact of overlapping clubs on the prospects for international cooperation. If as discussed above, a club is at least partly defined and identified by the goods it hopes to produce for its members, then to understand the prospects of cooperation across overlapping clubs, we need to examine: (1) the degree of overlap across clubs in terms of the goods desired by the members of the various clubs, (2) the overlap in club membership itself, and most fundamentally, (3) the commonality of political-economic values and interests that exist across the clubs and their constituent members.

Figures 12.1 and 12.2 display two very different degrees of overlap among three hypothetical international clubs. In each case, the area within the circle represents the array of acceptable policy outcomes for one club. The point labeled with an A, B, or C represents the hypothetical ideal outcome point for that club. In Figure 12.1 there exists a high degree of overlap in the desired policy spaces of the three clubs involved. As each looks at an international issue, the shaded area of the figure represents the potential for cooperative outcomes across the goals of the three clubs.

This overlap can be conceptualized in two ways. First, it can be understood as the overlap in membership that exists among the three clubs, which ultimately translates into a policy overlap, if that portion of the overlapping membership is able to control or at least strongly influence the decision-making process in each of the three clubs. In the example from above, the G-7 countries might well represent such an overlap group among the actors of the six clubs listed in Table 12.1.

The second way to conceptualize the shaded area is by considering it the overlap of preferred policy options and outcomes that satisfy the basic interests

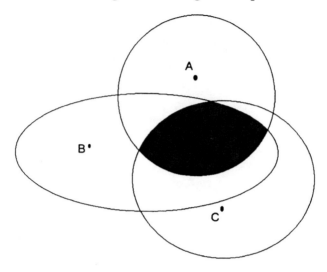

Figure 12.1
Club Space with Large Overlap

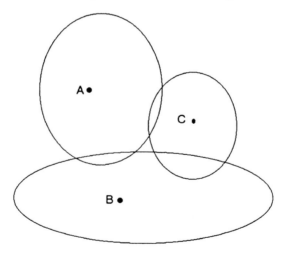

Figure 12.2
Club Space with Small Overlap

of the club's actors. This conceptualization allows the analysis to move beyond two dimensions, as we begin to think about the intersection of policy options and outcomes and individual club member positions in a policy space where many issues are being considered simultaneously. Obviously, the limits of the two-dimensional space shown in Figures 12.1 and 12.2 only allow the discussion of two policy dimensions using the second method of conceptualization. The following will focus primarily on the issue conceptualization of the club policy space.

It is intuitive to assert that the greater the overlap among the clubs in the policy space, the greater the likelihood that there will be cooperation among the clubs in search of common goals and policy outcomes. By extension, for issues that lie outside the shaded overlapping policy space, it is likely that as cooperation emerges on issues within the area of overlap, club members will tend to make decisions on other policy issues that are also in concert with overlap issues. In other words, cooperation on overlap issues may produce a policy environment that reinforces the overlap by bringing "outlying" policies in line with the club overlap. The primary reason for doing so would be to make sure that outlying policies do not contradict the overlap policies, thus causing problems for the fulfillment of the overlap set of goals.

This rosy picture of the prospects for transnational cooperation is tempered by several factors, however. The first tempering factor is that the model as shown is a static one. In reality, the overlapping identities of the three clubs shown in Figure 12.1 may be transient and thus the desire across clubs to coordinate interests may not be long-lived. Change of this sort will depend largely on the degree to which the identities constructed by international actors are changed from below by their constituent parts. The elements of identity may change from a focus on the satisfaction of interests held throughout the world (such as in the impact of international financial crises on local pension plans) to interests that reside much closer to home (such as protection against crime in the inner cities of a decaying urban environment). In the former situation, overlap will likely continue, while in the latter, the desire by constituents to focus on problems closer to home will likely pull attention and interest away from the rationale for cooperation and identification with broader transnational concerns. This tugging in opposite directions is witnessed today in many parts of American foreign policy, as some groups wish to pull back from transnational commitments, while others see as inevitable the need to coordinate activities on a global scale. These tendencies also fit closely with what Rosenau has identified as the simultaneous tendencies for fragmentation and integration in the contemporary system.[20]

But in contrast to thinking about the impact of change from below, a second way of thinking about change deals with the effects of systemic change. Change of this sort has a direct impact on the degree to which the values espoused by the dominant regime of the old system will continue into a new era when the dominant system is in decline. In some instances, it may be that the values of the old system have become institutionalized to such an extent that the "new" system is merely an adaptation of or symbolic change from the old. In others, it may be that the new or evolving system changes relationships among actors to such a degree that the overlap that existed across issues is substantially reduced at least in the short term. Ultimately, new constellations of actors will form new clubs to provide collectively desired goods and identify the overlapping commonalities shown among the clubs in Figure 12.1.

In the short-term during periods of systemic change, and in many other situations where little in the way of identifiable overlap is evident, club relationships may resemble a formation similar to that shown in Figure 12.2. In these types of cases, opportunities for cooperation across clubs are minimal and bargaining will likely be confrontational and difficult, as the clubs involved will negotiate over the small areas of overlap that exist between them. But in contrast to the case in Figure 12.1 (where there is a large amount of overlapping space across clubs), when overlap is small even successfully negotiated outcomes will likely be tenuous as they will exist in places relatively far from the ideal points for each club. Thus, they will likely only be short-term solutions to the problems facing the group of clubs.

In the contemporary system and more precisely in the series of overlapping clubs identified in Table 12.1, we can identify a core set of interests and desired goods among the dominant actors involved that are rooted in the creation of the post–World War II international political-economic system. These include among others:

- military stability, particularly as it serves commercial interests around the globe;
- bounded liberal trading policies; and
- international financial stability.

Numerous scholars have argued that the desirability of these club goods was inculcated by the hegemonic power throughout the Cold War period.[21] What remains to be seen in the future of cooperation among the various actors in the Table 12.1 clubs is whether these hegemonic system values will continue to form the core of the political-economic identity of the clubs in question. The most troublesome substantive issue appears to be whether or not liberal economic policy as espoused by the United States and its power in the World Trade Organization (WTO) and its predecessor the General Agreements on Tariffs and Trade (GATT) will remain a centerpiece in the wave of neomercantilist pressures witnessed through the rise of regional trading blocs and the pressure for domestic protection in many states. But even with much bluster over trade conflict in recent years between some of the dominant actors, it is worth noting that no major moves away from the policies espoused under the WTO have been witnessed and, if anything, more international actors are seeking entry into the system, thus serving to bolster the institutional framework for cooperation. Moreover, from the standpoint of understanding the solidity of the core interests in this area, the wave of anti-WTO (and IMF and World Bank) protests during 1999 and 2000 stemmed not primarily from state-based opposition, but rather from individual and NGO activity centering on particular issue problems, such as international environmental and labor standards.[22]

In another substantive venue, the complex constellation of overlapping interests and desired club goods that exist among the various international debtor and creditor clubs provides an opportunity for cooperative outcomes where there were few politically or economically viable ones fifteen years ago. It took creditor identification of financial vulnerability and interdependence with the debtors to move in this direction. Put simply, by 1990 creditor states had redefined their identities in a more transnational way than was the case earlier and this was at least partly the result of pressure from interests below the state level (banks and other investors worried about their financial commitments) to think in more than the narrow terms traditionally saved for perceptions of creditor financial positions.[23] The highly publicized series of Asian financial crises in recent years even hit these points home to many an average citizen who watched personal investments (such as retirement funds) vacillate widely in financial markets around the world.

Concluding Thoughts

International cooperation can be a fragile phenomenon in the ever-changing landscape of contemporary transnational relations. The foregoing essay has attempted to bring together a number of diverse concepts in the current field of international relations theory in an effort to understand better why cooperation is stable and lasting in some instances and elusive and fleeting in others. In many ways, this is a first venture toward integrating the rich fields of theory that have emerged in recent years regarding the ways collectives form and how they search for solutions to problems that transcend the boundaries of the state.

By using club theory, and public goods theory more generally, we are able to employ a linear understanding of how groups pursue goals in collective action situations and of whether or not they can be successful in the pursuit of those goals. But by introducing the concepts developed by Wendt, Ferguson, and Mansbach and others to the club goods approach to cooperation, an element of nonlinearity is introduced that focuses on the ways group identities can form, evolve, and span across multiple-policy dimensions. In addition, the inherent complexity of social constructs emphasized by these authors and the questioning of the validity of state-based conceptual approaches that they put forth also points to the conceptual limits of the narrower, and conventional, approach to club theory usually employed in the rational choice field.

It is in this complexity, and not the simple pursuit of a single policy good by a group in isolation from other groups and other policy arenas, where the prospects for transnational cooperation are rooted. The degree to which stable networks of overlapping interests exist among transnational actors and the sets of clubs to which they belong is ultimately the determining factor in the successful pursuit of transnationally cooperative policy outcomes.

What lies ahead for the contemporary international system is an unfinished story. Although one can speculate about the institutionalization and political solidification of the transnational values espoused and encapsulated in the series of relationships created during the era of undisputed American hegemony, it is merely that . . . speculation. Given the record of action and policy decisions made by nonhegemonic great powers over the past twenty years, there is certainly reason for optimism, muted though it must be, given the continuing competitive and conflictual urges that emerge among the dominant powers within the system.[24] Nonetheless, it is also obvious that the possibility for systemic and identity change to occur among the various actors and the clubs they form may lead the world in directions not charted by the series of relationships carved out in the American image in the early post–World War II era.

Notes

1. James Rosenau, *Turbulence in World Politics.* (Princeton: Princeton University Press, 1990).

2. Yale H. Ferguson and Richard W. Mansbach, *Polities: Authority, Identities, and Change.* (Columbia: University of South Caroline Press, 1996).

3. Alexander Wendt, "The Agent-Structure Problem in International Relations Theory," *International Organization,* 41(1987): 335–370; Alexander Wendt, "Anarchy Is What States Make of It: The Social Construction of Power Politics," *International Organization,* 46(1992): 391–425; Alexander Wendt, "Collective Identity Formation and the International State," *American Political Science Review,* 88(1994): 384–396.

4. Barry Buzan, Charles Jones, and Richard Little. *The Logic of Anarchy: Neorealism to Structural Realism.* (New York: Columbia University Press, 1993); Helen Milner (1991), "The Assumption of Anarchy in International Relations Theory: A Critique," *Review of International Studies,* 17(1991): 67–85.

5. Davis B. Bobrow and Mark A. Boyer, "International System Stability and American Decline: A Case for Muted Optimism," *International Journal*, 53(1998): 285–305; Davis B. Bobrow and Mark A. Boyer, "Maintaining System Stability: International Cooperation in the Foreign Aid Arena," *Journal of International Relations*, 4(1997): 84–111; Davis B. Bobrow and Mark A. Boyer, "Maintaining System Stability: Contributions to Peacekeeping Operations," *Journal of Conflict Resolution*, 41(1997): 723–748. Bobrow, Davis B. and Mark A. Boyer, "Maintaining System Stability: In Whose Debt?," paper presented at the annual meeting of the International Studies Association, Toronto, Ontario, 17–22 March, 1997.

6. Todd Sandler, *Global Challenges: An Approach to Environmental, Political, and Economic Problems.* (Cambridge: Cambridge University Press, 1997); Todd Sandler, "The Impurity of Defense: An Application to the Economics of Alliances," *Kyklos*, 30(1977): 443–460; Todd Sandler and John F. Forbes, "Burden-Sharing, Strategy and Design of NATO," *Economic Inquiry*, 18(1980): 425–444; Todd Sandler and James Murdoch, "Nash-Cournot or Lindahl Behavior? An Empirical Test for the NATO Allies," *Quarterly Journal of Economics*, 105(1990): 875–894; Todd Sandler and Keith Hartley, *The Economics of Defense.* (Cambridge: Cambridge University Press, 1995); Todd Sandler and Keith Sargent, "Management of Transnational Commons: Coordination, Publicness, and Treaty Formation," *Land Economics*, 71(1995): 145–62; John R. Oneal, "The Theory of Collective Action and Burden-Sharing in NATO," *International Organization*, 44(1990): 379–402; John R. Oneal, "Testing the Theory of Collective Action: NATO Defense Burdens, 1950–1984," *Journal of Conflict Resolution*, 34(1990):426–448; Glenn Palmer, "Corralling the Free-Rider: Deterrence and the Western Alliance," *International Studies Quarterly*, 34(1990): 147–164.

7. Mancur Olson, *The Logic of Collective Action.* (Cambridge: Harvard University Press, 1965).

8. Robert Gilpin, *War and Change in World Politics.* (Cambridge: Cambridge University Press, 1981); John J. Mearsheimer,"Back to the Future: Instability in Europe After the Cold War," in Sean M. Lynn-Jones and Steven E. Miller, eds. *The Cold War and After: Prospects for Peace,* expanded ed. (Cambridge: MIT Press, 1993), pp. 141–192.

9. Dussell Hardin, "Collective Action as an Agreeable n-Prisoners' Dilemma," in *Rational Man, Irrational Society? An Introduction and Sourcebook,* edited by Brian Barry and Russell Hardin. (Beverly Hills: Sage, 1982).

10. David H. Lumsdaine, *Moral Vision in International Politics: The Foreign Aid Regime, 1949–1989.* (Princeton: Princeton University Press, 1993).

11. Henry R. Nau, *The Myth of American Decline: Leading the World Economy in the 1990s.* (New York: Oxford University Press, 1990); Joseph S., Jr. Nye, *Bound To Lead: The Changing Nature of American Power.* (New York: Basic Books, 1990); Kagan, Robert. "The Benevolent Empire," *Foreign Policy*, 111(1998):24–36; G. John Ikenberry, and Charles A. Kupchan. "Socialization and Hegemonic Power," *International Organization*, 44(1990): 283–315.

12. Mark A. Boyer, *International Cooperation and Public Goods: Opportunities for the Western Alliance.* (Baltimore: Johns Hopkins University Press, 1993).

13. Milner (1991).

14. Wendt (1994), 386.

15. Barry Buzan, "From International System to International Society: Structural Realism and Regime Theory Meet the English School," *International Organization*, 47(1993): 327–352. Quoted from p. 339.

16. Milner (1991).

17. Wendt (1992).

18. Ferguson and Mansbach (1996).

19. I have chosen to use the abbreviation G-7 for clarity, as the addition of Russia as a member of the group has produced dynamics that are yet unknown in there implications for cooperation. Russia membership in the G-8 makes the club different in number and kind from the G-7 and is another example of the evolving nature of international club relationships.

20. Rosenau (1990).

21. See, for example, Ikenberry and Kupchan (1990); Nau (1990); and Nye (1990).

22. See for instance the special section on the Seattle WTO protests in the *Review of International Political Economy* edited by Jan Nederveen Pieterse, vol. 7(3):465–504.

23. Bobrow and Boyer (1997).

24. Bobrow and Boyer (1998).

CHAPTER 13

NGOs and Fragmented Authority in Globalizing Space

James N. Rosenau

There are good reasons for suggesting that the modern age had ended. Many things indicate that we are going through a transitional period, when it seems that something is on the way out and something else is painfully being born. It is as if something were crumbling, decaying and exhausting itself, while something else, still indistinct, were arising from the rubble.

—Vaclav Havel[1]

Assuming this observation is sound, little wonder that our collective understanding of the underlying nature of world affairs is deeply fractured. As students of international relations (IR), we lack consensus on whether profound transformations are fostering a new set of global arrangements, on whether any changes at work are moving in the direction of greater complexity or greater simplicity, on whether the essential structures of the international system are eroding, on whether states and national governments are undergoing a diminution of their capabilities, on whether transnational nongovernmental organizations (NGOs) are picking up any of the slack created by the diminution of state powers, and, indeed, on whether the concept of an NGO is vacuous or meaningful.

Such issues derive in part from paradigmatic differences—realists assess the capabilities of states differently than do transnationalists, to cite an obvious example—but they also have their roots in the diverse temperaments we bring to our observations. It may well be that these differences can never be bridged and that collectively we are destined to sustain a fractured understanding of the way the world works. But the impulse to build bridges across deep divides is hard to quell, as the ensuing analysis plainly demonstrates. Here I put aside paradigmatic differences and, instead, undertake to explore two lines of reasoning that may serve as building blocks for a more widespread consensus. One is to assess the conceptual underpinnings of each of the issues noted in the previous paragraph and the other is to focus on the concept of authority, which is central to all these issues and thus can serve as a bridge across which diverse analysts may be able to converge. In particular, since the role of NGOs in the emergent global system is both central and controversial, the authority that does or does not attach to them is probed as an example of the more encompassing issues.

Underlying Concepts

Achieving conceptual clarity is not an easy task. Temperamental differences can foster highly discrepant conclusions: where one observer sees change, another sees the recurrence of age-old patterns; where one discerns complex processes, another discerns regression toward a long-standing mean; where one perceives the operation of a dialectic, another perceives independent processes; where one analyst cites evidence of the emergence of new institutions, another interprets the same evidence as reflecting the adaptation of old institutions; where one treats governments as paralyzed by the growing complexity of globalized societies, another points to the stalemates as products of classic bureaucratic infighting; where one regards globalizing and localizing dynamics inextricably linked in deep dialectic processes, another presumes that localization derives from cultural origins unique to those who share a common territory.

Change

Perhaps no concept in the IR toolshed of analytic equipment is more fundamental to our understanding of how the world works than the concept of change, what it means, how it is measured, and when it is consequential. Despite its importance, however, the concept is used loosely and is not the focus of widespread agreement. It is almost as if some analysts temperamentally need to see the world as marked by pervasive constancies, while others are more suited to a perspective in which the dynamics of change are especially salient and still others need to take a middle position in which they acknowledge that profound transformations have occurred but argue that the changes have subsequently petered out and settled into predictable regularities. These temperamental differences are linked closely to our paradigmatic orientations and are thus central to our intellectual stances. Their operation can be readily discerned in the numerous analysts who assert that, yes, huge changes have occurred, but, no, these do not amount to fundamental changes.[2] Ambivalence of this sort can have enormous analytic consequences. It matters, for example, whether one views the transformations that underlay and accompanied the end of the Cold War as continuing to unfold or as having settled into routinized arrangements.

I would like to think that my perspective on the issue of change versus constancy derives from incisive empirical observations, but it is surely also a consequence of my own temperament, my sense that individuals and collectivities are endlessly adaptive, ever capable of learning, thus leading to a variability of human experience that allows for sharp turns in the paths of history. Accordingly, the pages that follow derive from an unequivocal conviction that the degrees of change unfolding throughout the world are so great as to lie beyond our full comprehension.

Although still accelerating at a rapid rate, the dynamics of change do seem well enough along to justify treating the world not as national and international arenas, but as a globalized space—a space that is not disaggregated in terms of specified geographic territories so much as it consists of a wide range of fast-moving, boundary-spanning actors whose activities cascade erratically across amorphous ethnoscapes, mediascapes, ideoscapes, technoscapes, and financescapes.[3] As indicated by the ensuing concern with NGOs and the authority they may or may not wield, I view this disaggregated system of diverse transnational collectivities as a multicentric world that competes, cooperates, or otherwise interacts with the state-centric world and, as such, constitutes an emergent world order, an order that is so decentralized that it does not lend itself either to hierarchy or coordination under hegemonic leadership.[4]

While it is thus difficult to specify precisely the nature of the global transformations underway at the outset of a new century, a general perspective on the transformative dynamics can be set forth. Whether they result from slow, evolutionary processes or sharp historical breakpoints, the changes of concern here are those that involve differences in kind, rather than in degree, compared to previous decades.[5] The distinction between the two kinds of change are conceived to reflect huge differences in the number, scale, scope, and rapidity through which the affairs of collectivities are conducted. Where the differences along these dimensions are regarded as involving patterns that are clearly discrepant with those of the past, changes in kind are deemed to have taken place. Lesser shifts along these dimensions—differences in degree—may eventually cumulate to differences in kind, but until they do, the analytic tasks can be carried out in familiar ways. It is the differences in kind that pose the most severe challenges to those who seek to develop adequate theories of world affairs. The scope of the challenges has been well described by David Held:

> [T]here is a fundamental difference between, on the one hand, the development of particular trade routes, and the global reach of nineteenth-century empires, and, on the other hand, an international order involving the conjuncture of a global system of production and exchange which is beyond the control of any single nation-state (even of the most powerful); extensive networks of transnational interaction and communication which transcend national societies and evade most forms of national regulation; the power and

activities of a vast array of international regimes and organizations, many of which reduce the scope for action of even leading states; and the internationalization of security structures which limit the scope for the independent use of military force by states. While in the eighteenth and nineteenth centuries trade routes and empires linked distant populations together through quite simple networks of interaction, the contemporary global order is defined by multiple systems of transaction and coordination which link people, communities and societies in highly complex ways and which, given the nature of modern communications, virtually annihilate territorial boundaries as barriers to socio-economic activity and relations, and create new political uncertainties.[6]

Related to these differences in kind are those that follow from the collapse of time and space through new technologies.[7] The latter are fostering processes of aggregation and disaggregation that are occurring and interacting so rapidly—more often than not instantaneously to the point of being simultaneous—that they can hardly be viewed as differences of degree. One need only compare the dynamics of organizational decision-making, societal mobilization, and intersocietal relationships in the present and previous eras to appreciate that the differences are not trivial, that they are so substantial as to be far more than merely updated repetitions of earlier patterns. Or, to use a more specific example, a comparison of the collapse of the Roman empire across centuries and of the British empire across decades with that of the Soviet empire across weeks and months will highlight how modern technologies have fostered differences in kind rather than degree.

Complexity

Closely related to the temperamental differences over the extent of change are those that relate to the extent to which the world is becoming increasingly complex. Those inclined to stress the constancy of human affairs are, naturally enough, disinclined to see them as marked by a deepening complexity, whereas those who emphasize transformative dynamics tend to perceive a world of ever greater intricacies. The latter are persuaded that whether or not linearity was ever the central tendency of human affairs, it now seems clear that we live in a nonlinear world in which causes and effects are so inextricably intertwined as to underlie central tendencies consisting of feedback loops, contradictory patterns, anomalous developments, and punctuated equilibria.

Happily, for those who are disposed to see the world undergoing vast transformations, a growing body of literature known as "complexity theory" has evolved that seems to offers a means of analytically probing the dynamics of change.[8] As I understand it, at the core of complexity theory is the complex adaptive system—not a cluster of unrelated activities, but a system; not a simple system, but a complex one; and not a static, unchanging set of arrangements, but a complex adaptive system. Such a system is distinguished by a set of inter-related parts, each one of which is potentially capable of being an autonomous agent that, through acting autonomously, can impact on the others, and all of which either engage in patterned behavior as they sustain day-to-day routines or break with the routines when new challenges require new responses and new patterns. The interrelationships of the agents is what makes them a system. The capacity of the agents to break with routines and thus initiate unfamiliar feedback processes is what makes the system complex (since in a simple system all the agents consistently act in prescribed ways). The capacity of the agents to cope collectively with the new challenges is what makes them adaptive systems. Such, then, is the modern urban community, the nation state, and the international system. Like any complex adaptive system in the natural world, the agents that comprise world affairs are brought together into systemic wholes that consist of patterned structures ever subject to transformation as a result of feedback processes from their external environments or from internal stimuli that provoke the agents to break with their established routines. There may have been long periods of stasis in history where, relatively speaking, each period in the life of a human system was like the one before it; but for a variety of reasons elaborated elsewhere,[9] the present period is one of turbulence, of social systems and their polities undergoing profound transformations that exhibit all the characteristics of complex adaptive systems.

Among the many insights into the nature of complex adaptive systems provided by complexity theory, four stand out as offering especially useful insights into the fragmentation of globalized space. First, such systems co-evolve with their environments as they adapt;[10] second, being adaptive, they are able to self-organize into an orderly whole and, as they do, they begin to acquire new attributes (what complexity theorists call emergent properties); third, their complexity is such that they are vulnerable to small events resulting in large outcomes (the so-called butterfly effect); and fourth, slight changes in their initial conditions can lead to very different outcomes.[11]

Structural Erosion

Although a preponderance of IR analysts agree that the system of anarchical states constitutes the essential structure of world affairs, important differences are discernible both with respect to the configuration of international structures and the possibility that another system has emerged to rival the international system. A large literature has evolved since the end of the Cold War in which questions whether international politics is dominated by a single hegemon, the United States, or whether it has become a multipolar system in which no single country can be meaningfully regarded as having achieved hegemonic status.[12] Another controversy revolves around the proposition that it is not so much states as it is civilizations that are the bases for the tensions and conflicts that sustain world affairs.[13] Still other differences focus on the possibility that while the interstate system continues to be a central feature of global structures, it now faces a structural rival composed of diverse nongovernmental collectivities that are active on the global stage—from NGOs to social movements, from ethnic minorities to transnational corporations, from professional societies to epistemic communities—and that form a sufficiently coherent structure to account for much of what happens in the course of events. As previously noted, those who attach importance to the advent of this multicentric world view the erosion of global structures as having occurred through a bifurcation wherein collectivities in the multi- and state-centric worlds endlessly interact.

Notwithstanding considerable evidence that can be cited (see below) in support of the predominance of the bifurcated system, again it is doubtless a mix of empirical evidence and temperamental inclinations that underlie my presumption that the erosion of long-standing global structures has resulted in the state system being supplemented (though not replaced) by a complex world of nongovernmental actors. Indeed, convinced that the word "international" no longer embraces much of what transpires across national boundaries, my comfort zone no longer tolerates use of the word.[14] Rather, I think of myself as a bifurcationist and have become habituated to the notion that once one moves beyond national boundaries one's focus turns to global politics or, perhaps more accurately, to politics on a global scale. Moreover, based on the presumption that politics on either side of national boundaries have become so inextricably linked as to render domestic and foreign affairs largely indistinguishable from each other, I am inclined to view all politics as global in scale.[15] This is why the ensuing analysis treats the question of the authority wielded by NGOs as central to our understanding of how the world works: reinforced by powerful data indicating a veritable organizational explosion at all levels of community throughout the world,[16] it seems inconceivable that the interstate system is still the sole arbiter of the course of events.

State Capabilities

An especially vigorous controversy revolves around the issue of whether states continue to be the dominant actors on the world stage, or whether for a variety of reasons their capabilities have undergone enough diminution to allow other collectivities, or even individuals, to exercise substantial power and influence in the construction and management of the global agenda. Numerous analysts acknowledge that states may not have the capabilities they once did, but they nevertheless resist interpreting such changes as an alteration of the predominance of states on the global scene. Yes, the argument goes, states have yielded substantial degrees of control over their economies to globalizing dynamics; yes, the microelectronic revolution has reduced their control over the flow of ideas and information that circulate domestically; yes, the trend toward decentralization to provincial and local levels of governance has lessened the capacities of central governments; and yes, the depletion of resources have made states increasingly dependent on external sources; but, no, such patterns and problems do not amount to a meaningful decrease of their central role in steering their societies through internal upheavals and external challenges.[17] On the other hand, a growing number of observers perceive these same trends—plus many others—as amounting to a significant decline in the capacities of states. A moderate form of this argument follows a line of reasoning that stresses "that what were once domains of authority exclusive to state authority are now being shared with other loci or sources of authority,"[18] whereas an unqualified expression of this perspective is plainly evident in the conviction of one analyst "that the nation-state as a complex modern political form is on its last legs. . . . Nation-states, as units in a complex interactive system, are not very likely to be the long-term arbiters of the relationship between globality and modernity. . . . [M]y persistent focus on the hyphen that links nation to state is part of an evolving argument that the very epoch of the nation-state is near its end."[19]

My analytic inclinations come out somewhere between these two perspectives. As indicated by the notion of global structures bifurcating into state- and multi-centric worlds, there continue to be important issue arenas in which states exercise authority and sustain their predominance, just as in other arenas they have been superseded, or at least rivaled, by collectivities in the multi-centric world. Given the dynamics of globalization and the counter-reactions in localizing directions,[20] it seems likely to me that the long-term trend favors an enduring bifurcation.[21]

NGO Capabilities

Although the definition of NGOs is not free of controversy (see below), whether their capabilities have expanded in proportion to any diminution of capabilities experienced by states is not so much a matter of dispute as it is a derivative of other differences. Few quarrel with the extensive literature in which NGOs are depicted as collectively playing an increasingly greater role in IR, but conclusions as to whether these new roles are intruding on and undermining the competencies of states derives from conceptions of how global structures and the capacity of states may or may not be changing. For those who tend to posit unchanging global structures and states as dominant actors, NGOs are seen as useful facilitators of the efforts of states to frame their policies and pursue their goals.[22] For those whose temperaments incline them to highlight the transformations that are fostering a bifurcation of the global system and a diminution of state capacities, NGOs are seen as "effective agents of change to the extent that they operate independently of states and do what states tend not to do," as having a "credible claim" on legitimacy when they do what "governments and corporations cannot."[23] Indeed, for some analysts, NGOs loom so large as major players on the global stage that they are viewed as taking over some the functions that states have long performed. As one observer puts it, "Groups like Amnesty International, Worldwatch, Greenpeace, and Doctors Without Borders—plus Mobil, Mitsubishi, CNN, and various cultural associations—will be writing the script for world history at least as much as most of the governments that now monopolize voting in the UN."[24]

Due to the advance of microelectronic technologies, moreover, the capabilities of NGOs have been extended considerably by their ability to coordinate their activities through the Internet, the fax machine, and the other gadgetry that marks the information revolution. In so doing, many have become members of vast networks with like-minded NGOs in other parts of the world, networks that carry more authority and influence than any of the NGOs do individually.[25]

To treat NGOs as major players, however, is not to imply that they are equally competent. As has been repeatedly noted, enormous variabilities mark their size, financial resources, influence, and coherence.[26] And it also seems clear that they cannot exercise nearly as much authority as do some states. Notwithstanding the variabilities in their capabilities, however, the thrust of the remainder of the paper is that more than a few NGOs are able to act authoritatively in the issue arenas where they are active.

The NGO Concept

The enormous variability in the purposes, resources, funding, size, and support of different NGOs underlies not only enormous problems of how to classify them for descriptive and analytic purposes,[27] but it also serves as a source of controversy over the meaning and utility of the concept. NGOs that are not officially recognized by the United Nations, for example, are considered to be no less relevant to the course of events than those that are, and yet the distinction can be easily misunderstood and, accordingly, is often rankling for those that lack UN status. One analyst succinctly captures this controversy and suggests an admittedly unworkable solution for it:

> The term "nongovernmental" has been resented by many organizations. It is indeed a manifestation of organizational apartheid—reminiscent of the "nonwhite" label so frequent in racist societies . . . the challenge is to discover the name . . . with which such bodies can identify. The problem may be insoluble, given the level of organizational apartheid practiced between organizations—even between NGOs. But if it is impossible to abandon the initials

"NGO," perhaps it is possible to reframe their significance in a more positive light. One candidate might be "Necessary-to-Governance Organizations". . . The corresponding reframing of "IGO" might then be "Insufficient-for-Governance Organizations."[28]

Not being an active member of any organization lacking an official UN affiliation, my temperament is to avoid conflicts surrounding the NGO concept by using it broadly and inclusively. With one exception, the analysis that follows treats any transnational organization not under the authority of a government as an NGO, and this formulation includes organizations that may actually receive funds from one or another government or IGO. It includes profit as well as voluntary or not-for-profit organizations, and it also collapses NGOs and GROs under the same rubric.[29] The only exclusion is that of organizations that openly reject the legitimacy of the political process and advocate or engage in violence.[30] The point is to focus on transnational organizations that lie outside the formal aegis of governments and states in order to assess the cross-currents and dynamics of the globalized space in which members of both the multi- and state-centric worlds frame and interactively sustain the global agenda.

Authority

If it is the case that the multicentric world is increasingly relevant as a source of global structures, and if it is also reasonable to treat states as undergoing a diminution of their capacity to cope with the dynamics of change and complexity in globalizing space, then more attention needs to be paid to NGOs, their variety, capacities, limitations, and influence as complex adaptive systems that are playing a role in configuring the emergent post–Cold War order. And, indeed, increasing attention is being focused on the sources and consequences of their actions. A rapidly growing literature has developed that is marked by both numerous case studies and several more general formulations.[31] Conspicuously missing from this literature, however, is the question of how much authority NGOs can command and how such authority as they may possess gets created, sustained, enlarged, diminished, and destroyed. While it is relatively easy to trace the influence and power exercised by NGOs and their advocacy networks, identifying and assessing their authority is more problematic.

Before undertaking this task, however, we need to clarify how authority relations differ from those based on power and influence. While there can be some overlap among the three types of relations—in the sense that each may be more effective if it is supported by either or both of the other two—there are important ways in which they are differentiated. Most notably, the compliance evoked by authority is a direct and voluntary response to a stimulus, whereas influence operates circuitously rather than through direct stimuli and power tends to obscure the voluntarism of the compliance because it is backed up by the threat or use of coercion. Consequently, the more authorities have to resort to the threat or use of force, the less voluntaristic is the compliance and the weaker is their authority. It follows that authority relations are to a large degree founded on habit, on an unthinking readiness to comply with directives, on a legitimacy that has been accorded the authorities by those toward whom their compliance efforts are directed. Authority relationships are thus not easily constructed or sustained inasmuch as the habits of compliance necessary to sustain them evolve only as they are repeatedly reinforced; and by the same token, such relationships can collapse quickly once the underlying tendencies toward habitual compliance are undermined by authoritative actions based on questionable legitimacy.[32]

The key to the effectiveness of an authority structure lies not in its formal documents but in the readiness of those toward whom authority is directed to comply with the rules and policies promulgated by the authorities. Formal authority is vacuous if it does not evoke compliance, whereas informal authority not backed by formal documentation can be stable and effective if its exercise produces compliance. This is especially so in the multicentric world where hierarchy is often less important than nonlinear feedback networks as the basis for coherence among those who make and implement decisions. Where hierarchy is minimal, as is the case for numerous collectivities in globalized space, compliance derives more from shared aspirations and practices generated by networking than from traditional obligations or coercive threats that foster an unthinking acceptance of directives.

In order to trace the flow of authority through horizontal networks, we need to view compliance as habitual responses to requests as well as directives. To comply repeatedly and unthinkingly with requests is not the same as engaging in cooperation. Whether they be in horizontal networks or hierarchical structures, cooperative acts result from calculations, from assessments as to how to achieve goals, from thinking through situations, whereas habitual responses to requests are grounded in an acknowledgment as to the location of authority in the relationship and thus do not require calculations to initiate or sustain the responses.

Locating authority relations in terms of varying kinds and degrees of compliance serves well the task of tracing authority in globalized space. Such a formulation allows for movement back and forth as particular authority structures change in response to the feedback loops and complex adaptation of collectivities in diverse situations. Moreover, it provides a context that can be applied equally to states and to collectivities in globalized space as diverse as crime syndicates, financial markets, nonprofit organizations, multinational corporations, coalitions of the willing, issue regimes, and so on. In the case of sovereign states, most possess both the formal and informal authority that enables them to compel compliance in their domains, but in the case of some states authority is fragile as developments undermine the habitual readiness of their citizens to comply. Likewise, the collectivities active in globalized space are located at various points along the compliance continuum, with a few (such as the European Union) having successfully created both formal and informal authority that can be effectively exercised, while some (such as Greenpeace) have evolved informal authority that relies on requests to evoke compliance on the part of their members and still others (such as crime syndicates) use threats, coercion, and other techniques toward the resistance extreme of the continuum to generate compliance. In short, wherever collectivities persist in globalized space, they have authority structures that enable them to mobilize and give direction to their memberships on behalf of their policies.

Types of Authority

Although NGOs vary greatly in their size, resources, goals, interests, and capacity to evoke habitual compliance, there are only a limited number of ways in which they can exercise authority. Lacking the weight of long-standing traditions, they can draw on five sources of habitual compliance: moral authority, knowledge authority, reputational authority, issue-specific authority, and what might be called affiliative authority. There is some overlap among these types, but they are sufficiently differentiated to illustrate separately.

Moral Authority

NGOs dedicated to alleviating torture, famine, and other forms of suffering are especially capable of generating habitual compliance. Neither people nor collectivities nor governments can readily resist appeals for support and money on behalf of the downtrodden, the exploited, or those victimized by nature's disasters. More accurately, when NGOs successfully make such appeals, it is because they are "portrayed as humanitarian, apolitical and representative of the best in motivations"[33] and thus backed by the moral authority that attaches high value to human rights, dignity, freedom, and well-being.[34] Some of the subjects of their exercise of authority—be they individuals giving money, groups offering services, or governments providing relief supplies—may waffle, need further persuasion, or be entirely unresponsive; but others are so sensitive to moral authority that they do not hesitate to comply with the requests. Such a pattern has recently been evidenced by the donor community in Rwanda and other African situations, by human rights groups that sponsored the disinvestment campaign against apartheid in South Africa, and by the fund-raising efforts of such NGOs as Amnesty International, Médicins Sans Frontièrs, CARE, and Oxfam. Indeed, habitual compliance to moral authority has become so thoroughgoing in the United States (and perhaps elsewhere) that some people now permit their donations to such organizations to be deducted automatically (and electronically) from their bank accounts every month.

While the moral authority of human rights and refugee organizations has expanded, however, the same cannot be said of governments. Torn by scandals, pervaded with corruption, buffeted by policy failures, many national governments appear to have lost all or most of any moral authority they once had, both with respect to each other and in relation to publics.[35] They still have authority they can exercise, but its effectiveness derives from sources other than high-minded appeals to values associated with human dignity and decency. Accordingly, as one analyst put it, "In this situation the human rights NGOs have to be the conscience of the world, as one government will often be reluctant to make accusations against another because of political alliances, commercial interests, or fear of the 'pot calling the kettle black.'"[36]

Knowledge Authority

Scientific associations and epistemic communities are clear-cut examples of how NGOs can use their knowledge to create authority that meets the habitual compliance test. Their expertise on medical, biological, and ecological issues is so scarce and specialized that private groups and governments are ready to comply with their recommendations about such issues. More accurately, if scientific communities can make pronouncements with a united voice on issues relevant to their expertise, then the world is poised to comply automatically with the policy implications of their advice. This is, of course, a big "if," as often such issues are divisive among the specialists, a circumstance that is likely to detract from the authority of their knowledge.[37]

While national governments tend to have access to more information and knowledge than NGOs, again it can be said that their authority in this regard has eroded. As previously indicated, one of the reasons for this erosion is the microelectronic revolution that has provided NGOs with access to a wide base of information and knowledge that is not so far removed from that available to counterparts in the government. But an equally important reason is that the mushrooming of cynicism toward government has tended to render any pronouncements they make—no matter how solid the evidence or how advanced the expertise they offer may be—objects of suspicion and ridicule.[38]

Reputational Authority

Closely linked to moral and knowledge authority is the kind that derives from a reputation for integrity and competence. A good illustration is the authority of credit-rating agencies. Their capacity to evoke habitual compliance is rooted in the impeccable reputation they build up for fairness and thoroughness, a reputation that appears to be so authoritative that defying it entails undue risks.[39] Consider, for example, this assessment of one such agency:

> Moody's is the credit rating agency that signals the electronic herd of global investors where to plunk down their money, by telling them which countries' bonds are blue-chip and which are junk. That makes Moody's one powerful agency. In fact, you could almost say that we live again in a two-superpower world. There is the U.S. and there is Moody's. The U.S. can destroy a country by leveling it with bombs; Moody's can destroy a country by downgrading its bonds.[40]

Following the above reasoning as to the authority governments can exercise through the knowledge they proffer, they surely fall far short of meeting the habitual compliance test when it comes to their reputational authority. The lack of trust and cynicism with which politics and governments are regarded today makes it very difficult for them to evoke compliance on the basis of a reputation for equity and even-handedness. And for many governments it may well be that this form of authority has eroded beyond repair.

Issue-Specific Authority

Some NGOs have established themselves so squarely in an issue arena that more often than not their authority evokes habitual compliance. In addition to any moral, special knowledge, or reputation that may undergird their authority, their actions are backed by the history and nature of the specific issues on which they focus—that is, by the weight of the path-dependent processes that led to the differentiation of their issue arena. The issues must have worldwide appeal and be based on concerns that lie beyond the aegis of governments. Sports offers an excellent illustration in this regard, particularly the International Olympic Committee (IOC) and the quadrennial games over which it exercises authority. The Olympics have not been free of politics, but the long-term tendency on the part of both athletes and governments is to comply with the IOC's rulings. It might be argued that the issue-specific authority of the IOC had its origins in the moral authority inherent in the ideals of amateur athletics as an activity where talent and sportsmanship predominates. While such an argument may have once carried weight, its foundations were undercut when the amateur rule was abandoned in 1992 and then further undermined when a corruption scandal engulfed the IOC in connection with the 2002 games in Nevada. Furthermore, because the Olympics are organized by country delegations, thus giving rise to nationalistic preoccupations, rather than concern for the athletes, the IOC's authority can hardly be regarded as a consequence of moral considerations. In the words of one analyst, "The Olympic movement has been forced to define its health in terms of the growth and size of its organizations rather than in terms of its ideals. The ideals have been made secondary but have been used as the primary justification for its existence."[41]

Has there been a loss in the issue-specific authority of governments? Probably not in the case of those issues, such as agriculture, finance, and immigration, where the regulatory capacities of governments remain intact. Of course, the trend toward deregulation and smaller government has doubtless reduced the scope of their issue-specific authority, but compared to their loss of the other forms of authority, that which attaches to issues that remain within the purview of governments would appear to still be capable of evoking habitual compliance.

Affiliative Authority

NGOs that serve the emotional needs of ethnic minorities, diaspora, and other groups with deep cultural roots can often evoke more than a little habitual compliance when they make requests of the groups they represent. Whether it be Jewish organizations in the United States responding to requests for funds from counterparts in Israel, Armenians in Los Angeles heeding requests from their homeland for supplies and manpower to cope with earthquakes, or Chinese in Southeast Asia being asked by the Chinese government to contribute their wealth, technological know-how, or otherwise help the country's development, the habitual compliance test is usually met quickly through the authority inherent in shared affiliations.[42] Indeed, common cultural or religious roots combined with a sense of being a beleaguered minority is perhaps the most effective source of authority on which any NGO can draw.

But quite the opposite conclusion obtains with respect to many national governments. The focus of skepticism and cynicism, wracked with internal divisions, and lacking a clear-cut external enemy, a number of governments cannot rely on loyalty to their country to achieve compliance with their policies. In the United States, prior to the September 2001 terrorist attack, for example, serious proposals were voiced questioning the virtues of patriotism.[43] A thoughtful proposal to rewrite the national anthem has even found its way into the public domain.[44] Stated differently, as the values of multiculturalism become increasingly ascendant throughout the world, the authority of states is bound to be weakened, with their capacity to sustain broad consensuses around shared goals diminished and their ability to concert the energies of citizens in support of policies reduced. Indeed, it is with respect to the breakdown of national consensuses and the subsequent diminution of national loyalties that governments may have incurred the greatest loss of authority. As Hegel once put it, "nothing assures the atrophy and corruption of the various organizations and structures of a state more than prolonged periods of peace. War with other countries generates that spirit of national unity which is indispensable for the health and stability of the state as an *organism which transcends and holds together its individual components*."[45]

Conclusions

The foregoing examples of different forms that the authority of NGOs can take are surely too few to prove anything. They are merely illustrative of the possibility that the transformations at work in world politics include a highly populated multicentric world in which NGOs can exercise authority and thereby add to their growing influence as players on the global stage. For both better and worse, their impact extends far beyond whatever authority they can exercise,[46] but it is crucial to an understanding of the dynamics of change that NGOs be seen as capable of evoking compliance under certain circumstances. And while it is also the case that "[f]actors such as operational experience, technical expertise, negotiating skills and precise objectives make all the difference between an effective NGO and one which enjoys less success, however worthy the cause or dedicated its representatives,"[47] the foregoing discussion suggests that effectiveness may also be linked to the moral, knowledge, reputational, issue-specific, and/or affiliative authority through which NGOs are linked to their supporters and the objects of their actions. Presumably the greater their authority in these respects, the more likely are they to accomplish their goals.

In short, while the perspective advanced here may not bridge the differences that divide the IR community of observers, hopefully the discussion points to the need to broaden our analytic lenses beyond the interactions of states and their systemic organizations. Clearly, we need to focus as well on the compliance that the diverse collectivities on the global stage can evoke in response to their goal-seeking endeavors.

Acknowledgments

I am grateful to David Johnson and Hongying Wang for their reactions to an earlier draft.

Notes

1. "The New Measure of Man," *New York Times*, July 8, 1994, p. 27A.

2. For an example in which states are conceived to have undergone profound changes that nevertheless have not altered their role and competence, see Eugene B.

Skolnikoff, *The Elusive Transformation: Science, Technology, and the Evolution of International Politics* (Princeton: Princeton University Press, 1993), p. 7.

3. These diverse "scapes" are the formulation of Arjun Appadurai, in *Modernity at Large: Cultural Dimensions of Globalization* (Minneapolis: University of Minnesota Press, 1996), p. 33.

4. For an analysis of the bifurcation that resulted in the multi- and state-centric worlds, see James N. Rosenau, *Turbulence in World Politics: A Theory of Change and Continuity* (Princeton: Princeton University Press, 1990), chap. 10.

5. It should be noted that I do not take the measurement problems associated with the differences in kind and degree lightly even though I assume they are solvable. Here, however, my concern is analytic clarity rather than empirical precision and thus no attempt is made to elaborate on how the differences might be measured.

6. David Held, "Democracy and the New International Order," in Daniele Archibugi and David Held (eds.), *Cosmopolitan Democracy: An Agenda for a New World Order* (Cambridge: Polity Press, 1995), p. 101.

7. One of the most recent—and among the most stunning—technological innovations is the advent of a new computer chip based on chemical processes that will reduce the size of a chip to that of a molecule and that promises to increase the speed of computers by 100 billion (repeat 100 billion) times. John Markoff, "Tiniest Circuits Hold Prospect of Explosive Computer Speeds," *New York Times*, July 16, 1999, p. A1.

8. For cogent analyses of complexity theory, see Roger Lewin, *Complexity: Life at the Edge of Chaos* (New York: Macmillan Publishing Co., 1992), and M. Mitchell Waldrop, *Complexity: The Emerging Science at the Edge of Order and Chaos* (New York: Simon and Schuster, 1992).

9. Rosenau, *Turbulence in World Politics*, chaps. 1, 5.

10. As one complexity theorist put it, referring to self-organization as a natural property of complex genetic systems, "There is 'order for free' out there." Stuart Kauffman, quoted in Lewin, *Complexity*, p. 25.

11. For an elaboration of these four premises, see James N. Rosenau, "Many Damn Things Simultaneously: Complexity Theory and World Affairs," in David S. Alberts and Thomas J. Czerwinski (eds.), *Complexity, Global Politics, and National Security* (Washington, D.C.: National Defense University, 1997), pp. 73–100.

12. For highlights of this debate, see Samuel P. Huntington, "The U.S.—Decline or Renewal?" *Foreign Affairs*, vol. 67 (Winter 1988–89), pp. 76–96; Bruce M. Russett, "The Mysterious Case of Vanishing Hegemony; or, Is Mark Twain Really Dead?" *International Organization*, Vol. 39 (Spring 1985), pp. 207–231.

13. This perspective is advanced in Samuel P. Huntington, *The Clash of Civilization and the Remaking of World Order* (New York: Simon & Schuster, 1996), and criticized in Symposium, "Responses to Samuel P. Huntington's 'The Clash of Civilizations,'" *Foreign Affairs*, vol. 72 (September/October 1993), pp. 2–26. For an especially virulent expression of this controversy, see Pierre Hassner and Samuel P. Huntington, "Clashing On," *The National Interest*, no. 48 (Summer 1997), pp. 105–111.

14. In other words, I am in full agreement with Susan Strange when she writes, "I have at last reached the final parting of the ways from the discipline of international relations. I have been involved with it now . . . over more than a half a century. But I can no longer profess a special concern with international politics if that is defined as a study different from other kinds of politics and which takes the state as the unit of analysis, and the international society of states as the main problematic." Susan Strange, *The Retreat of the State: The Diffusion of Power in the World Economy* (Cambridge: Cambridge University Press, 1996), p. xv.

15. This approach is elaborated at length in James N. Rosenau, *Along the Domestic-Foreign Frontier: Exploring Governance in a Turbulent World* (Cambridge: Cambridge University Press, 1997).

16. Lester M. Salamon, "The Global Associational Revolution: The Rise of the Third Sector on the World Scene," *Foreign Affairs*, vol. 73 (July/August 1994), pp. 109–122.

17. Recent and careful efforts to demonstrate the continuing viability and centrality of states and their international system are developed in Arie M. Kacowicz, "Reinventing the Wheel: The Attacks on the State and Its Resilience," a paper presented at the Annual Meeting of the International Studies Association (Chicago: February 22–25, 1995), and Georg Sorenson, "The State Is Still Decisive, OK? Security and Globalization," a paper presented at the Annual Meeting of the International Studies Association (Toronto: March 18–22, 1997).

18. Strange, *The Retreat of the State*, p. 82.

19. Appadurai, *Modernity at Large*, p. 19.

20. For a discussion of the interaction of globalizing and localizing dynamics, see James N. Rosenau, "Distant Proximities: The Dynamics and Dialectics of Globalization," in Bjorn Hettne (ed.), *International Political Economy: Understanding Global Disorder* (London: Zed Books, 1995), pp. 46–64.

21. For the reasoning that underlies this prime conclusion, see Rosenau, *Turbulence in World Politics*, pp. 453–454.

22. See, for example, Stephen D. Biggs and Arthur D. Neame, "Negotiating Room to Maneuver: Reflections Concerning NGO Autonomy and Accountability within the New Policy Agenda," in Michael Edwards and David Hulme (eds.), *Beyond the Magic Bullet: NGO Performance and Accountability in the Post–Cold War World* (West Hartford, CT: Kumarian Press, 1996), chap. 2.

23. Thomas Princen, Matthias Finger, and Jack P. Manno, "Translational Linkages," in T. Princen and M. Finger (eds.), *Environmental NGOs in World Politics: Linking the Local and the Global* (London: Routledge, 1994), p. 230.

24. Helena Cobban, "From Empires to NGOs," *Christian Science Monitor*, September 14, 1995, p. 20.

25. For example, see Margaret E. Keck and Kathryn Sikkink, *Activists Beyond Borders: Advocacy Networks in International Politics* (Ithaca: Cornell University Press, 1998).

26. These variabilities are even conspicuous in a particular issue area. For example, see Thomas Princen and Matthias Finger, "Introduction," in T. Princen and M. Finger (eds.), *Environmental NGOs in World Politics*, pp. 1–9.

27. A good insight into the conceptual and methodological problems inherent in mapping the NGO world is provided by the 1992/1993 edition of the *Yearbook of International Organizations* published by the Union of International Associations: it has no fewer than thirty-two pages of appendices (all with two columns of fine print) that elaborate the definitions and classification rules used to generate, compile, and classify the thousands of diverse organizations it identifies. For a summary of the main outlines of the data presented in the 1992/1993 edition of the *Yearbook* (Munich: K. G. Saur Verlag, 1992) as well as for data on transnational corporations and a discussion of the methodological problems that attach to gathering materials on a variety of types of NGOs, see James N. Rosenau, "Organizational Proliferation in a Changing World," in Commission on Global Governance, *Issues in Global Governance* (London: Kluwer Law International, 1995), pp. 265–294.

28. Anthony J. N. Judge, "NGOs and Civil Society: Some Realities and Distortions," *Transnational Associations* (May/June 1995), p. 178.

29. This broad conception is in contrast to numerous narrower ones that single out only certain organizational features as the basis for defining NGOs. For example, some analysts distinguish "between nongovernmental organizations (NGOs), which are intermediary organizations engaged in funding or offering other forms of support to communities and other organizations, and grassroots organizations (GROs), which are membership organizations of various kinds." Michael Edward and David Hulme, "Introduction: NGO Performance and Accountability," in M. Edwards and D. Hulme (eds.), *Beyond the Magic Bullet*, p. 15. Another narrower formulation involves positing NGOs as referring to "professionalized nonprofit organizations (with paid staff, fund-raising capabilities, and, except in highly repressive situations, juridical recognition)." Keck and Sikkink, *Activists Beyond Borders*, p. 218.

30. For a useful discussion of the problems that attend the task of defining and classifying NGOs, see Peter Willetts, "Introduction," in P. Willetts (ed.), *"The Conscience of the World,"* pp. 2–11.

31. Rosenau, *Along the Domestic-Foreign Frontier*, chap. 17.

32. For an interesting discussion of the links between legitimacy and compliance, see Timothy Dunne and Nicholas J. Wheeler, "Closing the Compliance Gap: Pluralist and Solidarist Readings of International Legitimacy," a paper presented at the Annual Meeting of the International Studies Association (Toronto, March 18–22, 1997).

33. Abdul Mohammed, "Responses of Non-Governmental Organizations to Conflict Situations," in Thomas G. Weiss, *Humanitarian Emergencies and Military Help in Africa* (London: The Macmillan Press, 1990), p. 101.

34. For an elaboration of the moral authority that attaches to the human rights regime, see James N. Rosenau, "Human Rights in a Turbulent and Globalizing World," a paper presented at the Annual Meeting of the American Political Science Association (Atlanta: September 4, 1999).

35. A compelling discussion of this point is presented in Ronnie D. Lipschutz, "(B)orders and (Dis)Orders: Sources and Sinks of Moral Authority in International Relations and Global Politics," a paper presented at the Annual Meeting of the International Studies Association (Toronto: March 18–22, 1997).

36. John Sankey, "Conclusions," in P. Willetts (ed.), *"The Conscience of the World,"* p. 273.

37. For a cogent analysis of the limits of authoritative nature of scientific expertise, as illustrated by the case of the 1987 Montreal Protocol on Substances that Deplete the Ozone Layer, see Karen T. Lifting, *Ozone Discourses: Science and Politics in Global Environmental Cooperation* (New York: Columbia University Press, 1994), pp. 5–7.

38. Satellite reconnaissance data may be an exception in this regard. Suspicion is hard to maintain in the face of photographic data depicting, say, Iraqi weapons facilities or Bosnian burial sites that prove accurate when subsequently checked on the ground. For a discussion of the role of proof in global affairs, see Rosenau, *Turbulence in World Politics*, pp. 198–209 and 425–429.

39. See, for example, Timothy J. Sinclair, "Passing Judgment: Credit Rating Processes as Regulatory Mechanisms of Governance in the Emerging World Order," *Review of International Political Economy,*" vol. 1 (April 1994), pp. 133–159.

40. Thomas L. Friedman, "Don't Mess with Moody's," *New York Times*, February 22, 1995, p. A19.

41. Richard Espy, *The Politics of the Olympic Games, with an Epilogue, 1976–1980* (Berkeley: University of California Press, 1981), p. 171.

42. For a insightful analysis of the authority that attaches to affiliations, see Joel Kotkin, *Tribes: How Race, Religion, and Identity Determine Success in the New Global Economy* (New York: Random House, 1993).

43. Joshua Cohen (ed.), *For Love of Country: Debating the Limits of Patriotism* (Boston: Beacon Press, 1996).

44. Hendrik Hertzberg, "Star-Spangled Banter," *The New Yorker,* July 21, 1997, pp. 4–5.

45. Quoted in G. Dale Thomas, "Historical Uses of Civil Society and the Global Civil Society Debate," a paper presented at the Annual Meeting of the International Studies Association (Toronto, March 18–22, 1997). Italics in original.

46. For a balanced assessment of the impact of transnational NGOs, see Ann Marie Clark, "Non-Governmental Organizations and Their Influence on International Society," *Journal of International Affairs*, vol. 48 (Winter 1995), pp. 507–525. Also see Sankey, "Conclusions," pp. 274–275.

47. Sankey, "Conclusions," p. 272.

CHAPTER 14

Practicing Democracy Transnationally

Rey Koslowski
and
Antje Wiener

Globalization and European integration have yielded "democratic deficits" emerging out of the transfer of sovereignty from elected national parliaments to unelected supranational institutions and the dispersion of authority from democratically governed states to nonstate actors. Nevertheless, globalization and European integration have opened new political spaces. Will these political spaces entail democratic practices? This paper explores the potential for democracy, outside of, along side of, and bypassing the nation-state by focusing on new transnational practices of interest groups, local governments, and even corporations.

The first section considers the lack of analysis of the democratic deficit in the International Relations (IR) literature and outlines the usefulness of a constructivist approach to transnationalism. By offering an assessment of democracy beyond the nation-state, we identify the practices, which stand to be routinized and, as such, will influence the rules of the game as new institutions in the future. The second section focuses specifically on the European Union (EU) because European integration not only prompted consideration of democratic deficits but in the EU "the incipient institutions of a 'democratic' transnational political community are faintly visible."[1] We look at four cases of democratic practices beyond national territory, including public hearings organized by the European Parliament, umbrella NGOs, individual NGOs, and comitology. The third section analyses the democratic potential in dimensions of globalization and the democratic content of newly emerging forms of global governance. We examine potential sites of democratic practice including: international non-government organizations (INGOs), transgovernmental networks of democratically elected subnational governments, and transnational corporations.

Of Theories and Practices

State-centric Theory, Globalization, and Democratic Deficits

Due to state-centric conceptualizations of most international relations (IR) theory transnational democratic practice is not a major concern of IR

theory. Neorealists and neoliberal institutionalists argue over conflict or cooperation among states in the condition of international anarchy but agree to stay
within a state-centric frame of reference. Upon opening the "black-box" of
domestic politics, theorists have primarily focused on the impact of domestic
politics on foreign policies of states, which collectively constitute international
politics as a whole or on the impact of the international environment on
domestic politics. Some who attribute international outcomes to domestic politics view democracy as an independent variable that explains peace.[2] Others
explain electoral outcomes[3] or economic policies of democratic states in terms
of changing international environments.[4] Nevertheless, the democratic deficit
and the democratic potential of global civil society may finally get onto the
mainstream IR theory research agenda.[5]

In the second half of the twentieth century the modern democratic context has changed.[6] The institutional settings of national states remained largely
stable but their citizenry and borders have not. Two developments were crucial.
First, border crossing by a variety of nonstate actors such as interest groups,
transnational corporations, as well as transnational flows of capital, products,
information, and migration have challenged the perception of a shared national
identity as the building block for the *demos*. Second, international interdependence expressed by institutional arrangements, which went beyond international treaties, international regimes, and, much more strikingly, the pooling of
sovereignty among states in the EU, have challenged the sovereign power of the
states. Similar democratic deficits have emerged as the scope of policy making
by democratically elected governments is increasingly constrained by the
unelected officials of the United Nations (UN), the International Monetary
Fund (IMF), and the World Trade Organization (WTO).[7] Whether these
processes are described as a series of external "disjunctures"[8] or the rise of
"McWorld"[9] democratic theorists have sounded the clarion call about the
threat of globalization to democracy.

Alternative Theoretical Approaches

By demonstrating the impact of nonstate actors on world politics and the
transformation of sovereignty, scholars of transnational relations and globalization[10] offer enabling conceptual frameworks to analyze these phenomena. The
larger questions about the increasing influence of transnational actors and any
corresponding diminution of state sovereignty on democracy remain insufficiently addressed. Susan Strange warned that the global diffusion of authority
to nonstate actors cumulatively produces a democratic deficit greater than that
of the EU noting "none of the non-state authorities to whom authority has
shifted, is democratically governed."[11] James Rosenau demonstrates just how
relevant NGOs are with references to the democratic deficit produced by the

gap between their increasing authority and lack of representativeness. Nevertheless, in contrast to Strange, he downplays the significance of this deficit by pointing to checks and balances on the power of the state provided by NGOs as well as the cross-cutting cleavages among the NGOs themselves.[12]

Traditionally, the formation of a democratic polity beyond that of the state has been approached within the framework of federalism, as it has been argued that federations of democratic states themselves form a new *demos* at a higher level. The oft-proposed solution to the democratic deficit is to make international organizations themselves "more democratic," for instance, in the EU by increasing the powers of the directly elected European Parliament vis-à-vis the unelected European Commission and Council of Ministers. Such reforms would replicate the representative institutions of the state at a higher level and, in effect, constitute a type of European federation.

In contrast to such analysis of political institutions in terms of formal structures, we take a constructivist approach and suggest a focus on practice, arguing that institutions are settled or routinized political practices that influence future politics and policy. Such an exclusively structural understanding of institutions makes the mere imagination of democracy outside of the state very difficult. In turn, thinking of institutions not only as structures but also as the outcome of political practice, allows for identifying political practices, informed by, for example, federal principles that may be routinized to become federal political institutions that are *not* federal states.[13] Similarly, democratic political practices may become institutionalized into new forms of democracy—including not only democracy that exists wholly within states, and/or federations of which they are consitutuent parts, but also in novel transnational arrangements.

Democratic theorists point to the democratic potential of civic associations, transnational communities, subnational administrations, and other non-state actors to constitute a "global civil society"[14] and become parts of "overlapping networks of power"[15] that can then serve as the agents of the "third democratic transition" beyond the nation-state that Robert Dahl had postulated.[16] Indeed, as he puts it, the complex set of institutions that evolved from the second transformation of democracy from the city-state to the nation-state is what "we commonly refer to as 'democracy.'"[17] As a "procedural minimal," this set of—formal—institutions has come to influence processes of transition from authoritarian rule across the globe and set standards for democratization.[18] With the increasing worldwide popularity of democracy this minimal set of formal conditions was increasingly found to be an insufficient frame for conditions for democracy.

A range of authors have argued that beyond the formal conditions for democracy such as constitutionally entrenched procedures and majoritarian rule, there are substantive conditions for democracy that cannot be overlooked. These conditions include structural factors, such as historically embedded cultural and social conditions.[19] Philippe Schmitter and Terry Karl point to the importance of such structural factors arguing that the "specific form democracy takes is contingent upon a country's socioeconomic conditions as well as its entrenched state structures and policy practices."[20] These factors have been applied within a theoretical context that operated on the underlying assumption of bounded polities. Indeed, Schmitter and Karl go on to stress the importance of boundaries for democratic practices pointing out that boundaries are "generated by competition among interest groups and cooperation within civil society."[21] While boundaries vary in different contexts, it is crucial for the practice of democracy that these boundaries are situated and constructed within this particular polity. The practice of interest groups then, is one condition for setting the boundaries of democratic space.

Both the formal and the substantive conditions for successful establishment of democracy are firmly situated within the bounded polities of nation-states. Current transnational interest group politics suggest, however, that as a practice, democracy need not necessarily be confined to the frame of a bounded national polity. If we are indeed facing a third transformation to democracy, which reaches beyond the boundaries of nation-states, other factors need to be taken into consideration, unless some form of superstate structure is the model. Since democratic rule is derived from the interplay between various factors, including practices, we question the exclusive focus on procedural factors once the context changes. Two such changes are crucial. First, if interest groups and associations are key actors in generating boundaries, then, a change in their activity may produce significant changes in the conceptualization of democracy. For example, once these actors move toward a transnational level, the bounded space is challenged. Second, democracy is challenged by the restructuring of state structures, or, due to new institutional limitations of democracy that are set by a nonstate polity. What does this imply for democratic practice? To capture the substance of democracy within such contexts in transition, we focus on political practices of actors within the respective processes

Sites of Transnational Democratic
Practice in the European Union

This section focuses on newly developing practices of democracy in the process of European integration. As a new model of governance beyond the nation-state, the EU provides one of the most interesting access points for thinking about deterritorialized democracy. We discuss four cases of interest groups that are engaged in transnational action, and, in the process have created new political spaces within the Euro-polity. They include (1) public hearings organized by the European Parliament, (2) umbrella NGOs, (3) individual NGOs, and (4) the practice of "comitology." These four cases operate beyond formal democratic institutions stressing the tension between new democratic practices and traditional institutional settings. In all cases, the *actors* share the characteristics of being transnational and not part of any specific societal group, the *arena* is a mixed (formal/informal) institutional setting, the *demands* are not exclusively directed to a state-centered authority, and the *action* is based on deliberation either direct (oral) or indirectly (written results of debate). This section is limited to identifying the practices of new transnational actors. Follow-up research is required to examine the institutional capacity of these practices, that is, do they set the rules of the game of democracy for future democratic practices?

Public Hearings

Parallel to the meetings of the representatives of the European Member States' governments during the Intergovernmental Conference (IGC), the European Parliament organized public hearings on various topics.[22] Open to NGOs and interest groups across the EU, they addressed points on the agenda of the IGC that were of main public concern, such as, citizenship, fundamental rights and cooperation in justice and home affairs, social policy, environment public health, and consumer policy. The hearings were held at two stages in Brussels: October 17–18, 1995 and February 26–27, 1996. About 500 organizations took part as speakers, observers, or both.[23]

The discussions focused on revising the Maastrich Treaty and eastern enlargement. Participating *actors* included transnational interest groups as well as different types of advocacy groups ranging from the Euro Citizen Action Service (ECAS) and the Federation of European Publishers to the Consumers' Association.[24] By encouraging and organizing the hearings, the European Parliament facilitated an *arena* for political deliberation. The multiple responses and the interest in participation demonstrated a high degree of organization within the "European" civil society. It is interesting to see that the *demands* of the advocacy groups were addressed to the IGC despite lacking formal channels for communication between the IGC and the groups. The *action* of these groups consisted of deliberating the demands within their local, regional, or national contexts and then discussing them in the newly created space at Brussels, or, absent an invitation to the hearings, sending them off to Brussels.

While a new space for public debate has thus been created, the initiative originated in the European Parliament's interest in legitimating EU governance. The debates among the transnational interest groups were then, primarily, enacted to facilitate legitimacy after the fact.[25] It stands to be shown, if and how this space is reenacted for further hearings and, what the impact of the hearings is on the groups' politics. At this point, we stress the fact that transnational politics is in the making, as new spaces and actors are observable. This type of transnational politics challenges the assumption that interest groups as key actors create boundaries of uncertainty *within* the context of a bounded state polity. However, the impact on Dahl's formal set of minimal procedures of democracy, as well as on the substantive aspect of democracy remains to be investigated.

Umbrella NGOs

The Permanent Forum on Civil Society is another type of transnational political actor in the EU.[26] The initiative was established in September 1995 at the initiative of the International European Movement. It gathers "more than a hundred NGOs and citizens' associations, working at the European, national or local level in different areas of activities (trade unions, environmental groups, social work, cultural action)."[27] The Permanent Forum held a first "Civil Convention" in Brussels on November 26, 1996 to launch a campaign to draw up a European Citizens' Charter. Its main forms of action consist in the organization of conventions to produce "collective writing" of European citizens, thus "keeping with a European tradition, where women and men intend to participate in declaring their rights and responsibilities." The goal of the activity is to create "participatory democracy."[28] The activities are meticulously reported on a well-kept and updated website, thus making the issues raised during the conventions, the papers adopted, and also ongoing processes of petitioning widely accessible to the computer literate and net-surfing public.

Individual NGOs

Another type of transnational interest group politics is performed by nongovernmental organizations themselves. Indeed, NGO politics on a transnational basis have been on the increase in the EU, particularly since the Maastricht IGC and the following treaty ratifications in the Member States as well as the Amsterdam IGC which was to revise some provisions of this much-debated Treaty. There are different types of NGOs, which need to be distinguished according to the contexts within which they were created.

One type of NGO includes independent nonprofit organizations that are devoted to the discussion of public issues, and focus on solving problems related to these issues. These groups are "political organizations that arise and operate outside the formal offices of the state, and are devoted to addressing public issues."[29] One example of this sort of NGO[30] is the ECAS group, which has been founded following a concern about citizens' rights in the EU. Its main activities include the organization of conferences, workshops, and meetings to facilitate public debate about the issue of citizenship. ECAS has, for example, drafted a blueprint of a "Chapter on European citizenship in a new Treaty."[31] Furthermore, the process of drafting this text has attracted the interest of a large number of associations that led to the formation of a coalition of citizens' associations called Voluntary Organizations of Citizens' Europe (VOICE). The participation of hundreds of advocacy groups in the Public Hearings, which were organized and facilitated by the European Parliament, was thus linked with this NGO activity.[32]

Another type of NGO is, if informally, linked with the formal set of governing institutions of the state. These NGOs receive funding, or, as is the case with many NGOs in the Euro-polity, were established precisely on the initiative of the Commission with a view to linking social forces to the European project.[33] Such NGOs are not strictly speaking independent from governmental organizations despite being nonprofit organizations.

For our purposes, the substantive differences among the groups are not significant since we seek to point out new actors and spaces for transnational democratic practices. The long-term question raised by these cases is whether and to what an extent can we characterize these practices as democratic in themselves? The immediate question is what do these new spaces and actors imply for existing perceptions of what according to Dahl is democracy in the common sense? More specifically, taking on Schmitter and Karl's point about the key role of interest groups in creating boundaries within a polity, what are the boundaries created by these groups' activities?

Comitology

The term "comitology" indicates mixed committee discussions over the process of adopting directives in various fields of EU policy.[34] The practice builds on the Council of Ministers' so-called Comitology Decision.[35] As such, it is part of the EU's *acquis communautaire,* or the EU's shared legal and procedural properties.[36] It presents an attempt to establish practices of governance in a new polity without a political center akin to the unitary administrative structure of national states. The effort to accommodate the political interests of the EU Member States within the otherwise 'highly administrative' committee task of overseeing policy implementation, has, accordingly, turned the committees into 'minicouncils'[37] representing an attempt to avoid clear shifts of power and authority. This form of political involvement by national actors, next to independent experts in the process of governance beyond the nation-state, is an interim solution that demonstrates the modern political actors' continuing struggle for survival in an increasingly postmodern, or for that matter, medieval political environment.[38] Both the arena and the actors involved in this political practice are transnational; the action is based on deliberation.

Potential Global Sites of Transnational Democracy

Democracy within International Nongovernmental Organizations

The rapid expansion of the numbers of INGOs has been heralded as evidence for the rise of a "global civil society."[39] New technologies that made it increasingly difficult for authoritarian regimes to suppress information reaching their citizens and contributed to the democratization of formerly Communist states also have the potential for providing a basis for transnational civil and political association. As the costs of microprocessors and cross-border communications drop precipitously, even small and relatively poor groups can organize on a global basis. This concept of global civil society promotes the notion that internet-empowered INGOs are potential checks on the power of not only states but also the international organizations they form and other nonstate actors like transnational corporations.[40] While pointing to the cumulative political impact of INGOs has a particularly Tocquevillian characteristic, taking another cue from Tocqueville, INGOs may be sites of transnational democratic practice in and of themselves. Moreover democratic practice within INGOs may have important indirect effects on the practice of democracy at other transnational sites.

Tocqueville argued that civil associations were necessary to the perpetuation of democracy because the art of association learned in civil society could then be applied to political association.[41] It was the self-government of political associations at all levels that represented the institutionalization of democratic practice. Tocqueville trained his attention to the local level—self-government, epitomized by the New England town meeting and the various local civil associations, which drew the individual into the public realm. While forms of democracy that exist within civil associations have been examined, the possibilities of the practice of democracy within civil associations and NGOs that span the international borders of states has not.

Anyone who has actually worked within an NGO knows that many NGOs are often founded by charismatic leaders who are loath to delegate authority, let alone give real decision-making powers to the entire membership. Nevertheless, the internal governance of INGOs may be a site of transnational democratic practice. They range from well-known activist groups such as Greenpeace and Amnesty International to more prosaic professional associations such as the International Studies Association (ISA) and the Institute of Electrical and Electronics Engineers (IEEE).[42] As anyone involved in professional associations knows, democracy often means single candidate ballots and leadership by those volunteers who were talked into thankless, but necessary, jobs nobody else wanted. Nevertheless, the internal politics of transnational professional organizations can also be very competitive, dynamic, and they have served as laboratories for democracy, as the IEEE did when it introduced approval voting in elections for its leadership.[43]

Global Localism: Democracy and Transgovernmental Relations

Transgovernmental relations refer to the relations between regions and localities within two or more states.⁴⁴ While they may be of a general nature, such as sister-cities programs, they may also be much more specifically focused on particular administrative functions. It was the move from the politics among nations to the transnational administration of things by international organizations that fueled hopes of functional integration that would eventually lead to a degree of interdependence that would make war unthinkable and states obsolete. The technocratic elites of the world's states, however, did not forsake their national identities in a frenzy of problem solving within international public administration. Nevertheless, transgovernmental contacts between public administrators persisted and as communication costs dropped precipitously, contacts between local, rather than national, level administrators dramatically expanded and they are overtaking national level contacts in terms of volume and practical accomplishments, if not in terms of symbolism. The intensity of this activity has inspired some observers to note that "the real new world order"⁴⁵ is being forged not within the international organizations formed by states, nor by the global civil society of INGOs, but rather in the much more mundane realm of functional cooperation among public agencies, localities, and regions.

Following the motto, "think globally, act locally," local authorities are interacting with local authorities in other states to learn from one another and to coordinate their actions. "Global localism" is institutionalized in the form of the International Union of Local Authorities (IULA). First established in 1913 as a union of national leagues of cities, IULA's membership now encompasses other types of urban associations as well as individual cities. The IULA has structured itself as a democratic organization, issued a 1993 "Worldwide Declaration of Local Self-Government," as a standard for democratic practice for the world's cities and localities, and it has provided international institutional support for a variety of practical initiatives of local administrations organized on a global basis.⁴⁶ The IULA also supports initiatives such as the International Council of Local Environmental Initiatives (ICLEI) through which local administrators from over 300 of the world's cities cooperate to more effectively deal with the practical problems confronted by their citizens, such as waste water treatment, toxic waste removal, and greenhouse gas emissions.⁴⁷

Transgovernmental relations may be a site for transnational democratic practice in several ways. First, the internal governance of International Local Governmental Organizations (ILGOs) like ICLEI may be democratic. Second, in as much as transgovernmental relations support local self-government, ILGOs may function as transnational intermediary institutions in the Tocquevillian sense. Participation of local authorities from nondemocratic states in projects with local authorities from democratic states may involve a degree of civil association that facilitates cross boundary learning of democratic practices and procedures that may, in turn, be applied to local self-government in general. Finally, such global localism is a form of political practice that uses federal principles but bypasses the state and is outside of the realm of an international federation of states.

Democracy within Transnational Corporations

Given that the expansion of transnational corporations since WWII is fundamental to the economic globalization that is undermining the sovereignty of democratic states, it may seem ludicrous to some to even mention democracy and transnational corporation in the same breath.[48] Susan Strange bluntly states, "Firms—the new players in transnational economic diplomacy—are hierarchies, not democracies."[49] It is not all that clear that the internal governance of all corporations is hierarchical and that hierarchy will remain the shape of the corporate future. Corporate governance is potentially less hierarchical and more decentralized, perhaps even more democratic, than one may think. Moreover, the practice of transnational collective decision-making by individuals within a corporation may indirectly facilitate democratic practice by those individuals at other sites of transnational democracy and vice versa.

When Tocqueville spoke of the civil associations in which the art of association was learnt he meant not only the community groups like the Rotary Club but also the emerging partnerships and corporations that were increasing in number in comparison to the individual capitalist entrepreneurs.[50] As corporations came to encompass ever-larger workforces, became central to their employees' livelihood and lives, and came to have an ever-greater influence on the governance of democratic states, democratic theorists like Dahl turned toward the internal governance of corporations and the idea of "workplace democracy," noting the gap in political participation between the economic haves and have-nots as well as the difference in actual influence on policy between the major corporations and the average citizen employee of those corporations. With this in mind, Dahl proposed an alternative form of democratic participation of citizens as employees within the corporation.[51] Given that the decision-making within the corporation may have an equal, if not greater, impact on the everyday life of the employee, such participation not only prepared the employee for participation in the public realm, it could potentially entail a form of direct empowerment over one's everyday life that has even greater meaning to the individual than the periodic election of legislators.

While in theory one could imagine how corporations could or should be run by their employees, Susan Strange makes a good point when she argues that corporations cannot be democratic because, "The multiple accountability of CEO's to shareholders, banks, employees, suppliers and distributors, not to mention strategic allies, means that like renaissance Princes, they can divide and rule."[52] In some cases, however, one division—between employees and shareholders—is being overcome. Employees are becoming owners of the firms they work for though Employee Stock Ownership Plans (ESOPs), 401(k) plans and stock options plans. For example, employees now own a majority of United Parcel Service and United Airlines stock. According to a study by the National Center for Employee Ownership, as of August 1997, employees controlled an estimated 8.3 percent of total corporate equity in the United States.[53] At this point, ESOPs and stock option plans of U.S. multinational corporations are often limited to their U.S. based employees, however, international ESOPs and stock option plans are beginning to be established.[54]

While proposals for workplace democracy offered by democratic socialists are aimed at the political goal of realizing democracy, corporations have economic objectives of increasing profits. Democratic governance and employee ownership provide practical means for firms to increase productivity, increase employee satisfaction, and retain skilled workers. Under the slogan of "empowerment" many corporations have razed their organizational hierarchies and given more decision-making authority to front-line workers to correct mistakes quickly, develop time- and labor-saving techniques and ensure product quality.[55] The move from manufacturing to postindustrial service economy has moved the share of valued-added by corporations away from the application of muscle, fossil fuel, and nuclear energy to raw material in the production of things for national markets toward the addition of knowledge in the development of better services that are more competitive in the global marketplace. Therefore, profits are increasingly dependent on corporations' human capital. In this context, the rise of the "knowledge worker," particularly in the high-technology sectors of postindustrial economies, is an important stimulus for democratization of governance in many corporations. Whereas the political object of realizing democracy may have only affected corporate governance on the margins, the economic object of increasing productivity and profits may have a much greater impact on corporate governance in the future.

This argument applies equally well to small corporations within national markets and transnational firms within global markets. Transnational firms operating in many different countries have additional hurdles to "empowering" their employees through forms of democratic governance. Authority within the organization must also be allocated across many divisions and subsidiaries, often acquired through mergers of firms that have not only their own corporate cultures but also national cultures and languages. Moreover, the major expansion of production in and for developing markets, such as China and India, has transformed the demography of many corporations' workforces (e.g., Asea Brown Boveri, ABB, cut the number of European employees by 40,000 and increased the number in Asia by 45,000 from 1996 to 1998) and this shift to multicultural demographics is also coming to management. It has been estimated that by the year 2010, upward of a third of the top 200 managers of many transnational corporations will probably not be from their home countries.[56] In many such cases, corporations have explicitly turned toward political theory for inspiration to deal with the challenges of governance in the face of increasing diversity, specifically to federalism.[57] Major transnational corporations such as ABB, Ciba-Geigy and Unilever have incorporated federal principles, including subsidiarity, into reforms of corporate governance. They have done so in order to maintain decentralization and self-governance of units while at the same time effectively delineating "jurisdictions" between units and providing means of dispute resolution between them, which in turn, reduces the temptation to reimpose power from above should major problems emerge. In this case, federalism at a global level has precious little to do with supranational state building.

Conclusions

After reviewing theoretical arguments about democracy in IR theory, we suggested that new insights from constructivist approaches as well as from new democratic theories offer a way of exploring the institutional building capacity of political practices. Transnational interest groups and subnational regional authorities within the EU are clearly increasing in number and diversity and they are increasingly being integrated into aspects of European governance. While the organizational density and impact of nonstate actors may not be as great on a global level as it is in Europe, the practice of these actors in Europe may resonate beyond. That is, beginning with the nation-state itself and the classical European system of states, the political organization of Europe has served as a model of sorts, whether imposed or voluntarily copied by the rest of the world. Whether the spread of transnational democratic practice within Europe will itself become routinized, let alone be emulated elsewhere, is very much an open question. In the meantime, however, one can see some potential of transnational democratic political practice filling the spaces opened by the processes of globalization. Given the current rate of globalization and corresponding impending displacement of authority from democratic states, it is doubtful that the potential transnational democracy identified in this paper can address the global democratic deficits emerging in new political spaces. If globalization cannot be "reversed," it is clear that democracy cannot continue on as before and it behooves all those concerned with the fate of democracy to more closely consider its practice transnationally.

Notes

1. Robert A. Dahl, *Democracy and Its Critics* (New Haven and London: Yale University Press, 1989), p. 320.

2. Bruce Russett, *Grasping the Democratic Peace* (Princeton, NJ: Princeton University Press, 1993).

3. Frances McCall Rosenbluth, "Internationalization and Electoral Politics in Japan," in Robert O. Keohane and Helen V. Milner, *Internationalization and Domestic Politics* (Cambridge, UK: Cambridge University Press, 1996).

4. Jeffry A. Frieden and Ronald Rogowski, "The Impact of the International Economy on National Policies: An Analytical Overview," and Geoffrey Garrett and Peter Lange, "Internationalization, Institutions, and Political Change," in Keohane and Milner, *Internationalization and Domestic Politics*.

5. Robert O. Keohane, "International Institutions: Can Interdependence Work?" *Foreign Policy*, 110 (Spring 1998): 82–96, especially pp. 91–94.

6. The following point draws on Antje Wiener, "Crossing the Borders of Order: Democracy Beyond the Nation-State?" in M. Albert, D. Jacobson and Y. Lapid, *Identities, Borders, Orders: New Directions in IR Theory* (Minneapolis: University of Minnesota Press, forthcoming).

7. Ralph Nader and Lori Wallach, "GATT, NAFTA and the Subversion of the Democratic Process," in Jerry Mander and Edward Goldsmith, eds., *The Case Against the Global Economy* (San Francisco: Sierra Club Books, 1996).

8. David Held, *Democracy and the Global Order* (Stanford: Stanford University Press, 1995), chaps. 5 and 6.

9. Benjamin R. Barber, *Jihad vs. McWorld* (New York: Random House, 1995), part 1 and chap. 16.

10. James N. Rosenau, *Turbulence in World Politics: A Theory of Change and Continuity* (Princeton: Princeton University Press 1990); Philip G. Cerney, *The Changing Architecture of Politics: Structure Agency and the Future of the State* (London: Sage, 1990); Haas, Peter M., ed., *Knowledge, Power and International Policy Coordination*, a special issue of *International Organization*, 46.1 (Winter 1992); Thomas, Risse-Kappen, ed., *Bringing Transnational Relations Back In: Non-State Actors, Domestic Structures and International Institutions* (Cambridge, UK: Cambridge University Press, 1995); Yale Ferguson and Richard Mansbach, *Polities: Authority, Identities and Change* (Columbia, SC: University of South Carolina Press, 1996).

11. Susan Strange, *Retreat of the State: The Diffusion of Power in the World Economy* (Cambridge, UK: Cambridge University Press, 1996), p. 197.

12. James N. Rosenau, *Along the Domestic-Foreign Frontier: Exploring Governance in a Turbulent World* (Cambridge, UK: Cambridge University Press, 1997), pp. 335–337, 403–412.

13. Rey Koslowski, "A Constructivist Approach to Understanding the European Union as a Federal Polity," *Journal of European Public Policy*, 6.4 (Special Issue 1999): 561–578.

14. Barber, *Jihad vs. McWorld*, pp. 276–288.

15. Held, *Democracy and the Global Order*, pp. 271.

16. Dahl, *Democracy and Its Critics*, part 3.

17. Dahl, *Democracy and Its Critics*, p. 2.

18. See Philippe C. Schmitter and Terry Karl, "What Democracy Is . . . And Is Not," in Larry Diamond and Marc E. Plattner, eds., *The Global Resurgence of Democracy* (Baltimore and London: Johns Hopkins University Press, 1996), p. 55; Guillermo O'Donnell, Philippe C. Schmitter, and Laurence Whitehead, *Transitions from Authoritarian Rule* (Baltimore: Johns Hopkins University Press, 1986); Samuel J. Valenzuela, "Democratic Consolidation in Post-Transitional Settings: Notion, Process, and Facilitating Conditions," in Guillermo O'Donnell and J. Samuel Valenzuela, Scott Mainwaring, eds., *Issues in Democratic Consolidation: The New South American Democracies in Comparative Perspective* (Notre Dame: University of Notre Dame Press, 1992).

19. Juan Linz and Alfred Stepan, *Problems of Democratic Transition and Consolidation: Southern Europe, South America, and Post-Communist Europe* (Baltimore: Johns Hopkins University Press 1996).

20. Schmitter and Karl, "What Democracy Is . . . And Is Not," p. 50.

21. Ibid., p. 57.

22. See the European Parliament's web page including topics, participating interest groups, and links to texts containing the demands of the respective participating interest groups http://www.europarl.eu.int/dg7/herarings/en/igc1/sommaire.htm, hereafter, Public Hearings 1998.

23. See Public Hearings 1998, Foreword by Mrs. Raymonde Dury and Mrs. Johanna Maij-Weggen.

24. For a list of the participating groups and the texts of their demands see Public Hearings 1998.

25. For example, then President of the European Parliament, Klaus Haensch emphasized the necessity to create an understanding among European citizens for the issues addressed by the EU. In an opening statement to the Public Hearings, he stressed that "if we want the citizens to understand and accept the pending reforms, then secrecy must be abandoned and public debate about these reforms has to take place" (translated from German by AW) See http://www.europarl.eu.int/dg7/hearings/en/igc1/begruss.htm (Public Hearings 1998, p. 1 of 2).

26. See http://www.eurplace.org/orga/forumsoc/index.html, hereafter: Permanent Forum 1998.

27. Permanent Forum 1998. For the participant groups see: http://www.eur-place.org/orga/forumsoc/ong.html.

28. Permanent Forum 1998.

29. Paul Wapner, "The Transnationalization of Environmental Activism: Searching for Governance in a Complex and Fragile World," Paper prepared for presentation at the *American Political Science Association Meeting,* Washington D.C. 1997, p. 3.

30. For information on ECAS, see http://europa.eu.int/en/agenda/igc-home/instdoc/ngo/ecasen.htm, hereafter, ECAS 1998. ECAS is a member of the umbrella organization with a concern for European citizens' rights, VOICE.

31. ECAS 1998, 1.

32. ECAS 1998, 1.

33. This is, for example, the case with the Migrant Forum and the Women's Lobby Group that have been founded on funding initiatives by the European Commission in the late 1980s, that is within the context of the social-democratic project of the Delors presidencies.

34. Most familiar is the case of such committee meetings in the foodstuff sector. See Christian Joerges and Juergen Neyer, "From Intergovernmental Bargaining to Deliberative Political Processes: The Constitutionalisation of Comitology," *European Law Journal* 3 (1997): 273–299.

35. See Council Decision, 87/373/EC OJ L197/87.

36. Joerges and Neyer, "From Intergovernmental Bargaining to Deliberative Political Processes."

37. Everson, Michelle. 1998. "Administering Europe?" *Journal of Common Market Studies,* pp. xx.

38. Ferguson and Mansbach, *Polities.*

39. Commission on Global Governance, *Our Global Neighborhood* (Oxford: Oxford University Press, 1995), pp. 253–263.

40. Rosenau, *Along the Domestic-Foreign Frontier,* pp. 332, 403–412.

41. Alexis de Tocqueville, *Democracy in America,* J. P. Mayer ed., George Lawrence trans. (Garden City, NY: Doubleday, 1969).

42. The IEEE is the world's largest technical professional society with 320,000 members operating in 150 countries. See http://www.ieee.org.

43. Brams, Steven J. and Jack H. Nagel, 1991. "Approval Voting in Practice," *Public Choice* 71 (August): 1–17.

44. Keohane, Robert O. and Joseph S. Nye, Jr. "Transgovernmental Relations and International Organizations," *World Politics* 27.1 (1974): 39–62.

45. Anne Marie Slaughter, "The Real New World Order," *Foreign Affairs*, Sept./Oct. 1997.

46. See http://www.iula.org.

47. See http://www.iclei.org.

48. See, for example, Nader and Wallach, "GATT, NAFTA and the Subversion of the Democratic Process."

49. Strange, *Retreat of the State*.

50. Tocqueville, *Democracy in America*, pp. 520–522.

51. Robert A. Dahl, *A Preface to Economic Democracy* (Berkeley: University of California Press, 1986).

52. Strange, *Retreat of the State*, p. 197.

53. See http://nceo.org/library/control_eq.html.

54. http://www.nceo.org/library/global.html.

55. Sumantra Ghoshal and Christopher A. Bartlett, *The Individualized Corporation: A Fundamentally New Approach to Management* (New York: HarperBusiness, 1997).

56. C. K. Prahalad and Kenneth Liberthal, "The End of Corporate Imperialism, *Harvard Business Review*, July–August 1998, pp. 69–79, at p. 78.

57. Handy, Charles, "Balancing Corporate Power: A New Federalist Paper," *The Harvard Business Review*, November–December 1992, pp. 59–72.

Contributors

John A. Agnew is Professor of Geography at the University of California, Los Angeles. He is the author of *Geopolitics: Revisioning World Politics* (1998); and co-author (with Stuart Corbridge) of *Mastering Space: Hegemony, Territory, and International Political Economy* (1995). A recent article is "Mapping Political Power Beyond State Boundaries: Territory, Identity and Movements in World Politics."

Mark A. Boyer is Professor of Political Science at the University of Connecticut. He is the co-author of *Negotiating a Complex World* (1999) and author of *International Cooperation and Public Goods: Opportunities for the Western Alliance* (1993). With Davis B. Brobow he is completing a book, *Pursuing Global Order*. Since 2000 he has been Editor of the International Studies Association's quarterly journal, *International Studies Perspectives*.

Stuart Corbridge is Professor of Geography at the London School of Economics, and also in the School of International Studies, University of Miami. He is the co-author of *Reinventing India: Liberalization, Hindu Nationalism and Popular Democracy* (2000) and *Mastering Space: Hegemony, Territory and International Political Economy* (1995); and the author of *Debt and Development* (1993) and *Capitalist World Development* (1986). His current project is a co-authored study of rural poverty, empowerment, and state performance in eastern India.

Ken Dark is Lecturer in International Relations, Department of Economics, at the University of Reading (UK), has taught at both the universities of Oxford and Cambridge, and holds honorary chairs and fellowships from several universities and research centers in Europe. He has published extensively in the fields of international relations, history, and archaeology, including *The Waves of Time: Long-Term Change and International Relations* (1998).

Yale H. Ferguson is Professor of Political Science and Co-Director of the Center for Global Change and Governance, Rutgers University-Newark. His books include several co-authored with Richard Mansbach: *Theory and Global Politics: The Elusive Quest Continues* (in press), *Polities: Authority, Identities, and Change* (1996), *The State, Conceptual Chaos, and the Future of International*

Relations Theory (1989), *The Elusive Quest: Theory and International Politics* (1988), and (also with D. Lampert) *The Web of World Politics: Nonstate Actors in the Global System* (1976).

K. J. Holsti is University Killam Professor of Political Science (emeritus) and a Research Associate in the Institute of International Relations at the University of British Columbia, Vancouver, Canada. His most recent books include *The State, War, and the State of War* (1996) and *Peace and War: Armed Conflicts and International Order, 1648–1989* (1991). Among his earlier works are *International Politics: A Framework for Analysis* (several editions) and *The Dividing Discipline: Hegemony and Diversity in International Theory* (1985).

R. J. Barry Jones is Professor Emeritus of the University of Reading, UK. His recent books include *The World Turned Upside Down?: Globalisation and the Future of the State* (2000) and a co-authored *Introduction to International Relations* (2001). In addition, he was General Editor of *The Routledge Encyclopaedia of International Political Economy* (2001). He was the founding Secretary of the British International Studies Association and the long-term Convenor of its Contemporary International Relations Group.

Rey Koslowski is Associate Professor of Political Science, Rutgers University-Newark. He has been a Visiting Fellow of the Center of International Studies at Princeton University (Fall 1999 and Fall 2000) and a Research Associate of the Center for German and European Studies at Georgetown University's School of Foreign Service (1996–97). He is the author of *Migrants and Citizens: Demographic Change in the European States System* (2000) and co-editor of *Global Human Smuggling: Comparative Perspectives* (2001).

Robert Latham is Director of the Social Science Research Council's Program on Information Technology, International Cooperation and Global Security, and he has taught at several New York area universities including Columbia University School of International and Public Affairs. He is the author of *The Liberal Moment: Modernity, Security, and the Making of Postwar International Order* (1997), and the co-editor of *Intervention and Transnationalism in Africa: Global/Local Networks of Power* (2001).

Richard Little is Professor of International Politics at the University of Bristol (UK). He is a former Editor of the *Review of International Studies* and is currently Chair of the British International Studies association. His most recent book (with Barry Buzan) is *International Systems in World History* (2000).

Richard W. Mansbach is Professor of Political Science at Iowa State University. In addition to his books co-authored with Yale Ferguson, he is the author of *The Global Puzzle: Issues and Actors in World Politics* (2000), co-author of *In Search of Theory: Toward a New Paradigm for Global Politics* (1981) and *Structure and Process in International Politics* (1973), and co-editor of *Global Politics in a Changing World* (2001). He is currently Co-Editor of the International Studies Association's *International Studies Quarterly*. Ferguson and he are completing two new books, *Remapping Global Politics* and *Ancient Polities*.

Ronen Palan is Lecturer in the Department of International Relations and Politics, University of Sussex (UK). He is the author of *The Offshore World: Virtual Spaces and the Commercialization of Sovereignty* (forthcoming), co-author of *The Imagined Economy: State, Globalization and Poverty* (forthcoming), and co-editor of *Global Political Economy: Contemporary Theories* (2000). He is also Co-Editor of the *Review of International Political Economy*.

James N. Rosenau is University Professor of International Affairs at The George Washington University. Among his many books, recent titles include *Distant Proximities; Dynamics Beyond Globalization* (forthcoming), *The Domestic-Foreign Frontier: Exploring Governance in a Turbulent World* (1997), and *Turbulence in World Politics: A Theory of Change and Continuity* (1990).

Saskia Sassen is the Ralph Lewis Professor of Sociology at the University of Chicago, and Centennial Visiting Professor at the London School of Economics. Her latest books include *The Global City* (2001, 1991), Guests and Aliens (1999), *Losing Control? Sovereignty in an Age of Globalization* (1996), the co-authored *Globalization and Its Discontents* (1998), and an edited volume *Cities and Their Cross-Border Networks* (2002). She is Co-Director of the Economy Section of the Global Chicago Project and the Chair of the newly formed Information Technology, International Cooperation and Global Security Committee of the Social Science Research Council.

Susan Strange, now deceased, ended her long career as Professor of International Political Economy at the University of Warwick (UK). She was a pioneer in establishing the field of international political economy (IPE) at the London Scool of Economics. Her books include *Mad Money: When Markets Outgrow Governments* (1998), *The Retreat of the State: The Diffusion of Power in the World Economy* (1996), *States and Markets* (1998), the co-authored *Rival States, Rival Firms Competition for World Market Shares* (1991), and *Casino Capitalism* (1986).

Antje Wiener is Associate Professor, Institute of European Studies at the Queen's University of Belfast (Northern Ireland). Her work explores the relationship between the political and the social, especially rights policy, polity-formation and constitutionalization in world politics. Among her publications are *"European" Citizenship Practice: Building Institutions of a Non-State* (1998) and a co-authored book on *The Social Construction of Europe* (2001).

List of Titles

American Patriotism in a Global Society—Betty Jean Craige

The Political Discourse of Anarchy: A Disciplinary History of International Relations—Brian C. Schmidt

From Pirates to Drug Lords: The Post—Cold War Caribbean Security Environment—Michael C. Desch, Jorge I. Dominguez, and Andres Serbin (eds.)

Collective Conflict Management and Changing World Politics—Joseph Lepgold and Thomas G. Weiss (eds.)

Zones of Peace in the Third World: South America and West Africa in Comparative Perspective—Arie M. Kacowicz

Private Authority and International Affairs—A. Claire Cutler, Virginia Haufler, and Tony Porter (eds.)

Harmonizing Europe: Nation-States within the Common Market—Francesco G. Duina

Economic Interdependence in Ukrainian-Russian Relations—Paul J. D'Anieri

Leapfrogging Development? The Political Economy of Telecommunications Restructuring—J. P. Singh

States, Firms, and Power: Successful Sanctions in United States Foreign Policy—George E. Shambaugh

Approaches to Global Governance Theory—Martin Hewson and Timothy J. Sinclair (eds.)

After Authority: War, Peace, and Global Politics in the Twenty-First Century—Ronnie D. Lipschutz

Pondering Postinternationalism: A Paradigm for the Twenty-First Century?—Heidi H. Hobbs (ed.)

Beyond Boundaries? Disciplines, Paradigms, and Theoretical Integration in International Studies—Rudra Sil and Eileen M. Doherty (eds.)

Why Movements Matter: The West German Peace Movement and U. S. Arms Control Policy—Steve Breyman

International Relations—Still an American Social Science? Toward Diversity in International Thought—Robert M. A. Crawford and Darryl S. L. Jarvis (eds.)

Which Lessons Matter? American Foreign Policy Decision Making in the Middle East, 1979—1987—Christopher Hemmer (ed.)

Hierarchy Amidst Anarchy: Transaction Costs and Institutional Choice—Katja Weber

Counter-Hegemony and Foreign Policy: The Dialectics of Marginalized and Global Forces in Jamaica—Randolph B. Persaud

Global Limits: Immanuel Kant, International Relations, and Critique of World Politics—Mark F. N. Franke

Power and Ideas: North-South Politics of Intellectual Property and Antitrust—Susan K. Sell

Money and Power in Europe: The Political Economy of European Monetary Cooperation—Matthias Kaelberer

Agency and Ethics: The Politics of Military Intervention—Anthony F. Lang, Jr.

Life After the Soviet Union: The Newly Independent Republics of the Transcaucasus and Central Asia—Nozar Alaolmolki

Theories of International Cooperation and the Primacy of Anarchy: Explaining U. S. International Monetary Policy-Making After Bretton Woods—Jennifer Sterling-Folker

Information Technologies and Global Politics: The Changing Scope of Power and Governance—James N. Rosenau and J. P. Singh (eds.)

Technology, Democracy, and Development: International Conflict and Cooperation in the Information Age—Juliann Emmons Allison (ed.)

The Arab-Israeli Conflict Transformed: Fifty Years of Interstate and Ethnic Crises—Hemda Ben-Yehuda

Systems of Violence: The Political Economy of War and Peace in Colombia—Nazih Richani

Debating the Global Financial Architecture—Leslie Elliot Armijo

Political Space: Frontiers of Change and Governance in a Globalizing World—Yale Ferguson and R. J. Barry Jones (eds.)

Crisis Theory and World Order: Heideggerian Reflections—Norman K. Swazo

Index

absolutist monarchs, 54
accountancy standards, global, 235
"acephalous units", 11
acquis communautaire, 287
actor interest and motivation, 250
adaptation, 70
Afghanistan, 102, 197
Africa, 144
Against Method, 203
age of imperialism, the, 145
agent-structure issue, 12, 91–93
agricultural based societies, 63
ahistorical conception of political space,
  46–48
airline registration, 221
Al-Queda, 99
Alexander the Great, death of, 49
Algeria, annexation by France, 200
alliances and networks, 96, 133
Amnesty International, 272, 288
Amsterdam Intergovernmental
  Conference of the EU, 286
anarchical political space, 47, 48, 49, 51
anarchical structures, 11
anarchy (international), 23, 50, 75, 92,
  190, 245, 249, 250
ancien regime, 99
"animal spirits," 194
annexations, 137
anthropology, 11
anthropomorphization, of states, 103
antitrust regulations, international convergence of, 176
ANZUS, 238
Arbitration, 51
Archeology, 11
arenas, international, 13, 132, 133, 134

aristocratic state, the, 99
Armenians in Los Angeles, 274
Armies, 136
Aron, Raymond, 19
Asea Brown Boveri, 292
Ashley, Robert, 123
Asian economic and financial crisis
  (1997–98), 101, 179, 193, 205,
  257
  response of USA, IMF and G10, 199
"Asian state," the, 100
Association of Petroleum Exporting
  Countries (APEC), 250
Associations, 284
Athens, 49, 53
atomic bomb, the, 28
atomism, 68
Austria, 10
Authorities, 105
Authority, 7, 17, 261–62, 268, 269–75
  affiliative, 274–75
  diffusion to nonstate actors, 282
  formal, 271
  higher order systems of, 122
  informal, 271
  issue-specific, 272–74
  knowledge, 272
  moral, 271–72
  reputational, 272–73
  wielded by Non Governmental
    Organizations, 266
autonomy, of political space, 54
Ayodhya, 154, 157
"Ayodhya procession," 155

Babari Masjid, the, 154
Bagehot, Walter, 195

Printed in the United States
68661LVS00004B/16-45